About the Authors

Dana Facaros and Michael Pauls have moved on from their Umbrian hilltop via a leaky old farmhouse in southwest France, and now live on the west coast of Ireland. They miss Italy; as their friend Santino always says about it: you cry twice, when you come, and when you leave. They have written over 30 guides for Cadogan.

About the Updater

Ros Belford is a travel writer who specialises in Italy but has also written about Greece and Spain. She founded the Virago Women's Travel Guides, and was shortlisted for the 1994 Thomas Cook Award. She broadcasts about food and travel on Radio 4.

Acknowledgements

Thanks to Richard and Rita for the use of Dolly, and to Anne and Santino for putting up with Corinne in the garden.

Please help us to keep this guide up to date

We have done our best to ensure that the information in this guide is correct at the time of going to press. But places and facilities are constantly changing, and standards and prices in hotels and restaurants fluctuate. We would be delighted to receive any comments concerning existing entries or omissions. Authors of the best letters will receive a copy of the Cadogan Guide of their choice.

Contents

The Italian Lakes and the old art towns of Lombardy invite all kinds of indulgences. Linger on a lakeshore terrace in the evening, over a saffron risotto and a glass of Bardolino or Franciacorta, as landscapes that inspired the backgrounds of Leonardo's greatest paintings dissolve and the scents of jasmine and night flowers fill the air. Golden lights come to life along the shore as if fastening a fairy necklace around the water; little islands seem to hover in the twilight over the glassy surface before melting into the total silhouette of night.

Introduction

Throughout history, the millions of frostbitten travellers, pilgrims, conquering armies, future popes and pushy emperors who lumbered over the treacherous passes of the Alps would be stopped in their tracks by a vision as powerful, terrible and beautiful as an epiphany: at their feet, wedged into the flanks of the snowcapped mountains, lay the Garden of Eden itself. Elegant, long lakes were its centrepiece, warmed by a glowing sun that had nothing in common with that old cheese in the sky they knew back home; on their chiselled shores lemons, figs, roses, pomegranates and palms grew in luxuriant abundance. And beyond these magical Mediterranean fjords the fertile Lombard plain spread its charms back to the edge of the horizon, dangling some of the richest art cities of Italy like diamonds across its bosom.

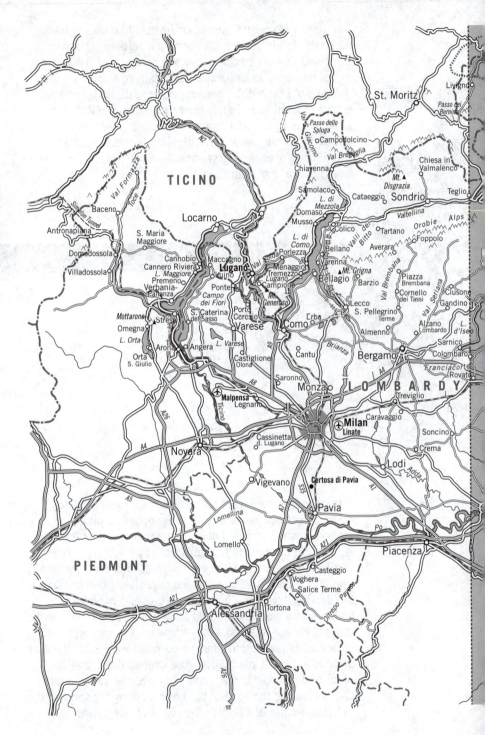

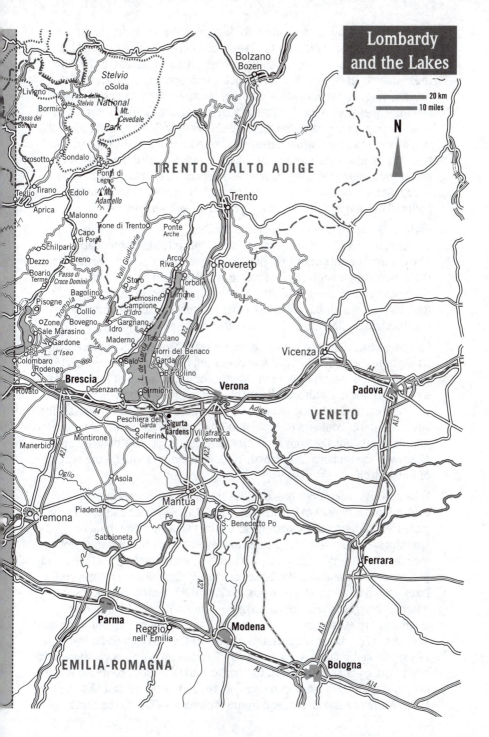

Lombardy
and the Lakes

20 km
10 miles

N

Bolzano
Bozen

Stelvio
Solda

Livigno

Passo dello
Stelvio

National

Bormio

Mt.
Cevedale

Passo dei
Bernina

Park

Grosotto
Sondalo

Sondrio

TRENTO—ALTO ADIGE

Teglio
Tirano

Edolo

Trento

Aprica

Ponti di
Legno

Mt.
Adamello

Malonno

Tione di Trento

Ponte
Arche

Capo
di Ponte

Schilpario

Arco
Riva

Rovereto

Dezzo
Breno

Storo

Torbole

Boario
Terme

Passo di
Croce Domini

Limone

Bagolino

Tremosine

Pisogne

Campione

Collio

L. d'Idro

Zone
Bovegno

Gargnano

Sale Marasino

Idro

Gardone

Maderno

Toscolano

Seo
L. d'Iseo

Torri del Benaco

Vicenza

Colombaro
Rodengo

Salo

Garda

Brescia

Bardolino

Padova

Rovato

Desenzano

Sirmione

Verona

Peschiera del
Garda

Sigurtà
Gardens

Adige

VENETO

Montirone

Solferino

Villafranca
di Verona

Manerbio

Oglio

Asola

Mantua

Cremona

Piadena

Po

S. Benedetto Po

Sabbioneta

Ferrara

Parma

Modena

Reggio
nell' Emilia

Bologna

EMILIA-ROMAGNA

Valli Giudicarie

Trompia

L. de Garda

The finished product, the Lombardy and Lakes we see today, is the result of primordial blasts of ice. In the last glacial period huge masses of ice rolled down from the Alps, ironing flat the Lombard plain. On the way they gouged out deep welts in the rock, far deeper than the level of the Adriatic sea, sculpting (there's no other word for it) some of the most sublime lakes anywhere. Lombardy's character was similarly formed by violence. Countless gangsters coveted this earthly Eden (not the least of whom were the Lombards themselves, who liked the odd swig of mead from the skulls of their enemies). Many invaders settled down to stay and turned their energy to farming and especially to trade, the natural occupation for people living at the crossroads between Italy, France, Switzerland and Austria, and the Tyrrhenian and Adriatic seas.

Early in the Middle Ages, mercantile Lombardy invented the idea of the *comune*, a kind of independent city-state, the antithesis of feudalism. The *comuni*'s new outlook on the world, freedom of action, wealth, and their increasingly sophisticated ruling families, keen on embellishing their palaces and cities with art, were leading factors in ushering in the Renaissance, which has left some of its greatest treasures behind in Milan, Mantua, Bergamo, Como and Brescia.

Lombardy has been making some big noises recently, adding more than its share to the contradictions and confusions besetting modern Italy. Pilgrims of old, descending from the Alps on this Garden of Eden, trod softly so as not to disturb God's angel with the fiery sword. Nowadays you can rest assured that he's run off to join the circus. Nevertheless, the advent of Berlusconi and the substitution of vague, soft-touch commercial mumbo-jumbo for the honest politics Italy needs suggests that the Tree of Knowledge remains untouched, still defended by a viper—the symbol of Milan itself.

Lake holidays faded from fashion after the last war, when a suntan evolved into a symbol of leisure instead of manual labour and summer's mass trek to the seashore became as instinctual as the drowning of lemmings. But the lakes are simply too lovely to stay out of fashion for long, and today a new generation is busily rediscovering what their grand-parents took for granted. For better or worse, the Italians have ringed the lakes with finely engineered roads, making them perhaps too accessible, whereas before visitors had to make do with small boats or leisurely steamers. Prices have risen with demand, and between July and September (the latter is generally considered the best month for the lakes) rest and relaxation may seem a Victorian relic, unless you book into one of the grander villa hotels. Calmer havens, however, continue to exist on the smaller, less developed lakes of Iseo and Orta, the east shores of Lakes Maggiore and Como, and in the mountain valleys to the north.

Travel

By Air from the UK and Ireland

Milan is the gateway for Lombardy. International flights use **Malpensa Airport**, about 50km northwest of the city; domestic and European flights use **Linate Airport** about 7km east. Direct scheduled flights to Milan are operated by **Alitalia**, ✆ (0171) 602 7111, and **British Airways**, ✆ (0345) 222 111. Besides London, you can also fly from Birmingham or Manchester in the summer. Alternatively, BA has two direct flights a day to Verona—which will bring you much closer to Lake Garda.

The real challenge is not so much finding a flight, but finding a bargain, especially in the high season (mid-May to mid-September); the trick is to start hunting well in advance, or, if you're a gambler, at the last moment. The advantages of shelling out for a full **scheduled** fare are that few restrictions are imposed on when you travel or how long you stay. To sweeten the deal, promotional perks like rental cars, discounts on domestic flights and accommodation, tours, etc. may also be included. **Children** travel for greatly reduced fares (10% for the under-twos on an adult's lap; 33% discount for children aged 2–11). *Bona fide* **students** with suitable ID also receive handsome discounts. Special fares booked in advance, however (PEX, APEX and so on), may save you as much as 50% of the cost. Typical fares to Milan on British Airways or Alitalia are currently around £250–£300 return in high season. Booking restrictions apply: you have to stay a Saturday night abroad. Ticket changes involve high penalties.

The direct flights from **Ireland** to Italy are from Dublin to Milan with **Aer Lingus**, ✆ (0645) 737 747, with connections for Cork and Galway on certain days (£250); or **Alitalia**, ✆ (01) 677 5171. Both fly twice daily, less often out of season. Alternatively, travel to London and fly from there. Even if their £10-plus-tax and similar fares are no longer up for grabs, the cheapest Dublin–London fares are usually to be found with **Ryan Air**, ✆ (0541) 569 569 (landing at Stansted or Luton), though **Aer Lingus** and **British Midland**, ✆ (0181) 745 7321, take you directly into Heathrow for around £75, which is more convenient and will probably save time and money in the end. From Belfast, both British Airways and British Midland operate to Heathrow. If you're a student, substantial discounts may be available: contact **USIT** at 12–21 Aston Quay, O'Connell Bridge, Dublin 2, ✆ (01) 679 8833, or Fountain Centre, College St, Belfast, ✆ (01232) 324 073.

charters, discounts and special deals

London is a great centre for discounted flights, and you should be able to find a good deal if you allow enough time. Seat-only charters to Milan may cost less than £100 return (inc. tax) off-peak; contact a reputable ABTA-registered agent (who won't bunk off with your cash and leave you stranded) such as **Trailfinders**, ✆ (0171) 937 5400, **STA**, ✆ (0171) 361 6161, **Lupus Travel**, ✆ 0171 287 1292, or **Campus Travel**, ✆ (0171) 730 3402. Alternatively you can book directly through a charter or holiday operator. The Italian specialist **Air Travel Group**, at 227 Shepherd's Bush Road, Hammersmith, London W6 7AS, ✆ (0181) 748 7575, incorporates Italy Sky Shuttle, Magic of Italy and Italian Escapades. Remember to check deals offered by scheduled airlines as well; both Alitalia and BA often have competitive fares, and GO (BA's new subsidiary) have fares from £100 return including tax.

Classified sections of weekend newspapers also advertise discounted fares (in London, get *Time Out* or other listings magazines, and the *Evening Standard* or the free newspapers like *TNT* or *Trailfinder* from near tube stations). Peak seasons are Easter and summer, when there are generally a couple of flights a day from London (book well ahead). The major charter agencies are **Italy Sky Shuttle**, ✆ (0181) 748 1333 (reservations), **Skybus**, ✆ (0171) 631 3444, and **LAI**, ✆ (0171) 837 8492. Rock-bottom fares are generally subject to restrictions, and departure or arrival times may be inconvenient or uncertain. STA and Campus Travel offer exceptionally good deals for students.

By Air from the USA and Canada

Transatlantic airlines **Delta**, ✆ (800) 241 414, **TWA**, ✆ (800) 892 4141, **United Airlines** ✆ (800) 241 6522, and **Air Canada**, USA ✆ (800) 776 3000, Canada ✆ (800) 555 1212, all have direct flights to Rome or Milan from a number of cities, including New York, Boston, Miami, Chicago, Los Angeles, Toronto or Montreal, but **Alitalia**, ✆ (800) 223 5730, has the most options. Summer round-trip fares from New York to Italy cost around $1300, from Montreal or Toronto about $1100 Canadian.

Alternatively, you may prefer to take a flight to London or some other European city (Paris or Amsterdam, for example) and change there, a reasonably economical option. APEX or SuperAPEX deals are better value than scheduled fares, though you may prefer to pay extra for security, flexibility and convenience on such a long jouney (9–15 hours' flying time). Beware the restrictions imposed on special fares, and plan well in advance. Obviously, low-season flights (between November and March) tend to be a great deal cheaper than peak-season ones, and mid-week fares are generally lower than at weekends.

As in Britain, a host of cheap deals are advertised in the travel sections of major newspapers like the *New York Times*, *LA Times* or *Toronto Star*. If you are prepared to take pot luck, try for a stand-by or consolidated fare, or consider a courier flight (remember you can only take hand luggage with you on these deals). **Now Voyager**, ✆ (212) 431 1616, is one of the main US courier flight companies (annual membership fee), based at Suite 307, 74 Varrick St, New York, NY 10013. Both **STA** and **Council Travel** are well worth contacting for cheaper charter flights and budget student travel. Both agencies have branches in several major US cities. In Canada, **Travel Cuts**, ✆ (416) 979 2406, specializes in discounted student fares. Numerous travel clubs and agencies also specialize in discount fares (you may have to pay a membership fee).

By Rail

Lombardy is easily accessible by rail from the UK. With Eurostar from London the journey time to Milan is about 12 hours; services run daily in summer. Return fares using Eurostar range from £170 to £250. Travelling by train and ferry takes about 24 hours, though you can stop off as often as you like. Fares range from £170 to £250, or £129 for the under-26s. Once you've added the cost of a couchette (£10 or so), rail travel is scarcely cheaper than flying unless you are able to take advantage of student or youth fares (£144 under 26). Discounts are available for families and young children. **Interail** (UK) or **Eurail** (USA/Canada) passes give unlimited travel throughout Europe for one or two months. If you are just planning to see

Italy, these passes may not be worthwhile (see 'Getting Around', below, for details on specifically Italian rail passes). A month's full Interail pass covering France, Switzerland and Italy costs £309, or £229 for the under-26s; for France and Italy only it costs £279, or £209 for the under-26s.

Various cheap youth fares (BIJ tickets etc.) are also available; you should organize these before you leave home. **Wasteels Travel**, in the UK located adjacent to Platform 2, Victoria Station, London SW1V 1JT, ✆ (0171) 834 7066, and in the US at 7041 Grand National, Suite 207, Orlando, 32819 Florida, ✆ (407) 351 2537, offer various passes. Italian rail passes currently cost £88 and are valid for up to 5 people for a maximum of 20 journeys or 3000km. The Italy Flexi Card allows 4 days' unlimited travel in any month for £84, 8 days for £116 or 12 days for £148 (with no extra costs). The Italy Rail Card allows 8 days' travel for £122, 15 days for £150, 21 days for £176 and 30 days for £210. Wasteels often have further discounts for students and under-26s using Eurostar. In the USA or Canada, contact **Rail Europe**, whose central office is at 226–230 Westchester Ave, White Plains, NY 10604, ✆ (914) 682 2999 or ✆ (800) 438 7245.

CIT offices, which act as agents for Italian State Railways, also offer various deals; contact them in the **UK** at Marco Polo House, 3–5 Lansdowne Rd, Croydon, Surrey, ✆ (0181) 686 0677, in the **USA** at 15 West 44th St, New York, NY 10036, ✆ (212) 730 2121, and in **Canada** at 1450 City Councillors St, Suite 750, Montreal H3Λ 2E6, ✆ (514) 845 4310.

In Italy, a good bet for discounted train tickets, flights etc. is **CTS**, Corso P. Ticinese 83, Milan, ✆ 02 837 2674.

A convenient pocket-sized **timetable**, detailing all the main and secondary Italian railway lines, is now available in the UK, costing £7 (plus 50p postage). Contact Accommodation Line Ltd, 11–12 Hanover Square, London W1, ✆ (0171) 409 1343; Y Knot Travel, Morley House, 1st Floor, 314/320 Regent St, London W1, ✆ (0171) 436 0448; or Italwings, Travel & Accommodation, 162–8 Regent St, London W1R 5TB, ✆ (0171) 287 2117. If you wait until you arrive in Italy, however, you can pick up the Northern Italy timetable at any station for about L4500.

By Road

Eurolines is the main international **bus** operator in Europe, with representatives in Italy and many other countries. In the UK they can be found at 52 Grosvenor Gardens, London SW1, ✆ (0171) 730 8235/(01582) 404511, and are booked through National Express. Regular services run to many northern Italian cities (on Wed or Sat), including Milan, where they will generally arrive at the Piazza Castello. Needless to say, the journey is long (24 hours) and the relatively small saving in price (a return ticket from London to Milan costs about £109 or £99 for under-26s) makes it a masochistic choice in comparison with a discounted air fare, or even rail travel. However, if it isn't pitch-dark, you'll catch a fleeting glimpse of Mont Blanc and Turin on the way.

To bring a GB-registered **car** into Italy, you need a vehicle registration document, full driving licence and insurance papers. Non-EU citizens should preferably have an international driving licence which has an Italian translation incorporated. Your vehicle should display a nationality plate indicating its country of registration.

It's the best part of 24 hours' driving time even if you stick to fast toll roads. The most scenic and hassle-free route is via the Alps, avoiding crowded Riviera roads in summer, but if you take a route through Switzerland expect to pay for the privilege (£14 or SF30 for motorway use). In winter the passes may be closed and you will have to stick to those expensive tunnels (one-way tolls range from about L22,000 for a small car). You can avoid some of the driving by putting your car on the train, though this is scarcely a cheap option. Express Sleeper Cars run to Milan from Paris or Boulogne (infrequently in winter). Milan is a major junction of Italy's motorways and many smaller national roads. Fog and snow can make it a hazardous winter destination. Foreign-plated cars are currently entitled to free breakdown assistance from the **ACI** (Italian Touring Club).

For information on driving in Italy, contact the motoring organisations: **AA**, ✆ (0990) 500600 or **RAC**, ✆ (0891) 347 333 (50p per minute), both in the UK, and **AAA**, ✆ (407) 444 4000, in the USA and ✆ (416) 221 4300 in Canada (Toronto).

Entry Formalities

Passports and Visas

EU nationals with a valid passport can enter and stay in Italy as long as they like. Citizens of the USA, Canada, Australia and New Zealand need only a valid passport to stay up to three months in Italy; this can be extended by obtaining a special visa in advance from an Italian embassy or consulate (*see* p.20).

By law you should register with the police within eight days of your arrival in Italy. In practice this is done automatically for most visitors when they check in at their first hotel. Don't be alarmed if the owner of your self-catering property proposes to 'denounce' you to the police when you arrive—it's just a formality.

Customs

EU nationals over the age of 17 can now import a limitless amount of goods for personal use, provided duty has already been paid. If you arrive from a non-EU destination, you have to pass through the Italian customs. How the frontier police manage to recruit such ugly, mean-looking characters to hold the submachine guns and drug-sniffing dogs from such a good-looking population is a mystery, but they'll let you be if you don't look suspicious and haven't brought along more than 200 cigarettes or 100 cigars, or more than a litre of hard drink or three bottles of wine, a couple of cameras, a movie camera, 10 rolls of film for each, a tape-recorder, radio, record-player, one canoe less than 5.5m, sports equipment for personal use, and one TV (though you'll have to pay for a licence for it at customs). Pets must be accompanied by a bilingual Certificate of Health from your local veterinary inspector. You can take the same items listed above home with you without hassle—except of course your British pet. US citizens may return with $400 worth of merchandise—keep your receipts.

Currency

There are no limits to how much money you bring into Italy: legally you may not export more than L20,000,000 in Italian banknotes, a sum unlikely to trouble many of us, and officials rarely check.

Tour Operators and Special Interest Holidays

UK operators offer holidays in the Lakes area, including many tours of gardens and villas, and painting courses. City and opera visits to Milan can also be arranged. Not all those operators listed below are necesssarily ABTA-bonded; check before booking.

in the UK

Abercrombie & Kent, Sloane Square House, Holbein Place, London SW1W 8NS, ✆ (0171) 730 9600. Milan in all seasons; gardens of the Veneto and Lombardy.

ACE Study Tours, Babraham, Cambridge CB2 4AP, ✆ (01223) 835 055. Italian Lakes, villas and gardens.

Citalia, Marco Polo House, 3–5 Lansdowne Rd, Croydon CR9 1LL, ✆ (0181) 686 5533, ✉ (0181) 681 0712.

Cosmos, Tourama House, 17 Holmesdale Rd, Bromley, Kent BR2 9LX, ✆ (0181) 464 3444. Lakes guided tours.

Cresta Holidays, Tabley Court, Victoria St, Altringham, Cheshire WA14 1EZ, ✆ (0161) 927 7000. Milan city tours; Como.

Crystal Holidays, Crystal House, The Courtyard, Arlington Rd, Surbiton, Surrey KT6 6BW, ✆ (0181) 390 5554. Lakes and gardens.

Eclipse Direct, First Choice House, Peel Cross Road, Salford, Manchester, M5 2AN, ✆ (0990) 010 203.

Italian Escapades, 227 Shepherds Bush Rd, London W6 7AS, ✆ (0181) 748 2116. Milan.

Italiatours, 9 Whyteleafe Business Village, Whyteleafe Hill, Whyteleafe, Surrey, CR3 0AT, ✆ 01883 623363. Milan opera and football.

JMB, Rushwick, Worcester WR2 5SN, ✆ (01905) 425 628, ✉ (01905) 420219. Opera.

Kirker, 3 New Concordia Wharf, Mill St, London SE1 2BB, ✆ (0171) 231 3333, ✉ (0171) 231 4771. Milan city breaks.

Magic of Italy, 227 Shepherds Bush Rd, London W6 7AS, (0181) 748 7575.

Martin Randall Travel, 10 Barley Mow Passage, Chiswick, London W4 4PH, ✆ (0181) 742 3355, ✉ (0181) 742 7766. Duchy of Milan and opera tours (guest lecturers).

Page & Moy, 136–140 London Rd, Leicester LE2 1EN, ✆ (0116) 250 7979. Gardens.

Prospect Music & Art, 454/458 Chiswick High Rd, London W4 5TT, ✆ (0181) 995 2151, ✉ (0181) 742 1969. Opera; villas and gardens.

Saga, The Saga Building, Middelburg Sq, Folkestone, Kent CT20 1AZ, ✆ (0800) 300 500, ✉ 01303 776647. Majesty of the Lakes.

Shearings, Miry Lane, Wigan, Greater Manchester WN3 4AG, ✆ (01942) 824 824, ✉ (01942) 230949. Lakes—accompanied tours.

STA, 74 & 86 Old Brompton Rd, London SW7, or 117 Euston Road, London NW1, ✆ (0171) 361 6161.

Travel for the Arts, 117 Regent's Park Rd, London NW1 8UR, ✆ (0171) 483 4466 ✉ (0171) 586 0639. Custom-made Milan opera holidays.

Venice Simplon-Orient Express, Sea Containers House, 20 Upper Ground, London SE1 9PF, ✆ (0171) 928 6000.

Wallace Arnold, Gelderd Rd, Leeds, LS12 6DH, ✆ (0113) 263 4234. Lakes (coach tours).

in the USA

CIT Tours, 342 Madison Ave, Suite 207, New York, NY 10173, ✆ (212) 697 2100, and 6033 West Century Blvd, Suite 980, Los Angeles, CA 90045, ✆ (310) 338 8616.

Dailey-Thorp Travel, 330 West 58th Street, New York, NY 10019, ✆ (212) 307 1555. Milan opera.

Maupintour, 1515 St Andrew's Drive, Lawrence, Kansas 66047, ✆ (785) 843 1211.

Olson Travelworld, 1145 Clark St, Stephen's Pt, Wisconsin 54481, ✆ (715) 345 0505.

Trafalgar Tours, 11 East 26th Street, New York, NY 10010, ✆ (212) 689 8977.

Travel Concepts, 62 Commonwealth Ave, Suite 3, Boston, MA 02116, ✆ (617) 266 8450. Wine and food.

For **camping** and **self-catering** specialists *see* pp.35 and 36.

Getting Around

Italy has an excellent network of airports, railways, highways and byways, and you'll find getting around fairly easy—until one union or another takes it into its head to go on strike (to be fair, they rarely do it during the high holiday season). There's plenty of talk about passing a law to regulate strikes, but it won't happen soon, if ever. Instead, learn to recognize the word in Italian: *sciopero* (*sho*-per-o), and do as the Romans do—quiver with resignation. There's always a day or two's notice, and strikes usually last only a day, just long enough to throw a spanner in the works if you have to catch a plane. Keep your ears open and watch for notices posted in the stations.

By Boat

All the major lakes are crisscrossed by a complex network of *battelli* (boats) and *aliscafi* (hydrofoils), some of which are regular ferries, others cruise or excursion boats either available for hire or operating to set schedules. All services are seasonal, and massively reduced during the winter. Day or longer passes allowing unlimited travel on any particular lake are available. Some services transcend frontiers and pass into Swiss waters. Ask for timetables at tourist offices, or if you're in Milan call in at the *Gestione Navigazione Laghi*, Via L Ariosto 21, ✆ 02 481 2086. Individual companies are listed by each lake.

By Train

FS Informa (train info from anywhere in Italy), 7am–9pm, ✆ (1478) 88088. www.fs-on-line.com

Italy's national railway, the **FS** (*Ferrovie dello Stato*), the most serendipitous national line in Europe, is well run, inexpensive and often a pleasure to ride. (Note that Lombardy also has several private rail lines, which, unlike the FS, won't accept Interail or Eurail passes). Possible

FS unpleasantnesses you may encounter, besides a strike, are delays, crowding (especially at weekends and in the summer), and crime on overnight trains, where someone rifles your bags while you sleep. The crowding, at least, becomes much less of a problem if you reserve a seat in advance at the *prenotazione* counter. The fee is small and can save you hours standing in some train corridor. On the upper-echelon trains, **reservations** are mandatory. Do check when you purchase your ticket in advance that the date is correct; unlike in some countries, tickets are only valid the day they're purchased unless you specify otherwise. A number on your reservation slip will indicate in which car your seat is—find it before you board rather than after. The same goes for sleepers and couchettes on overnight trains, which must also be reserved in advance.

Tickets may be purchased not only in the stations, but at many travel agents in the city centres. Fares are determined by the kilometres travelled. The system is computerized and runs smoothly, at least until you try to get a reimbursement for an unused ticket (usually not worth the trouble). Be sure you ask which platform (*binario*) your train arrives at; the big boards posted in the stations are not always correct. If you get on a train without a ticket you can buy one from the conductor, with an added 20% penalty. You can also pay a conductor to move up to first class or get a couchette. Try to avoid travel on Friday evenings, when the major lines out of the big cities are packed.

There is a fairly straightforward **hierarchy of trains**. At the bottom of the pyramid is the humble *locale* (euphemistically known sometimes as an *accelerato*) which often stops even where there's no station in sight; it can be excruciatingly slow. When you're checking the schedules, beware of what may look like the first train to your destination—if it's a *locale*, it will be the last to arrive. A *diretto* stops far less, an *expresso* just at the main towns. *Intercity* trains whoosh between the big cities and rarely deign to stop. *Eurocity* trains link Italian cities with major European centres. Both of these services require you to pay a supplement, some 30% more than a regular fare. Reservations are free but must be made at least five hours before the trip, and on some trains there are only first-class coaches. The real lords of the rails are the *ETR 450 Pendolino* trains, kilometre-eaters that will speed you to your destination as fast as trains can go (in Italy!). For these there is a more costly supplement and, on some only, first-class luxury cars.

The FS offers several **passes**. One, which you should ideally arrange at a CIT or Italian rail agent office (e.g. Wasteels) before arriving in Italy, is the 'Travel-at-Will' ticket (*Biglietto Turistico Libera Circolazione*), available only to foreigners. This is a good deal only if you mean to do some very serious train-riding on consecutive days; it does, however, allow you to ride the *Intercity/Eurocity* without paying a supplement. Tickets are sold for 8, 15, 21 or 30-day periods, first or second class, with 50% reductions for children under 12. At the time of writing, an 8-day second-class ticket is around £88 and the 30-day ticket is £152. A more flexible option is the 'Flexi Card' which allows unlimited travel for either four days within a nine-day period (second class £66, first class £98), 8 days within 12 (second class £94, first class around £140), or 12 days within 30 (second class £120, first class £190), and you don't have to pay any supplements. Another ticket, the *Kilometrico*, gives you 3000km of travel, made on a maximum of 20 journeys, and is valid for two months; one advantage is that it can be used by up to five people at the same time. Second-class tickets are currently £88, first-class £152; supplements are payable on *Intercity* trains. Other discounts, available only once you're in Italy, are 15% on same-day return tickets and 3-day returns (depending on the distance), and discounts for families of at least four travelling together. Senior citizens (men 65 and over, women 60) can also get a *Carta d'Argento* ('silver card') for L40,000 entitling them to a 20% reduction in fares. A *Carta Verde* bestows a 20% discount on people under 26 and also costs L40,000. *See* 'Getting There: By Rail', p.7.

Refreshments on routes of any great distance are provided by bar cars or trolleys; you can usually get sandwiches and coffee from vendors along the tracks at intermediary stops. Station bars often have a good variety of takeaway travellers' fare; consider at least investing in a plastic bottle of mineral water, since there's no drinking water on the trains.

Besides trains and bars, Italy's stations offer **other facilities**. All have a *deposito*, where you can leave your bags for hours or days for a small fee. The larger ones have porters (who charge L1500 per piece) and some even have luggage trolleys; major stations have an *albergo diurno* ('Day Hotel', where you take a shower, get a shave and have a haircut), information offices, currency exchanges open at weekends (not at the most advantageous rates, however), hotel-finding and reservation services, kiosks with foreign papers, restaurants, etc. You can also arrange to have a rental car awaiting you at your destination—Avis, Hertz, Aurotrans and Maggiore are the firms most widespread in Italy.

The FS is an honest crap shoot; you may find a train uncomfortably full (in which case stand by the doors, or impose on the salesmen in first class, where the conductor will be happy to change your ticket) or unexpectedly be treated to a dose of genuine Italian charm. If there's a choice, opt for one of the older cars, depressingly grey outside but fitted with comfortably upholstered seats, Art Deco lamps and old framed pictures. Now and then, you may just have a beautiful 1920s compartment all to yourself for the night—even better if you're travelling with your beloved—and be serenaded on the platform.

By Coach and Bus

Inter-city coach travel is sometimes quicker than train travel, but also a bit more expensive. The Italians aren't dumb; you will find regular coach connections only where there is no train to offer competition. Coaches almost always depart from the vicinity of the train station, and tickets usually need to be purchased before you get on. In many regions they are the only means of public transport and are well used, with frequent schedules. If you can't get a ticket before the coach leaves, get on anyway and pretend you can't speak a word of Italian; the worst that can happen is that someone will make you pay for a ticket. The base for all **country bus** lines will be the provincial capitals.

City buses are the traveller's friend. Most northern cities label routes well; all charge flat fees, at the time of writing around L1200, for rides within the city limits and in the immediate suburbs. Bus tickets must always be purchased before you get on, either at a tobacconist's, a newspaper kiosk, in bars, or from ticket machines near the main stops. Once you get on, you must 'obliterate' your ticket in the machines in the front or back of the bus; controllers stage random checks to make sure you've punched your ticket. Fines for cheaters are about L50,000, and the odds are about 12 to 1 against a check, so many passengers take a chance. If you're good-hearted, you'll buy a ticket and help some overburdened municipal transit line meet its annual deficit.

A car is certainly the best and most convenient way to get to the more remote parts of Lombardy, but quite unnecessary in Milan, where public transport is extremely efficient and parking is hell on wheels. Other large towns, like Bergamo, can also be a headache.

Third-party insurance is a minimum requirement in Italy. Obtain a Green Card from your insurer, which gives proof that you are covered. Also get hold of a **European Accident Statement** form, which may simplify things if you are unlucky enough to have an accident. Always insist on a full translation of any statement you are asked to sign.

Breakdown assistance insurance is obviously a sensible investment (e.g. AA's Five Star or RAC's Eurocover Motoring Assistance). Don't give the local police any excuse to fine you on the spot for minor infringements like worn tyres or burnt-out sidelights (such infringements could cost you L150,000 or more on a bad day). A **red triangular hazard sign** is obligatory; also recommended are a spare set of bulbs, a first-aid kit and a fire extinguisher. Spare parts may be tricky to find for non-Italian cars.

Petrol (*benzina*; unleaded is *benzina senza piombo*, and diesel *gasolio*) is very expensive, about L1800 a litre. Many petrol stations close for lunch in the afternoon, and few stay open late at night, though you may find a 'self-service' where you feed a machine nice smooth L10,000 notes. **Motorway** (*autostrada*) tolls are also quite high; the journey from Milan to Rome on the A1 costs around L80,000 at the time of writing. Rest-stops and petrol stations along the motorways stay open 24 hours. Other roads—*superstrade* on down through the Italian grading system—are free of charge.

Speed limits (generally ignored) are 130kph on motorways (110kph for cars under 1100cc or motorcycles), 110kph on main highways, 90kph on secondary roads and 50kph in built-up areas. Speeding fines may be as much as L500,000, or L100,000 for jumping a red light (a popular Italian sport).

Italians are famously anarchic behind a wheel, though perhaps a smidgeon less so in the Lombardy region than further south. Warnings, signals, and general rules of the road are frequently simply ignored; a two-lane carriageway becomes an impromptu three-lane road at a moment's notice. The only way to beat the locals is to join them. Bear in mind the ancient maxim that he/she who hesitates is lost (especially at traffic lights, where the danger of crashing into someone at the front is less great than that of being rammed from behind). All drivers, from boy racers to elderly nuns, tempt Providence by overtaking at the most dangerous of bends, and no matter how fast you are hammering along the *autostrada*, plenty of other drivers, headlights a-flashing, will fly past at supersonic rates. North Americans used to leisurely speed limits and gentler road manners may find the Italian interpretation of the highway code especially stressful.

If you are undeterred by these caveats, you may actually enjoy driving in Italy, at least away from the congested tourist centres. Signposting is generally good and roads are usually excellently maintained. Some of the roads are feats of engineering that the Romans themselves would have admired—bravura projects suspended on cliffs, crossing valleys on vast stilts, winding up hairpins. Milan is a major motorway junction, but take care on the A4 (Milan–Turin), very busy and an accident blackspot.

Buy a good road map (the Italian Touring Club series is excellent). The **Automobile Club of Italy** (ACI) is a good friend to the foreign motorist. They offer a free breakdown service, and can be reached from anywhere by dialling **116**—also use this number if you have to find the nearest service station. If you need major repairs, the ACI can make sure the prices charged are according to their guidelines.

hiring a car

Hiring a car or camper van (*autonoleggio*) is simple but not particularly cheap. There are both large international firms through which you can reserve a car in advance, and local agencies, which often have lower prices. Air or train travellers should check out possible discount packages. Most companies will require a deposit amounting to the estimated cost of the hire. VAT of 19% is applied, so make sure you take this into account when checking prices. Most companies have a minimum age limit of 21 (23 in some cases). A credit card makes life easier, and you will need to produce your licence and a passport. Current rates are around L250,000 per day for a medium-sized with unlimited mileage and collision damage waiver, including tax (hire for three days or longer is somewhat less pro rata). Most major rental companies have offices at Milan's airports or the Stazione Centrale. If you need a car for longer than three weeks, leasing may be a more economic alternative. The National Tourist Office has a list of firms in Italy that hire caravans (trailers) or camper vans. Non-residents are not allowed to buy cars in Italy.

By Taxi

Taxis are fairly expensive, so don't take too many of them if you're on a tight budget. The average meter starts at L6400, and adds L300 per kilometre. There are extra charges for luggage and trips to the airport; rates go up after 10pm and on Sundays and holidays. They usually don't stop if hailed on the streets; head for a taxi-rank (marked with a yellow line on the road). Radio-taxi services operate in Milan.

Hitchhiking

It is illegal to hitch on the *autostrade*, though you may pick up a lift near one of the toll booths. For the best chances of getting a lift travel light, look respectable and take your shades off. Hold a sign indicating your destination if you can. Never hitch at points which may cause an accident or obstruction; Italian traffic conditions are bad enough already! Risks for women are lower in northern Italy than in the more macho south, but it is not advisable to hitch alone. Two or more men may encounter some reluctance.

By Motorcycle or Bicycle

The means of transport of choice for many Italians, motorbikes, mopeds and Vespas can be a delightful way to see the country. You should only consider it, however, if you've ridden them before—Italy's hills and alarming traffic make it no place to learn. You must be at least 14 for a *motorino* (scooter) and 16 for anything more powerful. Helmets are compulsory. Costs for a *motorino* range from about L20,000 to L35,000 per day, scooters somewhat more (up to L50,000). Italians are keen cyclists as well, racing drivers up the steepest hills; if you're not training for the Tour de France, consider the region's topography well before planning a cycling tour, especially in the hot summer months. You can hire a bike in most Italian towns. Prices are about L10,000–L20,000 per day, which may make buying one interesting if you plan to spend much time in the saddle, either in a bike shop or through the classified ad papers put out in nearly every city and region. Alternatively, if you bring your own bike, do check the airlines to see what their policies are on transporting them. Bikes can be transported by train in Italy, either with you or within a couple of days—apply at the baggage office (*ufficio bagagli*).

Practical A–Z

Children

Even though a declining birthrate and the legalization of abortion may hint otherwise, children are still the royalty of Italy, and are pampered, often obscenely spoiled, probably more fashionably dressed than you are, and never allowed to get dirty. In spite of it all, most of them somehow manage to be well-mannered little charmers. If you're bringing your own *bambini* to Italy they'll receive a warm welcome everywhere. Many hotels offer advantageous rates for children and have play areas, and many larger cities have permanent **Luna Parks** or funfairs. Specifically child-orientated entertaiment is concentrated in the east: Lake Garda's **Gardaland** (Italy's approximation to Disneyland), the **Parco Minitalia** at Capriate S. Gervasio, the **Parco della Preistoria** (dinosaurs) at Rivolta d'Adda, and the **Parco Natura Viva**, near Lazise east of Lake Garda, which has another leisure park with still more dinosaurs (alas, concrete ones) and an autosafari park. A pair of **water-fun parks** compete in Valeggio sul Minci, south of Garda. On Lake Maggiore, the **Villa Pallavicino** in Stresa has a children's zoo with sea lions and zebras, and children may also like the **doll museum** at Anghera and the **puppet museum** on Isola Madre.There are several places around Lake Como to watch **silk spinning**, or perhaps a visit to the **motorcycle museum** in Mandello sul Lario is in order. Milan's **Natural History Museum** has not only stuffed rhinos, but also a good playground in the gardens nearby. Other good bets are **canal tours** or a trip to the top of the **Duomo** or the Luna Park rides at the Idroscalo.

Lake cruises, of course, are fun for everyone, and children travel half-price. If a **circus** visits town you're in for a treat; it will either be a sparkling showcase of daredevil skill or a poignant, family-run, modern version of Fellini's *La Strada*. At the time of writing a show featuring a giant octopus (La Piovra più Grande del Mondo!) and mermaids has been doing the rounds. We never quite caught up with it, but on the posters it looks great.

Climate and When to Go

Lombardy has the most exciting weather in Italy. Here the climate of the Alps meets the Mediterranean head-on and on the whole the latter wins, especially around the large lakes, shielded by the mountains from the worst of winter and large enough to maintain a Mediterranean microclimate at prealpine altitudes; olives and lemons and beautiful gardens brighten their shores. The Po valley is another story: chilly and fog-bound in winter, and a steam basket in August.

Winter is a good time not only for skiing but for seeing Milan at its liveliest, when you can meet more natives and find the sights blissfully uncrowded (if sometimes closed!). The Lakes themselves, however, may well be shrouded in mist for weeks on end. **Spring** brings warmer temperatures, blossoming trees and flowers—and few crowds apart from Easter. A few days of intermittent rain is about the worst that can happen. During the **summer** the Lakes are very crowded and there are scores of festivals and special events, though the cities are more or less abandoned to tourists in August and early September. It rarely rains (though isolated, dramatic thunderstorms may occur), and outside the plains the temperatures are usually remarkably pleasant. Early **autumn**, especially September, is perhaps the ideal time to go for the magnificent colours, the grape harvests and blue balmy days (though rain may intrude during October and November).

Average Temperatures in °C (°F)

	Jan	April	July	Oct
Milan	1.9 (35)	13.2 (55)	24.8 (76)	13.7 (56)
Lake Como	6.0 (43)	13.3 (55)	23.7 (74)	9.8 (50)
Lake Maggiore	5.2 (41)	12.9 (54)	23.9 (74)	10.1 (50)
Lake Garda	4.0 (39)	13.2 (55)	24.5 (76)	14.7 (58)

Average Monthly Rainfall in mm (in)

	Jan	April	July	Oct
Milan	62 (3)	82 (3)	47 (2)	75 (3)
Lake Como	74 (3)	47 (2)	12 (0.5)	20 (1)
Lake Maggiore	90 (4)	61 (3)	20 (1)	22 (1)
Lake Garda	31 (1)	62 (3)	72 (3)	89 (4)

Crime and Police Business

Police ✆ 113

Northern Italians tend to look down on what they perceive as the corruption and inefficiency of the south, in particular the central government in Rome. But Milan, Italy's second city, is an angel with very dirty hands and a pocketful of bribes, and in the last few years has even outscandalled Rome. This won't affect you, but a fair amount of petty crime might—purse snatchings, pickpocketing, minor thievery of the white-collar kind (always check your change) and car break-ins and theft—however, violent crime is rare.

Purse-snatchers can be discouraged if you stay on the inside of the pavement and keep a firm hold on your property (sling your bag-strap across your body, don't dangle it from one shoulder). Be aware that pickpockets strike in crowded buses and gatherings; don't carry too much cash, and split it so you won't lose the lot at once. In cities and popular tourist sights, beware groups of scruffy-looking women or children with placards, apparently begging for money. They use distraction techniques to perfection, and in general the smallest and most innocent-looking child is the most skilful pickpocket. If targeted, grab sharply hold of any vulnerable possessions or pockets and shout furiously—Italian passers-by or plain-clothes police will often come to your assistance if they realize what is happening. Be extra careful in train stations, don't leave valuables in hotel rooms, and always park your car in guarded lots or on well-lit streets, with temptations well out of sight. Purchasing small quantities of soft drugs for personal consumption is technically legal in Italy, though what constitutes a small quantity is unspecified and, if the police don't like you to begin with, it will probably be enough to get you into big trouble.

Political terrorism, once the scourge of Italy, has declined greatly in recent years, mainly thanks to special quasi-military squads of black-uniformed national police, the *carabinieri*. Local matters are usually in the hands of the *polizia urbana*; the nattily dressed *vigili urbani* concern themselves with directing traffic and handing out parking fines.

Disabled Travellers

Italy has been relatively slow off the mark in its provision for disabled visitors. Uneven or non-existent pavements, the appalling traffic conditions, crowded public transport and endless flights of steps in many public places are all disincentives. Progress is gradually being made. A national support organization in your own country may well have specific information on facilities in Italy. The Italian national tourist office or CIT (travel agency) can also advise on hotels, museums with ramps, etc. If you book your rail travel through CIT, you can request assistance if you are wheelchair-bound. If you need help while in Milan or around the Lakes, the local tourist offices can be very helpful and have even been known to find wheelchair-pushers on the spot.

In the UK, contact the **Royal Association for Disability & Rehabilitation** (RADAR), 12 City Forum, 250 City Rd, London ECIV 8AF, ✆ (0171) 250 3222, and ask for their guide *Getting There* (£5.00 inc. postage). Americans should contact **SATH** (Society for the Advancement of Travel for the Handicapped), 347 Fifth Ave, Suite 610, New York 10016, ✆ (212) 447 7284.

Embassies and Consulates

Italian consulates abroad

UK: 38 Eaton Place, London SW1X, ✆ (0171) 235 9371; 32 Melville St, Edinburgh 3, ✆ (031) 220 3695; 111 Piccadilly, Manchester, ✆ (0161) 236 9024.

Ireland: 63–65 Northumberland Road, Dublin, ✆ (01) 660 1744.

USA: 690 Park Avenue, New York, NY, ✆ (212) 737 9100; 12400 Wilshire Blvd, Suite 300, Los Angeles, CA, ✆ (310) 8200 622.

Canada: 136 Beverley St, Toronto, ✆ (416) 977 1566.

Australia: 61–69 Macquarie St, Sydney 2000, NSW, ✆ (02) 392 7900.

New Zealand: 34 Grant Rd, Thorndon, Wellington, ✆ (04) 473 5339.

consulates and embassies in Italy

UK: Via San Paolo 7, Milan, ✆ 02 723 001.

Ireland: Piazza San Pietro in Gessate 2, Milan, ✆ 02 5518 8848.

USA: Via Principe Amedeo 2/10, Milan, ✆ 02 2903 51.

Canada: Via Vittorio Pisani 19, Milan, ✆ 02 67581.

Australia: Via Borgogna 2, Milan, ✆ 02 777 041.

Festivals

Festivals in Italy are often more show than spirit (there are several exceptions to this rule), but they can add a special note to your holiday. Some are great costume affairs dating back to the Middle Ages or Renaissance; others recall ancient pre-Christian religious practices; and there are a fair number of music festivals, antique fairs and, most of all, festivals devoted to the favourite national pastime—food. Check with local tourist offices for precise dates: many dates are liable to slide into the nearest weekend.

Jan–July	Opera and ballet at La Scala, **Milan**
Jan 6	Three Kings Procession, **Milan**
Mid-Jan–May	Musical afternoons (*I pomeriggi musicali*), **Milan**
Jan 17	Sant'Antonio fair, with folklore and human chess game, **Mantua**; *I sarmenti ed i falò* at **Volongo** (Cremona): 'In a gigantic fire all the runners picked up by the young people are burnt. Meanwhile, the women prepare the characteristic '*torta dura*' (hard cake), aromatized with mint, then offered to all the people present.' Sounds risky!
Jan 19	San Bassiano fair, with free tripe, **Lodi**
Jan 26	Bonfire of the Giubiana, **Cantù** (Como), with fireworks
Jan 31	San Giulio, boat procession, **Lake Orta**
Feb	Carnivals at **Schignano** (Como) with a parade of *bei* or elegant figures and *brutt* (ragged ones), ending with a bonfire; **Bagolino** (Brescia); **Milan** (processions, floats, children's events etc.). **Bormio** has a good one, too, with masks
Ash Wednesday	Bigolada celebrations at **Castel d'Ario**, (Mantua): communal feasting on spaghetti with anchovies in main piazza)
Feb 11–12	San Bello at **Berbenno** (Sondrio), folk festival in honour of Fra' Benigno, a handsome local friar
Lent, 1st Sun	Traditional carnival with floats and food, **Grosio** (Sondrio)
Feb 15	San Faustino, **Brescia** patron saint fair and festival
March	Fashion collections, **Milan**; spring rites: 'calling up the plants', **Aprica**
Mid-March	Sant'Ambroggio carnival, **Milan**
Easter	Parade of Easter floats, **Bormio**
Mar–April	Concerts at San Maurizio church in Monastero Maggiore, **Milan**
April 9–10	Re-enactment of the Oath of the Lombard League (historical costumes and pageantry, **Bergamo**
End April/ 1st week May	Ortafiori flower festival, **Orta San Giulio**
April–May	Jazz festival Città di Milano, **Milan**
May	Piano competition, **Bergamo** and **Brescia**. Palio del Carroccio (medieval parade and horse-race), celebrating defeat of Barbarossa by the Lombard League in 1176, **Legnano** (Milan)
2nd Sun May	Asparagus festival and pig *palio*, **Cilavegna** (Pavia)
Corpus Christi	Processions with decorated streets, **Premana** (Como) and **Grosio** (Sondrio)
June	Festival Cusiano di Musica Antica, **Orta San Giulio**.
June 4	Navigli Festival, **Milan** Historical pageant and flag-tossing to commemorate imprisonment of François Ier, **Pizzighettone** (Cremona)
June 6	Festa of San Gerardo, **Monza** (feast of patron saint who once rescued the sick during a flood by turning his cloak into a raft)

June 23–24	300-year-old festival with illuminations in snail shells on Comacina, boat procession, and folk music, **Ossuccio** (Como)
June, last Sun	San Pietro, with fish, wine, and dancing, **Limone sul Garda**
July 2	Festa della Madonna della Foppa, **Gerosa** (Bergamo), marking an apparition of the Virgin
Early July	Piazza di Spagna fair, with concerts fireworks and donkey races in **Casalmaggiore** (Cremona); Feast of the Big Noses, with prizes for the biggest and strangest schnozes, **Gromo** (Bergamo)
July 16	**Contrada del Brodo**, 3-day festival at **Gallarate** (Varese)
July 29–30	Melon festival at **Casteldidone** (Cremona)
July, last Sun	*Pizzoccheri* festival, woodland feasting on grey noodles, **Teglio** (Sondrio).
August	Vacanze a Milano, **Milan**, theatre and musical events
Aug, 2nd Sun	Osei fair, hunting dogs, decoys, and nightingale imitations, at **Almenno San Salvatore** (Bergamo)
Aug 15	Ferragosto holiday, marked by the exhibition of the *madonnari*, pavement artists, **Mantua**
Aug 16	Feast of gnocchi and small salami, **Pognana Lario** (Como)
Aug, last wk	San Vito, with big fireworks, at **Omegna** (Lake Orta)
End Aug–Sept	*Settimane Musicali*, musical weeks at **Stresa** on Lake Maggiore
September	Italian Grand Prix, **Monza**; World Pumpkin Weigh-off, **Sale Marasino**, Lake Iseo
Sept, 1st Sun	Duck festival, with food, games and music, **Desenzano del Garda**
Sept, 2nd Sun	Centomiglia yacht race, **Gargnano**, Lake Garda; horse *palio* with Renaissance costumes at **Isola Dovarese** (Cremona); feast of the Missoltino, feast of sun-dried fish, **Mezzagra** (Como); polenta feasting and election of the 'Big Pot of Italy' (whoever eats the most sausages), at **Corno Giovine** (Milan)
Sept, 3rd Sun	Crotti festival at **Chiavenna** (Sondrio) with songs, dances, food and wine. *Il Grappolo d'Oro*, grape harvest festival, **Chiuro** (Sondrio); bean feast, dancing and handicrafts, **Gaverina Terme** (Bergamo)
October	Spring fashion collections, **Milan**; big food fair, **Morbegno** (Sondrio)
Oct–Nov	Organ concerts at San Maurizio in Monastero Maggiore, **Milan**
Oct, 1st Sun	Festa della Madonna del Rosario, **Montodine** (Cremona), with illuminated procession of boats down the River Serio and fireworks; duck and macaroni feasting at **San Benedetto Po** (Mantua)
Oct, 3rd Sun	Donkey palio and events at **Mezzana Bigli** (Pavia); feast of chicory, **Soncino** (Cremona)
December 7	La Scala opera season opens; Feast of Sant'Ambrogio and 'O Bei O Bei' antique market, **Milan**
Christmas Eve	Torchlight procession of the shepherds at **Canneto dell'Oglio** (Mantua); underwater Christmas crib at **Laveno** (Varese) until Epiphany; living crib with music and costumes, **Triangia** (Sondrio)
Dec–April	Stagione di Prosa, **Brescia** (theatrical performances)

There are those who eat to live and those who live to eat, and then there are the Italians, for whom food has an almost religious significance, unfathomably linked with love, *La Mamma* and tradition. In this singular country, where millions of otherwise sane people spend many of their waking hours worrying about their digestion, standards both at home and in the restaurants are understandably high. Few Italians are gluttons, but all are experts on what's what in the kitchen; to serve a meal that is not properly prepared is tantamount to an insult.

Breakfast (*colazione*) in Italy is no lingering affair, but an early-morning wake-up shot to the brain: a *cappuccino* (espresso with hot foamy milk, often sprinkled with chocolate—incidentally, first thing in the morning is the only time of day at which any self-respecting Italian will touch the stuff), a *caffè latte* (white coffee) or a *caffè lungo* (espresso with hot water), accompanied by a croissant-type roll, called a *cornetto* or *briosce*, or a fancy pastry. This repast can be consumed in any bar and repeated during the morning as often as necessary. Breakfast in Italian hotels seldom represents very good value, although buffets more in line with northern appetites are becoming increasingly popular.

Lunch (*pranzo*), generally served around 1pm, is the most important meal of the day for the Italians (except for many office workers in Milan who get by on a rapid snack). This consists of, at the bare minimum, a first course (*primo piatto*—any kind of pasta dish, broth or soup, or rice dish or pizza), a second course (*secondo piatto*—a meat dish, accompanied by a *contorno* or side dish, usually a vegetable, salad, or potatoes), followed by fruit or dessert and coffee. You can, however, begin with the *antipasti*—the appetizers Italians do so brilliantly, ranging from warm seafood delicacies to raw ham (*prosciutto crudo*), salami in a hundred varieties, lovely vegetables, savoury toasts, olives, pâté and many, many more. There are restaurants that specialize in *antipasti*, and they usually don't take it amiss if you decide to forget the pasta and meat and just nibble on these scrumptious hors-d'œuvres (though in the end it will probably cost more than a full meal). Most Italians accompany their meal with wine and mineral water—*acqua minerale*, with or without bubbles (*con* or *senza gas*), which supposedly aids digestion—concluding their meals with a *digestivo* liqueur.

Cena, or **supper**, is usually eaten around 8pm. This is much the same as *pranzo* although lighter, without the pasta (the Italians believe it lies too heavily on the stomach at night): a pizza, eggs or a fish dish and salad are common. In restaurants, however, they offer all the courses, so if you eat a light lunch you can still go for the works in the evening.

Lombard specialities

The Lombards like their food and they like it to be fairly substantial; they tend to use butter instead of olive oil, and there's a great fondness for cheese and frying in breadcrumbs. Some Lombard dishes, like the *costelleta alla Milanese*, are devoured with relish across Italy, while others are so quirky (the sweet tortellini of Crema, for instance) that you can only find them in one place. Favourite **antipasti** include meats (*salami di Milano*, carpaccio, prosciutto and *bresaola*—dried salt beef served with lemon, oil and parsley), *carciofi alla milanese* (artichokes with butter and cheese), mozzarella fried in breadcrumbs, *peperonata* (red pimentos, onions and tomatoes cooked in butter and olive oil).

First and often second courses are often based on **polenta** (yellow cornmeal, a bit like American cornmush), boiled until thick and served with butter and cheese, or cut in slices, or shaped and fried, baked or grilled. Lombard classics are *polenta e osei* (polenta slices topped with roast birds), *polenta alla Lodigiana* (round slices of polenta fried in breadcrumbs), *polenta pasticciata* (baked with cheese, meat and mushroom sauces) and Lake Iseo's famous baked polenta with tench.

As Europe's major producer of rice, Lombardy is also famous for its **risotti**, which are typically served as a first course. Look for traditional saffron-tinted *risotto alla milanese*, *risotto alla Monzese* (with sausage meat, tomato and Marsala) and Mantuan *risotto alla pilota*, with butter and onions, or more seasonal concoctions with porcini mushrooms or asparagus, or even fruit and raisins in some *cucina nuova* restaurants. Lombardy's **pasta** specialities may be served with gorgonzola, or stuffed with pumpkin and cheese, meat, fish, or spinach in melted butter and sage. If served *alla mantovana* the sauce will include meat, pounded walnuts, white wine and cream. Another local pasta speciality is *pizzoccheri* (buckwheat noodles from the Valtellina, served with butter and cheese).

A wide variety of **fish**, fresh or sun-dried, comes from the Lakes, especially trout, pike, perch, tench, chub, whitefish, barbel, bleak, eel, allice shad and, in Lake Garda, the prized *carpione*, a kind of plankton-feeding carp that lends its name to a common preparation, *in carpione* (fried and marinated with herbs); chefs in the better restaurants do magical things with them. Admirers of slippery dishes like eels, frogs or snails will find happiness in the lowlands of the Po. Donkey meat appears with alarming frequency on menus from Lake Orta to Mantua; even King Kong would balk before *stu'a'd'asnin cünt la pulenta* (stewed donkey with polenta). But don't despair—other **meat courses** include classics such as *ossobuco alla milanese* (veal knuckle braised with white wine and tomatoes, properly served with risotto) *costoletta alla milanese* (breaded cutlet—the Lombard wiener schnitzel), duckling (excellent in *Nedar*, with macaroni), *fritto misto* (veal slices, calves' liver, artichokes and zucchini, fried in bread-crumbs), *busseca* (tripe stew, with eggs, cheese and cream), *fritto alla lombardo* (rabbit pieces fried in breadcrumbs) and the hearty regional pork and cabbage stew, *cazzoela* or *cassuoela* (two of 25 different spellings).

Gorgonzola, Bel Paese and *grana padana* (like parmesan) are the region's most famous **cheeses**, and soft, creamy mascarpone, now achieving cult status in UK supermarkets, is also a Lombard product. Bitto, made of goat's and sheep's milk in the Valtellina, is well worth a try as well. Polenta is sneaks its way into **desserts**, but *torta di tagliatelle* (a cake with egg pasta and almonds) is perhaps more appealing. Each province has its own highly individual sweets, although the Milanese cake *panettone,* a light fruit cake with raisins and candied fruit, has become a Christmas tradition all over the country.

Eating Out

In Italy the various terms for types of **restaurants**—*ristorante, trattoria,* or *osteria*—have been confused. A *trattoria* or *osteria* can be just as elaborate as a restaurant, though rarely is a *ristorante* as informal as a traditional *trattoria.* Unfortunately the old habit of posting menus and prices in the windows has fallen from fashion, so it's often difficult to judge variety or cost. Invariably the least expensive type of restaurant is the *vino e cucina,* simple places serving simple cuisine for simple everyday prices. It is essential to remember that the fancier the fittings, the fancier the bill, though neither of these points has anything at all to do with the quality of the food. If you're uncertain, do as you would at home—look for lots of locals. When you eat out, mentally add to the bill (*conto*) the bread and cover charge (*pane e coperto*, between L2000 and L3000) and a 15% service charge. This is often included in the bill (*servizio compreso*); if not, it will say *servizio non compreso* and you'll have to do your own arithmetic. Additional tipping is at your own discretion.

People who haven't visited Italy for years and have fond memories of eating full meals for under a pound will be amazed at how much **prices** have risen; though in some respects eating out in Italy is still a bargain, especially when you figure out how much all that wine would have cost you at home. In many places you'll often find restaurants offering a *menu turistico*—full, set meals of usually meagre inspiration for L18,000–25,000. More imaginative chefs often offer a *menu degustazione*—a set-price gourmet meal that allows you to taste their daily specialities and seasonal dishes. Both of these are cheaper than if you had ordered the same food à la carte. When you leave a restaurant you will be given a receipt (*scontrino* or *ricevuto fiscale*) which according to Italian law you must take with you out of the door and carry for at least 60 metres. If you aren't given one, it means the restaurant is probably fudging on its taxes and thus offering you lower prices. There is a slim chance that the tax police (*guardia di finanza*) may have their eye on you and the restaurant, and if you don't have a receipt they could slap you with a heavy fine (L30,000).

Restaurant Price Categories	
very expensive	over L90,000
expensive	L60–90,000
moderate	L40–60,000
cheap	below L40,000

There are several alternatives to sit-down meals. The '**hot table**' (*tavola calda*) is a stand-up buffet where you can choose a simple prepared dish or a whole meal, depending on your appetite. The food in these can be impressive; many offer only a few hot dishes, pizza and sandwiches, though in every fair-sized town there will be at least one *tavola calda* with seats where you can contrive a complete dinner outside the usual hours. Little shops that sell pizza by the slice or weight are common in resorts and city centres. At any grocer's (*alimentari*) or market (*mercato*) you can buy the materials for countryside or hotel-room **picnics**; some places in the smaller towns will make the sandwiches for you. For really elegant picnics, have a *tavola calda* pack up something nice. And if everywhere else is closed, there's always the railway station—bars will at least have sandwiches and drinks, and perhaps some surprisingly good snacks you've never heard of before. Some of the station bars also prepare *cestini di viaggio*, full-course meals in a basket to help you through long train trips. Common snacks you'll encounter include *panini* of prosciutto, cheese and tomatoes, or other meats; *tramezzini*, little sandwiches of plain, square white bread that are always much better than they look; and pizza, of course.

Wine

Italy is a place where everyday wine is cheaper than Coca-Cola or milk, and where nearly every family owns some vineyards or has relatives who supply their daily needs—which are not great. Even though they live in one of the world's largest wine-growing countries, Italians imbibe relatively little; shockingly, teetotallers number in the millions.

To accompany its infinite variety of regional dishes, Italy produces an equally bewildering array of regional wines, many of which are rarely exported and best drunk young. Unless you're dining at a restaurant with an exceptional cellar, do as the Italians do and order a carafe of the local wine (*vino locale* or *vino della casa*). It's inexpensive, and you won't often be wrong. Most wines are named after the grape and the district they come from. If the label says **DOC** (*Denominazione di Origine Controllata*) it means that the wine comes from a specially defined area and was made according to a certain method.

Lombardy produces many commendable wines which are comparable with the more illustrious vintages of Piedmont and Tuscany, although its residents often snobbily prefer to drink wine from other regions, leaving the enterprising Swiss (many of whom own local vineyards) to snap up the most interesting vintages and whistle them over the border in their Mercedes car boots.

Lombardy's noblest wines come from the **Valtellina**, where the vines grow on immensely steep walled terraces, and cables are used to transfer the harvested grapes to the valleys below (*see* p.195). Delicious light sparkling wines, fresh white wines and mellow reds hail from the **Franciacorta** region, and are often found in restaurant carafes around the Lakes. Southwest Lombardy's Po valley produces a large quantity of wine, in a huge zone known as DOC **Oltrepò Pavese**, much sold through cooperatives; the three potent reds with funny names, Buttafuoco, Barbacarlo and Sangue di Giuda, go down especially well. Lake Garda is surrounded with vineyards, from the well known Bardolino and Bianco di Custoza to the elegant dry white Lugano.

Italians are fond of post-prandial digestives—the famous Stock or Vecchia Romagna **brandies** are always good. **Grappa** (*acquavitae*) is usually tougher, and often drunk in black coffee (a *caffè corretto*). **Fernet Branca**, **Cynar** and **Averno** are other popular aperitif/digestives; and liqueurs like **Strega**, the witch potion from Benevento, apricot-flavoured **Amaretto**, cherry **Maraschino**, aniseed **Sambuca**, as well as any number of locally brewed elixirs, often made by monks, are other popular choices.

Health and Emergencies

Fire © 115
Ambulance © 113

Non-emergencies can be treated at a *pronto soccorso* (casualty/first aid department) at any hospital clinic (*ambulatorio*), or at a local health unit (*unita sanitarial locale*—USL). Airports and main railway stations also have **first-aid** posts. Most Italian doctors speak at least rudimentary English, but if you can't find one contact your consulate. Standards of health care in Milan and Lombardy in general are high. If you have to pay for any health treatment, make sure you get a receipt to claim for reimbursement later.

You can insure yourself for almost any possible mishap—cancelled flights, stolen or lost baggage and health. Check your current policies to see if they cover you while abroad, and under what circumstances, and judge whether you need a special **traveller's insurance** policy (check student cards and credit cards to see if they entitle you to some medical cover abroad). Travel agencies as well as insurance companies sell traveller's insurance; they are not cheap.

Citizens of EU countries and Australia are entitled to **reciprocal health care** in Italy's National Health Service and a 90% discount on prescriptions (if you're British, bring **Form E111** with you). The E111 does not cover all medical expenses (e.g. no repatriation costs and no private treatment), and you may want to take out separate travel insurance for full cover. Note that there are no reciprocal agreements between Italy and New Zealand, Canada or the USA.

Dispensing **chemists** (*farmacia*) are generally open 8.30am–1pm and 4–8pm. Pharmacists are trained to give advice for minor ills. Any large city will have a *farmacia* that stays open 24 hours (in **Milan** it's at the Stazione Centrale); others take turns to stay open (the address rota is posted in the window). Prescriptions can be hard to match; bring any drugs you need regularly.

Maps and Publications

The maps in this guide are for orientation only, and to explore in any detail invest in a good, up-to-date regional map before you arrive. For an excellent range of maps in the UK, try **Stanford's**, 12–14 Long Acre, London WC2 9LP, ✆ (0171) 836 1321, the **Travel Bookshop**, 13 Blenheim Cres, London W11, ✆ (0171) 229 5260, or **Daunt Books**, 83 Marylebone High St, London W1, ✆ (0171) 224 2295. In the USA, try **The Complete Traveller**, 199 Madison Ave, New York, NY 10016, ✆ (212) 685 9007. Excellent maps are produced by the **Touring Club Italiano**, **Michelin** and the **Istituto Geografico de Agostini**. They are available at all major bookshops in Italy or sometimes on news-stands. Tourist offices can often supply area maps and town plans; those around the lakes often provide good walking maps and trail guides put out by the **Club Alpino Italiano**.

Books are expensive in Italy, and outside the cities the selection of English-language books is usually limited to paperback bestsellers at the larger news-stands. Milan's newspaper, the *Corriere della Sera*, is one of the country's best, with a nationwide distribution. Major English-language newspapers can be found in the cities and resort areas; *Time*, *Newsweek* and *The Economist* are also readily available.

Money

It's a good idea to order a wad of *lire* from your home bank to have on hand when you arrive in Italy, the land of strikes, unforeseen delays and quirky banking hours (*see* below), though take care how you carry it. Obtaining money is often a frustrating business involving much queueing and form-filling. The major banks and exchange bureaux licensed by the Bank of Italy give the best exchange rates for currency or traveller's cheques. Hotels, private exchanges in resorts and FS-run exchanges at railway stations usually have less advantageous rates, but are open outside normal banking hours. There are several weekend exchange offices in Milan, e.g. at **Banca Ponti**, Piazza del Duomo 19 (*Sat 8.30–1*), and exchange offices at both airports and the Stazione Centrale. Remember that Italians indicate decimals with commas and thousands with full points.

Besides traveller's cheques, most banks will give you cash on a recognized credit card or Eurocheque with a Eurocheque card (taking little or no commission), and automatic tellers (Bancomats) at nearly every bank spout cash if you have a PIN number. Read the instructions carefully or the machine may devour your card. MasterCard (Access) is much less widely acceptable in Italy. Large hotels, resort restaurants, shops, car hire firms and petrol stations will accept plastic as well; always check the signs on the door. Make sure you bring the correct number to call if you have lost your card: you will probably have to call the international operator and ask them to reverse the charges. **American Express** office in Milan: Via Brera 3, ✆ 7200 3694 (*open Mon–Thurs 9–5.30, Fri till 5*).

You can have money transferred to you through an Italian bank but this process may take over a week, even if it's sent urgent (*espressissimo*). You will need your passport as identification when you collect it.

Opening Hours

Italy (except for bars and restaurants) closes down at 1pm until 3 or 4pm to eat and properly digest the main meal of the day. Afternoon hours are from 4 to 7, often from 5 to 8 in the hot summer months. Most of Milan closes down completely during August, when locals flee from the polluted frying pan to the hills, lakes or coast.

Banks: Banking hours vary, but core times in Milan and Lombardy are more or less Monday to Friday from 8.30am to 1pm and 3 to 4pm, closed weekends and on local and national holidays (*see* below). Outside normal hours, you will usually be able to find a travel office or hotel or even a machine in a wall to change money for a small commission.

Shops: Shops are usually open Monday–Saturday from 8am to 1pm and 3.30pm to 7.30pm, though hours vary according to season and are shorter in smaller centres. In Milan, shopping capital of Italy (if not the universe), hours are longer. A few supermarkets and department stores stay open throughout the day.

Churches: Italy's churches have always been a prime target for art thieves and as a consequence are usually locked when there isn't a sacristan or caretaker to keep an eye on things. All churches, except for the really important cathedrals and basilicas, close in the afternoon at the same hours as the shops, and the little ones tend to stay closed. Always have a pocketful of coins for the light machines, or whatever work of art you came to inspect will remain shrouded in ecclesiastical gloom. Don't visit during services, and don't come to see paintings and statues in churches in the week preceding Easter—you will probably find them covered with mourning shrouds.

Museums and galleries: Many of Italy's museums are magnificent, many are run with shameful neglect, and many have been closed for years for 'restoration', with slim prospects of reopening in the foreseeable future. With two works of art per inhabitant, Italy has a hard time financing the preservation of its national heritage; it's as well to enquire at the tourist office to find out exactly what is open and what is 'temporarily' closed before setting off on a wild-goose chase.

In general, Sunday afternoons and Mondays are dead periods for the sightseer—you may want to make them your travelling days. Places without specified opening hours can usually be visited on request but it is best to go before 1pm. **Entrance charges** to Lombardy's star museums are quite steep but others are fairly low, and some sights are completely free. For museums and galleries the average is L5000 to L8000, for churches or cathedrals about L4000, and for castles, palaces, villas and their gardens around L6000. Prices that substantially exceed these amounts will be marked *adm exp*. EU citizens under 18 and over 65 get free admission to state museums, at least in theory.

Most museums, as well as banks and shops, are closed on the following national holidays:

1 January (New Year's Day), **6 January** (Feast of the Epiphany), **Easter Monday**, **25 April** (Liberation Day), **1 May** (Labour Day), **15 August** (Assumption, also known as *Ferragosto*, the official start of the Italian holiday season), **1 November** (All Saints' Day), **8 December** (Immaculate Conception), **25 December** (Christmas Day), **26 December** (*Santo Stefano*, St Stephen's Day).

The feast day of Saint Ambrose (*Sant'Ambroggio*) on **7 December** is the closest the hard-working Milanese have to a civic holiday.

Packing

It's hard to overdress in Italy; whatever grand strides Italian designers have made on the international fashion merry-go-round, most of their clothes are purchased domestically, prices be damned. It's not that the Italians are very formal; they simply like to dress up with a gorgeousness that adorns their cities just as much as those old Renaissance churches and palaces. The few places with dress codes are the major churches and basilicas (no shorts, sleeveless shirts or strappy sundresses—women should tuck a light silk scarf in a bag to throw over the shoulders), casinos and a few smart restaurants.

After agonizing over fashion, remember to pack small and light: transatlantic airlines limit baggage by size (two pieces are free up to 1.5m in height and width; in second class you're allowed one of 1.5m and another up to 1.1m). Within Europe limits are by weight: 20kg (44lbs) in second class, 30kg (66lbs) in first. You may well be penalized for anything larger. If you're travelling by train, you'll want to keep bags to a minimum: jamming big suitcases in overhead racks in a crowded compartment isn't much fun for anyone. Never take more than you can carry, but do bring the following: any prescription medicine you need, an extra pair of glasses or contact lenses if you wear them, a pocket knife and corkscrew (for picnics), a flashlight (for dark frescoed churches, caves and crypts), and a travel alarm (for those early trains). If you're a light sleeper, you may want to invest in earplugs. Your electric appliances will work in Italy if you adapt and convert them to run on 220 AC with two round prongs on the plug.

Photography

Film and **developing** are much more expensive than they are in either the UK or the USA. You are not allowed to take pictures in most museums and in some churches. Lombardy's light is less dazzling than in the vivid south, and clarity may be affected by Milanese air pollution or local mists, but allow for extra brightness reflected off the water if you're by the lakes. Most cities now offer one-hour processing if you're in a hurry.

Post Offices

Dealing with *la posta italiana* has always been a risky, frustrating, time-consuming affair. One of the scandals that mesmerized Italy in recent years involved the minister of the post office, who disposed of tons of backlog mail by tossing it in the Tiber. When the news broke, he was replaced—the new minister, having learned his lesson, burned all the mail the post office was incapable of delivering. Not surprisingly, fed-up Italians view the invention of the fax machine and Internet as gifts from the Madonna.

If you want to take your chances, post offices are usually open Monday to Saturday from 8am until 1pm, or until 6 or 7pm in a large city. To have your mail sent poste restante (general delivery), have it addressed to the central post office (*Fermo Posta*) and allow three to four weeks for it to arrive. Make sure your surname is very clearly written in block capitals. To pick up your mail you must present your passport and pay a nominal charge. Stamps (*francoboli*) may be purchased in post offices or at tobacconists (*tabacchi*, identified by their blue signs with a white T). Prices fluctuate. The rates for letters and postcards (depending how many words you write!) vary according to the whim of the tobacconist or postal clerk. You can also have money telegraphed to you through the post office; if all goes well, this can happen in a mere three days, but expect a fair proportion of it to go into commission.

Shopping

'Made in Italy' has become a byword for style and quality, especially in fashion and leather, but also in home design, ceramics, kitchenware, jewellery, lace and linens, glassware and crystal, chocolates, bells, Christmas decorations, hats, straw work, art books, engravings, handmade stationery, gold and silverware, bicycles, sports cars, woodworking, a hundred kinds of liqueurs, aperitifs, coffee machines, gastronomic specialities, and antiques (both reproductions and the real thing). And where more so than in glossy Milan, Italy's major shopping city, the cynosure of innovative style and fashion throughout the world? Surprisingly in this Aladdin's cave big-city competition keeps prices lower than most Italian cities and usually much lower than you'll find in posh resort boutiques.

If you are looking for antiques, be sure to demand a certificate of authenticity—reproductions can be very, very good. To get your antique or modern art purchases home, you will have to apply to the export department of the Italian Ministry of Education and pay an export tax; your seller should know the details. Be sure to save receipts for Customs.

Sports and Activities

Beaches: The beaches around the Lakes are mostly shingly strips—useful platforms for sunbathing or landing boats, but little more. Many of them shelve steeply and the water is never very warm. However sparkling the water may seem, some shores suffer from pollution and bathing may not be exactly as healthy as you think; Garda, one of the cleanest lakes in Europe, is the great exception, and has the longest beaches, too.

Casinos: A curious outpost in the centre of Lake Lugano, surrounded by the Swiss canton of Ticino, Campione d'Italia's *raison d'être* is a prosperous casino where the Swiss get a chance to throw caution and any spare francs at the croupiers. Other nationalities with money to burn are also welcome (take your passport and a jacket and tie).

Fishing: Lombardy's rivers are renowned for good fishing; to try your luck you need to purchase a year's membership card (currently L189,000) from the *Federazione Italiana della Pesca Sportiva*, which has an office in every province; they will inform you about local conditions and restrictions. Bait and equipment are readily available.

Football: Soccer (*calcio*) is a national obsession. For many Italians its importance far outweighs tedious issues like the state of the nation, the government or any momentous international event—not least because of the weekly chance of becoming an instant *lira* billionaire in the *Lotteria Sportiva*. The sport was actually introduced by the English but a similar game, like a cross between football and rugby, has existed in Italy since the Renaissance. Italian teams are known for their grace, precision and teamwork; rivalries are intense, scandals rife, racism an occasional problem, yet crowd violence is minimal compared with the havoc wreaked by Britain's lamentable fans. *Serie A* is the equivalent of the first division, comprising 18 teams; Milan's two teams, **Inter** and **AC Milan**, are at the top of the tree; details on match tickets are on p.90.

Golf: Lombardy has a wide variety of beautiful courses, particularly around Lake Como. Write or ring beforehand to check details before turning up. Most take guests and hire equipment (a selection of these is given below, but there are many others).

> **Bergamo** (27 holes): 24030 Almenno S. Bartolomeo, ✆ 035 640028
>
> **Carimate** (18 holes): 22060 Carimate, ✆ 031 790226
>
> **La Pinetina** (18 holes): 22070 Appiano Gentile, ✆ 031 933202
>
> **Menaggio e Cadenabbia** (18 holes): 22010 Grandola e Uniti, ✆ 0344 32103
>
> **Milan** (27 holes): 20052 Parco di Monza, ✆ 039 303081
>
> **Molinetto** (18 holes): 20063 Cernusco sul Naviglio, ✆ 02 92105128
>
> **Monticello** (36 holes): 22070 Cassina Rizzardi, ✆ 031 928055
>
> **Varese** (18 holes): 21020 Luvinate, ✆ 0332 229302
>
> **Villa d'Este** (18 holes): 22030 Montorfano, ✆ 031 200200

Hiking and mountaineering: These sports become steadily more popular among native Italians every year, and Lombardy now has a good system of marked trails and Alpine refuges run by the **Italian Alpine Club** (CAI) located in every province (even the flat ones, where they organize excursions into the hills). If you're taking some of the most popular trails in summer (especially in the Stelvio National Park or around the Lakes), you would be well advised to write beforehand to reserve beds in refuges. Walking in the Alps is generally practicable between May and October, after most of the snow has melted; all the necessary gear—boots, packs, tents—is available in Italy but for more money than you'd pay at home. The CAI can put you in touch with Alpine guides or climbing groups if you're up to some real adventure, or write to the Italian national tourist board for a list of operators offering mountaineering holidays.

Some Alpine resorts have taken to offering *Settimane Verdi* (Green Weeks)— accommodation and activity packages for summer visitors similar to skiers' White Weeks. Trails around Lakes Como and Iseo are particularly interesting. Other areas to head for are the **Parco Nazionale dell' Stelvio** and the **Val Malanca**. For more arduous climbing, the northern province of Valtellina is best.

Motor-racing: Monza hosts the Italian Grand Prix every September. The Formula 1 track, built in 1922, is 15km out of town, reached along Viale Monza from Piazzale Loreto.

Skiing and winter sports: Lombardy's most famous ski resort, **Bormio**, at the entrance to Italy's largest national park, has hosted world events in recent years, and doubles as a summer resort and spa too (glacier skiing is practised above the Stelvio pass). The Valtellina, Ossola and Bergamasque valleys have other skiing facilities; Monte Baldo on the east side of Lake Garda and the Grigna range near Lecco also have well-equipped resorts.

Facilities in Italy have improved greatly and now compare with other European skiing areas, but are usually less expensive. Prices are highest during Christmas and New Year holidays, in February and at Easter. Most resorts offer *Settimane Bianche* (White Weeks), off-season packages at economical rates. Other sports, such as ice-skating and bobsleighing, are available at larger resorts.

Watersports: Riva, on Lake Garda, is the main resort for swimming and watersports, with sailing, diving and windsurfing schools. Try Bouwmeester Windsurfing Centre by the Hotel Pier, ✆ 0464 554 230. Torbole nearby is another popular windsurfing spot. Contact Centro Windsurf, Colonia Pavese, ✆ 0464 505 385. Lake Como also has well-equipped sailing and windsurfing schools. **Waterskiing** is possible on all the major lakes.

Sailing: Fraglia della Vela, ✆ 0464 552 460, in Riva can provide plenty of information about sailing on Lake Garda. Yacht charters are available from Horca Myseria, Via Pelitti 1, 20126 Milan, ✆ 02 2552585. For further information, contact the **Italian State Tourist Office**.

Telephones

Public phones in Italy take either coins or phone cards (*schede telefoniche*) available in L5000, L10,000 or L15,000 amounts at tobacconists or news-stands; stock up for a long international call, or hunt out a metered *telefoni a scatti* (bars are a good place). In a city there are phones in the offices of SIP (*Società Italiana Telefoni*), the only place where you can make reverse-charge or collect calls (*a erre*). Try to avoid phoning from hotels, which often add 25% to the bill. Telephone numbers in Italy change with alarming regularity. Many places have public fax machines, but the speed of transmission make costs high.

Direct calls may be made by dialling the international prefix (for the UK 0044, Ireland 00353, USA and Canada 001, Australia 0061, New Zealand 0064). If you're **calling Italy from abroad**, dial the country code (39) and then the full dialling, including the initial zero. From the UK and Ireland call 00 39; from the USA and Canada 011 39; from Australia 0011 39; from New Zealand 00 44 39.

Time

Italy is one hour ahead of Greenwich Mean Time. From the last weekend of March to the end of September, Italian Summer Time (daylight-saving time) is in effect.

Toilets

Frequent travellers have noted a steady improvement over the years in the cleanliness of Italy's public conveniences, although as ever you will only find them in places like train and bus stations and bars. Ask for the *toilette* or *gabinetto*; in stations and the smarter bars and cafés there are washroom attendants who expect a few hundred *lire* for keeping the place decent. Don't confuse the Italian plurals: *signori* (gents), *signore* (ladies).

Tourist Information and the Internet

Tourist offices are known variously as EPT, APT or AAST, or more modestly as Pro Locos (for lunatics) and usually stick to shop hours, although in summer they often stay open on Saturday afternoons or even Sundays. They can provide hotel lists (most will call around and make bookings on the spot), town plans and information on local sights and transport. English is spoken nearly everywhere. If you're stuck, you may get more sense out of a friendly travel agency than an official tourist office. The Italian National Tourist Office (ENIT) can help before you leave home; in some countries, tourist information is also available from the offices of Alitalia or CIT (Italy's State Tourist Board).

UK: 1 Princes Street, London W1R 8AY, ✆ (0171) 408 1254, ✉ 493 6695.

USA: 630 Fifth Avenue, Suite 1565, New York, NY 10111, ✆ (212) 245 4822, ✉ 586 9249, or 12400 Wilshire Blvd, Suite 550, LA, CA 90025, ✆ (310) 820 0098, ✉ 820 6357.

Canada: 1 Place Ville Marie, Suite 1914, Montréal, Quebec H3B 3M9, ✆ (514) 866 7667, ✉ 3921429.

Japan: 2-7-14 Minimi, Aoyama, Minato-Ku, Tokyo 107, ✆ (813) 347 82 051, ✉ 347 99 356 (also responsible for Australia and New Zealand).

It can be fun and even useful to have a look at the **Internet** before you start your trip. The Italians are no slouches in cyberspace, though they're really only getting started; some day the Italian slice of the web may be as gaudy as Italian television—some day. And we do hope this information isn't out of date before it's printed!

Among the directories, Lycos is probably the best place to look for European cities and regions, with an index of sites in a few score of Italian towns; Yahoo and Infoseek (under travel: destinations) are also helpful. Several sites in these listings offer tips on accommodation, and hotel reservations in Milan and elsewhere. Milan is especially well covered on the web. A list of all cities and their sites can be found at *www.cilea.it/WWW-map/NIR-list.html.* The Milan Chamber of Commerce has an English-language site full of Chicagoish boosterism; Inter and AC Milan both keep up pages for their fans, and La Scala claims to have the 'first website of any opera theatre' (it includes a gift shop and ticket sales): *lascala.milano.it/.*

Some of the provincial APT tourist offices also maintain sites; Bergamo's (*spm.it/Bergamo/Aziende/Apt*) is one of the best. For Brescia, *www.numerica.it/Brescia/Bol/* makes a good introduction to the city, as does *www.systemy.it/pavia/home.html* for Pavia, with nice pictures.

Where to Stay

All accommodation in Italy is classified by the Provincial Tourist Boards. Price control, however, has been deregulated since 1992, leaving hotels to set their own rates, which means that in some places prices have rocketed. After a period of rapid and erratic price fluctuation, tariffs are at last settling down again to more predictable levels. In general, the quality of furnishings and facilities has improved in all categories in recent years. But you can still find plenty of older hotels and *pensioni* whose often charming eccentricities of character and architecture may frequently be at odds with modern standards of comfort or even safety. Milan has the most expensive and heavily booked hotels in Italy and a major trade fair could put all your travel plans in jeopardy.

Hotel Price Categories

Category		Double with Bath
luxury	★★★★★	L450–800,000
very expensive	★★★★	L250–450,000
expensive	★★★	L180–250,000
moderate	★★	L100–180,000
cheap	★	up to L100,000

Hotels and Guesthouses

Italian *alberghi* come in all shapes and sizes. They are rated from one to five stars, depending strictly on the facilities they offer. The star ratings are some indication of price levels, but for tax reasons not all hotels choose to advertise themselves at the rating to which they are entitled, so you may find a two-star hotel just as comfortable as, or more so than, a four-star one. Conversely, you may find that a hotel offers few stars in hopes of attracting budget-conscious travellers, but charges just as much as a higher-rated neighbour. *Pensioni* are generally more modest establishments, though nowadays the distinction between these and hotels is becoming blurred. *Locande* used to be an even more basic form of hostelry, but these days the term may denote somewhere chic.

Price lists, by law, must be posted on the door of every room, along with meal prices and any extra charges (such as air-conditioning, or even a shower in cheap places). Many hotels display two or three different rates, depending on the season. Low-season rates may be about a third lower than peak-season tariffs. Resort hotels tend to close down altogether for several months a year. During high season you should always book ahead to be sure of a room (a fax or phone reservation is less frustrating to organize than one by post). If you have paid a deposit your booking is valid under Italian law, but don't expect it to be refunded if you have to cancel. Tourist offices publish annual lists of hotels and pensions with current rates and will usually ring around if you show up without a place to sleep. Major railway stations also have accommodation booking desks.

If you arrive without a reservation, begin looking or phoning round for accommodation early in the day. If possible, inspect the room (and bathroom facilities) before you book, and check the tariff carefully. Italian hoteliers may legally alter their rates twice during the year, so printed tariffs or lists (and prices quoted in this book!) may be out of date. Hoteliers who wilfully overcharge should be reported to the local tourist office. You will be asked for your passport for registration purposes.

Prices listed in this guide are for double rooms; you can expect to pay about two-thirds the rate for single occupancy, though in high season you may be charged the full double rate in a popular resort. Extra beds are usually charged at about a third more than the room rate. Rooms without private bathrooms generally charge 20–30% less, and most offer discounts for children sharing parents' rooms, or children's meals. If you want a double bed, specify a *camera matrimoniale*. Breakfast is usually optional in hotels but obligatory in *pensioni*. You can usually get better value by eating breakfast in a bar, if you have any choice. In high season you may be expected to take half-board in resorts if the hotel has a restaurant, and one-night stays may be refused.

Youth Hostels

Alberghi or *ostelli per la gioventù* in Italian, these are few (you'll find them in **Milan, Bergamo, Menaggio, Mantua,** and **Como**) but they are pleasant and sometimes located in historic buildings. The *Associazione Italiana Alberghi per la Gioventù* (Italian Youth Hostel Association, or **AIG**) is affiliated to the International Youth Hostel Federation. For a full list of hostels, contact AIG at Via Cavour 44, 00184 Roma ✆ 06 4871152; @ 06 4880492. An international membership card will enable you to stay in any of them (cards can be purchased on the spot in many hostels). Rates are usually under L20,000, including breakfast. Discounts are available for senior citizens, and some family rooms are available. You generally have to check in after 5pm and pay for your room before 9am. Hostels usually close for most of the daytime and many operate a curfew. During the spring, noisy school parties cram hostels for field trips. In the summer it's advisable to book ahead. Contact the hostels directly.

Camping

Most of the official sites in Lombardy are near the lakes, though you can camp somewhere near most of the principal tourist centres (Milan's camp site is some way out of the city). Camping is not the fanatical holiday activity it is in France, for example, nor necessarily a bargain, but it is popular with holidaymaking families in August, when you can expect to find many sites at bursting point. Unofficial camping is generally frowned on and may attract a stern rebuke from the local police. Camper vans (and facilities for them) are increasingly popular. You can obtain a list of local sites from any regional tourist office. Camp site charges generally range from about L7000 per adult; tents and vehicles additionally cost between L7000 to L18,000 each, with plenty for L12,000 or less. Small extra charges may also be levied for hot showers and electricity. A car-borne couple could therefore spend practically as much for a night at a well-equipped camp site as in a cheap hotel. To obtain a camping carnet and to book ahead, write to the *Centro Internazionale Prenotazioni Campeggio*, Casella Postale 23, 50041, Calenzano, Firenze ✆ 055 882 382 or ✆ 055 882 3918 (ask for their list of camp sites as well as the booking form). The *Touring Club Italiano* (**TCI**) publishes a comprehensive annual guide to camp sites and tourist villages throughout Italy. Write to TCI, Corso Italia 10, Milan, ✆ 02 85261/852 6245.

UK operators offering camping or caravanning holidays in the Lakes include:

Caravan & Camping Service, 69 Westbourne Grove, London W2, ✆ (0171) 792 1944.

Caravan Club, East Grinstead House, East Grinstead, West Sussex RJ19 1UA, ✆ (01342) 326 944.

Eurocamp, Hertford Manor, Greenbank Lane, Northwich, Cheshire CW8 1HW, ✆ (01606) 787 878.

Select Sites Reservations, Travel House, 34 Brecon Rd, Abergavenny, Gwent NP7 5UG, ✆ (01873) 859 876.

Agriturismo

For a breath of rural seclusion, the normally gregarious Italians head for a spell on a working **farm**, in accommodation (usually self-catering) that often approximates to the French *gîte*. Often, however, the real pull of the place is the restaurant in which you can sample some home-grown produce (olives, wine, etc.). Outdoor activities may also be on tap (riding, fishing, cycling, and so forth). Prices are very reasonable: expect to pay around L40,000–60,000 for a double room; more for an apartment or cottage, which are usually rented by the week. *Agriturismo* is very popular around the Lakes. Local tourist offices will have information for their areas; otherwise contact **Agriturist Lombardia**, 27 Viale Isonzo, Milan, ✆ 02 5830 2122, or **Turismo Verdi**, Via Cornalia 19, Milan, ✆ 02 670 5544.

Alpine Refuges

The Italian Alpine Club operates refuges (*rifugi*) on the main mountain trails (some accessible only by *funivie*). These may be predictably spartan or surprisingly comfortable. Many have restaurants. For an up-to-date list, write to the **Club Alpino Italiano**, Via Fonseca Pimental 7, Milano, ✆ 02 2614 1378. Charges average L20,000–L25,000 per person per night, including breakfast. Most are open only from July to September, but those used by skiers are about 20% more expensive from December to April. Book ahead for August.

Self-catering Tour Operators

One of the most enjoyable and best-value ways of visiting Italy is to opt for self-catering accommodation. Centralized booking agencies exist in many countries as well as Italy, sometimes offering discounted air or ferry fares and fly-drive schemes to egg you on. Watch for the small ads, or see the list below. Lakeside cottages are the classic Lombard self-catering experience.

in the UK

The Apartment Service, 5–6 Francis Grove, Wimbledon, London SW19 4DT, ✆ (0181) 944 1444, ▨ (0181) 944 6744 for apartments in Milan; 96-page colour guide free on request.

Auto Plan, Auto Plan House, Stowe Court, Stowe St, Lichfield, Staffs WS13 6AQ, ✆ (01543) 257 777.

Eurovillas, 36 East St, Coggeshall, Essex CO6 1SH, ✆ (01376) 561 156.

Inghams, 10–18 Putney Hill, London SW15 6AX, ✆ (0181) 780 4400.

Interhome, 383 Richmond Rd, Twickenham, Middx TW1 2EF, ✆ (0181) 891 1294.

The Italian Connection, 1st Floor Suite, 68 Gloucester Place, London W1H 3HL, ✆ (0171) 486 6890, ▨ (0171) 486 6891, for hotel and self-catering bookings.

Lakes and Mountains Holidays, The Red House, Garstons Close, Titchfield, Fareham PO14 4EW, ✆ (01329) 844 405, ▨ (01329) 844 688.

in the USA

Rentals in Italy (and Elsewhere), Suzanne T. Pidduck, 1742 Calle Corva, Camarillo, CA 93010, ✆ (805) 987 5278 or ✆ (800) 726 6702, ▨ (805) 482 7976, *mail@rentvillas.com*

Hometours International, PO Box 11503, Knoxville, TN 37938, ✆ (423) 690 8484/ ✆ (800) 367 4668.

RAVE (Rent-a-Vacation-Everywhere), 135 Meigs St, Rochester, NY 14607, ✆ (716) 256 0760.

History

Quarrelsome Celts, Imperialistic Romans

The first known inhabitants of Lombardy, from about 3000 BC, left us something to remember them by: the thousands of mysterious symbols incised on the rocks of the Val Camonica north of Lake Iseo. In a remarkable example of cultural continuity, these inscriptions were made well into Roman times, while various peoples passed across the stage, notably the quiet folks who lived in Bronze Age villages built on piles over the water at Lakes Orta, Varese and Ledro.

By 400 BC, when most of the peninsula was inhabited by the '**Italics**'—a collection of distinct Indo-European tribes with similar languages—northwest Italy stood apart. Most of the area north of the Po was occupied by various Celtic and related Ligurian tribes. A century later, when the Romans arrived, they thought of this region as not Italy at all; their name for it was **Cisalpine Gaul**, 'Gaul this side of the Alps'. The two peoples were bound to come into conflict, and whenever there was war they usually found themselves on opposite sides. The Celts, skilled warriors who made whacking good swords, and gave the Romans their word for 'chariot', often got the best of it, notably in 390 BC when they occupied Rome itself; only the famous cackling of the geese, warning the Romans of a night attack on their last citadel within the city, saved Rome from complete extinction. From then on, though, the tide turned, and even the chariots couldn't keep out the legions a hundred years later, in a general Italian conflagration called the **Third Samnite War** that pitted the Romans against the Samnites, Northern Etruscans and Celts. The Romans beat everyone once and for all and annexed most of Italy by 283 BC. As in Italy, to solidify their hold the Romans founded colonies throughout Cisalpine Gaul and populated them with army veterans; these included Mediolanum (Milan), Brixia (Brescia), Como and Cremona.

Being a less developed area, Cisalpine Gaul suffered less from Roman misrule than other parts of Italy. There was little wealth to tax, and little for rapacious Roman governors to steal. The region managed to avoid most of the endless civil wars, famines and oppression that accompanied the death throes of the Roman Republic elsewhere. It did endure a last surprise raid by two Celtic tribes, the Cimbri and Teutones, who crossed over the Riviera and the Alps in a two-pronged attack in 102 BC. **Gaius Marius**, a capable though illiterate Roman general, defeated them decisively, using his popularity to seize power in Rome soon after.

The Height and Depths of Empire

In the Pax Romana of Augustus and his successors, the northern regions evolved from wild border territories to settled, prosperous provinces full of thriving new towns. Of these the most important was **Mediolanum**. The lakes became a favourite holiday destination for Rome's élite. Trade flourished along new roads like the Via Postumia to Cremona, and Mantua gave birth to Virgil just in time to put Rome's faith in its divine destiny into words. But after over two centuries at the glorious noonday of its history, in the 3rd century AD the Roman empire began to have troubles from without as well as within: a severe, long-term economic decline coinciding with a shift in military balance to the favour of the barbarians on the frontiers. **Diocletian** (284–305) completely revamped the structure of the state, converting it into a vast bureaucratic machine geared solely to meeting the needs of its army; Diocletian also initiated the division of the empire into western and eastern halves, for reasons of military and administrative necessity. The western emperors after Diocletian usually kept their court at army headquarters in Mediolanum, a convenient place to keep an eye on both the Rhine and

Danube frontiers. Through most of the 4th century that city was the western empire's *de facto* capital, while Rome itself decayed into a marble-veneered backwater.

Times were hard all over the west and, although northern Italy was relatively less hard-hit than other regions, cities decayed and trade disappeared, while debt and an inability to meet high taxes pushed thousands into serfdom or slavery. The confused politics of the time were dominated by **Constantine** (306–37), who ruled both halves of the empire, and adroitly moved to increase his political support by the Edict of Milan (313), declaring Christianity the religion of the empire. Later in the century Milan became an important centre of the new faith under its great bishop **St Ambrose**.

The inevitable disasters began in 406, when the Visigoths, Franks, Vandals, Alans and Suevi overran Gaul and Spain. Italy's turn came in 408, when Western Emperor Honorius had his brilliant general Stilicho (who was himself a Vandal) murdered. A Visigothic invasion followed; Alaric sacked Rome in 410; and in Milan St Augustine, probably echoing the thoughts of most Romans, wrote that it seemed the end of the world must be near. Italy should have been so lucky; judgement was postponed long enough for Attila the Hun to pass through in 451.

So completely had things changed, it was scarcely possible to tell the Romans from the barbarians. By the 470s the real ruler in Italy was a Gothic general named **Odoacer**, who led a half-Romanized Germanic army and probably thought of himself as the genuine heir of the Caesars. In 476 he decided to dispense with the lingering charade of the Western Empire. The last emperor, **Romulus Augustulus**, was retired to Naples, and Odoacer had himself crowned king at Italy's new Gothic capital, Pavia.

Fairly Good Goths and Really Nasty Lombards

At the beginning, the new Gothic-Latin state showed some promise; certainly the average man was no worse off than he had been under the last emperors. In 493 Odoacer was replaced (and murdered) by a rival Ostrogoth, **Theodoric**, nominally working on behalf of the Eastern Emperor at Constantinople. Theodoric proved a strong and able, though somewhat paranoid, ruler; his court witnessed a minor rebirth of Latin letters, most famously in the great Christian philosopher Boethius, while trade revived and cities were repaired. A disaster as serious as those of the 5th century began in 536 with the invasion of Italy by the Eastern Empire, part of the relentlessly expansionist policy of Emperor **Justinian**. The historical irony was profound: in the birthplace of the Roman Empire, Roman troops now came not as liberators, but foreign, largely Greek-speaking conquerors. Justinian's brilliant generals Belisarius and Narses ultimately prevailed over the Goths in a series of terrible wars that lasted until 563, but the damage to an already stricken society was incalculable.

Italy's total exhaustion was exposed only five years later with the invasion of the **Lombards**, a Germanic people who worked hard to maintain the title of Barbarian; while other, more courageous tribes moved in to take what they could of the empire, the Lombards had ranged on the frontiers like mean stray curs. Most writers, ancient and modern, mistakenly attribute the Lombards' name to their long beards; in fact, these redoubtable nomads scared the daylights out of the Italians not with beards but with their long *bardi*, or poleaxes.

Narses himself first invited the Lombards in, as mercenaries to help him overcome the Goths. Quickly understanding their opportunity, they returned with the entire horde in 568. By 571 they were across the Apennines; Pavia, one of the old Gothic capitals and the key to northern

Italy, fell after a long siege in 572. The horde's progress provided history with unedifying spectacles from the very start: King Alboin, who unified the Lombard tribes and made the invasion possible, met his bloody end at the hands of his queen, Rosmunda—whom he drove to murder by forcing her to drink from her father's skull.

They hadn't come to do the Italians any favours. The Lombards considered the entire population their slaves; in practice, they were usually content to sit back and collect exorbitant tributes. Themselves Arian Christians, they enjoyed oppressing both the orthodox and pagans. Throughout the 6th century their conquest continued apace. The popes, occasionally allied with the Lombards against Byzantium, became a force during this period, especially after the papacy of the clever, determined **Gregory the Great** (590–604), who in 603 managed to convert the Lombard queen **Theodolinda** and her people to orthodox Christianity. By then things had stabilized. Northern Italy was the Lombard kingdom proper, centred at Pavia and Monza, while semi-independent Lombard duchies controlled much of the peninsula.

In Pavia, a long succession of Lombard kings made little account of themselves. However, under the doughty warrior king **Liutprand** (712–44), Byzantine weakness made the Lombards exert themselves to try to unify Italy. Liutprand won most of his battles but gained few territorial additions. A greater threat was his ruthless successor **Aistulf**, who by 753 conquered almost all of the lands held by the Byzantines including their capital, Ravenna. If the Lombards' final solution was to be averted, the popes would have to find help from outside. The logical people to ask were the **Franks**.

Threshold of the Middle Ages

At the time, the popes had something to offer in return. The powerful **Mayors of the Palace of the Frankish Kingdom** longed to supplant the Merovingian dynasty and assume the throne for themselves, but needed the appearance of legitimacy that only the mystic pageantry of the papacy could provide. At the beginning of Aistulf's campaigns Pope Zacharias had foreseen the danger, and gave his blessing to the change of dynasties in 750. To complete the deal, the new king Pepin sent his army over the Alps in 753 and 756 to foil Aistulf's designs.

By 773 the conflict remained the same, though with a different cast of characters. The Lombard king was Desiderius, the Frankish king his cordially hostile son-in-law **Charlemagne**, who also invaded Italy twice, in 775 and 776. Unlike his father, though, Charlemagne meant to settle Italy once and for all. His army captured Pavia, and after deposing his father-in-law he took the Iron Crown of Italy for himself.

The new partnership between pope and king failed to bring the stability both parties had hoped for. With Charlemagne busy elsewhere, local lordlings across the peninsula scrapped continually for slight advantage. Charlemagne returned in 799 to sort them out, and in return got what must be the most momentous Christmas present in history. On Christmas Eve, while he was praying in St Peter's, Pope Leo III crept up behind him and deftly set an imperial crown on the surprised king's head. The revival of the dream of a united Christian empire changed the political face of Italy forever, beginning the contorted *pas de deux* of pope and emperor that was to be the mainspring of Italian history throughout the Middle Ages.

Charlemagne's empire quickly disintegrated after his death, divided among squabbling descendants, and Italy reverted to anarchy. Altogether the 9th century was a rotten time, with Italy caught between Arab raiders and the endless wars of petty nobles and battling bishops. To north Italians, the post-Carolingian era is the age of the *reucci*, the 'little kings', a profusion of puny rulers angling to advance their own interests. After 888, when the Carolingian line became extinct, ten little Frankish kings of Italy succeeded to the throne at Pavia, each with less power than the last. Their most frequent antagonists were the Lombard **Dukes of Spoleto**, though occasionally foreign interlopers like Arnolf of Carinthia (893) or Hugh of Provence (932) brought armies over the Alps to try their luck. Worse trouble for everyone came with the arrival of the barbarian **Magyars**, who overran the north and sacked Pavia in 924.

The 10th century proved somewhat better. Even in the worst times, Italy's cities never entirely disappeared. Maritime powers like Venice and Pisa led the way, but even inland cities like Milan were developing a new economic importance. From the 900s many were looking to their own resources, defending their interests against the Church and nobles alike. A big break for the cities came in 961 when **Adelheid**, the beautiful widow of one of the *reucci*, Lothar, refused to wed his successor, Berengar II, Marquis of Ivrea. Berengar had hoped to bring some discipline to Italy, and began by imprisoning the recalcitrant Adelheid in a tower by Lake Como. With the aid of a monk she made a daring escape to Canossa and the protection of the Count of Tuscany, who called in for reinforcements from the king of Germany, **Otto the Great**. Otto came over the Alps, got the girl, deposed Berengar and was crowned Holy Roman Emperor in Rome the following year. Not that any of the Italians were happy to see him, but the strong government of Otto and his successors beat down the great nobles, divided their lands and allowed the growing cities to expand their power and influence.

The Rise of the *Comune*

On the eve of the new millennium business was very good in the towns, and the political prospects even brighter. The first mention of a truly independent *comune* (a free city state; the best translation might be 'commonwealth') was in Milan, where in 1024 the first popular assembly (*parlamento*) met to decide which side the city would take in the imperial wars. And when that was done, Milan's archbishop Heribert invited the German Frankish king Conrad to be crowned in Milan, founding a new line of Italian kings.

During this period the papacy had declined greatly, a political football kicked between the emperors and the Roman nobles. In the 1050s a monk named **Hildebrand** (later Gregory VII) worked to reassert Church power, beginning a conflict with the emperors over investiture— whether the church or secular powers would name church officials. Fifty years of intermittent war followed, including the famous 'penance in the snow' of Emperor Henry IV in Canossa (1077). The result was a big revival for the papacy, but more importantly the cities of Lombardy and the north used the opportunity to increase their influence, and in some cases achieve outright independence, razing the nobles' castles and forcing them to move inside the town.

While all this was happening, the First Crusade (1097–1130) occupied the headlines, partially a result of the new papal militancy begun by Gregory VII. For Italy the affair meant nothing but profit. Trade was booming everywhere, and the accumulation of money helped the Italians to create modern Europe's first banking system. It also financed the continued independence of the *comuni*, who began to discover there simply wasn't enough Italy to hold them all. Cremona had its dust-ups with Crema, Bergamo with Brescia, while Milan, the biggest bully of them all, took on Pavia, Cremona, Como and Lodi with one hand tied behind its back.

By the 12th century, far in advance of most of Europe, Italy enjoyed prosperity unknown since Roman times. The classical past had never been forgotten: free *comuni* in the north called their elected leaders 'consuls', and artists and architects turned ancient Roman styles into the Romanesque. Even names were changing, an interesting sign of the growing national consciousness; suddenly the public records show a marked shift from Germanic to classical and biblical surnames: fewer Ugos, Othos and Astolfos, more Giuseppes, Giovannis, Giulios and Flavios.

Emperors and popes were still embroiled in the north. Frederick I—**Barbarossa**—of the Hohenstaufen or Swabian dynasty, was strong enough back home in Germany, and he made it his special interest to reassert imperial power in Italy. In 1154, he crossed the Alps for the first of five times, settling local disputes against Milan and Tortona in favour of his allies Pavia, Como and Lodi. As soon as he was back over the Alps, Milan set about undoing all his works, punishing the cities that had supported him. Back came Frederick in 1158 to starve Milan into submission and set up imperial governors (*podestàs*) in each *comune*; and, when Milan still proved defiant, he destroyed it utterly in 1161. And back over the Alps he went once more, confident that he had taught Lombardy a lesson.

What he had taught northern Italians was that the liberties of their *comuni* were in grave danger. A united opposition, called the **Lombard League**, included by 1167 every major city between Venice and Asti and Bologna (except Pavia), with spiritual backing in the person of Frederick's enemy Pope Alexander III. Twice the Lombard League beat the furious emperor back over the mountains, and when Frederick crossed the Alps for the fifth time in 1174 he was checked at Alessandria in Piedmont and forced by the league to raise his siege; then, in 1176, while his forces were in Legnano preparing to attack Milan, the Milanese militia surprised and decimated his army, forcing Frederick to flee alone to Venice to make terms with Pope Alexander. The truce he signed with the League became the **Peace of Constance**, which might as well have been called the Peace of Pigheads: all that the *comuni* asked was the right to look after their own interests and fight each other whenever they pleased.

Guelphs and Ghibellines, and the Renaissance

Frederick's grandson **Frederick II** was not only emperor but also King of Sicily, thus giving him a strong power base in Italy itself. The second Frederick's career dominated Italian politics for 30 years (1220–50). With his brilliant court, his half-Muslim army, his dancing girls, eunuchs and elephants, he provided Europe with a spectacle the like of which it had never seen. The popes excommunicated him at least twice. Now the battle had become serious. All Italy divided into factions: the **Guelphs**, under the leadership of the popes, supported religious orthodoxy, the liberty of the *comuni* and the interests of their emerging wealthy merchant class. The **Ghibellines** stood for the emperor, statist economic control and (sometimes) religious and intellectual tolerance. Frederick's campaigns and diplomacy in the north met with very limited success, and his death in 1250 left the outcome much in doubt.

His son Manfred, not emperor but merely King of Sicily, took up the battle with better luck. In 1261, however, Pope Urban IV set an ultimately disastrous precedent by inviting in Charles of Anjou, the ambitious brother of the King of France. As champion of the Guelphs, Charles defeated Manfred (1266), murdered the last of the Hohenstaufens, Conradin (1268), and held unchallenged sway over Italy until 1282. By now, however, the terms 'Guelph' and 'Ghibelline' had ceased to have much meaning; men and cities changed sides as they found expedient, and the old parties began to seem like the black and white squares on a chessboard.

Some real changes did occur out of all this sound and fury. As elsewhere around the peninsula, some cities were falling under the rule of military *signori* whose descendants would be styling themselves dukes, like the Visconti of Milan and the Gonzaga of Mantua. Everywhere the freedom of the *comuni* was in jeopardy; after so much useless strife the temptation to submit to a strong leader often proved overwhelming. And yet at the same time money flowed as never before; cities built new cathedrals and created incredible skylines of tower-fortresses, dotting the country with medieval Manhattans.

This paradoxical Italy continued through the 15th century, with a golden age of culture and an opulent economy side by side with continuous war and turmoil. With no threats over the border, the myriad Italian states menaced each other joyfully without outside interference. War became a sort of game, conducted on behalf of cities by *condottieri*, leading paid mercenaries who were never allowed to enter the cities themselves. The arrangement suited everyone well. The soldiers had lovely horses and armour, and no real desire to do each other serious harm. The cities were making too much money to really want to wreck the system anyway.

By far the biggest event of the 14th century was the **Black Death** of 1347–8, in which Italy lost one-third of its population. The shock brought a rude halt to what had been 400 years of almost continuous growth and prosperity, though its effects did not prove a permanent setback. In fact, the plague's grim joke was that it actually made life better for most of the Italians who survived; working people in the cities, no longer overcrowded, found their rents lower and their labour worth more, while in the country farmers were able to increase their profits by only tilling the best land.

In the north, the great power was the signorial state of Milan. Under the Visconti Milan had become rich and powerful, basing its success on the manufactures of the city (arms and textiles) and the bountiful, progressively managed agriculture of southern Lombardy. Its greatest glory came under **Gian Galeazzo Visconti** (1385–1402), who bought a ducal title from the emperor and came close to conquering all of north Italy before his untimely death, upon which the Venetians were able to snatch up tasty titbits on the fringe like Brescia and Bergamo.

And what of the Renaissance? No word has ever caused more mischief for the understanding of history and culture—as if Italy had been Sleeping Beauty, waiting for some Prince Charming to come and awaken it from a 1000-year nap. On the contrary, Italy even in the 1200s was richer, more technologically advanced and far more artistically creative than it had ever been in the days of the Caesars. The new art and scholarship that began in Florence in the 1400s and spread across the nation grew from a solid foundation of medieval accomplishment. The gilded Italy of the 15th century felt complacently secure in its long-established cultural and economic pre-eminence. The long spell of freedom from outside interference lulled the nation into believing that its political disunity could continue safely forever; except perhaps for the sanguinely realistic Florentine Nicolò Macchiavelli, no one realized that Italy was in fact a plum waiting to be picked.

Three Grim Centuries of Foreign Rule

The Italians brought the trouble down on themselves, when Duke Lodovico of Milan invited the French king **Charles VIII** to cross the Alps and assert his claim to the throne of Milan's enemy, Naples. Charles did just that, and the failure of the combined Italian states to stop him (at the inconclusive Battle of Fornovo, 1494) showed just how helpless Italy was at the hands of new nation-states like France or Spain. When the Spaniards saw how easy it was, they too marched in, and restored Naples to its Spanish king the following year. Before long the German emperor and even the Swiss, who briefly took control of Milan, entered this new market for Italian real estate. The popes did as much as anyone to keep the pot boiling. Alexander VI and his son **Cesare Borgia** carried the war across central Italy in an attempt to found a new state for the Borgia family, and Julius II's madcap policy led him to egg on the Swiss, French and Spaniards in turn, before finally crying, 'Out with the barbarians!' when it was already too late.

By 1516, with the French ruling Milan and the Spanish in control of the south, it seemed as if a settlement would be possible. The worst possible luck for Italy, however, came with the accession of the insatiable megalomaniac **Charles V** to the throne of Spain; in 1519 he emptied the Spanish treasury to buy himself the crown of the Holy Roman Empire, making him the most powerful ruler in Europe since Charlemagne. Charles wanted Milan as a base for communications between his Spanish, German and Flemish possessions, and the wars began anew, bloodier than anything Italy had seen for centuries, climaxing with the defeat of the French at Pavia in 1525 and the sack of Rome by an out-of-control imperial army in 1527. The French invaded once more in 1529, and were defeated, this time at Naples, by the treachery of their Genoese allies. All Italy save only Venice was now at the mercy of Charles and the Spaniards.

The final peace negotiated at Château-Cambrésis left Spanish viceroys in Milan and Naples, and pliant dukes and counts toeing the Spanish line almost everywhere else. The broader context of the time was the bitter struggles of the Reformation and Counter-Reformation. In Italy, the Spaniards found a perfect ally in the papacy; together they put an end to the last surviving liberties of the cities, while snuffing out the intellectual life of the Renaissance with the help of the Inquisition and the Jesuits.

Nearly the only place where anything creative came out of this new order was Lombardy. In Milan that incorruptible Galahad of the Counter-Reformation, Archbishop **Charles Borromeo** (1538–84), came out of the Council of Trent determined to make his diocese a working model of Tridentine reforms. One of the most influential characters in Italian religious history, he relentlessly went about creating an actively pastoral, zealous clergy, giving the most prominent teaching jobs to Jesuits and cleansing Lombardy of heresy and corruption. By re-establishing the cult of Milan's patron, St Ambrose, he developed a sense of Lombard regional feeling; with his nephew and successor **Federico Borromeo** he promoted sorely needed cultural and welfare institutions, instilling in the Lombard élite an industrious Catholic paternalism still noted in the region today.

Despite political oppression, the 16th century was a generally prosperous period for most of Italy, embellished with an afterglow of late-Renaissance architecture and art. After 1600, though, nearly everything started to go wrong for the Italians. The textiles and banking of the north, long the engines of prosperity, both withered in the face of foreign competition. The old mercantile economies built in the Middle Ages were failing, and the wealthy began to invest their money in land instead of risking it in business or finance.

Italy in this period hardly has any history at all; as Spain slouched into decadence, most of Lombardy dozed on as part of the Duchy of Milan, ruled by a Spanish viceroy. In 1713, after the War of the Spanish Succession, the Habsburgs of Austria came into control of the Duchy, and the tiny Duchy of Mantua. The Austrians improved conditions somewhat. Especially during the reigns of **Maria Theresa** (1740–80) and her son **Joseph II** (1780–92), two of the most likeable Enlightenment despots, Lombardy and the other Austrian possessions underwent serious, intelligent economic reforms—the head start over the rest of Italy that helped Milan to its industrial prominence today.

From Napoleon to Italian Unification

Napoleon, that greatest of Italian generals, arrived in 1796 on behalf of the French revolutionary Directorate, sweeping away the Austrians and setting up republics in Lombardy (the 'Cisalpine Republic') and elsewhere. Italy woke up with a start from its baroque slumbers, and local patriots gaily joined the French cause. In 1799, however, while Napoleon was off in Egypt, the advance through Italy by an Austro-Russian army, aided by Nelson's fleet, restored the status quo. In 1800 Napoleon returned in a campaign that saw the great victory at Marengo, giving him the opportunity to reorganize Italian affairs once more, and to crown himself King of Italy in Milan cathedral. Napoleonic rule lasted only until 1814, but in that time important public works were begun and laws, education and everything else reformed after the French model; Church properties were expropriated and medieval relics everywhere put to rest. The French, however, soon wore out their welcome through high taxes, oppression and the systematic looting of Italy's artistic heritage. When the Austrians came to chase the French out in 1814, no one was sad to see them go.

Though the postwar **Congress of Vienna** put the Italian clock back to 1796, the Napoleonic experience had given Italians a taste of the opportunities offered by the modern world, as well as a sense of national feeling that had been suppressed for centuries. Almost immediately revolutionary agitators and secret societies sprang up all over Italy; sentiment for Italian unification and liberal reform was greatest in the north, and in the decades of the national revival, the **Risorgimento**, Lombardy in particular would contribute more than its share.

In March 1848 a revolution in Vienna gave Italians under Austrian rule their chance to act. Milan's famous *Cinque Giornate* revolt began with a boycott of the Austrian tobacco monopoly. Some troops, conspicuously smoking cigars in public, caused fighting to break out in the streets. In five incredible days the populace of Milan rose up and chased out the Austrian garrison (led by Marshal Radetzky, he of the famous march tune). Events began to move rapidly. On 22 March revolution spread to Venice, and soon afterwards Piedmont's King Carlo Alberto declared war on Austria and his army crossed the Ticino into Lombardy. The Piedmontese won early victories, including one important one at Goito, on 30 May, but under the timid leadership of the king they failed to follow them up, and the Austrians were back in control by the end of July. The other Italian revolts, in Rome and Venice, were not put down until 1849.

Despite failure on a grand scale, the Italians knew they would get another chance. Unification, most likely under the House of Savoy that ruled Piedmont, was inevitable. In 1859, with the support of Napoleon III and France, the Piedmontese tried again and would have been successful had the French not double-crossed them and signed an armistice with Austria in the middle of the war; as a result, though, Piedmont gained Lombardy and Tuscany. That left the climactic event of unification to be performed by the revolutionary adventurer **Giuseppe Garibaldi**. When Garibaldi sailed to Sicily with a thousand volunteers in May 1860, nearly half his men were from Lombardy. Their unexpected success in toppling the Kingdom of Naples launched the Piedmontese on an invasion from the north, and Italian unity was achieved.

Lombardy Takes Off

While life under the corrupt and bumbling governments of the new Italian kingdom wasn't perfect, it was a major improvement over the Austrians. The integration of the northern industrial towns into a unified Italian economy gave trade a big boost, and Milan in particular saw its industry expand dramatically. Along with that came the beginnings of the socialist movement, stronger at first in Lombardy than anywhere else; the first socialist party, the **Partito Operaio Italiano**, was founded in Milan in 1882. Strikes and riots were common in the depression of the nineties; over a hundred people were killed in one clash in 1896. Nevertheless, a rapidly increasing prosperity was drawing the northern cities into the European mainstream. The decades before the First World War, a contented time for many Italians, came to be known by the slightly derogatory term *Italietta*, the 'little Italy' of bourgeois happiness, sweet Puccini operas, the first motor cars, blooming 'Liberty'-style architecture, and Sunday afternoons at the beach.

After the war Milan saw the birth of another movement, Fascism. **Mussolini** founded his newspaper there, the *Popolo d'Italia*, and organized bands of *squadri*, toughs who terrorized unions and leftist parties. The upper classes got on well enough with the Fascists, especially during the boom of the twenties, when big Milanese firms like Montecatini-Edison and Pirelli came into prominence. In the Second World War the industrial cities suffered heavily from Allied bombings after the capture of Sicily in July 1943. After the government signed an armistice with the Allies in September, the German army moved in massively to take control of the north. They established a puppet government, the Italian Social Republic, at the resort of Salò on Lake Garda, and re-installed Mussolini, though now little more than a figurehead.

The war dragged on for another year and a half, as the Germans made good use of Italy's difficult terrain to slow the Allied advance. Meanwhile Italy finally gave itself something to be proud of: a determined, resourceful Resistance that established free zones in many areas of Lombardy and other regions, and harassed the Germans with sabotage and strikes. The *partigiani* caught Mussolini in April 1945, while he was trying to escape to Switzerland; after shooting him and his mistress, they hung him by the toes from the roof of a petrol station in Milan where the Germans had shot a number of civilians a week before.

With a heavy dose of Marshall Plan aid and some intelligent government planning, Milan (and Turin) led the way for the 'economic miracle' of the fifties. Meaningful politics almost ceased to exist, as the nation was run in a constantly renegotiated deal between the Christian Democrats and smaller parties, but Lombard industry surged ahead, creating around Milan a remarkably diverse economy of over 60,000 concerns, from multinational giants like Olivetti to the small, creative, often family-run firms that are the model of what has been called 'Italian capitalism'. Milan's most glamorous industry, fashion, began to move to the city from Florence around 1968, owing to the lack of a good airport there. The climax of the boom came in 1987, when it was announced that Italy had surpassed Britain to become the world's fifth largest economy; '*Il Sorpasso*', as Italians called it, was a great source of national pride—even though it was later discovered that government economists had fiddled the figures to make the claim.

Finally in the Driver's Seat: Lombardy and Milan Today

With some 8,500,000 people, Lombardy is the most populous region of Italy. And also the richest by far; it produces a quarter of the gross national product and a third of Italy's exports.

The average income is twice that of the south, and higher than any region of Britain or France. Even in the current recession, Lombardy isn't doing badly; on Milan's frantic stock market the number of shares traded in a day occasionally exceeds New York's. Along with prosperity has come a number of serious worries: a big increase in corruption and crime, unchained suburban sprawl and pollution, in the air and in Europe's filthiest river, the Po. Some 250,000 immigrants from southern Italy and Sicily have moved to Milan since the war, and the inability of many of them to adapt and get ahead, largely thanks to the bigotry of the Lombards, fuels a host of intractable social problems.

The Milanese believe their city is the real capital of Italy—because it pays the bills. But, following its old traditions, the city has remained traditionally indifferent to politics and stolidly unproductive in the arts. Milan can offer fashion and industrial design—both of course highly profitable; it is the nation's publishing centre, and probably its art centre, with more galleries than anywhere else. Endlessly creative in business, it has so far had little else to offer the world.

In politics, at least, the indifference may be gone forever. The lid blew off Italy's cosily rotten political system and its Byzantine web of bribery and kickback in 1992 in Milan.

It will make a good film some day—no doubt somebody's already working on the screenplay. **Antonio di Pietro** was a poor boy from the most obscure region of Italy, the Molise. He worked in electronics while studying law at night in Milan, and became a judge in the early 1980s. The electronics background gave him a thorough knowledge of computers and what they could do, and he used them skilfully to pile up and collate evidence and connections between cases. He first made a name for himself in 1987, breaking open bribe scandals in the vehicle licence bureau and city bus company. In 1992 a divorced woman wrote him a letter complaining of how her ex-husband, an official in a city old age hospice, was driving around in a new Alfa and wearing silk suits while claiming he couldn't afford her alimony. That man was the now famous Mario Chiesa, a hapless grafter and Socialist party hack who had been skimming off L100,000 from undertakers for every corpse they took out of the place. He was had, and he squealed, revealing a wealth of interesting information about similar shady deals all over Milan.

One thing led to another—to put it mildly. Even di Pietro was amazed at how information on one racket tied in inevitably with others, each one bigger than the last. Four years into the affair, now known around the world as *Tangentopoli*, or 'Bribe City', hundreds of leading politicians and business magnates have been convicted or are awaiting their turn. One of the country's most respected business leaders, Raul Gardini, committed suicide in his cell. The Christian Democrat and Socialist parties have been utterly annihilated and the face of Italy's politics changed forever. No one is safe—now even di Pietro, after being chosen as the most popular man in Italy and serving briefly as minister of public works in the Prodi government in 1996, is under investigation, although nearly everyone believes the investigation has been thrown up as a warning to judges who tread on powerful toes.

Today, unfortunately for the Milanese, everyone knows where Bribe City really is. All along, it seems, the two extremities of the nation have had their separate and distinct ways of doing business—the Sicilians' was just a little more colourful. For every proud, honest citizen of the city of silk suits and Alfas, the events of the last four years must be a profound revelation. Paradoxically the tremendous drama of indictments, trials and retaliations, north and south, may become the greatest impetus towards a true Italian unity since Giuseppe Garibaldi.

Italians have only to look at what is happening to realize that they're all in the same boat, that Palermo and Milan aren't so different after all.

There are other spoons busily stirring the pot. Even before *Tangentopoli*, a new Lombard League, or Lega Lombarda, led by the noisy yet enigmatic **Umberto Bossi** (the only Italian political figure to dress badly since the time of King Aistulf), made its breakthrough in the 1990 elections, and became the leading party of the region in 1992. On most issues the Lega's position can change by the hour, but its basic tenet of federalism, to cut out the voracious politicians and bureaucrats in Rome and allow the wealthy north to keep more of its profits for itself, has understandably struck a deep chord in the Lombard soul; other 'leagues' have emerged and prospered in other northern regions, uniting in 1994 as the Lega Nord. In September 1996 Bossi attracted a lot of media attention by declaring the north (as far south as Umbria and the Marches) the independent Republic of Padania, accompanied by a triumphant three-day rally and march down the Po to Venice. The whole affair turned into a badly staged comedy—arguments about crowd counts, tiffs with journalists (Bossi and the media hate each other's guts), rumblings about just what might happen if Bossi's promised Padania militia turned out to be more than hot air. If nothing else, the threat of an independent Padania has moved the idea of federalism, perhaps on the Spanish model, up a notch on the Italian political agenda.

That leaves Milan's other gift to Italian politics, **Silvio Berlusconi**, in some ways the essence of Milan distilled into a single individual, the self-made man (self-made with the help of his connections, notably to now disgraced Socialist kingpin Bettino Craxi). Berlusconi's empire includes half of Italy's television audience, a third of its magazine readership, books, newspapers, a department-store chain and an influential political party, Forza Italia. Only a few years ago, no journalist or author ever dared to mention some of things about Italy that everyone knew—say, the close alliance between the Christian Democrats and the Mafia. Today, you won't find anyone looking very closely into how Berlusconi came by all these prizes, or more interestingly, into his membership of P2, the shadowy clique of top politicians, industrialists and security chiefs that managed Italy's institutional corruption in the last decades, and created or manipulated most of the terrorist groups of the 1960s and '70s.

Forza Italia exploded on the scene by winning the elections in 1994, only to rule in an uncomfortable and ultimately untenable coalition with the Lega Nord and Fini's neo-Fascist Alianza Nazionale. Berlusconi put on a not entirely convincing and occasionally shrill show as Prime Minister for a season; succeeded by Prodi's centre-left-Green Olive Tree Coalition, the media tycoon is now in the opposition, both in parliament and on the air waves, oily, smiling, and, like Milanese *busecca* or tripe stew, a bit uneasy on the national digestion.

Romano Prodi may lack Berlusconi's inside track, but he managed to stay in the driver's seat longer than anyone predicted. The Italians, who understandably place more hope in Europe than in their national leaders, bit the bullet and supported Prodi's stringent economic measures, allowing them to squeak into Euroland in January 1999. Prodi had little time to bask in the glory: the same strict measures led to the Communists withdrawing their support of his government in late 1998 and giving it to current prime minister and leftwing darling Massimo d'Alema of the DS (Democratia di Sinistra) party, forming Italy's 60th government since the Second World War.

Art & Architecture & Where to Find it

Like the rest of Italy, Lombardy is packed to the gills with notable works of art and architecture, and it's hard to find even the smallest village without a robust Romanesque chapel, curlicued baroque *palazzina*, or mysterious time-darkened painting by a follower of Leonardo or Caravaggio. Because the 'art cities' of this region flourished at different periods, there is no one dominant 'golden age' comparable to the Renaissance in Tuscany or Venice, or the baroque in Rome. On the other hand, you'll find examples of art of all periods, and of nearly every school. For what the Lombards didn't make, they had the money to buy, so their churches and galleries are endowed with masterpieces.

Prehistoric and Roman

The most remarkable works from the Neolithic period up to the Iron Age are the thousands of graffiti rock incisions left by the Camuni tribes in isolated Alpine valleys north of Lake Iseo, especially in the national park of the **Valle Camonica** (others are in the Upper Valtellina at **Teglio** and **Grósio**). Remains of Neolithic and Bronze Age pile-dwelling communities have survived on an islet in **Lake Varese** and by **Lake Ledro**. Apart from the odd menhir and pot the Ligurians and Celts have left few traces, and even the arches and amphitheatres erected by their Roman conquerors have almost disappeared as the towns and colonies grew into modern cities. **Brescia**'s forum has come down remarkably intact, and there are the sizeable remains of Roman villas on Lake Garda, at **Desenzano** and **Sirmione**; also *see* the archaeological museum in **Milan**.

Early Middle Ages (5th–10th centuries)

Although the brilliant mosaics such as those in Ravenna, Venice and Rome—the delight of this period in Italy—are rare here (*see* the chapels in Sant'Ambrogio and San Lorenzo Maggiore, both in **Milan**), the work of the native population under its Lombard rulers was certainly not without talent; *see* the treasury of 6th-century Lombard Queen Theodolinda in **Monza**; the 5th-century baptistry at **Lomello**; the Carolingian-era stuccoes and treasure in San Salvatore, **Brescia**; other Lombard stucco reliefs in San Pietro al Monte, above **Civate**; the 8th-century frescoes at **Castelséprio**; and those from the 10th-century San Vincenzo at Galliano, near **Cantù**.

The key work of the age, one that would become the great prototype of the Lombard Romanesque, Sant'Ambrogio in **Milan**, dates from the 880s, a design respected in its last rebuilding in the 1080s. The chief ingredients are all there: the broad, triangular façade, the decorative rows of blind arches, sometimes called 'Lombard arcading'; the passages under exterior porticoes; and a rib-vaulted interior, with the presbytery raised over the crypt, and aisles delimited by arches (in some churches supporting internal galleries)

Romanesque and Gothic (11th–14th centuries)

In many ways the Romanesque was the most vigorous phase in Italian art history, when the power of the artist was almost that of a magician. Lombardy shone in particular: even many of Tuscany's finest Romanesque churches were built and decorated by roving schools of builders and sculptors (the Maestri Comaschi and Maestri Campionesi) from Lakes Como and Lugano.

Prime examples of Lombard Romanesque, based on Milan's Sant'Ambrogio, are the cathedrals of **Cremona**, **Crema**, **Lodi** and **Monza**, Sant'Abbondio in **Como** (which also has an exceptionally pure Romanesque town hall or Broletto), Santa Maria Maggiore in **Lomello**, the church at **Agliate**, and San Michele and San Pietro in Ciel d'Oro in **Pavia**. Sometimes, however, architects built in the round, as in the old cathedral in **Brescia**, the Rotunda di San Lorenzo in **Mantua** and San Tomé at **Almenno San Bartolomeo**. Gabled porches supported by crusty lions (usually having a human for lunch) or hunchbacked telamones were a common fixture, even into the 14th century (Santa Maria Maggiore, **Bergamo**).

With such a strong local building tradition, it may not be surprising that Gothic ideas imported from France never made much of an impression and caught on only briefly—but long enough to reach a singular climax and size in the spire-forested cathedral of **Milan**. The transition from pointy, vertical Gothic to the more rounded, classically proportioned Renaissance reads like a textbook in the Duomo in **Como**, built half in one style, and half in the other.

Renaissance (15th–16th centuries)

The fresh perspectives, technical advances and discovery of the individual that epitomize the Renaissance were born in quattrocento Florence and spread to the rest of Italy at varying speeds. Wealthy Lombardy played a major role, although perhaps most notably in its capacity to patronize and appreciate talent. Outdoor frescoes—one of the most charming features of the region—were within the realm not only of the nobility but of merchants and bankers. Celebrated patrons of indoor art include Cardinal Branda Castiglioni, who hired the Florentine Masolino (*d.* 1447) to paint the charming frescoes in **Castiglione Olona**. The Duke of Milan, Lodovico il Moro, sponsored the Milanese sojourns of **Leonardo da Vinci**. Leonardo's smoky shading (*sfumato*) so dazzled the local painters that the next generation or two lay heavily under his spell. Most talented of his many followers (Boltraffio, Giampietrino, Cesare da Sesto, Andrea Solario, Salaino and Marco d'Oggiono) was **Bernardino Luini** (*d.* 1532), whose masterpiece is the fresco cycle in Santa Maria degli Angioli in **Lugano** (other great works are in San Maurizio and Brera Gallery in **Milan** and in **Saronno**). Even sculptors were inspired by Leonardo, among them **Cristoforo Solari** (1439–1525), whose tombs of Lodovico il Moro and Beatrice d'Este are among the many treasures at the **Certosa di Pavia**.

The perfect symmetry and geometrical proportions of Renaissance architecture were introduced into **Milan** in the 1450s by Francesco Sforza, who hired **Filarete** to design the city's revolutionary Ospedale Maggiore, modelled on Brunelleschi's Ospedale degli Innocenti in Florence. Lodovico il Moro brought architect **Donato Bramante** of Urbino (*d.* 1514) to Milan, where he designed the amazing, illusionistic 3ft-deep apse of Santa Maria presso San Satiro, the great tribune of Santa Maria delle Grazie and the cloisters of Sant'Ambrogio before going on to Rome. Most Tuscan of all, however, is the Cappella Portinari in Sant'Eustorgio, built for an agent of the Medici bank, perhaps by the Florentine Michelozzo.

Elsewhere in Lombardy, **Mantua**, thanks to its sophisticated, free-spending dukes, the Gonzaga, became one of Italy's most influential art cities of the Renaissance. The Gonzaga's court painter was **Andrea Mantegna** (*d.* 1506), the leading northern Italian artist of the day, along with his brother-in-law Giovanni Bellini; for the dukes Mantegna produced, among other works, the frescoes of the *Camera degli Sposi* (1474). Mantegna studied the ancients with an intensity only rivalled by Florentine theorist and architect **Leon Battista Alberti** (*d.* 1472), who designed two churches in Mantua, most notably **Sant'Andrea**, in an imaginative re-use of the forms of Vitruvius. Ideal cities, designed from scratch according to Renaissance theories of humanism, were a popular concept, but Vespasiano Gonzaga was one of few to ever actually build one, **Sabbioneta.**

Uncomfortable next to such classicizing idealism is the Mannerist masterpiece of Raphael's star pupil, **Giulio Romano** (*d.* 1546): Federico Gonzaga II's Mantuan pleasure palace, the **Palazzo Tè** (1527–34). Its beginning coincided with the 1527 Sack of Rome, an event that shook Italians to the core; some of the artists who witnessed it (like Rosso Fiorentino) went mad. Giulio Romano, a native of Rome, was safe in Mantua, but in the Palazzo Tè one can sense reverberations of the calamity: the limits of art and architecture become ambiguous; delight and illusion mingle with oppression; violent contrasts between light and dark echo the starkly defined good and evil of the Counter-Reformation.

Elsewhere in Lombardy, the region's traditional art of sculpture reached its florid epitome in the Renaissance in the person of **Giovanni Antonio Amadeo** of Pavia (*d.* 1522), best known for the extraordinary ornate façade of the **Certosa di Pavia** and for the design of the Colleoni Chapel in **Bergamo**. Even more prolific than Amadeo was his follower **Bergognone** (*d.* 1530s), sculptor and painter, whose calm, undramatic style is often enhanced by lovely landscape backgrounds (especially in the Incoronata in **Lodi**).

Brescia became a minor centre of Renaissance painting, beginning with **Vincenzo Foppa** (*d.* 1515), one of the leaders of the Lombard Renaissance, a school marked by a sombre tonality and atmosphere; Foppa was especially known for his monumental style (works in **Bergamo**'s Accademia Carrara and **Milan**'s Sant'Eustorgio). Later, when Brescia came under Venetian rule, its artists also turned east: Alessandro Bonvincino, better known as **Moretto da Brescia** (*d.* 1554), was more influenced by Titian, and painted the first-known full-length Italian portrait (1526; works in **Brescia** are the Duomo Vecchio and the Galleria Tosio-Martinengo). His Bergamasque pupil, **Giovanni Battista Moroni** (*d.* 1578), painted many run-of-the-mill religious works, but also penetrating portraits of the first calibre (in **Bergamo's** Accademia Carrara) as did Lorenzo Lotto of Venice (1480–1556) who spent many years in the city (Accademia Carrara and Santo Spirito in **Bergamo**). A third painter of this period was **Girolamo Romanino** (*d.* 1561), whose works combine the richness of Titian with the flatter Lombard style (Santa Maria delle Neve in **Pisogne** and **Cremona** cathedral). The rather naïve but sincere works of the prolific **Giovan Pietro Da Cemmo**, a quattrocento painter from Brescia's Valle Camonica, turn up in many a country parish and in the monastery of Sant'Agostino in **Crema**.

Besides the followers of Leonardo and assorted Brescian masters, Lombardy did produce two extraordinary native geniuses: Arcimboldo and Caravaggio. **Giuseppe Arcimboldo** (*d.* 1593) of Milan painted portraits made up entirely of seafood, vegetables or flowers which anticipate the surrealists and the collages of *objets trouvés*. Arcimboldo became the court painter to the Habsburgs in Prague and has left works only in **Milan** (Castello Sforzesco). More immediately influential, not only in Italy but throughout 17th-century Europe, was **Michelangelo Merisi da Caravaggio** (1573–1610) who, despite a headlong trajectory through life (perhaps the first true bohemian—anarchic, rebellious and homosexual, he murdered a man over a tennis game, was thrown out of Malta by the Knights, and was almost killed in Naples before dying on a Tuscan beach), managed to leave behind paintings of dramatic power. His use of light, of foreshortening, and of simple country people as models in major religious subjects were often copied but never equalled. Although most of his paintings are in Rome, where he moved in 1590, there are some works in **Milan** (Ambrosiana and Brera Gallery).

Baroque (17th–18th centuries)

Architecturally, in these centuries the real show in north Italy took place in Piedmont, notably in the revolutionary works of Juvarra and Guarini. In **Milan** these two centuries were far more austere, in part thanks to St Charles Borromeo, who wrote a book of guidelines for Counter-Reformation architects. **Fabio Mangone** (*d.* 1629) epitomized this new austerity (the façade of the Ambrosiana, Santa Maria Podone); the more interesting **Lorenzo Binago** (*d.* 1629) designed Sant'Alessandro, with its innovative combination of two domed areas. Most important of all baroque architects in Milan was **Francesco Maria Ricchino** (*d.* 1658), whose San Giuseppe follows Binago's Sant'Alessandro with its two Greek crosses; he created a style of crossings and domes that enjoyed tremendous success (other works include the Palazzo di Brera and the Collegio Elvetico, now the Archivo di Stato, the first concave palace façade of the baroque style).

Milan's best painters of the age all worked in the early 1600s—the mystic and somewhat cloying Giovanni Battista Crespi (called **Cerano**, *d.* 1632) and the fresco master of Lombardy's sanctuaries, Pier Francesco Mazzucchelli, called **Morazzone** (*d.* 1626; works at **Varese**). These two, along with the less interesting Giulio Cesare Procaccini, teamed up to paint the Brera Gallery's unusual 'three masters' painting of *SS. Rufina and Seconda*. A fourth painter, Antonio d'Enrico, **Il Tanzio** (d. 1635), was inspired by Caravaggio, with results that range from the bland to the uncannily meticulous.

After 1630, when Milan and its artists were devastated by plague, **Bergamo** was left holding the paintbrush of Lombard art, in the portraits of **Carlo Ceresa** (*d.* 1679) and **Evaristo Baschenis** (1617–77), whose precise still-life paintings of musical instruments are among the finest of a rather un-Italian genre. From **Brescia** came **Giacomo Ceruti** (active in the 1730s–50s), whose sombre pictures of idiots, beggars and other social outcasts are as carefully obsessive. In sculpture, **Antonio Fantoni** (1659–1734) from a big family of woodcarvers in Rovetta stands out with his scrolly, elegantly decorative rococo altarpieces and pulpits (works in Santa Maria Maggiore, **Bergamo**, and in the Valle Seriana, especially **Alzano Lombardo**).

Two late baroque painters marched to a different drummer: **Alessandro Magnasco** (1667–1749) of Genoa, who worked mainly in Milan and produced with quick, nervous brushstrokes weird, almost surreal canvases haunted by wraiths of light (Civic Museum, **Crema**) and **Giuseppe Bazzani** (1690–1769) of Mantua, who used similar quick brushstrokes to create the unreal and strange.

Neoclassicism and Romanticism (late 18th–19th century)

Baroque proved to be a hard act to follow, and in these centuries Italian art and architecture almost ceased to exist. Three centuries of stifling oppression had taken their toll on the national imagination, and for the first time Italy not only ceased to be a leader in art but failed even to a make a significant contribution. The period did sprinkle the shores of the lakes with superb private villas: one, the **Villa Carlotta**, on the banks of Lake Como, is a triumph of neoclassicism, with statues by the master of the age, **Antonio Canova**, and his meticulous follower **Thorvaldsen**. The Galleria Vittorio Emanuele in **Milan** is a 19th-century triumph of engineering; romantic-era Lombard artists, the *Scapigliati* ('Wild-haired ones'), are in **Milan**'s Civic Gallery of Modern Art.

20th Century

Italian Art Nouveau, or Liberty-style, left its mark in the grand hotels of the Lakes and the residential area around Corso Venezia in **Milan**, and reached an apotheosis in the spa of **San Pellegrino Terme** (*see* **Milan** p.78) But Liberty's pretty, bourgeoise charm and the whole patrimony of Italian art only infuriated the young **Futurists**, who produced manifestos and paintings which attempted to speed Italy into modern times (*see* **Milan**'s Civic Gallery of Modern Art, the Brera, and the Civico Museo dell'Arte Contemporanea). This same urge to race out of the past ('Never look back' was Mussolini's motto after the day he ran over and killed a child) also created modern Italy's most coherent and consistent sense of design. Fascist architecture may be charmingly Art Deco, or warped and disconcerting (**Brescia**'s Piazza della Vittoria, **Bergamo'**s Piazza Matteotti and around, or its domestic variety, D'Annunzio's villa in **Gardone Riviera**). A remarkable exception are the visionary works of Giuseppe Terragni (Casa Terragni, **Como**).

However uneven the Fascist contribution, modern Italian architects have yet to match it, hardly ever rising above saleable and boring modernism (Milan's 1960 **Pirelli Building** by Gio Ponti and Pier Luigi Nervi is the pick of the bunch). The aforementioned museums in Milan have collections of contemporary art—the bronzes of **Mariano Marini** in the Galleria d'Arte Moderna in **Milan** deserves special mention. But most artistic talent these days is sublimated into film, or the shibboleth of Italian design—clothes, sports cars, furniture—and even these consumer beauties often are more packaging than content.

Topics

Java had little to do with it, but *Il Caffè* had the same effect as an espresso on sleepy 18th-century Lombardy—a quick jolt of wakeful energy. This was in fact the name of Italy's first real newspaper. It was published for only two years in the 1760s, by brothers Pietro and Alessandro Verri and a small circle of young Milanese aristocrats who called themselves the *Accademia dei Pugni*, 'the Fists'.

The opinions it published derived from England and the philosophers and encyclopedists of France. They wrote of the need for economic, humanitarian and judicial reforms, not once challenging the authority of the absolute monarchy of the Austrian Habsburgs in Lombardy, or even suggesting anything as radical as Italian unity. But at a time when Italy was still languishing in the enforced ignorance of the Church and foreign rulers, this newspaper, such as it was, was revolutionary for merely encouraging people to think.

When *Il Caffè* was published only a few thousand lay Italians were literate enough to read it. But they were the élite of the system, and it was their opinions that the Verri brothers hoped to influence in their editorials. Also, conditions in Milan, if nowhere else in Italy, were ripe for change. Lombardy's sovereign, Maria Theresa of Austria, was a benevolent, enlightened despot prepared to tolerate a certain amount of local autonomy and opinion; while Milan was starting to wake up, on the verge of its great capitalist destiny, the rest of Italy snored away, festering under papal and Spanish Bourbon rule.

The most important fruit of the Fists' endeavours came from the youngest member of the Academy, a plump stay-at-home mamma's boy named Cesare Beccaria. Pietro Verri saw potential in this muffin that no one else could fathom and assigned him the task of writing a pamphlet on the group's opinions on justice—not a pleasant subject: torture was the most common way of extracting a confession and in Milan alone someone was executed nearly every day. There was even a strict hierarchy of death: nobles got a quick decapitation with a sharp axe and cardinals had the right to be strangled with a gold and purple cord, while the lower classes could expect to have their tongues and ears chopped off, their eyes put out and their flesh burned with hot irons before being allowed to die.

No one suspected Beccaria of any talent whatsoever, and all were astonished when he roused himself to produce the brilliant, succinct *Dei Delitti e delle Pene* (*Of Crimes and Punishments*), published in 1764 in Livorno, out of the reach of local censors. Although the Church hastily consigned the work to its Index of prohibited books, it can be fairly said that no other work on jurisprudence had such an immediate effect on the day-to-day lives of everyday men and women. Beccaria's eloquent logic against torture and the death penalty, his insistence on equality before the law and for justice to be both accountable and public, moved Voltaire to write in his commentary on the work that Beccaria had eliminated 'the last remnants of barbarism'. The absolute monarchs of the day (with the notable exception of Louis XVI) moved at once to follow Beccaria's precepts, at least in part: Maria Theresa in Austria, Charles III in Spain, Catherine the Great in Russia, Frederick the Great of Prussia, Ferdinand I in Naples and most of all Peter Leopold in Tuscany, who went the furthest of all by completely abolishing torture and capital punishment. Beccaria wrote of the 'greatest happiness shared by the greatest number', a phrase adopted by Jeremy Bentham and Thomas Jefferson, who used Beccaria's ideas of equal justice for all as a starting point in framing the American constitution.

The origins of the conflict between Guelphs and Ghibellines are lost in the mists of legend. One medieval writer blamed two brothers of Pistoia named Guelph and Gibel, one of whom murdered the other and began the seemingly endless factional troubles that to many seemed a God-sent plague, meant to punish the proud and wealthy Italians for their sins. Medieval Italy may in fact have been guilty of every sort of jealousy, greed and wrath, but most historians trace the beginnings of the party conflict to two great German houses, *Welf* and *Waiblingen* (Edmund Spenser, looking on amusedly from England, fancifully suggested the names were the origins of our 'Elfs' and 'Goblins').

Trouble was brewing even before the conflict was given a name. The atmosphere of contentious city states, each with its own internal struggles between nobles, merchants and commons, crystallized rapidly into parties. In the beginning, at least, they stood for something. The Guelphs, largely a creation of the newly wealthy bourgeois, were all for free trade and the rights of free cities; the Ghibellines from the start were the party of the German emperors, nominal overlords of Italy who had been trying to assert their control ever since the days of Charlemagne. Naturally, the Guelphs found their protector in the emperors' bitter temporal rivals, the popes.

Nothing unifies like a common enemy, though, and in 12th-century Lombardy the battle-lines between Guelphs and Ghibellines broke down in face of the terror sown by the biggest Goblin of them all, Emperor Frederick Barbarossa (1152–90). Barbarossa understood his election as a mission to restore the lost dignity of the Roman Empire. He even got the Bologna University masters of jurisprudence to proclaim that, according to ancient Roman law, only the emperor had power over the appointment of magistrates, taxes, ports and such.

To maintain the fond fiction that he was the heir of the Caesars required that Barbarossa possess Italy. His sheer ruthlessness in attempting to do so in seven different forays over the Alps was enough to make him one of Hitler's heroes: to subdue Crema, he captured a number of children and bound them to the front of his siege engine as a human shield, where their parents could hear their pathetic cries. But the Cremaschi hated Barbarossa so much that they fought determinedly on, and after a six-month siege Barbarossa razed their city to the ground—his usual technique in dealing with independent-minded city states. The original Lega Lombarda, or Lombard League, united against him and finally crushed the big thug at Legnano. (This victory over northern tyranny found an echo in the 19th-century struggles of the Risorgimento and in Verdi's rambunctious opera of 1848, *La Battiglia di Legnano*. Verdi's personality, and many of his operas, made him a rallying point for partisans of Italian unity. Crowds at the Scala in the 1850s would shout 'VERDI! VERDI!' whenever there were any Austrians around to hear it, and the composer probably didn't mind that the real message, as everyone knew, was 'Vittorio Emanuele, Re D'Italia!')

Ironically, Barbarossa himself was at that same time a symbol for those Germans who wanted their own national unity. The Germans will tell you that Barbarossa wasn't such a bad fellow after all, that the Italians simply invented most of the horror stories, as Italians are wont to do. In later legend—severely embroidered by Romantic poets—the old emperor slept under a mountain called the Kyffhäuser, like King Arthur; sitting around a table with his knights, his red beard growing through the table as he slept, he would wake up once every hundred years and the raven perched on the back of his throne would tell him whether Germany was yet united—only then could Barbarossa finally rest in peace.

After Legnano Barbarossa was forced to make peace with his arch enemy, Pope Alexander III, kneeling to pay him homage in the atrium of San Marco (the Venetians triumphantly installed a stone to mark the exact spot). The pope brokered the Peace of Constance of 1183, in which the *comuni* maintained their sovereign rights while recognizing the overall authority of the emperor. Perhaps this was some small consolation to Barbarossa, who shortly afterwards departed for the Crusades, only to fall off his horse crossing a shallow river in Turkey and drown in six inches of water.

The Best Fiddles in the World

The modern violin, developed in Cremona in the 16th century in the workshops of Guarneri, Stradivarius and the two Amatis, was the perfect instrument to usher in the opulent pageant of baroque style. Its rich, sonorous tone, its capacity for thrilling emotions and drama, equalled rarely even by the human voice, was enough to make the typical baroque dome's population of saints and angels pause on their soaring flight to heaven to let a tear fall for the earth they were leaving behind.

The sensuous shape of the violin and the very complexity of its manufacture are as baroque as its sound. Stradivarius and company used the finest wood from the Dolomites and from the dense groves that covered the Lombard plain. The main body of the violin was made from maple and spruce, the neck and other bits from poplar, pear and willow. The fluted edges and scrolls and the beautiful curves come straight from the vocabulary of Cremona's baroque architecture. Shaped and preserved with an alchemist's varnish, the violins made by the 16th- and 17th-century masters have mellowed and aged over the years like bottles of the finest Sauternes, to develop a quality of sound so powerful, rich and luscious that the violins themselves seem to have a soul. The priceless examples displayed in Cremona's Palazzo del Comune are taken out at least once a week and given a bit of exercise, a caress over the old strings, because there is something alive in them.

The year after Andrea Amati fathered the first violin prototype (1566), Cremona gave birth to Claudio Monteverdi. Growing up amid the rich music flowing from the violinmakers' shop must have had a seminal influence on his career. As a pioneer composer of opera and *maestro di cappella* of St Mark's in Venice, his sumptuous polyphonic music for four to six choirs got him in trouble with the Church, which complained that no one could make out a word of the sacred texts. But that's baroque for you—the beauty and feeling is the meaning. And perhaps it's not surprising, in our strange modern baroque world, that an organization called the *Associazione Cremonese Luitai Artigiani Professionisti* is attempting to revive the intricate, painstaking craftsmanship that made Cremona's violins the happiest of all instruments of passion.

Romans of the Lakes

Pliny the Elder (Gaius Plinius Secundus), born in Como in the year AD 23, was a man with an endless capacity for collecting facts, gossip and hearsay. The result can be read in his greatest work, the 37 books of the *Historia Naturalis*, the world's first encyclopedia, which he himself proudly claimed contained '20,000 matters worthy of consideration'. Though above all a scholar and a natural scientist, Pliny died with his boots on—he was the admiral of the fleet in Campania when Vesuvius erupted in AD 70, and as he went closer to inspect the phenomenon he was suffocated in the fumes.

There's hardly a subject Pliny failed to expound on in his master work—geography, botany, agriculture, mineralogy, zoology and medicine are all there, much of it taken from lost Greek works. What can be traced back to an original source shows that what he read was often ill-digested, and that he failed to apply much critical judgement; the truth is, much of the *Historia Naturalis* is pure poppycock—like the accounts of blue men in India who hopped around on a single foot, or others who fed only on the scent of flowers—although that hardly stopped it from being one of the most plagiarized works of all time.

Less known, perhaps, is the influence wielded in the Renaissance by Pliny's entries on art and artefacts (again from Greek sources—the Romans themselves were far too practical to theorize about such things). In the 15th and 16th centuries, most artists were of humble origin, and got about as much respect as the local baker. In Pliny (translated into Italian in 1473) they found justifications for their obsession with mathematics, for painting nude figures and for their search for ever more accurate illusions of reality. Best of all to their minds were Pliny's anecdotes on the honour and respect given by the ancient Greeks to artists. One of their favourites was the story of how Alexander the Great gave his mistress Campaspe to Apelles, when he noticed that the artist had fallen for her while painting her in the nude.

If the Greeks that the Elder Pliny studied so intensely were great classicists in their shunning of all excess and search for beauty in simple, everyday things, the Romans always preferred realism (their finest achievements in sculpture were portrait busts showing all the warts and wrinkles, exactly the opposite of the idealizing Greeks). Long doses of ugly realism, however, are hard to bear and lead almost inevitably to an escape into the imagination, into romance. Although today we tend to lump all Greek and Roman literature together as 'classics', the greatest Roman writers in the golden age of Augustus were, as the very name suggests, the first Romantics, from Virgil (born in Mantua in AD 70) down to Petronius.

Perhaps the immeasurable, excessive beauty of Lake Como and Lake Garda had something to do with the fact that two other important Roman romantics grew up on their shore. Pliny's own nephew, Pliny the Younger (born in AD 61 in Como), was a famous lawyer and consul whose *Letters* are an invaluable source for his times. But he also wrote of his quiet villas on the lake, to evoke the magic of the scenery—not something the Romans had ever paid much attention to, except when working out where to build the next aqueduct.

To Garda, however, goes the honour of hosting the most highly strung Romantic of them all, the poet Catullus, born in AD 87 in Verona, although he spent most of his time at the family villa at Sirmione—the delicious descriptions by the Younger Pliny of fishing out of his bedroom window resulted in a veritable craze among the first century's smart set to build their own holiday homes there. Catullus' burning, tortured poems for his mistress Lesbia deserve a chapter of their own in the literature of love; she is a grand married woman of the world living on the Palatine Hill, who is gradually won by the young poet's passionate verses. But she soon tires of him and takes new lovers by the score; in despair Catullus flees to Sirmione, only to be summoned back to Rome a decade later by the ageing Lesbia for one last bitter fling. He finds her holding reckless orgies, and about to go on trial for having murdered her husband; in his final poem, shortly before his early and perfectly romantic death from consumption and unrequited love, he leaves a picture of his old flame worthy of a final scene in a Puccini opera:

> *Caelius, Lesbia—she, our Lesbia—Oh, that*
> *only Lesbia, whom Catullus only*
> *loved as never himself and all his dearest,*
> *now on highways and byways seeks her lovers,*
> *strips all Rome's noble great-souled sons of their money.*

trans. by Edith Hamilton

The Immortal Fool

The first recorded mention of Arlecchino, or Harlequin, came when the part was played by a celebrated actor named Tristano Martinelli in 1601—the year that also saw the début of *Hamlet*. Theatre as we know it was blooming all over Europe in those times: Shakespeare and Marlowe, Calderón and Lope de Vega in Spain, the predecessors of Molière in France. All of these learned their craft from late-Renaissance Italy, where the *commedia dell'arte* had created a fashion that spread across the continent. The great companies, such as the Gelosi, the Confidenti and the Accesi, toured the capitals, while others shared out the provinces. Groups of ten or twelve actors, run as cooperatives, they could do comedies, tragedies or pastorals to their own texts, and provide music, dance, magic and juggling between acts. The audiences liked the comedies best of all, with a set of masked stock characters, playing off scenes between the *magnificos*, the great lords, and the *zanni*, or servants, who provided the slapstick, half-improvised comic relief. To spring the plot there would be a pair of lovers or *innamorati*—unmasked, to remind us that only those who are in love are really alive.

It had nothing to do with 'art'. *Arte* means a guild, to emphasize that these companies were made up of professional players. The term was invented in 1745 by Goldoni (who wrote one of the last plays of the genre, *Arlecchino, servitore di due padroni*); in the 1500s the companies were often referred to as the *commedia mercenaria*—they would hit town, set up a stage on trestles and start their show within the hour. Cultured Italians of the day often deplored the way the 'mercenary' shows were driving out serious drama, traditionally written by scholarly amateurs in the princely courts. In the repressive climate of the day, caught between the Inquisition and the Spanish bosses, a culture of ideas survived only in free Venice. Theatre retreated into humorous popular entertainment, but even then the Italians found a way to say what was on their minds. A new stock character appeared, the menacing but slow-witted 'Capitano', who always spoke with a Spanish accent, and Italians learned from the French how to use Arlecchino to satirize the hated Emperor Charles V himself—playing on the French pronunciation of the names *harlequin* and *Charles Quint*.

Arlecchino may have been born in Oneta, a village north of Bergamo (*see* p.213), but he carries a proud lineage that goes back to the ancient Greeks and Romans. From his character and appearance, historians of the theatre trace him back to the antique *planipedes*, comic mimes with shaved heads (everyone knew Arlecchino wore his silly nightcap to cover his baldness). Other scholars note his relationship to the 'tricksters' of German and Scandinavian mythology, and it has even been claimed that his costume of patches is that of a Sufi dervish. No doubt he had a brilliant career all through the Middle Ages, though it was probably only in the 1500s that he took the form of the Arlecchino we know. At that time, young rustics from the Bergamasque valleys would go to Venice, Milan and other cities to get work as *facchini*, porters. They all seemed to be named Johnny—*Zanni* in dialect, which became the common term for any of the clownish roles in the plays; it's the origin of our word 'zany'.

The name 'Arlecchino' seems actually to have been a French contribution. At the court of Henri III, a certain Italian actor who played the role became a protégé of a Monsieur de Harlay, and people started calling him 'little Harlay', or Harlequin. The character developed into a stock role, the most beloved of all the *commedia dell'arte* clown masks: simple-minded and easily frightened, yet an incorrigible prankster, a fellow as unstable as his motley dress. His foil was usually another servant, the Neapolitan Puricinella, or Puncinella—Punch—more serious and sometimes boastful, but still just as much of a buffoon. Try to imagine them together on stage, and you'll get something that looks very much like Stan Laurel and Oliver Hardy. No doubt these two have always gone through the world together, and we can hope they always will.

Bella Figura

The longer you stay in Italy, the more inscrutable it becomes. Nothing is ever quite as it seems, and you'll find yourself changing your ideas about things with disconcerting frequency. Part of the reason why is the obsession to *fare una bella figura*, 'to make a good impression or appearance', one of the most singular traits of the Italian people. You notice it almost immediately upon arrival. Not only is every Italian an immaculately smart fashion victim (they are by far the biggest consumers of their own fashion industry), but they always seem to be modelling their spiffy threads—posing, gesturing, playing to an audience when they have one, which is nearly always because Italians rarely move about except in small herds. Their cities are their stage, with perfectly arranged piazze and streets designed like movie sets, with lights suspended over the middle. Long-time observers of the phenonemon have even noted that each city's women tend to dress themselves in colours that complement the local brick or stone.

The Italians' natural grace and elegance may be partly instinctive; even back in the 14th century foreigners invariably noted their charming manners and taste for exquisite clothes. Many a painting of the Madonnna not only served piety, but also advertised the latest Milanese silks cuts or Venetian brocades. Appearance supplanted reality in a thousand ways in the Renaissance, especially after the discovery of artificial perspective, which made artistic representations seem much more clever and interesting than the real thing. Fake, painted marble supplanted real marble, even if the fake cost more; Palladio built marble palaces out of stucco; *trompe l'œil* frescoes embellished a hundred churches; glorious façades on cathedrals and palaces disguise the fact that the rest is shabby, unfinished brick. Even castles were built more to impress rather than keep out the enemy, in a day when battles had become brilliant bloodless games, and gorgeous Italian armour deflected few blows.

The gentleman's bible of the day, Castiglione's *The Courtier*, advises that it is no use doing a brave and noble deed unless someone is watching; honour, like almost every other virtue, is something bestowed from without. After the French and Spanish burst the Italians' lovely soap-bubble of superiority in the 16th century, the country's history becomes a saga of trying to do everything to keep up appearances, of nobles desperately mending their socks in the dim light to save up the money for hiring a servant when they expected visitors.

Bella figura pleases the eye but irritates just about everything else. Fashionable conformity has a way of spreading from mere clothing and gestures to opinions, especially in the provinces; the Italians remain the masters of empty flattery and compliments (don't think for a moment that a Roman bartender is mistaking you for someone else when he addresses you as 'duke' or 'cavalier'), and will say anything to please: 'Yes, straight ahead!' they'll often reply when you need directions, hoping it will make you happy even if they've never heard of your destination.

Nor does fashion slavery show any sign of abating; now that more Italians have more money than ever before, they are using it for fur coats, rarely necessary in most of the country's winters, and for designer clothes for the whole family. Even little children go to bed with visions of fashion dancing in their heads; Italy is the last stand of Barbie and Ken dolls, where each little girl owns at least a dozen.

Milan

La Scala

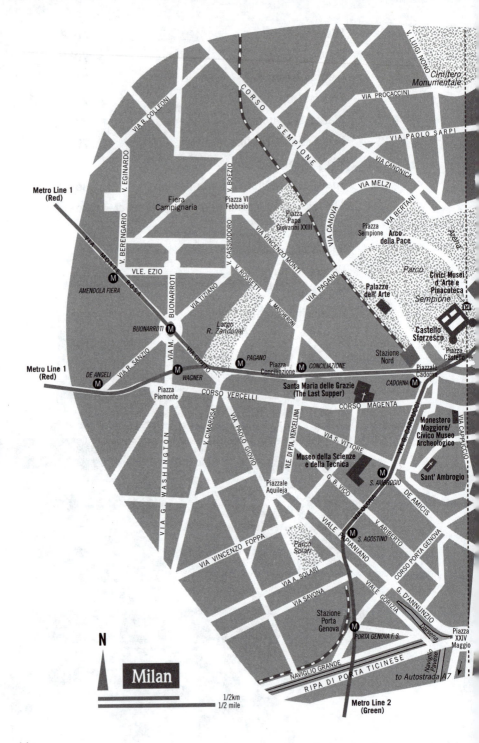

Most tourists don't come to Italy looking for slick and feverishly busy Milan, and most of those who find themselves here take in only the obligatory sights—Leonardo's *Last Supper*, La Scala, the Duomo, and the Brera Gallery—before rushing off to shop. The Italians (apart from the 4,000,000 Milanese, that is) have little good to say about their second city, either: all the Milanese do is work, all they care about is money, they are just as corrupt as everyone else, and they defiantly refuse to indulge even in the myth of *la dolce vita*.

The Italians who deride Milan (most of whom work just as many hours themselves) are mostly envious, and the tourists who whip through it in a day are mostly ignorant of what this great city has to offer. Milan is certainly atypical, devoid of the usual Italian daydreams and living-museum mustiness. Like Naples it lives for the present, but not in Naples' endearing total anarchy; as one of Europe's major financial centres and a capital of fashion, Milan dresses in a well-tailored, thoroughly cosmopolitan three-piece suit. The skills of its workers, above all in the luxury clothing trades, have been known for centuries—as evoked in the English word *millinery*.

And yet, as the Milanese are the first to admit, Milan has made its way in the world not so much by native talent as through the ability to attract and make use of those from other places, from St Ambrose and Leonardo da Vinci to its most celebrated designer of the moment. It has produced no great music of its own, but La Scala opera house is the world's most prestigious places to sing; it has produced very few artists of its own but has amassed enough treasures to fill four superb galleries. Milan is the Italian melting pot, Italy's picture window on the modern world, where the young and ambitious gravitate to see their talents appreciated and rewarded. Here history seems to weigh less; here willowy Japanese models slink down the pavement with natty young gents whose parents immigrated from Calabria. Roiling, moiling, toiling, constantly evolving, Milan is *sui generis*; in Milanese dialect they have said simply, long before Gertrude Stein's 'a rose is a rose', *Milan l'e Milan*, Milan is Milan.

History

Milan was born cosmopolitan. Although located far from any sea or river, in the midst of the fertile but vulnerable Lombard plain, it occupies the natural junction of trade routes through the Alpine passes, from the Tyrrhenian and Adriatic ports and from the River Po. This commercially strategic position has also put Milan square in the path of every conqueror tramping through Italy.

Mediolanum, as it was called for its first millennium and a half, first became prominent in the twilight of Rome when, as the headquarters of the Mobile Army and the seat of the court and government of the West, it became the *de facto* capital of the empire; Diocletian preferred it to

Rome, and his successors spent much of their time here. The official Christianization of the empire began here in 313, when Constantine the Great established religious toleration with his Edict of Milan.

St Ambrose (Sant'Ambrogio)

No sooner had Christianity received the imperial stamp of approval than it split into two hostile camps: the orthodox, early-Catholic traditionalists and the followers of the Egyptian bishop Arius. Arians denied that Christ was of the same substance as God; the sect was particularly widespread among the peoples on the fringes of the Roman Empire. An early bishop of Milan was an Arian and persecutor of the orthodox, and a schism seemed inevitable when he died. When the young consular governor Ambrose spoke to calm the crowd during the election of the new bishop, a child's voice suddenly piped up: 'Ambrose Bishop!' The cry was taken up, and Ambrose, who hadn't even been baptized, suddenly found himself thrust into a new job.

According to legend, when Ambrose was an infant in Rome, bees had flown into his mouth, attracted by the honey of his tongue. Ambrose's eloquence as bishop (374–97) is given much of the credit for preserving the unity of the Church; when the widow of Emperor Valentine desired to raise her son as an Arian, demanding a Milanese basilica for Arian worship, Ambrose and his supporters held the church through a nine-day siege, converting the empress's soldiers in the process. His most famous convert was St Augustine, and he also set what was to become the standard in relations between Church and Empire when he refused to allow Emperor Theodosius to enter church until he had done penance for ordering a civilian massacre in Thessalonika.

Ambrose left such an imprint on Milan that to this day genuine Milanese are called Ambrosiani. Their church, which was practically independent from Rome until the 11th century, still celebrates Mass according to the Ambrosian rite and holds its own carnival of Sant'Ambrogio in March.

The Rise of the *Comune*

During the barbarian invasions of the next few centuries 'Mediolanum' was shortened to Mailand, the prized Land of May, for so it seemed to the frostbitten Goths and Lombards who came to take it for their own. In the early 11th century Milan evolved into one of Italy's first *comuni* under the leadership of another great bishop, Heribert, who organized a *parlamento* of citizens and a citizen militia. The new *comune*, Guelph in defiance of imperial pretensions, at once began subjugating the surrounding country and especially its Ghibelline rivals Pavia, Lodi, and Como. To inspire the militia Heribert also invented that unique Italian war totem the *carroccio*, a huge ox-drawn cart that bore the city's banner, altar and bells into battle, to remind the soldiers of the city and church they fought for.

It was Lodi's complaint about Milan's bullying to Holy Roman Emperor Frederick Barbarossa that first brought old Red Beard to Italy in 1154. It was to prove a momentous battle of wills and arms between the emperor and Milan, one that would define the relationship of Italy's independent-minded *comuni* towards their nominal overlord. Barbarossa besieged and sacked Milan in 1158; the Ambrosiani promised to behave but attacked his German garrison as soon as the emperor was back safely over the Alps. Undaunted, Barbarossa returned again and for two years laid waste to the countryside around Milan, then grimly besieged the defiant city. When it surrendered he was merciless, demanding the surrender of the *carroccio*, forcing the citizens to kiss his feet with ropes around their necks, and inviting Milan's bitterest enemies, Lodi and Como, to raze the city to the ground, sparing only the churches of Sant'Ambrogio and San Lorenzo.

But this total humiliation of Milan, meant as an imperial lesson to Italy's other *comuni*, had the opposite effect; it galvanized them to form the Lombard League against the foreign oppressor (only Pavia hated Milan too much to join). Barbarossa, on his next trip over the Alps, found the *comuni* united against him, and in 1176 he was soundly defeated by the Lombard League at Legnano. Now the tables had turned and the empire itself was in danger of total revolt. To preserve it, Barbarossa had to do a little foot-kissing himself in Venice, the privileged toe in this case belonging to Pope Alexander III, whom Barbarossa had exiled from Rome in order to set up another pope more malleable to his schemes. To placate the Lombard *comuni* the Treaty of Constance was signed after a six-year truce in 1183, in which the signatories of the Lombard League received all that they desired: their municipal autonomy and the privilege of making war—on each other! The more magnanimous idea of a united Italy was still centuries away.

The Age of the Big Bosses

If Milan was precocious in developing government by the *comune*, it was also one of the first cities to give it up. Unlike their counterparts in Florence, Milan's manufacturers were varied in their trades (though mainly involved in textiles and armour) and limited themselves to small workshops, failing to form the companies of politically powerful merchants and trade associations that were the power base of a medieval Italian republic. The first family to fill Milan's vacuum at the top were the Torriani (della Torre), feudal lords who became the city's *signori* in 1247, only to lose their position to the Visconti in 1277.

The Visconti, created dukes in 1395, made Milan the strongest state in all Italy, and marriages into the French and English royal houses brought the family into European affairs as well (they fêted a certain Geoffrey Chaucer, in town to find a princess for a Plantagenet). Most ambitious of all the Visconti was Gian Galeazzo (1351–1402), married first to the daughter of the king of France and then to the daughter of his powerful and malevolent uncle Bernabò, whom Gian Galeazzo neatly packed off to prison, before conquering northern Italy, the Veneto, Romagna and Umbria. His army was ready to march on Florence, the gateway to the rest of the peninsula, when he suddenly died of plague. In his cruelty, ruthlessness and superstitious dependence on astrology, and in his love of art and letters (he founded the Certosa of Pavia, began the Duomo, held a court second to none in its lavishness, and supported the University of Pavia) Gian Galeazzo was one of the first 'archetypal' Renaissance princes. The Florentines and the Venetians took advantage of his demise to carry off pieces of his empire and, while his sons, the obscene Giovanni Maria (who delighted in feeding his enemies to the dogs) and the grue-some, paranoid Filippo Maria, did what they could to regain their father's conquests, Milan's influence was eventually reduced to Lombardy, which its leaders ran as a centralized state.

Filippo Maria left no male heirs, but a wise and lovely daughter named Bianca, whom he betrothed to his best *condottiere*, Francesco Sforza (1401–66). After Filippo Maria's death the Milanese declared the Golden Ambrosian Republic, which crumbled without much support after three years, when Francesco Sforza returned peacefully to accept the dukedom. One of Milan's best rulers, he continued the scientific development of Lombard agriculture and navigable canals and hydraulic schemes, and kept the peace through a friendly alliance with the Medici. His son, Galeazzo Maria, was assassinated, but not before fathering Caterina Sforza, the great Renaissance virago, and an infant son, Gian Galeazzo II.

Lodovico il Moro

It was, however, Francesco Sforza's second son, Lodovico il Moro (1451–1508), who took power and became Milan's most cultivated ruler, helped by his wife, the delightful Beatrice d'Este, who ran one of Italy's most sparkling courts until her early death in childbirth. Lodovico was a great patron of the arts, commissioning from Leonardo the *Last Supper*, engineering schemes and magnificent theatrical pageants. But Lodovico also bears the blame for one of the greatest political blunders in Italian history, when his quarrel with Naples grew so touchy that he invited Charles VIII of France to come and claim the Kingdom of Naples for himself. Charles took him up on it and marched unhindered down Italy. Lodovico soon realized his mistake, and joined the last-minute league of Italian states that united to trap and destroy the French at Fornovo. They succeeded, partially, but the damage was done: the French invasion had shown the Italian states, beautiful, rich, in full flower of the Renaissance, to be disunited and vulnerable. Charles VIII's son, Louis XII, took advantage of a claim on Milan through a Visconti grandmother and captured the city, and Lodovico with it. The Duke of Milan died a prisoner in a Loire château, an unhappy Prospero, covering the walls of his dungeon with bizarre graffiti that perplexes visitors to this day. After more fights between French and Spanish, Milan ended up a strategic province of Charles V's empire, ruled by a Spanish viceroy.

In 1712 the city came under the Habsburgs of Austria and with the rest of Lombardy profited from the enlightened reforms of Maria Theresa, who did much to improve agriculture (especially the production of rice and silk), rationalize taxes and increase education; her rule saw the creation of La Scala, the Brera Academy and most of central neoclassical Milan. After centuries of hibernation the Ambrosiani were stirring again, and when Napoleon arrived the city welcomed him fervently. With a huge festival Milan became the capital of Napoleon's 'Cisalpine Republic', linked to Paris via the new Simplon Highway.

The Powerhouse of United Italy

After Napoleon's defeat in 1814 the Austrians returned, but Milan was an important centre of Italian nationalist sentiment during the Risorgimento and rebelled against the repressive Habsburg regime in 1848. The city's greatest contribution during this period, however, was the novelist Manzoni, whose masterpiece *I Promessi Sposi* caused a nationwide sensation and sense of unity in a peninsula that had been politically divided since the fall of Rome (*see* p.186).

After joining the new kingdom of Italy, Milan rapidly took its place as the country's economic and industrial dynamo, attracting thousands of workers from the poorer sections of Italy. Many of these workers joined the new Italian Socialist Party, which was strongest in the regions of Lombardy and Emilia-Romagna. In Milan, too, Mussolini founded the Fascist Party and launched its first campaign in 1919. The city was bombed heavily in air raids during the Second World War. In May 1945 Milan's well-organized partisan forces liberated it from the Germans before the Allies arrived, and when Mussolini's corpse was hung up on a meat hook in the Piazzale Loreto the Milanese turned out to make sure that the duke of delusion was truly dead before beginning to rebuild their battered city on more solid ground.

Milan was, again, *the* centre of Italy's postwar economic miracle when it began to take off in the late fifties, drawing in still more thousands of migrants from the south. Despite economic ups and downs and a few hiccups, the city's wealth has continued to grow by near-mathematical progression ever since, while its political affairs were dominated from the seventies onwards by the Socialists and their ineffable boss Bettino Craxi. Since the beginning of the nineties, however, as anyone exposed to any of the Italian media has not been allowed to forget for even one minute, the whole structure has come crashing down, for it was in Milan, too, that the first allegations of the large-scale taking of *tangenti* (bribes) came to light, initially involving the Socialists, though the mud later spread to touch all the established parties. Craxi and his cronies have disappeared from the political map (Craxi disappeared from Italy altogether, and is holed up in Tunisia) and power in Milan is now disputed between a left/green alliance and Umberto Bossi's Lega Nord.

Getting There

The transport hub of northern Italy, Milan is well served by a full range of international services—with two international **airports**, several **train stations** and many long-distance **coach** services. Milan's expanding Metro network is, as well as one of the quickest means of getting from A to B, a very useful orientation aid, and stops (indicated **Ⓜ**) are listed in the text below.

from the airport

Milan has two main airports, **Linate** (8km from the centre) and the larger **Malpensa** (50km to the west), both of which receive national and international flights. As a rule, intercontinental flights use Malpensa while Linate handles most of the European and domestic traffic—but check. For flight information for both airports, call ✆ 02 7485 2200. STAM buses (L4500) run every 20 minutes from 5.40am to 7pm between Linate and the Stazione Centrale. City bus 73 (L1500) also runs to Linate from Piazza San Babila (**Ⓜ** *line 1*) in the city centre.

Air Pullman bus shuttles (✆ 02 4009 9260) link Malpensa to the Stazione Centrale and Linate in about an hour, approximately once an hour from 7am to 10.15pm (L13,000). Between 7.30am and 12.30pm a second shuttle bus runs hourly from Piazza Castello, and goes by way of the Trade Fair during exhibitions. Beware that taxis from Malpensa to Milan cost a bomb.

Charter flights may use a third airport, **Orio al Serio**, near Bergamo, ✆ 035 326 325. STAB buses ✆ 035 318 472 (they're harmless, really) link it to Milan's Stazione Centrale (L15,000) and vice versa, leave the Stazione Centrale 3 hours before each charter flight.

by rail

Milan's splendiferous main **Stazione Centrale** (Ⓜ *lines 2, 3*), designed in the thirties with the travelling Fascist satrap in mind, dominates the Piazza Duca d'Aosta northeast of the centre. Centrale (switchboard ✆ 02 63711) handles nearly all international trains, as well as most of the domestic routes. Useful trams and buses from Centrale include tram 1 to Piazza Scala and Nord Station, and 33 to Stazione Garibaldi and the Cimitero Monumentale; bus 60 goes to Piazza del Duomo and Castello Sforzesco and bus 65 runs down Corso Buenos Aires, Corso Venezia and through the centre to Corso Italia. The **Left Luggage** at Centrale is open 24 hours a day; **Lost and Found**, ✆ 02 6371 2667.

Stazione Garibaldi (Ⓜ *2*) is the terminus for car-train services, as well as trains for Pavia, Monza, Varese, Como and Bergamo. **Stazione Lambrate** (Ⓜ *2*), on the east side of the city, has connections to Genoa, Bergamo and towards the Simplon Pass. **Stazione Cadorna** (Ⓜ *Cadorna*) is the main station of Lombardy's regional Milan Nord railway (✆ 02 7202 2343) with connections to Como, Varese, Saronno, Erba and Laveno (Lake Maggiore).

by coach

Inter-city coaches arrive in the Piazza Castello (Ⓜ *Cairoli*), where several companies have their offices. Contact the tourist office (*see* below) for information on destinations, schedules and prices.

Getting Around

Even though Milan looks like a bloated amoeba on the map, the city marks its age in rings, like a tree, and most of its sights are in the highly walkable innermost ring, the *Cerchia dei Navigli*. Milan is not a difficult place to find your way around—unless you've brought a car: the one-way system, no traffic zones in the centre and expensive parking make driving distinctly unfun.

by bus and tram

The buses and rather dashing Art Deco trams and trolleys run by the Milan transport authority (ATM, ✆ 02 8901 0797) are convenient and their routes well marked. Purchase **tickets** (L1500, or carnets of 10 tickets, L14,000) in advance at tobacco shops, news-stands, metro stations or in the coin-gobbling machines at the main stops, and stamp them in the machines on board; a ticket is valid for 75 minutes' travel anywhere on the network, regardless of how many transfers you make. Most bus routes run from about 6am to midnight, after which time special night bus routes operate with reasonable frequency.

If you plan to be riding around a fair bit, buy a one-day pass (L5000), or two-day pass (L9000), valid for buses, trams and the Metro. The ATM also publishes a very useful map showing all the bus routes and metro stops, the *Guida Rete dei trasporti pubblici*, available at the tourist office and the Stazione Centrale.

by metro

The **Metropolitana Milanese** (Ⓜ), begun in the sixties, is sleek and well run, and a boon for the bewildered tourist. There are three lines, the Red (Ⓜ*1*), Green (Ⓜ*2*), and Yellow (Ⓜ*3*), the last of which was completed in 1990. The Metro is open from 6am to midnight daily, and tickets are the same as those used for the buses or trams.

by taxi

Milanese taxis are yellow (but soon to be white) and their drivers generally honest and reliable. If it's not possible to flag a free cab down they can be found waiting at ranks in the Piazza del Duomo, by the Stazione Centrale, and in several other central piazzas. Alternatively, book a taxi on ✆ 02 8585, ✆ 02 6767 or ✆ 02 5353.

by car

Driving in Milan requires chutzpah, luck and good navigation skills. One-way streets are the rule, signs are confusing, parking impossible, and bringing a vehicle into the city centre between 7am and 7pm is not only foolhardy but illegal *unless* you have a foreign number plate. If you must bring a car into the centre, look for ATM car parks on the outskirts, or dump your car in one of the large parking lots at the termini of the metro lines.

Tourist Information

The main tourist office is in the Piazza del Duomo on Via Marconi 1, ✆ 02 7252 4300, ✉ 02 7252 4360 (*open Mon–Fri 8.30am–8pm, Sat 9–1 and 2–7, Sun 9–1 and 2–5*). It has a branch office at the Stazione Centrale (*open Mon–Sat 8am–7pm, Sun 9–12.30 and 1.30–6*). Both will make free hotel reservations on the spot and provide good city maps and other practical information. Tourist SOS: Via Adige 11, ✆ 02 545 6551.

Piazza del Duomo

In the exact centre of Milan towers its famous **Duomo**, a monument of such imposing proportions (third largest in the world after St Peter's and Seville Cathedral) that on clear days it is as visible from the distant Alps as the Alps are visible from its dome. Bristling with 135 spires, defended by 2244 marble saints and one cheeky sinner (Napoleon, who crowned himself King of Italy here in 1805), guarded by 95 leering gargoyles, energized by sunlight pouring through the largest stained-glass windows in Christendom, Milan Cathedral is a remarkable bulwark of the faith. And yet for all its monstrous size, for all the hubbub of its busy piazza, traversed daily by tens of thousands of Milanese and tourists, the Duomo is utterly ethereal, a rose-white vision of pinnacles and tracery woven by angels. In Vittorio de Sica's *Miracle in Milan* (1950) it serves its natural role as a stairway (or rather launching pad) to heaven for the broomstick-riding heroes.

Gian Galeazzo Visconti began the Duomo in 1386 as a votive offering to the Mother of God, hoping that she would favour him with an heir. His prayers for a son were answered in the form of Giovanni Maria, a loathsome degenerate assassinated soon after he attained power; as the Ambrosiani have wryly noted, the Mother of God got the better of the deal.

The Making of a Cathedral

Gian Galeazzo Visconti was the Man Who Would Be King—King of Italy, or whatever fraction of it he could snatch. A well-nigh psychotic ambition drove the frantic career of this paradigm of Renaissance princes, and such an ambition required a fitting symbol. Milan was to have a new cathedral, the biggest in Italy, dedicated to the greater glory of God, Milan and the Visconti. The demolition of a huge part of the city centre made a space ready for it by 1386, when building began.

All Gian Galeazzo's schemes and aggressions came to nothing, as the little empire he built disintegrated after his death, but Milan did get its cathedral as a kind of consolation prize. From the beginning, the Duke called in all the most skilled builders of the day who were available. Their names are recorded: men such as Bonino da Campione and Matteo da Campione, two of the Campionese masters, and also a number of foreigners—Gamodia of Gmünd, Walter Monich and Peter Monich from Germany, and a Parisian known as Mignot. In the court of the Duke, they argued over the sacred geometry appropriate to the task, over the relative merits of beginning the work *ad triangulum* or *ad quadratum*, that is, whether the plans and the measures should be based on the proportions of the equilateral triangle or the square. The latter, the more common form, was decided on, and in the lodge constructed for them the builders would have set up a large open space on the floor, for tracing out the detailed plan and elevation with compass and straight-edge. After that, over the years to come, they would work out all the details, every vault, column, buttress and pinnacle, from the same set of proportions.

The building would be a major drain on Gian Galeazzo's budget—almost as expensive as his endless wars. A normal, modest cathedral would have been a sufficiently difficult project. To get the Candoglia marble they wanted, for example, the master builders had to build roads and even canals, to bring the stone down from the quarries north of Lake Maggiore. The duke's passion for decoration made it even more difficult; he demanded angelic hosts of statuary—over 2000 on the exterior and 700 more inside. As many as 300 sculptors found employment at one time in the cathedral workshops. These too came from all over Europe; names like Pietro di Francia and Fritz di Norimberga on the pay lists are a reminder of the Christian, pan-European universality of the age. Men might speak different tongues, but for all the language of faith and art were the same.

How did Milan and the duke pay for all this? The records mention a big campaign by local church authorities to sell religious indulgences, while the state contributed sums from a steep increase in fines in the courts. It wouldn't have been enough. The financing would have been a formidably complex matter, no doubt partially arranged by loans from the Lombard and Tuscan bankers, but no one can say exactly how deeply the Duke dug into his own pockets, how much he coaxed or squeezed out of the other great families, how much the pope, Milan's ally, threw in and how much was wrung out of the poor. New technology helped to lower the costs, especially the machines invented by a Master Giovanni da Zellino for hoisting stone more easily—it's often forgotten how the late Middle Ages was a time of dizzying technological progress, creating advances in everything from navigation to farming to the first mechanical clocks. For all the complexity, the duke and his builders knew what they were about; the cathedral was substantially complete by 1399.

However, by the time they got to the façade, the Gothic style—which the Italians never liked much to begin with—had become unfashionable. This bewildered front went through several overhauls of Renaissance and baroque, then back to Gothic, with the end result, completed in 1809 under Napoleon's orders, resembling a shotgun wedding of Isabelline Gothic with Christopher Wren. In the 1880s there were plans to tear it down and start again, but no one had the heart, and the Milanese have become used to it. Walk around, though, to the glorious Gothic apse, to see what its original builders were about. The subjects of the bas-reliefs on the bronze doors, all cast in this century, are a Milanese history lesson: the Edict of Constantine, the Life of St Ambrose, the city's quarrels with Barbarossa and the history of the cathedral itself.

The Interior

The remarkable dimensions of the interior challenge the eye to take in what seems like infinity captured under a canopy. Its tremendous volume is defined into five aisles by 52 pillars of titanic dimensions, crowned by rings of niches and statues, and is dazzlingly lit by acres of stained glass; the windows of the apse, embellished with flamboyant Gothic tracery, are among the most beautiful anywhere. All other decorations seem rather small, but you may want to seek out in the right transept Leoni's fine Mannerist tomb of Gian Giacomo de' Medici, *Il Medeghino*, the pirate of Lake Como—erected by his brother Pope Pius IV. In the same transept you'll find one of the most peculiar of the cathedral's thousands of statues: that of San Bartolomeo holding his own skin, with an inscription assuring us that it was made by Marco Agrate and not by Praxiteles, just in case we couldn't tell the difference. Other treasures include the 12th-century Trivulzio Candelabrum by Nicola da Verdun, as well as medieval ivory, gold and silverwork in the Treasury, located below the main altar by the crypt, where the mastermind of the Counter-Reformation, St Charles Borromeo (nephew of Il Medeghino; *see* p.44) lies in state.

Near the cathedral entrance a door leads down to the **Baptistry of St Ambrose** (*open daily 9.45–12.45 and 2–5.45; adm*), excavated in the 1960s, containing the octagonal baptismal font where St Ambrose baptized St Augustine. Throughout the Duomo you can see the alchemical symbol adopted as the Visconti crest, now the symbol of Milan: a twisting serpent in the act of swallowing a man; the story goes that in 1100, in the Second Crusade, the battling bishop Ottone Visconti fought a giant Saracen, and when he slew him he took the device from his shield.

For a splendid view of Milan, take a walk through the enchanted forest of spires and statues on the **cathedral roof** (*open daily 9–5.30; steps or lift from outside the cathedral; adm*). The 15th-century dome by Amadeo of Pavia, topped by the main spire with the gilt statue of *La Madonnina* (who at 12ft really isn't as diminutive as she seems 354ft from the ground), offers the best view of all—on a clear morning, all the way to the Matterhorn.

Museo del Duomo and Palazzo Reale

On the south side of the cathedral, the Palazzo Reale was for centuries the headquarters of Milan's rulers, from the Visconti down to the Austrian governors, who had the place redone in their favourite neoclassical style. In one wing, the **Museo del Duomo** (*open Tues–Sun 9.30–12.30 and 3–6; adm*) contains art and artefacts made for the cathedral over the past six centuries, including some of the original stained glass and fine 14th-century French and German statues and gargoyles, tapestries, and a Tintoretto. Other rooms document the cathedral's construction, including a magnificent wooden model from 1519, designs from the 1886 competition for the façade, and castings from the bronze doors.

In the main core of the Palazzo Reale is the **Cívico Museo dell'Arte Contemporanea** (**CIMAC**) (*open Tues–Sun 9.30–5.30*), with temporary exhibits on the second and the main collection on the third floor. The concentration is on Italian art of this century, with early works by the futurists (especially Boccioni), as well as others by Modigliani, de Chirico, Morandi, de Pises, Melotti, Carrà, and current artists like Tancredi and Novelli; Kandinsky, Mondrian, Matisse, Picasso and Klee also check in.

Behind the palace, on Via Palazzo Reale, be sure to note the beautiful 14th-century **campanile di San Gottardo**, formerly belonging to the palace chapel. The porticoes around the Piazza del Duomo are occupied by some of the city's oldest bars; in the centre of the square old Vittorio Emanuele II on his horse looks ready to charge into action.

The Galleria and La Scala

The king lent his name to Milan's majestic drawing room, the elegant **Galleria Vittorio Emanuele**, a glass-roofed arcade linking Piazza Duomo and Piazza della Scala. It was designed by Giuseppe Mengoni, who tragically slipped and fell from the roof the day before its inauguration in 1878. Here are more elegant bars (especially the venerable **Salotto**, serving perhaps Milan's best cup of coffee) and some of the city's finest shops. In the centre, under a marvellous 48m (157ft) glass dome, is a mosaic figure of Taurus; the Milanese believe it's good luck to step on the bull's testicles.

The Galleria opens up to the **Piazza della Scala**, address of one of the world's great opera houses, the neoclassical **Teatro alla Scala**, its name derived from the church of Santa Maria alla Scala which formerly stood on the site. Inaugurated in 1778 with Salieri's *Europa Riconosciuta*, La Scala saw the premieres of most of the 19th-century classics of Italian opera; when bombs smashed it in 1943, it was rebuilt as it was in three years, reopening under the baton of its great conductor Arturo Toscanini. The **Museo Teatrale alla Scala** (*open June–Oct daily, 9–12.30 and 2–5.30; Nov–May Mon–Sat only; adm*), entered through a door on the left, has an excellent collection of opera memorabilia (especially on Verdi) including scores, letters, portraits and photos of legendary stars, and set designs; there's even an archaeological section related to ancient Greek and Roman drama. From the museum you can look into the beautiful 2800-seat theatre, with its great chandelier; try to imagine the scene in 1859, when the crowded house at a performance of Bellini's *Norma* took advantage of the presence of the Austrian governor to join in the rousing war chorus.

An unloved 19th-century statue of Leonardo stands in the middle of the Piazza della Scala, while opposite the theatre the imposing **Palazzo Marino** is a fine 16th-century building hiding behind a 19th-century façade; now the Palazzo Municipale, it has one of the city's loveliest courtyards. A few steps away, on Via Catena, the unusual 1565 **Casa degli Omenoni** was built by sculptor Leone Leoni for his retirement, and is held up by eight uncomfortable telamones; around the corner of cobblestoned Piazza Belgioioso, at Via Morone 1, the handsome old home of Alessandro Manzoni (1785–1873) is now a shrine, the **Museo Manzoniano** (*open Tues–Fri 9–12 and 2–4*), filled with items relating to the Milanese novelist's life and work, including illustrations from *I Promessi Sposi* and an auto-graphed portrait of his friend Goethe. For more on the man, *see* p.186.

Museo Poldi-Pezzoli

In front of La Scala runs one of Milan's busiest and most fashionable boulevards, the **Via Manzoni**. Verdi lived for years and died in a room in the Grand Hotel (No.29); at No.10 is the lovely 17th-century palace of Gian Giacomo Poldi-Pezzoli, who rearranged his home to fit his fabulous art collection, then willed it to the public in 1879. Repaired after bomb damage in the war, the **Museo Poldi-Pezzoli** (*open Tues–Sun 9.30–12.30 and 2.30–6; Sat till 7.30; April–Sept closed Sun pm; adm*) houses an exquisite collection of 15th- to 18th- century paintings, including one of Italy's best-known portraits, the 15th-century *Portrait of a Young Woman* by Antonio Pollaiuolo, depicting an ideal Renaissance beauty. She shares the most elegant room of the palace, the Salone Dorato, with the other jewels of the museum: Mantegna's Byzantinish *Madonna*, Giovanni Bellini's *Pietà*, Piero della Francesca's *San Nicolò* and, from a couple of centuries later, Guardi's *Grey Lagoon*. Other outstanding paintings include Vitale da Bologna's *Madonna*, a polyptych by Cristoforo Moretti and works by Botticelli, Luini, Foppa, Turà, Tiepolo, Crivelli, Lotto, Cranach (portraits of Luther and wife) and a crucifix by Raphael. The collection is also rich in decorative arts: Islamic metalwork and rugs—note the magnificent Persian carpet (1532) depicting a hunting scene in the Salone Dorato—medieval and Renaissance armour, Renaissance bronzes, Flemish tapestries, Murano glass, antique sun dials, lace and more.

Via Monte Napoleone

Just up Via Manzoni is the entrance to Milan's high-fashion vortex, concentrated in the palace-lined **Via Monte Napoleone** and elegant **Via della Spiga**. Even if you're not in the market for astronomically priced clothes by Italy's top designers, these exclusive lanes make for good window-shopping and perhaps even better people-watching. It's hard to remember that up until the 1970s Florence was the centre of the Italian garment industry. When Milan took over this status—it has the airports Florence lacks—it added the essential ingredients of business savvy and packaging to the Italians' innate sense of style to create a high-fashion empire rivalling Paris, London and New York.

There are three museums in the sumptuous 18th-century Palazzo Morando Bolognini, on Via S. Andrea 6, between 'Montenapo' and Via della Spiga: the **Civico Museo di Milano** and the **Civico Museo di Storia Contemporanea** (*both open Tues–Sun 9–6*), the first with paintings of old Milan, the second devoted to Italian history between the years 1914 and 1945; the third, the **Civico Museo Marinaro Ugo Mursia**, (*open Tues–Sun 9.30–5.30*) has a collection of nautical models, English figureheads, scrimshaw and mementoes, founded by a Milanese scholar obsessed with Joseph Conrad. A fourth museum, still in the ozone of chic, the **Museo Bagatti Valsecchi**, Via Santo Spirito 10 (*open Tues–Sun 1–5; adm exp; half-price Wed*) was the life's work of two brothers, Fausto and Giuseppe Bagatti Valsecchi, who built a neo-Renaissance palace to integrate the period fireplaces, ceilings and friezes that they had collected, carefully disguising such 19th-century conveniences as the bathtub.

Near the intersection of Via della Spiga and Via Manzoni, the **Archi di Porta Nuova**, the huge stone arches of a gate, are a rare survival of the 12th-century walls. The moat around the walls was enlarged into a canal to bring in marble for building the cathedral; it was covered in the 1880s when its stench outweighed any economic benefit. (A useful bus, no.96/97 from the Piazza Cavour, makes the circuit of the former canal and is convenient for reaching the Castello Sforzesco, Santa Maria delle Grazie or Sant'Ambrogio.)

The Giardini Pubblici

From Piazza Cavour, Via Palestro curves between the two sections of Milan's Public Gardens. The romantic **Giardini di Villa Reale** (**Ⓜ** *Palestro*) were laid out in 1790 for the Belgiojoso family by Leopoldo Pollak, who later built the Villa Reale, Napoleon's residence while in the Cisalpine Republic. The villa is now the **Civica Galleria d'Arte Moderna** (*open Tues–Sun 9.30–5.30*) where, at the time of writing, only the first floor Vismara collection of paintings (works by Picasso, Matisse, Modigliani, de Pisis, Tosi, Morandi and Renoir) and the Mariano Marini sculpture collection are open; Marini (*d. 1980*), generally acknowledged as the top Italian sculptor of the 20th century, spent most of his career in Milan, and in 1973 he gave the city many of his sensuous, acutely observed bronzes, as well as paintings and graphic works. When the rest of the gallery reopens (one section, the Pavilione d'Arte Contemporanea, was bombed in 1993), look for paintings by Lombard neoclassicists, the self-consciously Romantic *Scapigliati* (the 'Wild-haired Ones') of Milan, Italian Impressionists, the futurists and more. Other works are French: by Millet, Corot, Cézanne, Gauguin, Manet and Toulouse-Lautrec.

The **Giardini Pubblici** proper, a shady Arcadia between Via Palestro and the Corso Venezia, was laid out in 1782; artificial rocks compensate for Milan's flat terrain. A good place to take children, with its zoo, swans, pedal cars and playgrounds, it is also the site of Italy's premier **Natural History Museum** (*open Tues–Fri 9.30–5.30, Sat, Sun and hols till 6.30*), near the Corso Venezia; another victim of the war, it has been rebuilt in its original neo-medieval style. Look out for the Canadian cryptosaurus, the Colossal European lobster, the Madagascar aye-aye and the 40-kilo topaz. The gardens also contain the recently reopened **Museo del Cinema**, Viale Manin 2 (*open Tues–Fri 3–6; adm*), with a small collection on early animation techniques, posters, cameras and so on.

Corso Venezia itself is lined with neoclassical and Liberty-style palaces—most remarkably, the 1903 **Palazzo Castiglione** at No.47 and the neoclassical **Palazzo Serbelloni**, Milan's press club, on the corner of Via Senato. The district just west of the Corso Venezia was the city's most fashionable in the 1920s, and there are a smattering of rewarding buildings: the **Casa Galimberti** with a colourful ceramic façade at Via Malpighi 3, off the Piazza Oberdan; the good Art Deco foyer at Via Cappuccini 8; the eccentric houses on Via Mozart (especially No.11); and the romantic 1920s **Palazzo Fidia** at Via Melegari 2.

Lo stile Liberty

'Liberty style' is the name given in Italy to Art Nouveau, the short-lived artistic and architectural movement that flourished in many European countries around the turn of the century. It refers, curiously, to Liberty's, the London shop, whose William Morris-influenced, flower-patterned fabrics and ceramics were some of the first articles in the style imported into Italy, and became enormously popular at the time (the style is also, less commonly, known as the *stile floreale*). The ethos behind the movement was an avoidance of architectural precedents, an embracing of 'naturalistic' ornament and smooth, flowing lines, and a desire to 'integrate' all the arts—hence the importance given not just to painting and fine art, but also to architecture and interior and practical design. Decoration, an integral part of every design, was the key.

Liberty style was never as important in Italy as were its equivalents in France, Austria or Catalunya—nor was it usually as extravagant as they often were—but it did for a time become the vogue among the newly wealthy middle classes of Italy's industrializing north. As the prosperity of this class grew in the 1900s, so too did demand for Liberty buildings and products—seen most notably in the hotels and villas around the lakes or along the Riviera. Perhaps the most important figure working in the style in Italy was Giuseppe Sommaruga (1867–1917), whose achievements include the Palazzo Castiglione, a pair of villas at Sárnico on Lake Iseo, and Hotel Tre Colli near Varese, characterized by their richly ornamental lines and an uninhibited use of space. In a similar style, but more refined, is the architecture of Raimondo D'Aronco (1857–1932), who worked mainly on public buildings, particularly for conferences and exhibitions. His most famous work is the Palazzo Comunale in Udine.

Northwest of the Giardini Pubblici, the **Piazza della Repubblica** has many of the city's hotels; the Mesopotamian-scale **Stazione Centrale** (1931), blocking the end of Via Vittor Pisani, is the largest train station in Italy. The nearby skyscraper, the **Pirelli Building**, is one that the Milanese are especially proud of, built in 1960 by Gio Ponti, while Pier Luigi Nervi designed the concrete structure. It's now the seat of Lombardy's regional government, and you can see most of the city from its terrace (call ahead, *©* 02 67651). Further to the north-west, at Via Petteri 56, the Palazzo Martinitt houses the **Museo del Giocattolo e del Bambino** (**Ⓜ** *Lambrate; open Tues–Sat 9am–9.45pm, Sun 9–12.45 and 2.30–7.45; adm*) with a beautiful display of toys dating back to 1700.

Brera and its National Gallery

Another street alongside La Scala, Via G. Verdi, leads into the Brera, one of the few old neigh-bourhoods to survive in central Milan. Although some of the old cobblestoned streets of Brera have maintained their original flavour (especially Corso Garibaldi), local trendies are busily turning the remainder into Milan's version of Greenwich Village, full of antique and curiosity shops, late night spots and art galleries.

At the corner of Via Brera and the piquantly named Via Fiori Oscuri ('Street of the Dark Flowers') is the elegant courtyard of the **Galleria Nazionale di Brera** (**Ⓜ** *Lanza* or *Monte Napoleone; open Tues–Sat 9am–9.45pm, Sun 9–12.45 and 2.30–7.45; adm; free on 1st, 3rd Sun and 2nd, 4th Sat of each month*), one of world's finest hoards of art. The collection was compiled by Napoleon, whose bronze statue, draped in a toga, greets visitors as they enter; a firm believer in centralized art as well as centralized government, he had northern Italy's churches and monasteries stripped of their treasures to form a Louvre-like collection for Milan, the capital of his Cisalpine Republic. The museum first opened in 1809; ongoing improve-ments and restorations since 1988 may lead to certain sections being closed.

Perhaps the best known of the Brera's scores of masterpieces is Raphael's *Marriage of the Virgin*, a Renaissance landmark for its evocation of an ideal, rarefied world, where even the disappointed suitor snapping his rod on his knee performs the bitter ritual in a graceful dance step, all acted out before a perfect but eerily vacant temple in the background. In the same room hangs Piero della Francesca's last painting, the *Pala di Urbino*, featuring among its holy personages Federico da Monfeltro, Duke of Urbino, with his famous nose. The Venetian masters are well represented: Carpaccio, Veronese, Titian, Tintoretto, Jacopo Bellini and the Vivarini, but especially Giovanni Bellini, with several of his loveliest Madonnas and the great *Pietà*, as well as a joint effort with his brother Gentile of *St Mark Preaching in Alexandria*; there are luminous works by Carlo Crivelli and Cima da Conegliano; and several paintings by Mantegna, including his remarkable study in foreshortening, the *Cristo Morto*. Other famous works include *Christ at the Column* by Bramante, Caravaggio's striking *Supper at Emmaus*, the *Pala Sforzesca* by a 15th-century Lombard artist, depicting Lodovico il Moro and his family; a polyptych by Gentile da Fabriano; and fine works by the Ferrarese masters da Cossa and Ercole de' Roberti.

Outstanding among the non-Italians are Rembrandt's *Portrait of his Sister*, El Greco's *St Francis* and Van Dyck's *Portrait of the Princess of Orange*. When the Great Masters become indigestible, take a breather in the new 20th-century wing of the gallery, populated mainly by futurists like Severini, Balla and Boccioni, who believed that to achieve speed was to achieve success, and the metaphysical followers of De Chirico, who seem to believe just the opposite.

Brera's other principal monument is **San Simpliciano**, just off Corso Garibaldi to the north. Perhaps founded by St Ambrose, it retains its essential palaeo-Christian form in a 12th-century wrapping, with an octagonal drum. The apse has a beautiful fresco of the *Coronation of the Virgin* (1515) by Bergognone, and the larger of the two cloisters, from the mid-16th century, is especially charming with its twin columns.

Castello Sforzesco

Marking the western limits of the Brera quarter, the Castello Sforzesco (Ⓜ *Cairoli* or *Cadorna*) is one of Milan's best-known landmarks. It was originally a fortress within the walls; the Visconti made it their base, and as a symbol of their power it was razed to the ground by the Ambrosian Republic in 1447. Three years later, under Francesco Sforza, it was rebuilt; after air raids in the war damaged it and its treasures it was rebuilt again, this time disguising water cisterns in its stout towers.

Today the castle houses the city's excellent collections, the **Civici Musei d'Arte e Pinacoteca del Castello** (*open Tues–Sun 9.30–5.30*). The entrance, by way of a tower rebuilt on a design by Filarete (1452) and the huge Piazza d'Armi, is through the lovely Renaissance Corte Ducale and the principal residence of the Sforza. There are intriguing fragments of Milanese history—the equestrian tomb of Bernabò Visconti and a beautiful 14th-century monument of the Rusca family; reliefs of Milan's triumph over Barbarossa, and the city's gonfalon. Leonardo designed the ilex decorations of the **Sala delle Asse**; the next room, the **Sala dei Ducali**, contains a superb relief by Duccio from Rimini's Tempio Malatestiano; the Sala degli Scarlioni contains the two finest sculptures in the museum, the *Effigy of Gaston de Foix* (1525) by Bambaia and Michelangelo's unfinished **Rondanini Pietà**, a haunting work that the aged sculptor worked at off and on during his last nine years, repudiating all of his early ideals of physical beauty in favour of such blunt, expressionistic figures; the difference between this and his *Pietà* in St Peter's couldn't be greater.

Upstairs, most notable among the fine collection of Renaissance furnishings and decorative arts are the 15th-century Castello Roccabianca frescoes illustrating the popular medieval tale of Patient Griselda. The **Pinacoteca** contains a tender *Madonna with Child* by Giovanni Bellini, his brother-in-law Mantegna's more austere, classical Madonna in the *Pala Trivulzio*, and the lovely *Madonna dell'Umiltà* by Filippo Lippi. Lombards, not surprisingly, predominate: Foppa, Solario, Magnasco (who spent most of his life in Milan), Bergognone (especially the serene *Virgin with SS. Sebastian and Gerolamo*) and Bramantino, with an eerie *Noli me tangere*. There's a room of Leonardo's followers, and then the *Primavera,* by Milanese Giuseppe Arcimboldo (1527–1593), who was no one's follower at all, but the first surrealist—the Primavera is a woman's face made up entirely of flowers. From 18th-century Venice, Francesco Guardi's *Storm* looks ahead to another school—Impressionism.

The castle's third court, the beautiful **Cortile della Rocchetta**, was designed by the Florentines Bramante and Filarete, both of whom worked for several years for Francesco Sforza. The basement of the courtyard is filled with an extensive **Egyptian collection** of funerary artefacts and the **prehistoric collection** of items found in Lombardy's Iron Age settlements, most notably the 6th-century BC bronzes from the tomb of the warrior of Sesto Calende. The first floor houses the **Museum of Musical Instruments** with a beautiful collection of 641 string and wind instruments, and a spinet that was played by Mozart. The **Sala della Balla**, where the Sforza danced, now contains the *Tapestries of the Months* designed by Bramantino.

Parco Sempione and Cimitero Monumentale

Behind the Castello stretches the **Parco Sempione**, Milan's largest park, where you can find De Chirico's **Metaphysical Fountain**; the 1930s **Palazzo dell'Arte**, used for exhibitions, especially the Milan Triennial of modern architecture and design; the **Arena**, designed in 1806 after Roman models, where 19th-century dilettantes staged mock naval battles; and an imposing triumphal arch, the **Arco della Pace**, marking the terminus of Napoleon's highway (Corso Sempione) to the Simplon Pass. Originally intended to glorify Napoleon, the Austrians changed the dedication to peace. At Corso Sempione 36 the **Casa Rustici** (1931), designed by Giuseppe Terragni of Como on the proportions of the Golden Rule, is often considered Milan's finest modern building.

Further out (*tram 4 from Piazza Scala*) the **Cimitero Monumentale** (*open daily 8.30–5*) is the last rendezvous of Milan's well-to-do burghers. Their lavish monuments—Liberty-style temples and pseudo-ancient columns and obelisks—are just slightly less flamboyant than those of the Genoese, the Italian champs for post-mortem splendour. The cemetery keeper has guides to the tombs—Manzoni, Toscanini and Albert Einstein's father are among the best-known names; the memorial to the 800 Milanese who perished in German concentration camps is the most moving.

West of the Duomo

Milan's greatest painting, Leonardo da Vinci's *Last Supper* (or the *Cenacolo*), is in the refectory of the convent of **Santa Maria delle Grazie** (**Ⓜ** *Cadorna, then Via Boccaccio and left on Via Caradosso; open Tues–Sat 8–1.45 and 7–10, Sun 8–1.45 and 5–8; adm; expect a long queue as only 30 visitors are admitted at a time*). But before entering, get into the proper Renaissance mood by first walking around the 15th-century church and cloister. Built by Guiniforte Solari, with later revisions by Bramante under Lodovico il Moro, it is perhaps the most beautiful Renaissance church in Lombardy, its exterior adorned with fine brickwork and terracotta. Bramante's greatest contribution is the majestic Brunelleschi-inspired tribune, added in 1492; he also designed the choir, the unusual crossing under the hemispherical dome, the sacristy and the elegant little cloister, all simple, geometric and pure.   ﹒

The Last Supper

Leonardo painted three of his masterpieces in Milan, the two versions of the mystery-laden *Virgin of the Rocks* and the *Last Supper*. The former two are in London and the Louvre; the latter would have been in Paris too, had the French been able to figure out a way to remove the wall. Unfortunately for posterity, the ever-experimental genius was not content to use proper, established fresco technique (where the paint is applied quickly to wet plaster) but painted with tempera on glue and plaster as if on wood, enabling him to return over and over to achieve the subtlety of tone and depth he desired. The result was exceedingly beautiful, but almost immediately the moisture in the walls began its deadly work of flaking off particles of paint. Although it was considered a 'lost work' by the 17th century, various restorers have tried their hand at this most challenging task, with mixed success. In the Second World War the refectory was massively damaged by a bomb, and the *Last Supper* was only preserved thanks to piles of mattresses and other precautionary measures. In 1977 restorers began cleansing the work of its previous restorations and stabilizing the wall to prevent further damage; in April 1995 the last scaffolding was taken down.

Deterioration or no, the Last Supper still thrills. Painted at the moment when Christ announces that one of his disciples will betray him, it is a masterful psychological study, an instant caught in time, the apostles' gestures of disbelief and dismay captured almost photographically by one of the greatest students of human nature. According to Vasari, the artist left the portrait of Christ purposely unfinished, believing himself unworthy to paint divinity; Judas was another problem, but Leonardo eventually found the proper expression of the betrayer caught guiltily unawares but still nefariously determined and unrepentant.

Monastero Maggiore and the Archaeology Museum

From Santa Maria delle Grazie the Corso Magenta leads back towards the centre; at the corner of Via Luini stands the Monastero Maggiore. The monastery's pretty 16th-century church of **San Maurizio** (*open Wed, Sat and Sun 9.30–12 and 3.30–6.30; closed June–Sept*) contains exceptional frescoes by Bernardino Luini, one of Leonardo's most accomplished followers. The former Benedictine convent (entrance at Corso Magenta 15) houses the city's Etruscan, Greek and Roman collections in the **Civico Museo Archeologico** (*open Tues–Sun 9.30–5.30*). As important as Milan was in the late Roman Empire (there's a model of the city inside), relatively little has survived the frequent razings and rebuildings: the 3rd-century tower in the garden, Roman altars, sarcophagi, stelae, glass, ceramics, bronzes and mosaics. Other sections are Greek, Etruscan, Indian (from Gandhara), Goth and Lombard.

Sant'Ambrogio

Located just off San Vittore and Via Carducci (Ⓜ *Sant'Ambrogio*), the stern towers of the 12th-century gate, the **Pusterla di Sant'Ambrogio**, bristle, perhaps appropriately enough, with the armour, antique weapons and torture instruments of the **Museo della Criminologia e Armi Antichi** (*open daily 10–1 and 3–7.30; adm*). The Pusterla guards the last resting place of Milan's patron saint and the city's holy of holies, the beautiful church of Sant'Ambrogio. Founded by Ambrose himself in 379, it was enlarged and rebuilt several times (most notably by Archbishop Anspert in the 870s, when it became the prototype of the Lombard Romanesque basilica). Its current appearance dates from the 1080s.

S. Ambrogio - Milano

The church (*open Mon–Fri 8–12 and 2.30–7, Sat and Sun 2.30–6*) is entered through a porticoed **atrium**, which in 1140 replaced the original Carolingian paved court or *parvis*. It sets off the simple, triangular façade with its rounded arches and towers; the one to the right, the Monks' Campanile, was built in the 9th century, while the more artistic Canons' Campanile on the left was finished in 1144. The bronze doors, in their decorated portals, date from the 10th century. In its day the finely proportioned if shadowy interior was revolutionary for its new-fangled rib vaulting; rows of arches divide the aisles, supporting the women's gallery or Matroneum. On the left, look for the 10th-century bronze serpent (the ancient symbol of health, or perhaps representing Moses' staff) and the richly sculpted **pulpit**, a vigorous masterpiece carved in 1080, set on an enormous late Roman sarcophagus. The apse is adorned with 10th–11th-century mosaics of the Redeemer and saints, while the sanctuary contains two ancient treasures: the 9th-century *Ciborium* on columns, and a magnificent gold, silver, enamel and gem-studded **altarpiece** (835), both signed by a certain 'Wolvinus magister phaber'. In the crypt below moulder the bones of Saints Ambrose, Gervasio and Protasio. At the end of the south aisle the 4th-century **Sacello di San Vittore in Ciel d'Oro** ('in the sky of gold') contains brilliant 5th-century mosaics in its cupola and a presumed authentic portrait of St Ambrose.

After working on Santa Maria delle Grazie, Bramante spent two years on Sant'Ambrogio, contributing the unusual **Portico della Canonica** (entered from the door on the left aisle) and the two cloisters, now incorporated into the adjacent Università Cattolica; these display Bramante's new interest in the ancient orders of architecture, an interest he was to develop fully when he moved to Rome. In the upper section of the Portico is the **Museo della Basilica di Sant'Ambrogio** (*open Mon–Fri 10–12 and 3–5; closed Tues pm; Sat and Sun 3–5; adm*), housing illuminated manuscripts, the saint's bed, Romanesque capitals, ancient fabrics and vestments called the 'Dalmatiche di Sant'Ambrogio' dating back to the 4th century, tapestries, and frescoes by Luini and Bergognone. The 1928 **War Memorial** in the Piazza Sant'Ambrogio was designed by Giovanni Muzio and inspired by Athens' Tower of the Winds.

Museum of Science and Technology

From Sant'Ambrogio, Via San Vittore leads to the Olivetan convent of San Vittore, repaired after the War to house the **Leonardo da Vinci Museo Nazionale della Scienza e Tecnica** (*open Tues–Sun 9.30–5, weekends till 6.30; adm*). Most of this vast and diverse collection, still arranged in its original 1950s format, is rather mysterious for the uninitiated, and if you're not keen about smelting and the evolution of batteries you may want to head straight for the **Leonardo da Vinci Gallery**, lined with pretty wooden models and explanations of his machines and inventions.

Leonardo in Milan

In 1481 Leonardo wrote to Lodovico il Moro, applying for a job in his court. He had been recommended to the duke as musician and player of the lyre, of all things; in his letter of introduction Leonardo boasts of his ability to design war machines, and mentions only at the end of the letter that he could paint too, if required. In fact, exactly what he did and for whom seemed to matter little. 'I work for anyone who pays me,' he said, and to prove it directly after his Milan period he worked with the nefarious Cesare Borgia. For Leonardo, at any rate, the results of his genius weren't half as important as the quest. In Milan he filled notebook after notebook (many are on display in the Ambrosiana) with studies of nature, weather and anatomy and ideas for inventions in the applied sciences. His most practical work in canal-building Milan, however, was in hydraulic engineering. He painted occasionally; besides the Virgin of the Rocks and the Last Supper, he did a range of portraits including one of Sforza's mistress, Cecilia Gallerani, called the Lady with an Ermine (in Cracow). Although the effortless master of the most beautiful painting technique of his time, Leonardo was chiefly interested in solving problems in composition and, once solved, he often left the painting unfinished out of boredom. Yet more than any other painter he was responsible for the intellectualizing of what had hitherto been regarded as a mere craft—culminating the Renaissance evolution that began with the rediscovery of the works of the Elder Pliny (see pp.58–60).

Other rooms include musical instruments and displays on optics, radios, computers, clocks and astronomy; downstairs you can push buttons and make waterwheels turn. Another building is devoted to trains, and another to ships and naval history.

Milan's Financial District

For centuries, the area between Sant'Ambrogio and the Duomo has been the headquarters of Milan's merchant guilds, bankers, and financiers, concentrated in the bank-filled **Piazza Cardusio** (Ⓜ *Cardusio*), Via degli Affari and Via Mercanti, just off Piazza del Duomo. Milan's imposing **Borsa** (stock exchange) in Piazza Affari was founded by Napoleon's viceroy Eugène de Beauharnais and is now the most important in Italy. On Via Mercanti, the **Palazzo della Ragione** (1233), the old Hall of Justice, was given an extra floor with oval windows by Maria Theresa. On the side facing Piazza Mercanti, look for a beautiful early 13th-century equestrian relief; while facing Via Mercanti don't miss the bas-relief of a sow partly clad in wool, discovered when the foundations for the palazzo were dug. According to legend, a tribe of Gauls under their chief Belloveso defeated the local Etruscans in the 6th century BC and wanted to settle in the area. An oracle told them to found their town on the spot where they found a sow half-covered in wool, and to name it after her. The sow was eventually discovered, and when the Romans conquered the Gauls, they translated the Celtic name of the town into the Latin *Mediolanum*, 'half-woolly'—which is, honestly, even sillier than the name of the city Milan is often compared to, Chicago, which means 'Stinky Onions'.

The Ambrosiana

Still in the financial district, in Piazza Pio XI (off Via Spadari and Via Cantù), the Ambrosiana is Milan's most enduring legacy of its leading family, the Borromei. Cardinal Federico Borromeo (cousin of Charles) founded one of Italy's greatest libraries here in 1609, containing 30,000 rare manuscripts, including ancient Middle Eastern texts collected to further the cardinal's efforts to produce a translation of the Bible; a 5th-century illustrated *Iliad*; Leonardo da Vinci's famous *Codex Atlanticus*, with thousands of his drawings; early editions of *The Divine Comedy*; and much, much more (*to arrange a visit, call ℭ 02 8645 1436*).

After years of restoration, the Cardinal's art collection or **Pinacoteca** (*open Mon–Fri and Sun 10–6; adm*), housed in the same building, has recently been reopened. Although paintings have been added over the centuries, the gallery is essentially a monument to one man's taste—which showed a marked preference for the Dutch, and for the peculiar, and ranges from the truly sublime to some of the funniest paintings ever to grace a gallery. Here are Botticelli's lovely *Tondo,* and his *Madonna del Baldacchino* nonchalantly watering lilies with her milk; a respectable *Madonna* by Pinturicchio; paintings by Bergognone (including the altar from Pavia's San Pietro in Ciel d'Oro), a lovely portable altar by Geertgen tot Sint Jans, and the strange, dramatic *Transito della Vergine* by Baldassarre Estense. Further along an *Adoration of the Magi* by the Master of Santo Sangue is perhaps the only one where Baby Jesus seems properly thrilled at receiving the very first Christmas presents. A small room, illuminated by a pre-Raphaelitish stained-glass window of Dante by Giuseppe Bertini (1865), contains the glove Napoleon wore at Waterloo, a 17th-century bronze of Diana the Huntress, so ornate that even the stag wears earrings, and entertaining paintings by the Cardinal's friend Jan Brueghel the Younger, who delighted in detail and wasn't above putting a pussycat in Daniel's den of lions.

These are followed by more masterpieces: a *Page*, perhaps by Giorgione, Luini's *Holy Family with St Anne* (from a cartoon by Leonardo), Leonardo's *Portrait of a Musician*, a lovely portrait of Beatrice d'Este attributed to Ambrogio da Predis, and then Bramantino's *Madonna in Trono fra Santi*, a scene balanced by a dead man on the left and an enormous dead frog on the right. Challenging this for absurdity is the nearby *Female Allegory* by 17th-century Giovanni Serodine, in which the lady, apparently disgruntled with her lute, astrolabe and books, is squirting herself in the nose.

The magnificent cartoon for Raphael's *School of Athens* in the Vatican is as interesting as the fresco itself; the copy of Leonardo's *Last Supper* was done by order of the Cardinal, who sought to preserve what he considered a lost work (the copy itself has recently been restored). A 16th-century *Washing of Feet* from Ferrara has one Apostle blithely clipping his toenails. Another room contains pages of drawings from Leonardo's *Codex Atlanticus.* The first Italian still-life, Caravaggio's *Fruit Basket*, is also the most dramatic; it shares the space with more fond items like Magnasco's *The Crow's Singing Lesson*. Further on is Titian's *Adoration of the Magi*, painted for Henri II of France, and still in its original frame.

San Satiro

On the corner of Via Spadari and busy Via Torino, a 19th-century façade conceals the remarkable Renaissance church of **San Satiro** (officially Santa Maria presso San Satiro), rebuilt by Bramante in 1476, his first project in Milan. Faced with a lack of space in the abbreviated, T-shaped interior, Bramante came up with the ingenious solution of creating the illusion of an apse with *trompe l'œil* stucco decorations. Bramante also designed the beautiful octagonal **Baptistry** off the right aisle, decorated with terracottas by Agosto De Fondutis; to the left the 9th-century **Cappella della Pietà** is one of the finest examples of Carolingian architecture in north Italy, even though it was touched up in the Renaissance, with decorations and a *Pietà* by De Fondutis. San Satiro's equally antique **campanile** is visible on Via Falcone.

South of the Duomo: Porta Romana

This corner of Milan, the main traffic outlet towards the *autostrada* to the south, can be busy. Tram 13 will take you to **San Nazaro Maggiore** on Corso Porta Romana, a church that has undergone several rebuildings since its 4th-century dedication by St Ambrose, and was last restored in the Romanesque style. The most original feature of San Nazaro is the hexagonal **Cappella Trivulzio** by Bramantino, built to contain the tomb of the *condottiere* Giangiacomo Trivulzio, who wrote his own epitaph, in Latin: 'He who never knew rest now rests: Silence.' Trivulzio did have a busy career; a native Milanese who disliked Lodovico Sforza enough to lead Louis XII's attack on Milan in 1499, he became the city's French governor, then went on to lead the League of Cambrai armies in thumping the Venetians at Agnadello (1509).

Just behind San Nazaro, in Via Festa del Perdono, the **Ospedale Maggiore** was commissioned by Francesco Sforza in 1456. He asked Filarete (who wrote an architectural treatise on the ideal city called *Sforzinda* in honour of his patron) to design one building to incorporate all the little hospitals spread across Milan. The result, now the centrepiece of the Università degli Studi, is a beautiful early Renaissance work with ornate brickwork and terracotta and the first cross-shaped wards; inside are over 900 portraits of hospital benefactors since 1602.

On **Corso Italia**, another main artery south, **Santa Maria presso San Celso** (1490–1563) offers a fine example of the Lombard love of ornament, which reaches almost orgiastic proportions in the Certosa di Pavia (*see* pp.104–5). Within, beyond an attractive atrium, the interior is paved with an exceptional marble floor and decorated with High Renaissance paintings by Paris Bordone, Bergognone and Moretto; on the day of their marriage Milanese brides and grooms traditionally stop by to pray in the chapel of the Madonna. The adjacent 10th-century church of **San Celso** has a charming interior restored in the 19th century and a good original portal.

South Milan: The Ticinese and Navigli Districts

Southwest of the city centre, Via Torino leads into the artsy quarter named for the Ticino river, traversed by the main thoroughfare, Corso di Porta Ticinese (*tram 15 from Via Torino*). In the Ticinese you can find pieces of Roman *Mediolanum*, which had its forum in modern **Piazza Carrobbio**. There's a bit of the Roman circus on Via Circo, off Via Lanzone, and the **Colonne di San Lorenzo**, on the Corso: 16 Corinthian columns, now a favourite teenager hangout but originally part of a temple or bath, were transported here in the 4th century to construct a portico in front of the **Basilica di San Lorenzo Maggiore**. The oldest church in Milan, it acquired its octagonal form, encircled by an ambulatory and crowned with a dome, in the 4th century, predating the church it resembles most, San Vitale in Ravenna. Carefully spared by Barbarossa in the sack of Milan in 1164, it has since suffered severe fires, and in the 16th century, when it was near total collapse, it was rebuilt, conserving as much of the old structure as possible. Luckily, the beautiful **Cappella di Sant'Aquilino** (*adm*) has come down intact, with 4th- or 5th-century mosaics of Christ and his disciples and an early Christian sarcophagus.

A green walkway, the Parco delle Basiliche, links San Lorenzo to the **Basilica di Sant'Eustorgio**, rebuilt in 1278 along the lines of Sant'Ambrogio, with a lofty campanile (1309). The pillars along the naves are crowned with good capitals, and the chapels, added in the 15th century, are finely decorated with early Renaissance art. One chapel is dedicated to the Magi, where a large Roman sarcophagus held the relics of the Three Kings until Frederick Barbarossa hauled them off to Cologne.

The highlight of the church, however, is the pure Tuscan Renaissance **Cappella Portinari** (1468) built for Pigello Portinari, an agent of the Medici bank in Milan. Attributed to Michelozzo and often compared with Brunelleschi's Pazzi Chapel in Florence in its elegant cubic simplicity and proportions, the chapel is crowned by a lovely dome, adorned with stucco reliefs of angels. This jewel is dedicated to the Inquisitor St Peter Martyr (who was axed in the head on the shores of Lake Como in 1252), whose life of intolerance was superbly frescoed on the walls by Vincente Foppa and whose remains are buried in the magnificent marble *Arca di San Pietro Martire* (1339) by the Pisan Giovanni di Balduccio. Balduccio also added the relief of saints on the nearby 14th-century **Porta Ticinese** built in the Spanish walls.

The colourful Navigli district (Ⓜ *Porta Genova, tram 8 or 19*) is named for its navigable canals, the **Naviglio Grande** (linking Milan to the river Ticino, Lake Maggiore and the Candoglio marble quarries) and **Naviglio Pavese** (to Pavia) that meet to form the docks, or *Darsena*, near Porta Ticinese. Up until the 1950s Milan, through these canals, handled more tonnage than seaports like Brindisi, and, like any good port, the Navigli was then a funky working-class district of warehouses, workshops, sailors' bars and public housing blocks. Although some of this lingers, the Navigli is now a relaxed, fashionably bohemian zone, where many of the city's artists work, where the restaurants are cheaper and you can hear jazz in the night.

Shopping

Most shops are closed all day Sunday, Monday mornings, and in August. Food stores close on Monday afternoons.

Milan is Italy's best shopping city hands down, and most especially for clothes and everything else capable of being designed in one way or another. Italians have always liked to put on the dog, *la bella figura*; it's in their blood. The hype machine has turned this traditional trait into a national obsession—there are countless Italian fashion magazines (most of them emanating from Milan, naturally), and a weekly television programme devoted to *La Moda*. After an hour of window-shopping, however, only a die-hard fashion slave would disagree with Walter Benjamin's 'Monotony is nourished by the new'. The **big sales** begin the second week of January and around 10 July.

the Quadrilateral

Many of the big names in fashion have their boutique 'headquarters' in what is known as the Quadrilatero, defined by Via Monte Napoleone, Via della Spiga, Via S. Andrea and Via Borgospesso (Ⓜ *Monte Napoleone*). Nearly all the shops here have branch offices elsewhere in Milan and in other cities. You may just find the latest of the latest designs on Monte Napoleone, but be assured they'll soon show up elsewhere, expensive enough but without the high snob surcharges. The **jewellers** were actually here first, in the 1930s; since then, an address on Via Monte Napoleone has meant status and quality. Have a look in the windows at **Buccellati** (No.4), considered by many the best jewellery designer in Italy, featuring exquisitely delicate gold work and jewels, each piece individually crafted. Other classics, all on Monte Napoleone, are **Faraone** (No.7a), **Martignietti** (No.10) and **Cusi** (No.21a); for antique jewellery, try **Romani Adami**, Via S. Andrea 7.

The artsy displays of clothing and accessories are a window-shopper's paradise. **Missoni's** ravishing knits for women and men are at Monte Napoleone 8; **Valentino** and his classics are at Via Santo Spirito 3; **Armani's** chief Milanese outlet is at Via Durini 24; **Laura Biagiotti** at Via Borgospesso 19; **Versace** display their innovations at Monte Napoleone 11.

Via della Spiga is chock-a-block with top designers: **Byblos, Krizia, Luciano Soprani** and **Dolce e Gabbana** are all there. Via Monte Napoleone has its share as well: **Alberta Ferretti, Ferragamo, Prada** and **Gucci**; as does Via Durini: **Chanel, Prada** (again), **Helmut Lang, Fendi**; and Via S. Andrea: **Ferre, Gigli** and **Krizia**. Milan's bad boy of fashion, **Moschino**, is at Via Durini 14. If you don't like anything new, try **Mercatino Michela**, Via della Spiga 33, for **second-hand designer fashions**.

Italian **leather** is known in most parts of the world simply through the name **Gucci**, Monte Napoleone 5; you can also have a look at the **Bottega Veneta**, Via della Spiga 5, and **Nazareno Gabrielli**, Monte Napoleone 23. Other Quadrilateral shops worth a browse include **Lorenzi**, Monte Napoleone 9, the city's most refined pipe and male accessories shop. **Il Salumaio**, at No.12, has an infinite array of nearly every gourmet item imaginable.

the city centre

Besides the great Galleria Vittorio Emanuele, several minor *gallerias* branch off the Corso Vittorio Emanuele, each a shopping arcade lined with good quality and reasonably priced shops. In Piazza del Duomo a monument almost as well known as the cathedral itself is Milan's biggest and oldest department store, **La Rinascente**; it's also the only one to have been christened by Gabriele D'Annunzio. La Rinascente has six floors of merchandise, with especially good clothing and domestic sections, offering a wide array of kitchen gear dear to the heart of an Italian cook. The cafeteria on the top floor has great views over the cathedral. Other shops in the centre include **Guenzati**, Via Mercanti 1, which will make a velvet-lover's heart flutter; they also do made-to-order clothes. Near the Duomo, Via Spadari and Via Speroni are a food shopper's heaven, beginning with the **Casa del Formaggio**, Via Speronari 3, where the best cheeses, from the most exotic to the most everyday, have been sold since 1894. **Rizzoli**, Galleria Vittorio Emanuele 79, is one of the city's best-stocked bookshops (with many English titles), owned by the family that founded the *Corriere della Sera*. In the Galleria del Corso, **Messaggerie Musicali** is one of the best in town for musical scores and recordings; the **Virgin Megastore**, Piazza Duomo 8 has a huge selection of music.The shops on busy Via Torino have some of Milan's more affordable prices, especially in clothes and footwear.

elsewhere in Milan

Brera offers some of Milan's most original shops and boutiques, as well as old standbys like **Surplus**, Corso Garibaldi 7, with a marvellous array of second-hand garments, and the big **COIN** department store, Corso Garibaldi 72, a good bet for reasonably priced Italian fashions. On **Corso Buenos Aires** (Ⓜ *Lima*), one of Milan's longest and densest shopping thoroughfares, you can find something of every variety and hue; one unusual shop is **Le Mani d'Oro**, Via Gaffurio 5 (near Piazzale Loreto), which specializes in *trompe l'œil* objects and decorations, while **Guerciotti**, Via Tamagno 55 (parallel to Corso Buenos Aires) makes bicycles to order. Another shopping street with excellent merchandise and reasonable prices is **Via Paolo Sarpi** (Ⓜ *Moscova*), formerly the city's Chinatown. For an excellent selection of books in English, try either **The English Bookshop**, Via Mascheroni 12, ✆ 02 469 4468 (Ⓜ *Conciliazione*) or **The American Bookstore**, Largo Cairoli, near the castle, 02 878 920 (Ⓜ *Cairoli*). If you're interested in the latest designs in furniture, Milan has a major concentration of showrooms and stores near the centre: well worth a look are **Artemide**, Corso Monforte 19; **De Padova**, Corso Venezia 14; **Dilmos**, Piazza San Marco 1; and **Alias**, Via V. Monti 2.

markets

The tourist office publishes a complete list of markets in Milan: most are open mornings from 9 to 1, with the exception of the huge **Saturday clothes markets** in Viale Papiniano (Ⓜ *S. Agostino*) and Via Osoppo (Ⓜ *Gambara*) that continue until 6pm. **Flea markets** include the Fiera di Senigallia, in Viale D'Annunzio every Saturday from 8.30 to 5 (Ⓜ *S. Agostino*) and the Via Lorenzini market on Sunday mornings (Ⓜ *Lodi Tibb*). For **antiques**, there's the enormous Mercatone dell'Antiquariato every last Sunday of the month, along the Naviglio Grande (Ⓜ *Porta Genova*) and the Mercato Antiquariato di Brera in Via Fiori Chiari on the third Saturday of each month (Ⓜ *Lanza*). On Sunday morning, a **Postcard, Stamp and Coin Market** is held in the Cordusio Arcade in Piazza Duomo (Ⓜ *Duomo*). Do note that nearly all markets are non-existent in August.

Sports and Activities

A dip in one of Milan's public **swimming pools** can make a hot day of summer sightseeing far more tolerable: two of the nicest and most convenient are situated in the **Parco Solari**, Via Montevideo 11 (Ⓜ *Sant'Agostino*), and the outdoor **Lido di Milano**, Piazzale Lotto 15 (Ⓜ *Lotto*). East of town, the **Parco dell'Idroscalo**, built around an artificial lake designed as a 'runway' for seaplanes in the 1920s, has a lovely complex of three pools known as Milan's Riviera (Viale dell'Idroscalo 1), reached by a special bus ID departing from San Babila. The **Luna Park** at Idroscalo has water slides and rides for the kids.

The best **golf** course in the Milan area is the **Golf Club Milano**, in the delightful Parco di Monza in Monza, a short distance north of the city (*see* p.96). A popular **bicycle excursion** from Milan is to pedal along the Naviglio Grande canal from the Darsena to the Ticino river (around 40km), passing by way of **Cassinetta di Lugagnano**, home of one of Italy's top restaurants (*see* p.93). Like the Venetians with their villas along the Brenta canal, the 18th-century Milanese built sumptuous summer houses along the Naviglio. Only one, the 15th-century frescoed **Villa Gaia** in

Robecco, is open to visitors, and only if you call ahead (𝄞 02 947 0512). **Bicycles** can be rented for any period of time from Vittorio Comizzoli's shop in Via Washington 60, 𝄞 02 498 4694 (Ⓜ *Wagner*).

Milan's two prestigious first-division football clubs, AC Milan and Inter, play on alternate Sundays during the September-May season at **San Siro** stadium, Via Piccolomini 5 (Ⓜ *Lotto*, then walk, or tram 24 or buses 95, 49 or 72). Tickets are available at the stadium, or from Milan Point, 𝄞 02 782 768, Largo Corsia dei Servi 11. For Inter matches, you can also buy tickets at branches of Banca Popolare di Milano; for AC games from branches of the Banca Cariplo. American football (the 'Rhinos') and rugby are semi-professional and can often be seen at the Giurati sports centre. Milan has a good basketball team, which plays in the Super Palatenda sports facility on Via Sant'Elia. There are two race tracks, the Ippodromo and the Trottatoio for trotters, both near San Siro.

Where to Stay

Milan has basically two types of accommodation: smart hotels for expense accounts, and seedy dives for new arrivals from the provinces. This bodes ill for the pleasure traveller, who has the choice of paying a lot of money for an up-to-date modern room with little atmosphere, or paying less for a place where you may not feel very comfortable (or, worse, very safe). Reserve in advance, because the exceptions to the rule are snapped up fast. Tourist offices (*see* p.72) provide a free hotel reservation service. Bear in mind also that in August much of Milan closes down, so that at this time it can be surprisingly easy to find a hotel. On the other hand, during the trade fairs (especially the big fashion shows in March and autumn, and the April Fair) you may find no room at the inn.

luxury

★★★★★ **Four Seasons**, Via Gesù 8, ✉ 20121 𝄞 02 77088, ✆ 02 7708 5000, is a beautiful hotel in a 17th-century monastery. The church is the lobby, breakfast is served in the refectory, and most of the spacious rooms look over the cloister; enormous bathrooms, great plush sofas around the blazing fire in the winter; private garage.

★★★★★ **Principe di Savoia**, Piazza della Repubblica 17, ✉ 20124, 𝄞 02 6230, ✆ 02 659 5838, is the most elegant and prestigious of the CIGA hotels, originally built in 1927 and since lavishly redecorated. The rooms and service are designed to please even the most demanding clients—when Margaret Thatcher and Jerry Lewis visited Milan, they stayed here. The hotel has its own airport bus, divine restaurant and a private garage.

★★★★★ **Grand Hotel et de Milan**, Via Manzoni 29, ✉ 20121, 𝄞 02 723 141, ✆ 02 8646 0861, has been a favourite with everyone from Verdi to Hemingway since it opened in 1863. Nowadays the Grand is the fashion headquarters of Naomi Campbell (whose favoured suite is decorated with Duchess of Windsor memorabilia) and Kate Moss. Rooms are individually furnished with antiques, and the atmosphere is grand and gracious without being stuffy.

★★★★ **Cavour**, Via Fatebenefratelli 21, ✉ 20121, ✆ 02 657 2051, ✆ 02 659 2263. An elegantly furnished hotel in the Brera, a few blocks from Via Monte Napoleone.

★★★★ **De La Ville**, Via Hoepli 6, ✉ 20121, ✆ 02 867 651, ✆ 02 866 609. Modern, located between the Duomo and La Scala, it has antique furnishings and courteous service, comfortable lounges, bar and excellent restaurant; great weekend rates.

★★★★ **Diana Majestic**, Viale Piave 42, ✉ 20129, ✆ 02 2951 3404, ✆ 02 201 072 (Ⓜ *Porta Venezia*) is a fashionable, stylish Liberty-style hotel built at the turn of the century, with charming rooms, views over a garden and a lovely breakfast buffet.

★★★★ **Excelsior Gallia**, Piazza Duca d'Aosta 9, ✉ 20124, ✆ 02 6785, ✆ 02 6671 3239, near the Stazione Centrale, has hosted visiting potentates since it first opened in 1932. Spruced up with briarwood furnishings and oriental rugs, its spacious, elegant, air-conditioned rooms are equipped with satellite television; the Health Centre offers Turkish baths, and beauty treatments, and the Baboon Bar (it got the name during the War; ask how) is a mellow place to spend an evening.

★★★★ **Manin**, Via Manin 7, ✉ 20121, ✆ 02 659 6511, ✆ 02 655 2160, faces the Giardini Pubblici, in one of central Milan's quieter corners; reception is friendly and the rooms modern and comfortable.

expensive

★★★ **Ariosto**, Via Ariosto 22, ✉ 20145, ✆ 02 481 7844, ✆ 02 498 0516, has more character than most, and is conveniently close to Ⓜ *Conciliazione*. An early 20th-century mansion, it has a lovely little courtyard, overlooked by the nicer rooms.

★★★ **Ariston**, Largo Carrobbio 2, ✉ 20123, ✆ 02 7200 0556, ✆ 02 7200 0914, at the south end of Via Torino, is an environmentalist's dream: 100% cotton futons, hydro-massage water-saving showers, recycled everything and ion-emitting machines in every room; there's a no-smoking floor and bicycles to borrow. *Closed Aug.*

★★★ **Manzoni**, Via Spirito Santo 20, ✉ 20121, ✆ 02 7600 5700, ✆ 02 784 212. Book in advance for this pleasant hotel, one of the most privileged locations in Milan—on a quiet street in easy walking distance of Monte Napoleone and La Scala, with the plus of a private garage. Soundproofed rooms, bright baths. *Closed late July–Aug.*

★★★ **Soperga**, Via Soperga 24, ✉ 20127 ✆ 02 669 0541, ✆ 02 6698 0352, just east of the Stazione Centrale, is comfortable, soundproof, and serves big breakfasts.

moderate

★★★ **Gala**, Viale Zara 89, ✉ 20159 ✆ 02 6680 0891, ✆ 02 6680 0463. Near Ⓜ *Zara*, set in a quiet garden, a fine moderate-sized hotel with wrought iron beds. *Closed Aug.*

★★★ **Giulio Cesare**, Via Rovello 10, ✉ 20121 ✆ 02 7200 3915, ✆ 02 7200 2179, on a quiet street near the London, is a pleasant and wholesome example of Milan's cheaper accommodation; it even has air-conditioning.

★★ **Antica Locanda Solferino**, Via Castelfidardo 2, ✉ 20121, ✆ 02 657 0129, ✆ 02 657 1361. This atmospheric 19th-century inn in Brera is at the top of the moderate range, but the most enjoyable, too. All 11 rooms are different, though the baths are spartan; breakfast is brought to your room. Book well in advance. *Closed Aug.*

★★ **London**, Via Rovello 3, ✉ 20121, ✆ 02 7202 0166, 🖷 02 805 7037. On a quiet street near the castle: air conditioning, satellite TV and parking. *Closed Aug.*

★ **Valley**, Via Soperga 19, ✉ 20127, ✆ 02 669 2777, 🖷 02 6698 7252. Good budget hotels are thin on the ground, but this one, a short distance from the Stazione Centrale, has comfortable rooms (some with baths) at the lower end of moderate.

cheap

★ **Alba d'Oro**, Viale Piave 5, ✉ 20129, ✆ 02 7602 3880 (Ⓜ *Palestro*). 'The Golden Dawn' is small and safe; baths down the hall.

★ **Casa Mia**, Viale Vittorio Veneto 30, ✉ 20124, ✆ 02 657 5249, 🖷 02 655 2228. A good choice just north of the Giardini Pubblici (Ⓜ *Piazzetta Venezia*).

★ **San Marco**, Via Piccinni 25, ✉ 20131, ✆ 02 2951 6414, 🖷 02 2951 3243. Rooms with bath are in the moderate range, but all have TVs (Ⓜ *Loreto*).

★ **Speronari**, Via Speronari 4, ✉ 20123, ✆ 02 8646 1125, 🖷 02 7200 3178 is adequate and just southwest of the Duomo; rooms with bath cost a bit more.

Ostello Piero Rotta, Via Salmoiraghi 2, ✆ 02 3926 7095, is Milan's modern youth hostel, near San Siro stadium and Ⓜ *QT8*. An IYHF card is required (can be bought on the spot). *Open all year 7–9.30 and 3.30–midnight; L26,000 per person per night, including breakfast; 3-bed room L90,000; maximum stay 3 days.*

Eating Out

In moneyed Milan you'll find some of Italy's finest restaurants and the widest range of international cuisine; on the down side, an average meal will cost you considerably more than it would almost anywhere else in Italy. That said, you will still pay less than you would in comparable London restaurants. Presume unless otherwise stated that all are **closed in August**; so few restaurants remain open that their names are printed in the paper. At other times, the best places to find a selection of cheaper restaurants are in the Brera, Ticinese and Navigli districts.

Saffron is Milan's fetish spice, and appears in most dishes *alla milanese*. The origins of its use go back to a Belgian stained-glass maker, working on the Duomo in 1574, who was called 'Saffron' by his fellows because he always sprinkled a bit of the stuff in his mixes to make the glass colours deeper and richer. The other glassworkers laughed and joked that he loved saffron so much that he would soon be adding it to his food. During the wedding of Saffron's daughter, his apprentice, meaning to play a prank, actually had the chef put saffron in the rice; everyone was astonished at the yellow concoction, but it was delicious, and the Milanese have been making their saffron *risotto alla milanese* ever since.

Savini, in the Galleria Vittorio Emanuele, ✆ 02 7200 3433 (since 1867), is a bastion of Milanese tradition, where you can try Lombard classics at the pinnacle of perfection—especially the *secondi*. The often-abused *cotoletta* and risotto retain their primordial freshness, as do the more earthy *cassoeula* and *ossobuco*. *Closed Sat lunch, and Sun*.

Another culinary bastion is **La Scaletta**, Piazzale Stazione Porta Genova 3, ✆ 02 5810 0290, the workshop of Italy's *nuova cucina* sorceress, Pina Bellini, who does exquisite things to pasta and risotto, fish and rabbit, all beautifully presented. Excellent desserts and wines finish off a truly memorable meal. *Closed Sun and Mon; reservations strongly advised*.

Peck, Via Victor Hugo 4, ✆ 02 876 774, is a name that has meant the best in Milan for over a hundred years, either in its epicurean delicatessen and shop at Via Spadari 9, or here at its modern cellar restaurant, which offers such a tantalizing array of delights that you hardly know where to begin. Their unctuous *risotto alla Milanese* is hard to beat. *Closed Sun and hols and 3 weeks in July, but open in Aug*.

One of Milan's most elegant restaurants, **Nino Arnaldo**, Via Carlo Poerio 3, ✆ 02 7600 5981, is the base of one of the city's most creative chefs: his pasta dishes are original and the limited dessert selection holds some real jewels—the cinnamon ice cream and *zabaione* are exquisite. *Closed Sat noon and Sun*.

If you need a break from Italian cuisine, **Suntory**, Via G. Verdi 6, ✆ 02 869 3022, serves some of the best Japanese food in all Italy, which may not be saying a lot, but it is much patronized by Milan's large Japanese business community. There are good set meal deals at lunchtime. *Closed Sun, and two weeks in Aug*.

Although it's 20km from Milan, along the Naviglio Grande in Cassinetta di Lugagnano, the **Antica Osteria del Ponte**, ✆ 02 942 0034, is known as a holy temple of Italian cuisine that shouldn't be missed by any serious gourmet, featuring heavenly dishes like ravioli filled with lobster and zucchini, fresh foie gras, marvellously prepared fish, cassata with pistachio sauce and perfect little pastries—nearly every dish is based on Italian traditions. The décor is beautiful, intimate and elegant. *Closed Sun and Mon*.

expensive

Aurora, Via Savona 23 (in the Navigli), ✆ 02 8940 4978, has lovely *belle époque* dining rooms and equally lovely Piemontese cuisine, with an emphasis on mushrooms and truffles; another speciality is the cart of boiled meats, from which you can choose from a vast array of sauces. Yet another cart will overwhelm you with its bewildering array of cheeses, although you might prefer to save some room for the superb *tarte tatin*. Exceptional value, and lovely on summer evenings in the cool shade. *Closed Mon*.

Pigs are trendy, and so is **Al Vecchio Porco**, Via Messina 8, ✆ 02 313 862, a pizzeria serving such delights as pizza with ricotta, tomatoes and olives, or the 'del Porco' with sausage, gorgonzola and egg. *Closed Sun lunch, and Mon*.

The Ticinese quarter has several restaurants offering equally good regional dishes at affordable prices. Soak in the romantic old-world bistrot atmosphere at **Ponte Rosso**, 23 Ripa Ticinese, ✆ 02 837 3132: the cuisine is simple but excellent. There's a fixed menu at lunch; at dinner choose from dishes such as cannellini bean and radicchio soup, pasta with zucchini and saffron, or a scrumptious lemon tart. *Closed Sun.* Arrive early to avoid the queues at **Al Pont de Ferr**, 55 Via Ripa Ticinese, ✆ 02 8940 6277, to sample the smoked salami, dishes such as pigeon with mushrooms and polenta, and delicious wines. *Closed Sat lunch, and Sun.*

Trattoria Toscana, 58 Corso Porta Ticinese, ✆ 02 8940 6292, is a jolly place, with music and drinks in the garden, and dishes like gnocchi filled with ricotta and sword-fish with thyme. *Open till 3am. Closed Sat lunch and Sun.* Still in the Ticinese, **Trattoria all'Antica**, Via Montevideo 4, ✆ 02 837 2859, serves abundant Lombard fare prepared simply, but with the freshest ingredients. *Closed Sun.*

One of business Milan's secrets, **San Fermo**, Via S. Fermo della Battaglia 1, in the centre, ✆ 02 2900 0901, serves light, tasty economic lunches and affordable full dinners; often busy, but service is fast and efficient. *Closed Sun.*

Besides the places listed below, Milan is well endowed with American and Italian fast-food places, for those without the money or time for an Italian sit-down feast. Prize-winning championship pizzas, with a vast selection to choose from, are the speciality at **Da Rino Vecchia Napoli** , Via Chavez 4 (between Stazione Centrale and Parco Lambro), ✆ 02 261 9056; they also do good *antipasti*, gnocchi, and fish dishes; it's best to book. *Closed Sun lunch and Mon.*

Another name in Milanese pizza lore is **Geppo**, Viale Brianza 30, ✆ 02 284 6548, with 50 kinds to choose from, including a Milanese with saffron, rocket and porcini mushrooms (Ⓜ *Loreto*). *Closed Sun.* At lunchtime, the atmospheric **Osteria del Treno** (a former railway workers' club) Via S. Gregorio 46, ✆ 02 669 1706 has an excellent self-service that shouldn't be more than L25,000, although the excellent sit-down dinners are in the moderate range (Ⓜ *Lima*). *Closed Sat.*

For vegetarian food, you can eat very well for around L20,000 at **Govinda**, 3/5 Via Valpetrosa, ✆ 02 862 417 (*closed Sun, Mon lunch*) and **Il Naviglio**, 5 Via Casale, ✆ 02 8940 0768 (*closed Mon, Tues evening*).

Entertainment and Nightlife

Check listings in the daily *Corriere della Sera* and *La Repubblica*'s Wednesday *Tutto Milano* magazine. For clubs with live music check under the heading 'Ritrovi'; if you want to see a film in English, make sure it says *versione originale*. Other sources include the free *What's On in Milan* and *Milano Mese*, available at the main tourist office. **Tickets** are sold at the Virgin Megastore, Piazza Duomo 8; Ricordi, in the Galleria Vittorio Emanuele and Corso Beunos Aires 33; at La Biglietteria, Corso Garibaldi 81, and in a kiosk in Stazione Cadorna.

For many people, an evening at **La Scala** is in itself the reason for visiting Milan. The season runs from 7 December, St Ambrose's Day, to mid-July; and mid-September through mid-November. For information on how to book by phone, ✆ 02 7200 3744. Note that you can only order two tickets at a time. Both the tourist office in Via Marconi and CIT office in the Galleria Vittorio Emanuele, ✆ 02 863 701, have a certain number of tickets to sell to foreign tourists. Finding a good seat at a moment's notice is all but impossible; try through your hotel's concierge, or show up at the box office an hour before the performance to see what's available; chances are it'll be a vertiginous gallery seat, just squeezed in under the ceiling, or standing room only. More **classical music** is performed in the Giuseppe Verdi Conservatorio, Via del Conservatorio 12, ✆ 02 762 1101 or ✆ 02 7600 1854. *Closed July–mid-Sept.* The city sponsors a series of **Renaissance and baroque music concerts** in the lovely church of San Maurizio on Corso Magenta and in San Marco, Piazza San Marco; *adm free or around L20,000*; the tourist office has programmes.

Milan is also the home of Italy's best **theatre** company, the **Piccolo Teatro**, Via Rovello 2, near Via Dante, ✆ 7233 3222. Founded after the Second World War and run for years by brilliant director Giorgio Strehler, the Piccolo is ideologically sound, with a repertory ranging from *commedia dell'arte* to the avant-garde. Tickets are priced low so anyone can go—but reserve in advance as far as possible. Sometimes the Piccolo performs at the much larger **Teatro Lirico**, near the Duomo at Via Larga 14, ✆ 02 809 665. The **Teatro Nazionale**, Piazza Piemonte 12, ✆ 02 4800 7700, puts on both plays and musicals. **Films** in English are shown regularly at the Anteo, Via Milazzo 9, ✆ 02 659 7732, Arcobaleno, Viale Tunisia, ✆ 02 2940 6054, and Mexico, Via Savona 57, ✆ 02 4895 1802.

jazz

Nearly all the jazz clubs are in the Navigli district, and the first three have restaurants as well. One of the best is **Scimmie**, Via Ascanio Sforza 49, ✆ 02 8940 2874, with diverse but high-quality offerings from Dixieland to fusion; in the summer the action moves to a canal barge. *Closed Tues.* The more informal **Capolinea**, Via Lodovico il Moro 119, ✆ 02 8912 2024, at the end of the no.19 tramline, has low prices and often excellent sessions; also check the listings for **Grillo Parlante**, Alzaia Naviglio Grande 36, ✆ 02 8940 9321. **Tangram**, Via Pezzotti 52, ✆ 02 8950 1007, schedules a mix of jazz, funk, rhythm and blues. *Closed Sun.* **Blues House**, 26 Via S. Uguzzone, ✆ 02 2700 3621, plays exclusively blues. *Closed Mon.*

cafés, gelaterie and bars

Milan has some good, lively bars that stay open late. The old rendezvous of artists and intellectuals in the twenties and thirties, **Jamaica**, is still open for business at Via Brera 26, as is another old bar, **Moscatelli**, Corso Garibaldi 93, a beloved Milanese oasis for the fashion-weary.

Even the Milanese like to take an evening promenade topped off with a stop at the *gelateria.* Some of the best ice cream in Milan is scooped out at the minuscule **Rossi,**

Viale Romagna 23 (exquisite chocolates and tiramisù) (*closed Tues*); **Viel**, Foro Buonaparte 71, has the most surprising flavours (*closed Wed*); while totally natural ingredients go into the treats at the **Ecologica**, Corso di Porta Ticinese 40 (*closed Wed*).

For a sophisticated drink try **Magenta**, Via Carducci 13, near **Ⓜ** *Cadorna*, where models swan about in a young and trendy crowd. In the Navigli area two of the most popular bars are the **Grand Café Fashion**, Corso di Porta Ticinese, and **Cocquetel**, Via Vetere 14, with hundreds of cocktails. Homesick Brits will find heartier relief at the **Matricola Pub**, Viale Romagna 43, a Guinness-owned place with the black stuff on tap plus full pub lunches and 'English' breakfasts. *Closed Sun.* Another lively pub, **Pogue's Mahones**, Via Salmini 3, hosts occasional live Irish bands.

Brera's Corso Garibaldi/Corso Como area jumps at night: in spots include the fashionable **Atiemme**, in a former train station at Bastioni Porta Volta 15, with good cocktails and music. The nearby **Lollapaloosa** is loud and Irish at Corso Como 15; **Tropical Latino**, Corso Como 2, is loud and Mexican, with food, lots of imported Mexican beer and salsa. Arrive early to avoid queueing.

clubs and discos

The **club scene** in Milan, as in the rest of Italy, is often concerned more with appearance than dancing and having a good time. However, it is possible to discover some places where the emphasis is reversed—though you have to look hard. Generally, clubs open every day until 3am (though this is often extended at weekends), and the pricy admission fee entitles you to one free drink.

At the time of writing, two discos are hot among fashion victims, models and designers: **Hollywood**, Corso Como 15 (*closed Mon*) and **Shocking**, Via Bastioni di Porta Nuova 12 (*closed Sun*).

The wonderful, bizarre and very chic **Plastic**, Viale Umbria 120, is small and shiny with a very eclectic clientele, drag-queen shows and fussy doormen; Thursday is gay night. *Open Thurs–Sat; adm.* Milan's foremost gay club, though, and the biggest in the country, is the often heavy **Nuova Idea**, Via De Castilla 30. *Open Thurs–Sun.* Another gay hotspot is **Sottomarino Giallo**, Via Donatello 2, with disco music for women only on Sat. *Closed Thurs.*

Latin American sounds, live music, shows and dancing are on the evening menu at **Sabor Tropical**, 18 Via Molino delle Armi. *Closed Mon and Tues.*

Short Excursions from Milan: Monza and Saronno

Only a hop and a skip from Milan, Monza seems to be unfairly slighted by most visitors to Lombardy. Monza attracts throngs in early September when it hosts the Italian Grand Prix; otherwise you may have its venerable monuments to yourself.

Getting Around

Monza is 15 minutes by train from Milan's Garibaldi Station, or 20 minutes by ATM bus from the same place; CTNM buses link Monza and Saronno.

Monza: Palazzo Comunale, Piazza Roma, ℂ/✆ 039 323 222. *Closed Sat pm.*

Monza

Back in the late 6th century Monza was the darling of the Lombard Queen Theodolinda, who founded its first cathedral after her conversion from Arianism by Pope Gregory the Great. Rebuilt in the 13th century, the **Duomo** on Via Napoleone bears a lovely green and white striped marble façade by the great Matteo da Campione (1396). The massive campanile dates from 1606, when the interior was given its baroque facelift. To the left of the presbytery, **Theodolinda's chapel** has charming 1444 frescoes by the Zavattari brothers, depicting the life of the queen who left Monza its most famous relic, preserved in the high altar: the gem-encrusted **Iron Crown of Italy** (*open 9–11.30 and 3–6.30, closed Mon; adm*). The story goes that when his mother Helena unearthed the True Cross in Jerusalem, Emperor Constantine had one of its iron nails embedded in his crown. It became a tradition in the Middle Ages for every newly elected emperor to stop in Monza or Pavia to be crowned King of Italy before heading on to Rome to receive the Crown of Empire from the pope—a tradition Napoleon briefly revived when he had himself crowned in Milan's Duomo in 1805. The cathedral's **museum** (*same hours; combined adm available*) contains Theodolinda's treasure: a processional cross given to her by Gregory the Great, the 5th-century ivory diptych of Stilicho, her crown and the famous silver hen and seven chicks symbolizing Lombardy and its provinces, as well a precious Syriac cross belonging to her son Agilgulfo (it's not hard to see why Lombard names soon fell out of fashion) and Gian Galeazzo Visconti's goblet.

Just north of the Duomo, the 13th-century Palazzo Comunale or **Arengario** is the city's finest secular building. From here, Via C. Alberto leads north to the beautiful 800ha **Parco di Monza** (*open 7–7, till 8.30 in the summer*) one of greater Milan's 'lungs', home to a horse-racing course, the 1922 Autodromo, site of the Italian Grand Prix and the 27-hole Golf Club Milano, as well as other recreational facilities. Until 1806 the park was the grounds of the neoclassical **Villa Reale**, built by Archduke Ferdinand of Austria and the favourite residence of Napoleon's viceroy Eugène de Beauharnais (*open for visits by appointment May–Oct, ℂ 039 322 086*). The single sombre note is struck behind the 18th-century residence—an expiatory chapel built by Vittorio Emanuele III that marks the spot where his father Umberto was assassinated by an anarchist in 1900.

North of Monza near Carate, **Agliate** has one of the earliest of many Romanesque churches modelled on Milan's Sant'Ambrogio, the 9th–10th-century basilica of **San Pietro**: inside rough 5th-century columns define the three naves, while the presbytery (with remains of the original frescoes) is raised over the choir and three apses. The proximity of a **baptistry** to the south forms what would soon become the archetypal Lombard temple complex; it too conserves its 10th-century frescoes and its original font.

Alfa Romeos and Saronno

Northwest of Milan, on the road and rail line to Varese, **Arese** has since 1910 been the home town of Lombardy's car industry, the *Associazione Lombarda Fabbrica Automobilistiche*, or Alfa Romeo, when a group of Lombard magnates bought up the French

Darracq manufacturer. Alfa, in turn, has recently been bought up by Fiat, but in Arese you can visit the six floors of the 'family album', the **Museo Storico di Alfa Romeo** (*ring ahead to visit, © 02 9339 2303*).

Further along towards Varese Saronno is synonymous with *amaretto*, either in the cocktail glass or in the biscuits, but students of Lombard Renaissance art will recognize it at once for its **Santuario della Madonna dei Miracoli**, built by Giovanni Antonio Amadeo in 1498. The façade with its trumpeting angels was added in the next century by Pellegrini, while highlights in the rich interior include the dome's startling, innovative fresco, the *Concert of Angels* by Gaudenzio Ferrari (1534) and Bernadino Luini's beautiful frescoes in the chapel of the Madonna (1531).

Where to Stay and Eating Out

Monza ✉ 20052

Overlooking the park, Monza's excellent ★★★★**Hotel de la Ville**, Viale Regina Margherita 15, © 039 382 581, ✆ 039 367 647 (*expensive*) is a cosy place with its own garden and the town's finest food in its Derby Grill restaurant: try the ravioli with rocket and ricotta in pepper and pistachio sauce. *Closed Sat and Sun lunch, and Aug.* For something less pricy, try ★★**Dell'Uva**, Piazza Carrobiolo 2, © 039 323 825 (*moderate*).

Pavia

The Lombard Plain

The three small capitals of the Lombard plain are among Italy's most rewarding art cities, each maintaining its individual character: Pavia, the capital of the ancient Lombards and the region's oldest centre of learning, embellished with fine Romanesque churches and its famous Renaissance Certosa; Cremona, the graceful city where the raw medieval fiddle was reincarnated as the lyrical violin; and Mantua, the dream shadow capital of the wealthy Gonzaga dukes and Isabella d'Este.

Pavia

Pavia is a distinctly serious no-monkey-business town. It is one of those rare cities that had its golden age in the three-digit years before the millennium, that misty half-legendary time that historians have shrugged off as the Dark Ages. But these were bright days for Pavia, when it served as capital of the Goths and saw Odoacer proclaimed King of Italy after defeating Romulus Augustulus, the last Roman Emperor in the West. In the 6th century the heretical Lombards led by King Alboin captured Pavia from the Goths and formed a state the equal of Byzantine Ravenna and Rome, making Pavia the capital of their *Regnum Italicum*, a position the city maintained into the 11th century; Charlemagne came here to be crowned (774), as did the first King of Italy, Berenguer (888), and Emperor Frederick Barbarossa (1155). At the turn of the millennium the precursor of Pavia's modern university, the *Studio*, was founded, and among its first students of law was the first Norman Archbishop of Canterbury, Lanfranc, born in Pavia in 1005.

Pavia was a Ghibelline *comune*, the 'city of a hundred towers' and a rival of Milan, to whom it lost its independence in 1359. It was favoured by the Visconti, especially by Gian Galeazzo, who built the castle housing his art collection and founded the striking Certosa di Pavia. It, with many other churches in the city, bears the mark of Pavia's great, half-demented sculptor-architect of the High Renaissance, Giovanni Antonio Amadeo.

Getting to and from Pavia

There are **buses** roughly every 45 minutes between Milan and Pavia, and this is also the best way to travel if you wish to stop off and visit the Certosa, some 8km north of Pavia. Buses arrive in and depart from Via Trieste, in the brand-new station-cum-shopping centre. Frequent **trains** link Pavia to Milan (30mins) and Genoa (1½ hours), and there are less frequent services to Cremona and Mantua, Alessandria and Vercelli, and Piacenza. The train station is a 10-minute walk from the centre, at the end of Corso Cavour and Viale Vittorio Emanuele II.

By **car**, Pavia can be reached very quickly from Milan by the A7 *autostrada*, or in a more leisurely fashion by the SS35, which has the advantage of passing by the Certosa.

Tourist Information

A couple of streets from the station, at Via Filzi 2, ✆ 0382 22156, 🖷 0382 32221.

The Duomo and San Michele

Through traffic has been banished from Pavia's core, which retains its street plan from the days when it was the Roman city of Ticinum, the cardus (Corso Cavour) and the decumanus (Corso Strada Nuova) intersecting by the town hall or **Broletto**, begun in the 12th century, and the **Duomo**, a front-running candidate for the ugliest church in all Italy. Begun in 1488, the cathedral owes its imposing design to Amadeo, Leonardo da Vinci, Bramante and a dozen others (definite proof that too many cooks spoil the broth) and its strange, unfinished appearance—it looks as if it's covered with corrugated cardboard—to an understandable lack of interest in ever finishing it. The last two apses in the transept were added only in 1930, while the vast cupola that dominates the city skyline was added in the 1880s. Next to the cathedral is the rubble of what was once the singularly unattractive 12th-century **Torre Civica**, the collapse of which in 1989 prompted serious attention to its rather more famous Pisan relation.

From the Duomo, the Strada Nuova continues south down to the river and the pretty **Covered Bridge**, which has replaced the original Renaissance model damaged during the last war. From Strada Nuova, Via Maffi leads to the small brick 12th-century **San Teodoro**, notable for its early 16th-century fresco of Pavia when it still had a forest of a hundred towers and the original covered bridge.

East of the Strada, Via Capsoni leads in a couple of blocks to Pavia's most important church, the Romanesque **Basilica di San Michele Maggiore**, founded in 661 but rebuilt in the 12th century after its destruction by lightning. Unlike the other churches of Pavia, San Michele is made of sandstone, mellowed into a fine golden hue, though the weather has been less kind to the intricate friezes that cross its front like comic strips, depicting a complete 'apocalyptic vision' with its medieval bestiary, monsters and human figures involved in the never-ending fight between Good and Evil. Mermaids are especially prominent—one impassively holds up her forked tail, a Romanesque conceit nearly as popular as the two lions by the main door. Such mermaids, displaying the entrance to the womb, with birds or dragons whispering in their ears, come straight from medieval mysticism, perhaps as a symbol of the cosmic process: the sirens, representing desire, become the intermediaries by which nature's energy and inspiration (here represented by the birds) are conducted into the conscious world.

The solemn interior, where Frederick Barbarossa was crowned with the Iron Crown of Italy, contains more fine carvings on the capitals of the columns; the most curious, the fourth on the left, portrays the 'Death of the Righteous'. Along the top runs a Byzantine-style women's gallery, while the chapel to the right of the main altar contains the church's most valuable treasure, a 7th-century silver crucifix.

The University and Castello Visconteo

The great yellow neoclassical quadrangles of the **University of Pavia**, famous for law and medicine, occupy much of the northeast quadrant of the ancient street plan. The ancient Studio was officially made a university in 1361. St Charles Borromeo, a former student, founded a college here (still supported by the Borromei in Milan), while Pope Pius V founded another, the Collegio Ghislieri, in 1569. In the 18th century Maria Theresa worked hard to bring the university back to life after scholarship had hit the skids and financed the construction of the main buildings. Three of Pavia's medieval skyscrapers or **Torri** survive in the middle of the university, in the Piazza Leonardo da Vinci; the roof in the Piazza shelters what is believed to be

Pavia

300 metres
250 yards

the crypt of the demolished 12th-century **Sant'Eusebio church**; nearby you can meet some of the university's 17,000 students (many of whom commute from Milan) at the Bar Bordoni, on Via Mentana. In the Piazza San Francesco d'Assisi, northeast of the main university, the 1228 **San Francesco d'Assisi** was one of the first churches in Italy dedicated to the saint; it has an unusual façade, adorned with lozenge patterns and a triple-mullioned window.

At the top of Strada Nuova looms the mighty **Castello Visconteo**, built in 1360 by the Campionese masters for Gian Galeazzo II, but partially destroyed in the Battle of Pavia on 24 February 1525, when Emperor Charles V captured Francis I of France, who succinctly described the outcome in a letter to his mother: 'Madame, all is lost save honour'. Three sides of the castle and its beautifully arcaded courtyard with terracotta decorations managed to survive as well, and now house Pavia's **Museo Civico** (*open Tues–Sun, 10–12 and 2.30–4; Dec and Jan, July and Aug Tues–Sun 9–1 only*). The archaeological and medieval sections contain finds from Roman and Gaulish Pavia, as well as robust Lombard and medieval carvings salvaged from now-vanished churches, and colourful 12th-century mosaics. One room contains an impressive wooden model of the cathedral, built by the architect Fugazza in the early 16th century. The picture gallery on the first floor contains works by Giovanni Bellini, Correggio, Foppa, Van der Goes and others.

San Pietro in Ciel d'Oro

Behind the castle, Via Griziotti (off Viale Matteotti) leads to Pavia's second great Romanesque temple, **San Pietro in Ciel d'Oro** ('St Peter in the Golden Sky'), built in 1132 and named for its once-glorious gilded ceiling, mentioned by Dante in Canto X of the *Paradiso*. The single door in the façade is strangely off-centre; within, the main altar is one of the greatest works of the Campionese masters, the **Arca di Sant'Agostino**, a magnificent 14th-century monument built to shelter the bones of St Augustine which, according to legend, were retrieved in the 8th century from Carthage by the Lombard king Luitprand, staunch ally of Pope Gregory II against the iconoclasts of Byzantium. Luitprand himself is buried in a humble tomb to the right, and in the crypt lies another Dark Age celebrity, the philosopher Boethius, slain by Emperor Theodoric of Ravenna in 524.

There are two other notable churches in Pavia. In the centre of town (walk down the Piazza Petrarca from Viale Matteotti) **Santa Maria del Carmine** (1390s) is an excellent example of Lombard Gothic, with a fine façade and rose window and, inside, a beautifully sculptured lavabo by Amadeo. Outside the centre, to the west (Corso Cavour to Corso Manzoni and Via della Riviera) it's a 15-minute walk to the rather plain, vertical, 13th-century **San Lanfranco**, especially notable for its lovely memorial, the *Arca di San Lanfranco*, sculpted by Amadeo in 1498, his last work (though Archbishop Lanfranc was actually buried in Canterbury); the same artist helped design the church's pretty cloister.

The Certosa di Pavia

The pinnacle of Renaissance architecture in Lombardy, and according to Jacob Burckhardt 'the greatest decorative masterpiece in all of Italy', the Certosa or Charterhouse of Pavia was built over a period of 200 years. Gian Galeazzo Visconti laid the cornerstone in 1396, with visions of the crown of Italy dancing in his head, and the desire to build a splendid pantheon for his hoped-for royal self and his heirs. Although many architects and artists worked on the project (beginning with the Campionese masters of Milan cathedral), it bears the greatest imprint of

Giovanni Antonio Amadeo, who with his successor Bergognone worked on its sculptural programme for 30 years and contributed the design of the lavish façade.

Napoleon disbanded the monastery, but in 1968 a small group of Cistercians reoccupied the Certosa. The monks of today live the same style of contemplative life as the old Carthusians, maintaining vows of silence. A couple, however, are released to take visitors around the complex (*open in summer Tues–Sun 9–11.30 and 2.30–6; spring and autumn until 5; winter until 4; weekends are often very crowded*). If you arrive by the Milan–Pavia bus, the Certosa is a 1½km walk from the nearest stop, a beckoning vision at the end of the straight, shaded land, surrounded by well-tended fields and rows of poplars once part of the vast game park of the Castello Visconteo in Pavia.

Once through the main gate and **vestibule** adorned with frescoes by Luini, a large grassy court opens up, lined with buildings that served as lodgings for visitors and stores for the monks. At the far side rises the sumptuous, detailed façade of the **church**, a marvel of poly-chromatic marbles, medallions, bas-reliefs, statues, and windows covered with marble embroidery from the chisel of Amadeo, who died before the upper, less elaborate level was begun. The interior plan is Gothic but the decoration is Renaissance, with later baroque addi-tions. Outstanding works of art include Bergognone's five statues of saints in the chapel of Sant'Ambrogio (sixth on the left); the tombs of Lodovico il Moro and his young bride Beatrice d'Este, a masterpiece by Cristoforo Solari; the beautiful inlaid stalls of the choir; and the tomb of Gian Galeazzo Visconti, all works of the 1490s and surrounded by fine frescoes. The old sacristy contains a magnificent early cinquecento ivory altarpiece by the Florentine Baldassarre degli Embriachi, with 94 figures and 66 bas-reliefs.

From the church, the tour continues into the **Little Cloister**, with delicate terracotta decora-tions and a dream-like view of the church and its cupola, a rising crescendo of arcades. A lovely doorway by Amadeo leads back into the church. The **Great Cloister** with its long arcades is surrounded by the 24 house-like cells of the monks—each contains a chapel and study/dining room, a bedroom upstairs and a walled garden in the rear. The frescoed **Refectory** contains a pulpit for the monks who read aloud during otherwise silent suppers.

Pavia ✉ *27100* **Where to Stay**

Most people visit Pavia as a day trip from Milan, but light sleepers or budget-minded souls could always take in Milan as a day trip from Pavia.

expensive and moderate

The ★★★★**Moderno**, Viale Vittorio Emanuele II 45, ✆ 0382 303 401, ✉ 0382 25225, is the most comfortable, if expensive, hotel in town, next to the railway station. The ★★★★**Ariston**, Via A. Scopoli 10/d, ✆ 0382 34334, ✉ 0382 25667, is conveniently centrally located and has a slightly more old-fashioned touch, with air-conditioning, private bath and television in each room, for much less than you'd pay in Milan. The ★★★**Excelsior**, Piazzale Stazione 25, ✆ 0382 28596, ✉ 0382 26030, also conveniently located, is slightly cheaper.

cheap

There are not many options in this category, but the ★★**Aurora**, Via Vittorio Emanuele II 25, ✆ 0382 23664, ✉ 0382 21248, is another hotel near the station, which has showers in all the rooms. The elderly but friendly ***Splendid**, Via XX Settembre 11, ✆ 0382 24703, has plenty of rooms, though none of them has a bath.

Eating Out

Pavia is well endowed with good restaurants. Specialities include frogs, salami from Varzi and *zuppa pavese* (a raw egg on toast drowned in hot broth); good local wines to try are from the Oltrepó Pavese region, one of Lombardy's best. Cortese is a delicious dry white, Bonarda a meaty, dry red, Pinot a fruity white.

expensive

For excellent, innovative cuisine, eat at the small but chic **Locanda Vecchia Pavia**, right under the cathedral on Via Cardinal Riboldi 2, ✆ 0382 304 132; its young chefs base the day's menu on what looks good in the market, with some surprising but delicious results like gratin of scallops and red mullet, truffle-filled ravioli, and equally fine desserts. *Closed Mon and Wed lunch, and Aug*. Pavia's other temple of fine cuisine is **Al Cassinino**, Via Cassinino 1, ✆ 0382 422 097, just outside the city on the Giovi highway. Sitting on the Naviglio, the restaurant is done out in the style of a medieval inn, complete with rare antiques. Dishes are whatever the market provides—try the fresh pasta with seasonal vegetables, or the pâté of sea bass and salmon. *Closed Wed, and Christmas*. Not far from **Bereguardo**, in the tiny village of **Zelata** in **Parco di Ticino**, taste the gastronomic delights of **La Zelata**, ✆ 0382 928 178, a family-run restaurant serving traditional Lombard dishes for the last twenty years. Various types of risotto are the house speciality, but save room for chocolate mousse or *tarte tatin*. *Closed Sun, and Mon lunch*.

moderate–cheap

Antica Osteria del Previ, Via Milazzo 65, ✆ 0382 26203, on the banks of the Ticino, is an old-fashioned place serving home-made salami, risotto with frog or radicchio and speck, and for *secondi* river-fish, frog and snails. *Closed Wed and lunchtimes in summer*. The **Osteria del Naviglio**, Via Alzaia 39, ✆ 0382 460 392, has a vast selection of wines to be sampled with delicacies such as a *sformato* (kind of hearty mousse) of potato and porcini or seasonal vegetables, or pappardelle with duck. Desserts are also excellent—try the sorbets or hazelnut *semifreddo*. *Closed Mon, open eves only*.

In the old 16th-century mill of the Certosa, the **Vecchio Mulino**, Via al Monumento 5, ✆ 0382 925 894, serves up delicious food with ingredients garnered from the fertile countryside—risotto with sweet peppers, tomato and oregano, crêpes filled with artichokes, and much more. The wine list has nearly every label produced in Lombardy. *Closed evenings Sun and Mon*.

Around Pavia: Lomello and Vigévano

West of Pavia and the Certosa lies the little-known Lomellina, a major rice-growing and frog-farming district, irrigated by canals dug by order of the Visconti in the 14th century. The feudal seat, **Lomello**, retains some fine early medieval buildings, most notably a lovely little 5th-century polygonal **Baptistry** near the main church, the 11th-century **Basilica di Santa Maria**. Also in the Lomellina is the old silk town of **Vigévano** (better known these days for its high-fashion footwear manufacturers), the site of another vast **castle** of the Visconti and Sforza clans; it was the birthplace of Lodovico il Moro, and for the past few years has been undergoing a lengthy restoration process. Below it lies the majestic rectangular **Piazza Ducale**, designed in 1492 by Bramante (with help from Leonardo) as Lombardy's answer to Venice's Piazza San Marco. Originally a grand stairway connected the piazza to one of the castle towers, though now the three sides are adorned with slender arcades, while on the fourth stands the magnificent concave baroque façade of the **cathedral**, designed by a Spanish bishop, Juan Caramuel de Labkowitz. Inside there's a good collection of 16th-century paintings and a 15th-century Lombard polyptych on the life of St Thomas of Canterbury, and an especially rich treasury (*open 3–5pm public holidays only, or upon request*) containing illuminated codices, Flemish tapestries and golden reliquaries. There is a **Shoe Museum** on Corso Cavour (*open Sun only*) which is stacked with weird and wonderful footwear.

Cremona

Cremona is famous for four things that have added to the sum total of human happiness: its Romanesque cathedral complex, Claudio Monteverdi, nougat, and violins. It has been the capital of the last-mentioned industry since 1566, when Andrea Amati invented the modern violin from the old medieval fiddle. It quickly became fashionable, and demand across Europe initiated a golden age of fiddle-making, when Andrea's son Nicolò Amati, and his pupils Stradivarius and Giuseppe Guarneri, made the best violins, ever. Walking around Cremona you can easily pick out in the elegant curves and scrolls on the brick and terracotta palaces that inspired the instrument's baroque form, while the sweetness of the violin's tone seems to have something of the city's culinary specialities in it, not only nougat but *mostarda di Cremona*—candied cherries, apricots, melons and so on in a sweet or piquant mustard sauce, served with boiled meats. Today some 50 *liutai* (violin-makers) keep up the tradition, using similar methods and woods (poplar, spruce, pear, willow and maple); a school and research institute are devoted to the craft, and every third October (next in 2000) the city hosts a festival of stringed instruments.

violin making

Milan captured the once feisty *comune* of Cremona in 1344 and in 1441 gave the city to Bianca Maria Visconti as her dowry when she married Francesco Sforza, marking the change of the great Milanese dynasties. The city enjoyed a happy, fruitful Renaissance as the apple of Bianca's eye, producing Monteverdi, the father of opera, the prolific Campi family of painters, and Sofonisba Anguissola, the recently rediscovered Renaissance portrait painter admired by Michelangelo, Van Dyck and Philip II (who summoned her to work in Spain) for her ability to depict a sitter's soul.

Even Cremona's railway station is delightful: there are frequent **train** services from Milan (about 2 hours), Pavia, Mantua, Brescia and Piacenza, as well as three times a day from Bergamo. The station lies north of the centre, at the end of Via Palestro. **Buses** arrive at and depart from the bus station in Via Dante, next to the train station. Leave your **car** in the Via Villa Glori car park in exchange for free use of a bicycle. **Boating** on the Po is possible at **SNI**, Via Robolotti 7, ✆ 0372 25546.

Piazza del Comune 5, ✆ 0372 23233, 📠 0372 21722. If you're in the market for a violin or just want to visit a workshop, ask for their free list of *Botteghe Liutarie.*

Via Palestro to the Piazza del Comune

Cremona can be easily visited on foot, starting from the station and the Via Palestro. Here, behind a remodelled baroque façade at Via Palestro 36, the **Palazzo Stanga Trecco**'s 15th-century courtyard is an excellent introduction to the Cremonese fondness for elaborate terracotta ornament. The **Museo Stradivariano** nearby at No.17 (*open Tues–Sat 8.30–6, Sun 9.15–12.15 and 3–6; closed Aug; adm*) is an equally good introduction to the cream of Cremona's best-known industry, featuring casts, models, items from the master's workshop and drawings explaining how Stradivarius did it. Just around the corner, on Via U. Dati 4, the Palazzo Affaitati (begun in 1561) houses a grand theatrical staircase added in 1769 and the **Museo Civico** (*same hours*), which has sections devoted to some amazingly dreary paintings by the Cremonese school (Boccaccino and the Campi family). The archaeology section includes a fine labyrinth mosaic with Theseus and the Minotaur in the centre (*c.* 2nd century AD) from the Roman colonia at Cremona; another section houses the cathedral treasury, with some fine illuminated codices and corals. The palace opposite, at Via U. Dati 7, has a pretty frescoed courtyard.

Via Palestro becomes Corso Campi, and at an angle runs into the boxy, Mussolini-era Galleria Venticinque Aprile, leading to the **Piazza Roma**, a little park; along Corso Mazzini is Stradivarius' red marble tombstone, transferred from a demolished church. Corso Mazzini forks after a block; near the split, at Corso Matteotti 17, is Cremona's prettiest palace, the 1499 **Palazzo Fodri** (*now owned by the Banca d'Italia; ask the guard to unlock the gate*), with a courtyard adorned with frescoed battle scenes and terracottas.

Piazza del Comune: The Torrazzo and Duomo

Cremona's lovely medieval Piazza del Comune is seductive enough to compete in any urban beauty contest. By now you've probably caught at least a glimpse of its biggest feature, the curious pointed crown of the tallest bell tower in Italy, the 370ft **Torrazzo** (*open April–Oct, Tues–Sun 10.30–12 and 3–6; Nov–Feb, Sat only 3–6; adm*). Only slightly shorter than Milan cathedral, the Torrazzo was built in the 1260s, has battlements as well as bells, and even tells the time thanks to a fine astronomical clock added in 1583 by Giovanni Battista Divizioli. The stout-hearted can ascend 487 steps to the top for an eye-popping view; the less ambitious can purchase a famous Cremona TTT postcard (Torrazzo, *torrone* and tits) to send home. The lower level houses a reproduction of a violinmaker's shop of Stradivarius' time, and in summer a man is on hand to show how it's done.

Linked to the Torrazzo in 1525 by a double loggia, the **Portico della Bertazzola**, the **Duomo** is the highest and one of the most exuberant expression of Lombard Romanesque, with a trademark Cremonese flourish in the graceful scrolls added to the marble front. Built by the Comacini masters after an earthquake destroyed its predecessor in 1117, the main door or **Porta Regia** remains as it was originally, flanked by two nearly toothless lion telamones and four flat prophets, and crowned by a small portico known as the Rostrum, where 13th- and 14th-century statues of the Virgin and two saints silently but eloquently hold forth above a frieze of the months by the school of Antelami.

The cathedral was begun as a basilica, but as Gothic came into fashion it was decided to add the arms of a Latin cross; the new transepts, especially the north one, are almost as splendid from the outside as the main façade. The interior is undergoing a major restoration, revealing primitive frescoes under the opulent 16th-century works by Romanino, Boccaccino and Pordenone (who painted the Crucifixion under the rose window); the right transept has some endearing sweet and simple paintings on the ceiling and Flemish tapestries. The twin pulpits have nervous, delicate reliefs attributed to Amadeo or Pietro da Rho. The choir has exquisite stalls inlaid in 1490 by G.M. Platina, with nearly all secular scenes, views of Cremona and still lifes. In the crypt, with the tomb of Ombrono Tucenghi, patron saint of tailors (*d.* 1197), note the painting of old Cremona with its Manhattan skyline of towers.

Completing the sacred ensemble in Piazza del Comune is the octagonal **Battistero di San Giovanni** (1167), with another pair of lions supporting the portico, and two sides of marble facing to match the cathedral. Across from the Duomo, the **Loggia dei Militi** (1292) was used as a rendezvous by the captains of the *comune*'s citizen militia; the outdoor pulpit between two of the arches is a relic of the charismatic, itinerant preachers like San Bernadino of Siena, whose sermons were so popular they had to be held outside. Behind it, the **Palazzo del Comune** (*open Tues–Sat 8.30–6, Sun 9.15–12.15 and 3–6; adm*) was begun in 1206 as the lavish seat of the Ghibelline party and now serves as Cremona's town hall. To see are paintings salvaged from churches, a superb marble fireplace of 1502 by Giovan Gaspare Pedone, baroque furniture and the **Saletta dei Violini,** with the town's violin collection, starring Stradivarius' golden 'Cremonese 1715', which retains its original varnish—as mysterious as the embalming fluids of ancient Egypt. Another of the master's secrets was in the woods he used for his instruments; like Michelangelo seeking just the right piece of marble in the mountains of Carrara, Stradivarius would visit the forests of the Dolomites looking for perfect trees that would one day sing. Other violins include 'Charles IX of France' by Andrea Amati, one of 24 violins commissioned in the 1560s by the French sovereign from the father of modern fiddles; the 'Hammerle', by Nicolò Amati (1658); Giuseppe Guarneri's 'Del Gesù' (formerly owned by Pinchas Zukerman); and the 1689 'Quarestini', also by Guarneri.

Back Towards the Station

Behind the Palazzo del Comune lie Piazza Cavour and Corso Vittorio Emanuele, leading to the River Po. En route it passes one of Italy's earliest and most renowned small-town theatres,

N

300 metres
250 yards

VIA BERGAMO

Station

Piazza
Stazione

Bus
Station

VIA F. GHINAGLIA

Piazza
Risorgimento

CORSO GARIBALDI

San Luca

VIA BERTESI

VIA G. FAERNO

VIA

Piazza
Fiume

Palazzo
Raimondi

Palazzo Stanga
Trecco

VIA GRADO

Museo
Stradivariano

Piazza
XXIV
Maggio

VIA DEI MILLE

Palazzo
Cittanova

Sant'
Agata

PALESTRO

CORSO GARIBALDI

VIA

Palazzo
Trecchi

VIA STEFANO LEONIDA BISSOLATI

VIA VILLA GLORI

VIA MILAZZO

VIA RUGGIERO MONNA

Sant'
Agostino

VIA PLASIO

MASSAROTTI

VIA TREBBIA

Piazza
S. Lucia

Piazza
Luigi Cadorna

Teatro
Ponchielli

San Pietro
al Po

VIA DEL GIORDANO

Piazza
San Pietro

VIALE PO

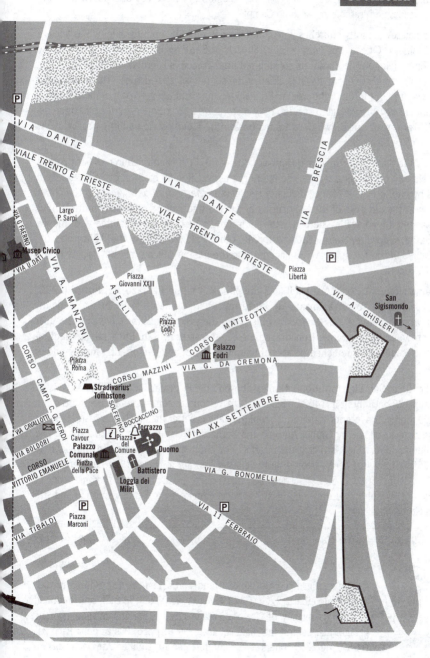

P

VIA DANTE

VIALE TRENTO E TRIESTE

VIA DANTE

VIALE TRENTO E TRIESTE

VIA BRESCIA

VIA G FAERINO

Largo
P. Sarpi

Museo Civico

VIA U.DATI

VIA A. MANZONI

VIA A.

VIA ASELLI

Piazza
Giovanni XXIII

Piazza
Lodi

VIA A. GHISLERI

San
Sigismondo

Piazza
Libertà

P

CORSO MATTEOTTI

CORSO CAMPI C. G. VERDI

Piazza
Roma

CORSO MAZZINI

Palazzo
Fodri

VIA G. DA CREMONA

VIA CAVALLOTTI

Stradivarius'
Tombstone

SOLFERINO

BOCCACCINO

VIA XX SETTEMBRE

VIA BOLDORI

Piazza
Cavour

Torrazzo

Piazza
del
Comune

Duomo

Palazzo
Comunale

Piazza
della Pace

CORSO
VITTORIO EMANUELE

Battistero

VIA G. BONOMELLI

Loggia dei
Militi

P

Piazza
Marconi

P

VIA TIBALDI

VIA II FEBBRAIO

111

the **Teatro Ponchielli**, built in 1734 and rebuilt after a fire in 1808, named for Amilcare Ponchielli (*see* below) who premiered several of his operas on its little stage. A street to the right of the theatre leads back to Piazza San Pietro and **San Pietro al Po**, coated with 16th-century stuccoes and frescoes by Antonio Campi.

Cremona has several lofty churches with interiors that look like nothing as much as ancient Roman basilicas. One is the 14th-century church of **Sant'Agostino**, north of the Corso Vittorio Emanuele, on Via Plasio. Its striking red brick façade is adorned with fine terracotta decorations, and the centre nave is lined with statues of the virtues. There are good Renaissance frescoes in the right aisle by Bonifacio Bembo and a lovely *pala* of the *Madonna with Saints* (1494) by Perugino (*undergoing restoration at the time of writing*). For something different, seek out the sinuous terracottas on the Liberty-style building nearby at Via Milazzo 16.

Further up Via Plasio joins the Corso Garibaldi, site of the 11th-century church of **Sant'Agata**, hiding behind a neoclassical façade; the interior, a perfect Roman basilica, contains excellent frescoes by Giulio Campi of the singularly unpleasant *Martyrdom of St Agata* in the choir, a painting in the left aisle of the holy family by Lucia Anguissola, sister of the more famous Sofonisba, and a medieval masterpiece, the 13th-century wooden panel painted with the life of St Agatha. Opposite, the recently restored Gothic **Palazzo Cittanova** (1256) was the headquarters of the Guelph party: adjacent, note the flamboyant but phoney façade of the **Palazzo Trecchi**.

Continuing along, at Corso Garibaldi 178 the pink and white **Palazzo Raimondi** (1496) houses the **Scuola Internazionale di Liuteria**, where students learn to make violins (*open by appointment, ☎ 0372 38689*) while across the street stands the city's most peculiar palace, crowned with strange iron dragons. Near the station, **San Luca** has a beautiful terracotta façade and a detached octagonal temple of 1503, a votive offering for the end of a plague.

One last church, **San Sigismondo**, is 1km east beyond the Piazzale Libertà, on Via A. Ghisleri (*take bus nos.2 or 3*). Built in 1463 by Bianca Maria Visconti to commemorate her marriage to Francesco Sforza, the interior is delicious proof that fake is better than real: rich pastel frescoes and *trompe l'œil* décors by Giulio, Antonio and Bernardino Campi, Camillo Boccaccino and Bernardino and Gervasio Gatti coat the interior. The choir stalls, by Domenico and Gabriele Capra (1590), have just been restored; in the cloister look for a fresco of the *Last Supper* by Tommaso Aleni (1508). Bianca's marriage also occasioned the invention of *torrone*, made of almonds, honey and egg whites—the gastronomical equivalent to San Sigismondo and still made in Cremona today.

Cremona ✉ *26100*

Where to Stay

expensive

The modern, comfortable, friendly and central ★★★★**Continental**, Piazzale Libertà 27, ☎ 0372 434 141, @ 0372 454 873, sets the mood with its display of Cremona-made fiddles; parking available in the garage. Just behind the main square ★★★★**Impero**, Piazza della Pace 21, ☎ 0372 460 337, offers stylish comfort in a streamlined Art Deco palace.

On a pedestrian-only street facing the cathedral, **★★★Duomo**, Via Gonfalonieri 13, ✆ 0372 35242, 🖷 0372 458 392, has a very nice restaurant (with a reasonably priced set menu) as well as comfortable rooms. For a bit less, try **★★★Astoria**, Via Bordigallo 9, ✆ 0372 461 616, 🖷 0372 461 810, a very pleasant hotel in a quiet street close to the Duomo.

★Albergo Touring, Via Palestro 3, ✆ 0372 36976, is a good, simple old-fashioned choice midway between the centre and the station with high ceilings, shared baths and a little parking garage. Right by the station **★Bologna**, Piazza Risorgimento 7, ✆ 0372 24258, has cheap singles but no doubles; nearby the gloomy **★Ideale**, Viale Trente e Trieste 2, ✆ 0372 38668, has clean, if rather noisy, doubles.

Eating Out

Just behind the baptistry, **Aquila Nera**, Via Sicardo 3, ✆ 0372 25646 (*expensive*) enjoys an enviable reputation for its regional dishes, starting with melt-in-your-mouth *antipasti, tortelli di zucca* and zesty *secondi* featuring meat or seafood. *Closed Sun eve, Mon and Aug.* An older, rather more traditional restaurant on the west end of town, **Trattoria Mellini**, Via Bissolati 105, ✆ 0372 30535 (*moderate*) features dishes to make animal-lovers foam at the mouth—casseroled donkey and baby horse, or raw baby horse with truffle. Less controversial fare includes a kind of risotto with salami and savoy cabbage, fresh pasta with sausage, and other hearty regional fare. *Closed Sun eve, Mon and July.*

The family-run **Porta Mosa**, Via Santa Maria in Betlem 11, ✆ 0372 411 803, is a tiny place serving delicious traditional dishes such as tortelli stuffed with squash and locally caught sturgeon steamed with herbs and capers. They also concoct a mean *tiramisu*. *Closed Sun, and mid-Aug–mid-Sept*. If your party can't decide between pizza, Thai or Chinese, the new **Hai Xia**, Corso Garibaldi 85, ✆ 0372 39153 (*cheap*) serves all three, and all are delicious—especially the Thai. *Closed Mon.*

Around Cremona

Soncino and Paderno Ponchielli

Lying between the rivers Po and Oglio, the rich and strategic agricultural province of Cremona is well fortified with castles and towers that recall the glorious days when the Italian *comuni* had nothing better to do than beat each other up. The most imposing of the surviving castles, the **Rocca Sforzesca** (*open Tues–Sun 10–12; summer Sat and Sun 10–12.30 and 3–7, winter Sat and Sun 10–12.30 and 4.30–5.30*) rears up over **Soncino**, a walled town north of Cremona on the Oglio. Built in the 12th century, it was greatly enlarged in 1473 by Galeazzo Maria Sforza as an advance base against the Venetians, who were holed up in the Brescian town of Orzinuovi directly across the river. The moat and sinister beetling towers survive intact, as well as the dungeon, which in 1259 hosted the most ferocious and hated man in

Italy: Emperor Frederick II's henchman, Ezzelino da Romano. Ezzelino was severely wounded when his own army and Ghibelline allies turned on him as he crossed the Oglio on his way to surprise Milan; at age 65, he kept his reputation as a tough *hombre* to the end, refusing to speak or receive any medical treatment, ripping the bandages from his wounds until he died in agony.

On a rather more cheerful note, admire the watermill under the castle walls, and the delicious painted terracottas and frescoes (*c.* 1500) by Giulio Campi and others that cover the interior of **Santa Maria delle Grazie**. In the late 15th century the Sforzas invited a community of Jewish refugees to settle in Soncino, one of whom, Israel Nathan, founded a press and printed his first ornate book in Hebrew in 1483, and the first complete Old Testament in Hebrew in 1488: the site of the press is now a little **Museo della Stampa** (*open same hours as the castle*).

Between Cremona and Crema (the two Italian towns that most sound like dairy products) you'll find **Paderno Ponchielli**, birthplace of 'the Italian Tchaikovsky', Amilcare Ponchielli (1834–86). Italy has produced scores of one-opera composers, but Ponchielli can claim two that are performed with some frequency: *La Gioconda* and *Marion Delorme*; and as the teacher of Puccini and Mascagni can claim to be grandfather of many others. His humble birthplace is now the **Museo Ponchiellano**, devoted to his life and works (*open Mon–Wed 3–7, Sat and Sun by appointment,* © *0374 67404*).

Crema

It was in 1159, during Frederick Barbarossa's third war with Milan, that the emperor, realizing that he lacked suffcient troops to besiege the big city, turned his German army on little Crema, Milan's staunch ally. Four hundred Milanese came to Crema's defence, but Frederick wasn't in the mood for a fair fight. He hanged all of his adult hostages from Crema and Milan outside the gates, hoping to horrify Crema into surrendering, and when that didn't work he strapped the littlest ones to his moving siege towers, so that the Cremaschi could not repulse the towers without harming their own children. The histories tell how the parents asked their fellow citizens to kill them, to avoid witnessing their children's torture, while at the same time shouting to their children to be brave and boldly give up their lives for their country. In spite of Frederick's merciless tactics Crema held out for another six months, but at last, starving and exhausted, it surrendered on the condition that the citizens could withdraw to Milan as their town was razed to the ground.

Three hundred years later, in 1449, Francesco Sforza offered the most loyal town of Crema to Venice when the Serenissima offered to support his dukedom. It proved to be a more pleasant occupation, enduring for three centuries and endowing Crema with a tidy elegance rare in the Lombard plain. To this day it bears a white Istrian marble lion of St Mark on its gates and town hall, the latter by the pink brick **Duomo**, a delightful Romanesque Gothic work built after Barbarossa sent the original up in flames. Its high 'wind façade' from the 1300s has windows finely decorated with curling vines, little turrets and blind arcading: next to it stands the whimsical, almost Moorish campanile of baked clay that so ravished John Addington Symonds.

Crema's narrow streets are lined by neat but secretive façades that often hide pretty courtyards and gardens. There are quite a few tidy palaces, and the uncompleted but utterly romantic baroque **Palazzo Terni de' Gregori** (or Bondenti) in Via Dante, opposite the former convent of Sant' Agostino. This now houses the library and **Museo Civico** (*open Tues–Fri 2.30–6.30, Sat and Sun 10–12 and 4–6*) with everything from medieval Lombard armour discovered in Aufoningum (Offanengo) in 1963, Risorgimento mementoes, and scores by local composers, to two dramatic paintings of the *Miracles of Christ* by Alessandro Magnasco with backgrounds by Clemente Spera, an expert on painting theatrical landscapes of ruins, and other works by local talent, including a really gross 17th-century *Martyrdom of San Erasmo* and aquafortes by Federica Galli, who lives just outside town. Ask the curators to unlock the refectory to see the recently restored frescoes of the *Last Supper* and *Crucifixion* (1498) by Giovan Pietro da Cemmo.

An architect from Cremona, Faustino Rodi, designed the fine neoclassical gate by the river, the **Porta Serio**, while just north of the walls, at the end of a long tree-lined avenue, an apparition of the Virgin is marked by the basilica of **Santa Maria della Croce** (1490–1500), a lovely Renaissance drum church inspired by Bramante. Encircled by three orders of loggias and four polygonal chapels with spherical cupolas, the interior is octagonal and contains a fine Assumption by Diana. Crema's Venetian period also saw the construction of fine palaces and villas, of which the 18th-century **Villa Ghisetti-Giavarina** in **Ricengo** just to the north is the most beautiful and stately, with frescoes inside (*to arrange a visit, ring the Pro Loco in Ricengo, ✆ 0373 267 708*).

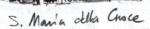

S. Maria della Croce

West of Crema towards Milan, **Pandino** has a large 14th-century Visconti hunting lodge-cum-castle, currently under restoration, while **Rivolta d'Adda**, 8km further on, has an 11th-century church of **San Sigismondo**, dwarfed by its battlemented campanile and containing some good carvings. Rivolta also offers Jurassic-era fun in its **Parco della Preistoria** (*open Mar–Nov daily, 9–dusk; adm*), where a zoo train chugs past 23 life-size reproductions of dinosaurs, prowling the wooded banks of the Adda.

Crema ✉ *26013*   ### Where to Stay and Eating Out

Crema has three hotels, all *expensive*: small ★★★★**Il Ponte di Rialto**, Via Cardorna 7, ✆ 0373 82342, ✐ 0373 83520, is the nicest; somewhat cheaper is the ★★★★**Palace**, Via Cresmiero 10, ✆ 0373 81487, ✐ 0373 86876. As for food, the local speciality, *tortelli cremaschi*, is decidedly different: pasta filled with *amaretti*, raisins, citron, peppermint, nutmeg and cheese, and served in melted butter, sage and cheese.

Try it at the **Trattoria Gobbato**, Via Podgora 2, ✆ 0373 80891 (*cheap*) a funky little place which has been feeding local railway workers for decades. It also serves great local salami, *pasta e fasoi* (pasta with beans), vegetable lasagne and hare with polenta. *Closed Mon; open daily July and Aug.*

Mantua (Mantova)

Mantua's setting hardly answers to one's great expectations of Italy, sitting in the midst of a fertile, table-flat plain, on a wide thumb of land protruding into three swampy, swollen lakes formed by the River Mincio. Its climate is moody, soggy with heat and humidity in the summer and frosty under blankets of fog in the winter. The local dialect is harsh, and the Mantuans, when they feel chipper, dine on braised donkey with macaroni. Verdi made it the sombre setting of his opera *Rigoletto*. And yet this former capital of the art-loving, fast-living Gonzaga dukes is one of the most atmospheric old cities in the country—'a city in the form of a palace' as Castiglioni called it—masculine, dark and handsome, with few of neighbouring Cremona's sweet architectural arpeggios—poker-faced but holding in its hand a royal flush of dazzling Renaissance art.

History

Mantua gained its fame in Roman times as the beloved home town of the poet Virgil, who recounts the legend of the city's founding by the Theban soothsayer Manto, daughter of Tiresias, and her son, the hero Ocnus. Virgil was born around 70 BC, and not much else was heard from Mantua until the 11th century, when the city formed part of the vast domains of Countess Matilda of Canossa. Matilda was a great champion of the pope against the emperor; her advisor Anselmo, Bishop of Lucca, became Mantua's patron saint. Even so, as soon as Mantua saw its chance it allied itself with the opposition, beginning an unusually important and lengthy career as an independent Ghibelline *comune*, dominated first by the Bonacolsi family and then the Gonzaga.

Naturally defended on three sides by the Mincio, enriched by river tolls and enjoying the protection and favour of the emperor, Mantua became prominent as a neutral buffer state between the expansionist powers of Milan and Venice. The three centuries of Gonzaga rule, beginning in 1328, brought the city unusual peace and stability, while the refined tastes of the marquesses brought out artists of the highest calibre: Pisanello, Alberti and especially Andrea Mantegna, who was court painter from 1460 until his death in 1506. Gianfrancesco I Gonzaga invited the great Renaissance teacher Vittorino da Feltre to open a school in the city in 1423, where his sons and courtiers, side by side with the children of Mantua's poorer families, were taught according to Vittorino's educational theories, which gave equal emphasis to the intellectual, the physical and the moral. His star pupil was Ludovico (1412–78), one of the most just princes of his day, who did much to create Mantua according to Florentine humanist principles. Ludovico's grandson, Gianfrancesco II, was a military commander who led the Italians against the French at Fornovo, but is perhaps best known in history as the husband of the brilliant and cultivated Isabella d'Este, the foremost culture vulture of her day as well as an astute diplomat, handling most of Mantua's affairs of state for her not very clever husband.

The family fortunes reached their apogee under Isabella's two sons. The eldest, Federico II (1500–40), godson of Cesare Borgia, married Margherita Palaeologo, the heiress of Monferrato, acquiring that duchy for the family as well as a ducal title for the Gonzaga. He hired Raphael's assistant, the Mannerist Giulio Romano ('that rare Italian master', Shakespeare called him in *The Winter's Tale*) to design and adorn his pleasure dome, the Palazzo Tè. When he died his brother, Cardinal Ercole, served as regent for his son Guglielmo, and both of these men, too, proved to be busy builders and civic improvers. The last great Gonzaga,

Vincenzo I, was a patron of Rubens, Fetti and Monteverdi, who composed the first modern opera, *L'Orfeo*, for the Mantuan court in 1607.

But times got hard and in 1628 Vincenzo II sold off many of the Gonzaga's treasures to Charles I of England, including Mantegna's *Triumphs of Caesar*, now at Hampton Court. It's just as well that he did; two years later Mantua suffered a near mortal blow when the Gonzaga's claims to Monferrato came into conflict with the Habsburgs, who were never ones for legal niceties and sent imperial troops to capture and sack the town. The duchy, under a cadet branch of the family, limped along until the Austrians snatched Mantua in 1707, eventually making it the southwest corner of their Quadrilateral.

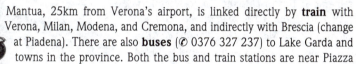

Getting There and Around

Mantua, 25km from Verona's airport, is linked directly by **train** with Verona, Milan, Modena, and Cremona, and indirectly with Brescia (change at Piadena). There are also **buses** (℘ 0376 327 237) to Lake Garda and towns in the province. Both the bus and train stations are near Piazza Porta Belfiore, at the end of Corso Vittorio Emanuele, about 10 minutes' walk from the centre.

Tourist Information

On the corner of Piazza dell'Erbe/Piazza Mantegna 6, ℘ 0376 328 253.

Piazza Mantegna

From the station, Corso Vittorio Emanuele and Corso Umberto I lead straight into the Renaissance heart of Mantua, where the narrow cobbled streets are lined with inviting porticoes, shielding strollers from the sun or rain. Rising up above the rest of the city in Piazza Mantegna is the great basilica of **Sant'Andrea**, designed by the great Florentine humanist Leon Battista Alberti in 1472 to house the Gonzaga's most precious holy relic: two ampoules of Christ's blood, said to have been given to St Andrew by St Longinus, the Roman centurion who pierced Christ's side with his lance. Ludovico Gonzaga had asked Alberti to create a truly monumental edifice to house the relic and form a fitting centrepiece for the city, and Alberti complied. In Florence Alberti had found himself constrained as an architect by his patrons' tastes, but in Mantua he was able to experiment and play with the ancient forms he loved. Sant'Andrea is based on Vitruvius's idea of an Etruscan temple, with a single barrel-vaulted nave supported by side chapels, fronted with a unique façade combining a triumphal arch and a temple. The lofty dome, designed by Juvarra, was completed in 1782. The interior is as grand and imposing as the outside. Andrea Mantegna (*d.* 1506) is buried in the first chapel on the left, with decorations by his followers and a rather stern self-portrait in bronze. The other chapels have fine altarpieces as well, especially the second one on the left, by Lorenzo Costa.

On the east side, the unfinished flank of the basilica is lined with the porticoes and market stalls of the delightful **Piazza dell'Erbe**. Sunk below the level of the modern pavement, the **Rotonda di San Lorenzo**, modelled on the Church of the Holy Sepulchre in Jerusalem, was built by the Countess Matilda in 1082; an ambulatory supports a matroneum for the ladies and there are damaged Romanesque frescoes by the altar. Opposite the tourist office, the **Casa di**

Boniforte da Concorezzo has elegant stucco decoration, almost unchanged since it was built in 1455, while the 13th-century **Palazzo della Ragione** has a stout clock tower topped by an odd little temple and astronomical clock, added during Ludovico's restoration of the palace in 1475. The piazza is closed by the **Broletto**, built in 1227, faces the Piazza del Broletto; note the niche holding a 13th-century statue of Virgil seated near the door. In Piazza Broletto another local hero, this time a racing driver, is remembered in the **Museo Tazio Nuvolari** (*open 10–1 and 3.30–6.30; closed Mon and Thurs; Feb and Mar Sat and Sun only; adm*).

An archway leads into the grand cobbled **Piazza Sordello**, traditional seat of Mantua's bosses. On one side rise the sombre palaces of the Bonacolsi, the Gonzaga's predecessors, with their

Piazza delle Erbe

Torre della Gabbia, named for the iron torture cage they kept to suspend prisoners over the city (though the Mantuans claim it was only used once). At the head of the piazza stands the **Duomo**, with a silly 1756 façade topped by wedding-cake figures that hides a lovely interior with five naves designed by Giulio Romano in 1545. Renaissance tapestries hang in the choir, and the enormous *Trinity* in the apse is by Domenico Fetti, another Roman painter who worked in Mantua in the early 17th century. The 15th-century house at No.23 has become the '**Casa di Rigoletto**' to satisfy the longings of Verdi buffs; opposite, a new archaeology museum is in the works.

The Palazzo Ducale

Open Tues–Sat 9–2 and 2.30–6, Sun 9–2; May–Sept Sun 9–2 and 4–10; to see Camera degli Sposi book in advance, © 0376 320 283; adm exp.

Opposite the Bonacolsi palaces stands that of the Gonzaga, its unimpressive façade hiding one of Italy's most remarkable Renaissance abodes, both in sheer size and the magnificence of its art. The insatiable Gonzaga kept on adding on until they had some 500 rooms in three main structures—the original **Corte Vecchia**, first built by the Bonacolsi in 1290, the 14th-century **Castello**, with its large towers overlooking the lake, and the **Corte Nuova**, designed by Giulio Romano. Throw in the Gonzaga's **Basilica di Santa Barbara** and you have a complex that occupies the entire northeast corner of Mantua. If you go in the winter, dress warmly—it's as cold as a dead duke.

Although stripped of its furnishings and most of its moveable art, the Palazzo Ducale remains imposing, majestic and seemingly endless. One of the first rooms on the tour, the former **chapel**, has a dramatic, half-ruined 14th-century fresco of the Crucifixion, attributed by some to Tommaso da Modena, while another contains a painting of a battle between the Gonzaga and the Bonacolsi in the Piazza Sordello, in which the Gonzaga crushed their rivals once and for all in 1328—although the artist, Domenico Monore, painted the piazza as it appeared in 1494. Even more fascinating than this real battle is the vivid **fresco of Arthurian knights** by

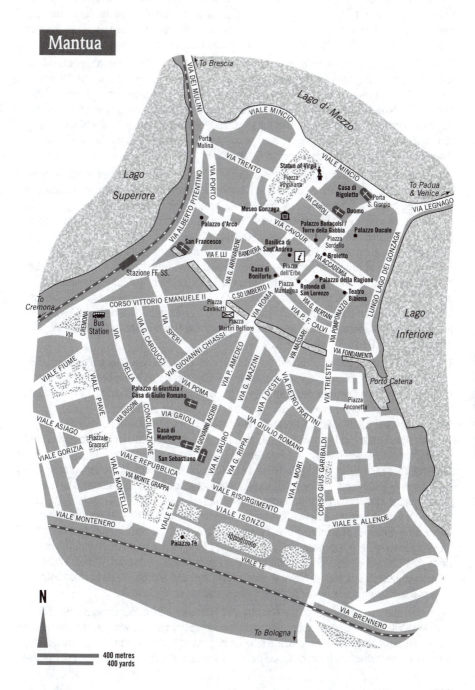

Mantua

To Brescia

VIA DEI MULINI

Lago di Mezzo

VIALE MINCIO

Porta Mulina

VIA TRENTO

VIALE MINCIO

Statue of Virgil

Piazza Virgiliana

Casa di Rigoletto

Porta S. Giorgio

To Padua & Venice

VIA LEGNAGO

Lago Superiore

VIA ALBERTO PITENTINO

VIA PORTO

VIA CAIROLI

Museo Gonzaga

Duomo

VIA CAVOUR

Palazzo d'Arco

Palazzo Bonacolsi / Torre della Gabbia

Palazzo Ducale

San Francesco

VIA F. LLI BANDIERA

VIA G. ARRIVABENE

Basilica di Sant'Andrea

Piazza Sordello

Broletto

VIA ACCADEMIA

LUNGO LAGO DEI GONZAGA

Stazione FF. SS.

Casa di Boniforte

Piazza dell'Erbe

Palazzo della Ragione

Piazza Mantegna

Rotonda di San Lorenzo

Teatro Bibiena

To Cremona

CORSO VITTORIO EMANUELE II

C.SO UMBERTO I

VIA ROMA

VIA G. BERTANI

VIA POMPONAZZO

Lago Inferiore

VIA CREMONA

VIA

Bus Station

Piazza Cavallotti

Piazza Martiri Belfiore

VIA P. F. CALVI

Porto Catena

VIA G. CARDUCCI

VIA G. SPERI

VIA GIOVANNI CHIASSI

VIA P. AMEDEO

VIA G. MAZZINI

VIA MASSARI

VIA TRIESTE

VIA FONDAMENTA

Piazza Anconetta

VIALE FIUME

VIA DELLA

VIA DUGONI

VIA POMA

Palazzo di Giustizia / Casa di Giulio Romano

VIA GIOVANNI ACERBI

VIA I D'ESTE

VIA PIETRO FRATTINI

Piazza

VIALE PIANE

VIA GRIOLI

Casa di Mantegna

San Sebastiano

VIA N. SAURO

VIA G. RIPPA

VIA GIULIO ROMANO

CORSO GIUS GARIBALDI

VIALE ASIAGO

Piazzale Gramsci

VIA CONCILAZIONE

VIALE REPUBBLICA

VIA A. MORI

VIALE GORIZIA

VIA MONTE GRAPPA

VIALE MONTELLO

VIALE TE

VIALE RISORGIMENTO

VIALE ISONZO

VIALE S. ALLENDE

VIALE MONTENERO

Ippodromo

Palazzo Te

VIALE TE

VIA BRENNERO

To Bologna

N

400 metres
400 yards

Pisanello, Italy's International Gothic master. Recorded as damaged in the 1480s, the fresco was believed lost until 1969, when layers of plaster were stripped away to reveal a remarkable work commissioned by Gianfrancesco Gonzaga in 1442 to commemorate his receiving from Henry VI the concession to use the heraldic SS collar of the House of Lancaster, an insignia that forms the border of Pisanello's mural, mingled with marigolds, a Gonzaga emblem.

Beyond this are the remodelled **neoclassical rooms**, holding a set of Flemish tapestries from Raphael's Acts of the Apostles cartoons (now in the Victoria and Albert Museum). Woven in the early 1500s, these copies of the Vatican originals are in a much better state of preservation. Beyond, the **Sala dello Zodiaco** has vivacious 1580 frescoes by Lorenzo Costa; the **Sala del Fiume** is named for its fine views over the river; and the **Galleria degli Specchi** has mirrors and mythological frescoes and, by the door, a note from Monteverdi on the days and hours of the musical evenings he directed there in the 1600s.

The Gonzaga were mad about horses and dogs and had one room, the **Salone degli Arcieri**, painted with *trompe l'œil* frescoes of their favourite steeds standing on upper ledges; the family used to play a kind of guessing game with them, when curtains would be drawn over the figures. Sharing the room are works by Tintoretto and a family portrait by Rubens, court painter under Vincenzo I, a picture so large that Napoleon's troops had to cut it up to carry it off. The duke's apartments hold a fine collection of classical statuary: busts of the emperors, a Hellenistic torso of Aphrodite, and the 'Apollo of Mantova', inherited from Sabbioneta after Vespasiano's death. The **Sala di Troia** has vivid 1536 frescoes by Giulio Romano and his pupil, Rinaldo Mantovano, while another ducal chamber has a beautiful 17th-century labyrinth painted on the ceiling, each path inscribed in gold with 'Maybe Yes, Maybe No'. From some of the rooms you can look out over the grassy **Cortile della Cavallerizza**, with rustic façades by Giulio Romano.

The oldest part of the palace complex, the 14th-century **Castello San Giorgio**, is reached by a low spiral ramp, built especially for the horses the Gonzaga could never bear to be without. Here, in the famous **Camera degli Sposi**, are the remarkable frescoes painted by Mantegna in 1474, who like a genie captured the essence of the Gonzaga in this small bottle of a room. Restored to their brilliant original colours, the frescoes depict the life of Ludovico Gonzaga, with his wife Barbara of Brandenburg, his children, dwarves, servants, dogs and horses, and important events—greeting his son Francesco, recently made a cardinal, and playing host to Emperor Frederick III and King Christian I of Denmark. The portraits are unflattering and solid, those of real people not for public display, almost like a family photo album. The effect is like stumbling on the court of the Sleeping Beauty; only the younger brother, holding the new cardinal's hand, seems to suspect that he has been enchanted. Wife Barbara and her stern dwarf stare out, as if determined to draw the spectator into the eerie scene. And there is a lingering sorcery here, for these frescoes are fruit of Mantegna's fascination with the myste-rious new science of perspective. The beautiful backgrounds of imaginary cities and ruins reflect Mantegna's other love, classical architecture, but add another element of unreality in their realistic vividness, as do his *trompe l'œil* decorations on the ceiling.

From here the tour continues to the **Casetta dei Nani**, residence of the dwarfs, tiny rooms with low ceilings and shallow stairs, although there are party-poopers who say the rooms had a pious purpose, and were meant to bring the sinning dukes to their proud knees. The last stop is the **suite of Isabella d'Este**, designed by her as a retreat after her husband's death. In these little rooms Isabella held court as the Renaissance's most imperious and demanding patron, practically commanding Leonardo and Titian to paint her portrait; at one point she commissioned an allegorical canvas from Perugino so exacting that she sketched what she wanted and set spies to make sure the painter followed orders. Given an excellent classical education in her native Ferrara, she surrounded herself with humanists, astrologers, poets and scholars. Her fabulous art collection has long gone to the Louvre, but the inexplicable emblems and symbols she devised with her astrologers remain like faint ghosts from a lost world on the ceiling.

Around Town

There are several sights within easy walking distance of the Palazzo Ducale. At Via Accademia 47, east of the Broletto, the **Teatro Accademico Bibiena** (*open Mon–Sat 9.30–12.30 and 3–6; adm*) is a gem built by Antonio Galli Bibiena, a member of the famous Bolognese family of theatre builders. Mozart, aged 13, performed at the inaugural concert in 1770; father Leopold said it was the most beautiful theatre he had ever seen.

West of the Piazza Sordello, Via Cairoli leads to the city's main park, the **Piazza Virgiliana**, with a marble statue of Virgil from 1927 (in time for the poet's 2000th birthday) and the **Museo Gonzaga** (*open April–June Tues–Sun 9.30–12 and 2.30–5; July and Aug Thurs, Sat, Sun only; Nov–Mar Sun only; adm*), containing artefacts and treasures that once belonged to the family. Further west, in the Piazza d'Arco, the **Palazzo d'Arco** (*open Nov–Feb Sat 10–12.30 and 2–5, Sun 10–5; Mar–Sept Tues–Fri 10–12.30 and 2.30–6, Sat and Sun 10–6; adm*) was rebuilt in 1784 over a 15th-century palace for the arty counts from Garda's north shore and has been left more or less as it was, complete with furnishings, paintings, instruments, a superb kitchen and, in a room preserved from the original palace, fascinating frescoes of the zodiac, attributed to Giovanni Maria Falconetto of Verona and painted *c.* 1515 in the period between Mantegna's death and Giulio Romano's arrival. The nearby church of **San Francesco** (1304) was rediscovered in 1944, when a bomb hit the arsenal that had disguised it for a century and a half. Restored to its original state, it contains frescoes by the excellent Tommaso da Modena in the last chapel on the right.

South of the medieval nucleus, just off main Via Principe Amedeo at Via Poma 18, the **Casa di Giulio Romano** was designed by the artist himself in 1544 while working on the Palazzo Tè. He also gets credit for the quaint palace decorated with monsters nearby; the heavy **Palazzo di Giustizia** at No. 22 was built in the 1620s. Mantegna also designed his dream house, the **Casa del Mantegna**, in the same neighbourhood, at Via Acerbi 47 (*open daily 10–12.30 and 3–6 when an exhibition is on; otherwise Mon–Fri 10–12.30*). Designed as a cube built around a circular courtyard, he intended it partially as his personal museum and embellished it with classical 'Mantegnesque' decorations. Opposite stands the rather neglected **San Sebastiano** (1460), the second church in Mantua designed by Alberti, this one in the form of a Greek cross.

A Renaissance Pleasure Dome: the Palazzo Tè

Open Tues–Sun 9–6, Mon 1–6; adm exp.

At the end of Via Acerbi is Giulio Romano's masterpiece, the marvellous Palazzo Tè , its name derived not from tea, but from the rather less savoury *tejeto*, a local word for a drainage canal. On a former swamp, drained for a horsey Gonzaga pleasure ground, work began in 1527 when Federico II had Giulio Romano expand the stables to create a little palace for his mistress, Isabella Boschetti, of whom his mother, Isabella d'Este, disapproved. The project expanded over the decades to become a guest house suitable for the emperor Charles V, who visited twice.

Giulio Romano had moved from Rome to Mantua in 1524 to escape prison for designing a series of pornographic prints. In his Palazzo Tè, one of the very first great Mannerist buildings, he had the same desire to shock and amaze and upset the cool classicism exemplified in Mantua by Alberti, and along the way he created one of the great Renaissance syntheses of architecture and art, combining *trompe l'œil* with a bold play between the structure of the room and the frescoes. Most of the art still has classical themes: the **Sala della Metamorfosi** is inspired by Ovid and Roman frescoes, which Giulio discovered with his master Raphael in Nero's Golden House in Rome. Gonzaga emblems fill the **Sala delle Imprese**: putti holding a cup, a belt, a bird catching fish, a muzzle, Mt Olympus, the salamander (a symbol of Federico's love, which is consumed, but doesn't burn); the chariot of the sun on the ceiling is a first hint of Giulio's love of wacky perspectives. The next room has more life-size Gonzaga horses up on ledges, and in the next, the **Sala di Psiche**, all glory bursts forth in the intense colours and exuberance of the scenes from *The Golden Ass* of Apuleius. The **Camera dei Venti** was Federico's private study, designed with the most precious materials and with a complex iconographic programme based on ancient astrological texts, each scene illustrating a prediction linked to a rising constellation.

The **Loggia di Davide**, quickly thrown up for Charles V's second visit in 1532, is decorated with scenes dear to Federico's heart—he identified himself with the king, and his Isabella with Bathsheba, both of whom were relieved of their husbands in suspicious circumstances. The next room has incredible antiquizing stuccoes by Francesco Primaticcio, who later went on to Fontainebleau to work for François I. The climax, however, is the famous **Sala dei Giganti**, Giulio's most startling work, entirely frescoed from floor to ceiling. Above, Zeus and Co. rain lightning, thunder, boulders and earthquakes down on the uppity Titans, creating so powerful an illusion of chaos that it seems as if the very room is about to cave in around the spectator.

Activities

Several **boat** companies operate on Mantua's lakes and the River Mincio, including **Motonavi Andes**, Piazza Sordello 8, © 0376 322 875, ✆ 322 869. A pleasant 1½hr trip past Gonzaga castles, a beautiful bridge designed by Nervi, water-lilies, water chestnut farms and flocks of egrets costs L14,000, children L10,000; the company also sails to San Benedetto Po (*see* below)

Mantua ✉ *46100*   **Where to Stay**

Do book: Mantua's few hotels tend to fill up fast.

expensive

★★★★   **San Lorenzo**, Piazza Concordia 14, © 0376 220 500, ✆ 0376 327 194, is housed in a restored late Renaissance building in the central pedestrian zone, with views over the Piazza dell'Erbe. The rooms have most comforts; guests have free access to a gym, and from the terrace there are views across to the dome of Sant'Andrea.

★★★★ Rechigi, Via Calvi 30, ✆ 0376 320 781, 🖃 0376 220 291, is conveniently located in the historic centre; all rooms have satellite TV, air-conditioning and comfortable furnishings. The hotel has ample parking and hires out bikes.

moderate

★★★ Due Guerrieri, Piazza Sordello 52, ✆ 0376 321 533, 🖃 0376 329 645, is housed in an older building overlooking the Palazzo Ducale. There are baths in every room, and a parking garage nearby.

★★★ Bianchi Stazione, Piazza Don Leoni 24, ✆ 0376 326 465, 🖃 0376 321 504. Near the station and recently renovated.

★★ ABC, Piazza le Stazione 25, ✆ 0376 323 347, 🖃 0376 322 329, by the station, has small cell-like rooms arranged around an inner courtyard with space for parking; those without en suite baths fall into the inexpensive category.

cheap

★ Maragò, just outside the centre at Virgiliana, ✆ 0376 370 313, has 13 simple rooms, not all with bath, and parking.

Ostello Sparafucile, Lunetta di San Giorgio, ✆ 0376 372 465, is an exceptional hostel, just outside the city on the Lago di Mezzo. Occupying a 15th-century castle, popularly believed to be the headquarters of the baddie in *Rigoletto*, the interior has been remodelled, but without losing any of its character. Cheap meals are also available. *Closed 15 Oct–1 April; take bus nos.2 or 9 from Piazza Cavallotti.*

Villa-farmhouses in the province of Mantua have been developed as inexpensive accommodation, averaging around L40,000 per person per night; book well in advance. Some of the most convenient for the city include **Corte Schiarino-Lena**, ✆ 0376 398 238, at Sant'Antonio, on the other side of Lago Superiore from Mantua, where rooms around a 16th-century courtyard have been converted into apartments. **Corte Bersaglio**, Via L. Guerra, at Migliaretto, just outside Mantua, ✆ 0376 320 345, has a stable with plenty of opportunities for a canter in the countryside. On the cycling route to Peschiera on Lake Garda, **Corte Prada Alta**, Strada San Girolamo 9, ✆ 0376 391 144, hires bikes. **Corte Feniletto**, 13km from Mantua at Rodigo, ✆ 0376 650 262, is a fully functioning farm in the midst of the Regional Park of the Mincio which offers boating excursions on the river.

Mantua ✉ *46100*   ***Eating Out***

During the long reign of the Gonzaga the Mantuans developed their own particular cuisine, which other Italians regard as a little peculiar. The notorious *stracotto di asino* (donkey stew) heads the list, but the Mantuans also have a predilection for adding Lambrusco to broth and soup. The classic Mantuan *primi* include *agnoli* stuffed with bacon, salami, chicken livers and cheese cooked in broth, *risotto alla pilota* (with onion, butter and local grana cheese), *risotto con salamelle* (with fresh salami) or *tortelli di zucca* (little pasta caps stuffed with pumpkin, mustard and cheese, served with melted butter). The local lake and river fish—catfish, eel, crayfish, pike (the delicious *luccio in salsa* is prepared with peppers and capers) and bass—and crispy deep-fried frog's legs are traditional second courses.

Mantua is also a good place to taste true, natural Lambrusco, which must be drunk young (a year or so old) to be perfectly lively and sparkling; the test is to see if the foam vanishes instantly when poured into a glass. There are three main kinds: the grand *Lambrusco di Sorbana*, the mighty *Lambrusco di Santa Croce* and the amiable *Lambrusco di Castelvetro*.

expensive

The lovely **Aquila Nigra**, Vicolo Bonaclosi 4, ✆ 0376 327 180, with its marble and traces of frescoes, serves exquisitely prepared regional dishes and others; the pasta courses (ravioli filled with truffled duck, for instance) are a joy, and there's a wide choice of seafood as well as meat dishes. A large selection of Italian and French wines, cheeses and delicious desserts like chestnut torte round off a special meal. *Closed Sun, Mon, Aug*. **Trattoria dei Martini**, Piazza d'Arco, ✆ 0376 327 101, overlooks an inner garden and has a menu that changes according to season, although solidly based on local cuisine—tagliatelle with duck, lamb casseroled with herbs, or roast guinea fowl; around L60,000. *Closed Mon, Tues, and first part of Aug*.

moderate

In a superbly renovated 14th-century palace, **San Gervasio**, Via San Gervasio 13, ✆ 0376 327 077, offers an excellent *menu mantovano* at L60,000 and has lunch bargains as well. *Closed Wed and Sun eve, and Aug*. In the summer, the tables fill up early at the **Ristorante Pavesi dal 1918**, Piazza delle Erbe ✆ 0376 323 627, where the service is friendly and they do a particularly good *gnocchi alla gorgonzola*. *Closed Thurs*. Away from the obvious tourist areas, the small **Trattoria Quattrotette**, Vicolo Nazione, ✆ 0376 329 478, squeezes in hordes of local clientele who cherish the dishes of vegetables and salads—*melanzana grillata, carciofi alla giudia* and *peperonata* —steaming hot bowls of pasta, and pasticceria. *Closed Sun*. **Al Garibaldini**, Via S. Longino 7, ✆ 0376 328 263, is in the historic centre, in a fine old house with a shady garden for al fresco dining. The menu features many Mantuan dishes, with especially good risotto and *tortelli di zucca*, fish and meat dishes. *Closed Wed, Jan*.

cheap

For no atmosphere but delicious Mantuan cooking at a very accessible price try the **Trattoria al Lago**, Piazza Arche 5, ✆ 0376 323 300. *Closed Mon*. **Due Cavallini**, Via Salnitro 5 (near Lago Inferiore, off Corso Garibaldi), ✆ 0376 322 084, is the place if you want to bite into some donkey meat—though it has other less ethnic dishes as well. *Closed Tues, and late-July –late-Aug*. **Il Portichetto**, Via Portichetto 14, ✆ 0376 360 747, is run by a former left-wing activist who has turned his hand to cooking. The results are excellent. The menu revolves around local river-fish—mixed *antipasti*, tagliatelle with perch or pike in salsa verde—and there are lots of vegetarian options. *Closed Sun eve, and Mon*. **L'Ochina Bianca**, Via Finzi 2, ✆ 0376 323 700, has an ever-changing menu which might include such treats as smoked beef dressed with superb olive oil, deep-fried zucchini flowers, delicate home-made pasta and succulent meat dishes. *Closed Mon and Tues lunch*.

Mantua's western lake, **Lago Superiore**, is noted for its delicate lotus blossoms, planted in the 1930s as an experiment. They have since thrived, and turn the lake violet and pink in July and August around the city's park, the **Valletta Belfiore**. Another park, the **Bosco della Fontana** (*open Oct–Mar daily 9.30–5.30, April–Sept daily 8.30–7.30; adm weekends*) lies 5km to the north off the road to Brescia. Once a Gonzaga hunting reserve, with a moated little castle built as a hunting lodge in 1595, the Bosco's ancient, broad-leafed trees are a last relic of the ancient forest that once covered the Po plain, and its shady paths and streamlets are a tempting retreat from the afternoon heat. If you're in Mantua on 15 August be sure to visit the **Sanctuary of the Madonna delle Grazie**, on the banks of Lago Superiore at Curtatone, where there's an unusual art competition for the *madonnari*—artists who draw sidewalk chalk portraits of the Madonna—among other diversions. Built as a votive offering by Francesco I after the plague of 1399, the church has a 15th-century frescoed ceiling, paintings by Lorenzo Costa, and a great hotchpotch of votive offerings, including a stuffed crocodile.

San Benedetto Po

Some 22km southeast of Mantua (connected in the summer by boats, sailing down the Mincio to the Po), San Benedetto Po grew up around the Benedictine abbey of **Polirone** (*open daily 8–12 and 2.30–7*), the 'Monte Cassino of the North', established in the year 1007 by the Canossa counts of Turscany. It was especially favoured by the last of their line, the feisty Countess Matilda (*d. 1115*), whose alabaster sarcophagus survives in the richly appointed **Basilica di San Benedetto**, rebuilt in the 1540s by Giulio Romano and linked to the 12th-century church of **Santa Maria**, which preserves a fine mosaic of 1151. There are three cloisters and a refectory with frescoes by Correggio, now part of the **Museo dell'Abbazia** (*open April–May Mon–Fri 9–12.30 and 2.30–5, Sat and Sun 9–12.30 and 2.30–6; June–mid-Nov Sat 2.30–6, Sun 10.30–12.30 and 3.30–7; rest of year Sat 2.30–6, Sun 10–12 (Mar 10.30–12.30) and 2.30–6; adm*). Another part of the monastery contains the **Museo della Cultura Popolare Padana**, ✆ 0376 615 977 (*open June–mid-Nov Mon–Fri 9–12.20 and 2.30–5.50, Sat and Sun 9–12.20 and 3.30–7.50; Mar Mon–Fri 9–12.20 and 2–5.20, Sat and Sun 9–12.20 and 2.30–5.50; April–May Mon–Fri 9–5.20, Sat and Sun 9–12.20 and 2.30–5.50; adm*), devoted to the traditions and culture of the surrounding countryside. Countess Matilda also built the handsome Romanesque **San Lorenzo** near the cemetery in **Pegognaga**, 9km southwest.

Sabbioneta

Set midway between Mantua, Cremona and Parma, Sabbioneta was a rural village backwater until 1556, when its new prince, Vespasiano Gonzaga Colonna, decided to rebuild it from scratch as the capital of his little Ruritania. A member of a cadet branch of the Gonzaga family, Vespasiano had earned his title fighting and building fortifications for Philip II of Spain, but he never forgot his Gonzaga grounding in the classics. His Sabbioneta would be a rational expression of humanistic ideals, with a content and a military, civic and cultural function, a walled 'Little Athens' on the Po plain. He gets credit as the first to consider urban planning as an act of government. It seemed like a good idea at the time.

A New Renaissance City

The idea of building a whole new city in the lifetime of a single man had already been made possible by technological advances on the construction site. Many of these techniques first came into being during the construction of Brunelleschi's dome over Florence Cathedral; one thing Brunelleschi did was abolish the medieval 'mechanical' system, composed of skilled workers working under master masons, in favour of a 'liberal' system in which there was only one planner and his manual labourers.

Equally fundamental was the evolution of the city from the Middle Ages, when it was an organic body, founded on a community of interest between the merchants and craftsmen who lived in it, to the 15th and 16th centuries, when it lost its liberties and became nothing more than the seat of a higher power, a *signore* or a king—a reflection of his greater glory. Public buildings became increasingly grand, and open spaces were arranged as a stage for the ceremonies of church and state. Architects and artists were inspired by Leon Battista Alberti's monumental *De re aedificatoria* (1452), which drew on Vitruvius in its aim to orchestrate the humanist recreation of the ancient city and its monuments. For the first time since antiquity, changes in a city's structure and plan were brought about from above by an absolute prince and his architects.

Architectural treatises of the time are filled with geometrical designs of ideal cities, usually set in massive defensive works around polygonal walls, often star-shaped, the better to deflect bullets and cannonballs. According to Alberti, single buildings must always be conceived in their urban context, the whole plan of which must follow the rule of perspective, proportion and symmetry—leading to the fanciful urban backgrounds of many Renaissance paintings. Vespasiano Gonzaga was one of the few readers of Alberti ever actually to build his city and apply his ideals. One of these was a great tolerance and respect for ancient learning, something that attracted many Jewish settlers. The press the Foà family established in Sabbioneta between 1551 and 1590 was famous for the excellence of its Hebrew editions.

The Tour

Unfortunately for Sabbioneta, humanism was out of fashion even before the city was built. When its creator died without an heir his principality reverted to Mantua and became a backwater once more, a little museum city of unfulfilled expectations with the haunting, empty air of a De Chirico painting. In the last 15 years, however, interest in Sabbioneta has been rekindled, and much has been restored; antique shops and restaurants have begun to fill some of the houses. The fascinating interiors of the principal monuments, however, can only be seen by guided tour (1½ hours) from the Pro Loco at the end of the brick atrium on Via V. Gonzaga 31, ✆ 0375 52039 (*open April–Sept Tues–Sat 9.30–12.30 and 2.30–6, Sun 9.30–12.30 and 2.30–7; Oct–Mar Tues–Sat 9.30–12.30 and 2.30–5, Sun 9.30–12.30 and 2.30–6; ring ahead to book a tour in English; adm*).

Vespasiano laid out Sabbioneta in polygonal star-shaped walls with two gates linked by the central axis of the main street. The street plan is rectangular, harking back to the style of an ancient Roman *castrum*, although tricks such as two off-centred main squares, irregular blocks and streets that narrow at their ends lend an illusion of greater space within the walls. In the larger square, Piazza Castello, Vespasiano constructed his castle (demolished in the 18th century) and erected a column topped with a statue of Sabbioneta's patroness, the goddess of wisdom, Athena, a classical Greek work that his father Rodomonte is said to have picked up in the infamous Sack of Rome. Along one side of the Piazza Castello runs a long brick atrium to Vespasiano's pleasure palace, a mini-version of the Palazzo Tè in Mantua called the **Palazzo del Giardino**. Its elegant marbled façade, its original windows and doors and gardens are long gone, but the rich frescoes and stuccoes by the school of Giulio Romano and Bernardino Campi remain fairly intact: grotesques, mythologies, urban perspectives (onewas apparently used for the stage of the Teatro all'Antica), imitation arbours that once led out to real garden arbours, monochrome Caesars, beautifully detailed animals, Roman circuses, landscapes in the Room of Mirrors, and a room dedicated to myths and Gonzaga *imprese*: uprooted branches, muzzles, dogs looking backwards and a burning temple, a reference to the Sack of Rome.

The Palazzo del Giardino was linked to the castle by way of the **Galleria degli Antichi,** a long frescoed corridor or *ambulacrum*, the height of architectural fashion in Renaissance France and Italy; Sabbioneta's, at 317ft, is the third longest after the Vatican's Map Gallery and Florence's Galleria degli Uffizi. The portico underneath allowed enjoyment of the gardens in inclement weather, while Vespasiano used the upper gallery to display his extensive collection of classical art (now in Mantua's Palazzo Ducale). *Trompe l'œil* perspectives on either end of the gallery make it seem even longer, while allegorical figures frescoed over the 26 windows represent virtues, sciences and seasons; they are attributed to Pietro Martire Pesenti, a master of the subtle art of painting *contrapposto* figures and architectural backgrounds that seemingly change their position, depending on the angle from which they are viewed.

The next stop on the tour, the **Teatro all'Antica** (1588), was designed by Vicenzo Scamozzi, Palladio's greatest pupil, inspired by Palladio's famous Teatro Olimpico in Vicenza and Sebastiano Serlio's *L'Idea dell'Architettura Universale* (1538), one of Vespasiano's chief sources for building his ideal city. Sabbioneta's theatre was abandoned at Vespasiano's demise; the roof crashed down on the stage and destroyed the permanent imaginary city set, and it was used as a cinema until the 1960s. What survived all these vicissitudes has been restored: the rectangular orchestra, backed by a peristyle topped with twelve plaster statues of the gods, while around the balcony where the duke and the nobility sat are busts and monochrome frescoes of the Caesars standing in alcoves. Other frescoes show scenes of Rome, and around the orchestra *trompe l'œil* boxes of chatting spectators and musicians in 16th-century costumes watch the performance. Note the man with the scissors near the stage: a barber-surgeon, he was immortalized for trepanning Vespasiano to relieve the painful pressure on his brain. The hole in his skull was successfully reopened four times; the fifth time killed the prince at age 60.

The tour continues to the octagonal church of the **Incoronata** (1586) with its impressive *trompe l'œil* dome from 1769 (Vespasiano originally intended it to be gilded) and Vespasiano's tomb in rare and antique marbles, with a bronze statue of the prince in Roman garb by Michelangelo's student Leone Leoni (1588). Vespasiano's hand is held out, as if to mould his city; the statue was originally intended for the Piazza Ducale. In 1988 the tomb was excavated, revealing not only the prince's trepanned skull but his collar of the Order of the Golden Fleece, now in the Museo dell'Arte Sacra.

Sabbioneta's second piazza contains the **Palazzo Ducale**, the first building erected by Vespasiano. Although much damaged, changed and ham-handedly restored over the centuries, it has kept its simple stately façade with five arches. A number of frescoed rooms with intricately carved Venetian ceilings have survived, one—the Sala d'Oro—completely covered with gold leaf. The large Room of the Eagles contains four wooden equestrian statues of Vespasiano and his direct ancestors, made in Venice; originally there were ten, but only four horsemen survived intact (along with five busts) from a fire in the 19th century. Vespasiano's private study is decorated with stucco reliefs of his more illustrious ancestors. The Sala degli Elefanti has a rare portrayal of elephants in a triumphal march, and two frescoes, of Genoa and Constantinople, surviving of the original ten paintings of port towns. The palace shares the square with the pink and white marble checked church of the **Assumption**, its interior given a delightful rococo treatment in the 18th century; the artistic fireworks are in the Bibiena chapel, with its fretwork double dome with a blue sky background and a reliquary cabinet full of wax martyrs.

A small **Museo dell'Arte Sacra** contains some sleepy religious paintings, brass band instruments and the Collar of the Golden Fleece, awarded to Vespasiano in 1585 by Philip II. This is an exceedingly rare authenticated example of the highest honour of Spanish knighthood and has become the prototype by which all others are judged. Near here the **Synagogue**, rebuilt in the 1820s and still consecrated, has displays tracing the history of Judaism in the region.

Sabbioneta ✉ *46018*   ### Where to Stay and Eating Out

In the centre **★★Al Duca**, Via della Stamperia 18, ✆ 0375 52474, 🖷 0375 22021 (*cheap*) offers largish, comfortable enough rooms with en suite baths and TV sets; similar if more simple facilities may be had at **★Giulia Gonzaga**, Via V. Gonzaga 65, ✆ 0375 528 164 (*cheap*) for less.

Of the many restaurants the two best are just outside the city walls: the elegant **Parco Cappuccini**, Via Santuario 30, ✆ 0375 52002, 🖷 0375 220 056 (*expensive*) occupies an 18th-century villa with a veranda on the park, an inviting place to linger over classic Italian cuisine. *Closed Mon and Wed eve.* **Il Capriccio**, Via Solazzi 51 (the Mantua–Parma road), ✆/🖷 0375 52722 (*moderate*) serves delicious creative dishes based on Mantuan tradition, with a L25,000 lunch menu. *Closed Tues eve and Wed.*

For a real treat (close to the very expensive price range) drive 20km north to Canneto sull'Oglio (just beyond Piadena), where you can feast at one of Lombardy's finest and most tranquil restaurants, **Dal Pescatore**, Località Runate 13, ✆ 0376 70304 (*very expensive; book well in advance*). In an elegant country villa, filled with antiques and oriental rugs, the ever-inventive Nadia Santini—Italy's most talented woman chef—enchants the privileged few (the dining room with its charming fireplace holds a maximum of 30 people) with her exquisite light cuisine using the best and freshest of produce, much of it picked that morning at the Santini family farm. Mantovan favourites like *tortelli de zucca* reach a kind of epiphany, served up with the best wines, the most civilized service and a bill at the end hovering around L110,000 per person excluding wine. *Closed Mon, Tues, much of Aug, and two weeks in Jan.*

Lakes Orta and Maggiore

The westernmost lakes, Orta and Maggiore, evoke a soft, dreamy image of romance and beauty, a Latin Brigadoon of counts, dowagers, poets and opera composers strolling through gardens, sketching landscapes, and perhaps indulging in a round of whist on the villa veranda in the evening. The backgrounds to their fond pleasures are scenes woven of poetry: of mountains tumbling steeply into ribbons of blue and islands floating enticingly just offshore; of mellowed villas under the palms, with perfect gardens tended for hundreds of years; of spring's excess, when the lakes become drunken with colour, as a thousand varieties of azalea, rhododendron and camellia spill over the banks, blooming even at the foot of the starlit Alps.

This chapter also takes in the lovely alpine valleys of the Ossola north of Orta and Varese, increasingly a bedroom suburb of Milan but one with a few surprises up its sleeve.

Lake Orta and Domodossola

Lake Orta (the Lacus Cusius of the Romans), the westernmost lake and the only one totally in the confines of Piedmont, is relatively pint-sized, stretching a mere 13km at its longest point. But what it lacks in volume it compensates with an exceptional dose of charm: a lake 'made to the measurements of man' that can be encompassed by a glance, surrounded by hills made soft with greenery, a haven from the excesses of tourism that sometimes scar the major lakes. Nietzsche, not a man to fall in love, did so on its soft green shores. He didn't get the girl, but the world got *Thus Spake Zarathustra.*

The waters of Lake Orta are enchanted in the moonlight, and in the centre they hold a magical isle, illuminated on summer nights to glow like a golden fairy castle in the dark. On a more mundane level, Orta's villages produce bathroom taps, saxophones, coffee pots and some of its finest chefs; so many come from Armeno that the second Sunday each November it holds an annual reunion of cooks and waiters.

Getting Around

The main lake resorts, Orta San Giulio, Pettenasco and Omegna, are easily reached from Turin or Milan on **trains** heading north to Domodossola and the Simplon Pass. Orta is also easy to reach from Lake Maggiore: a rail line links Stresa to Arona and **buses** run from Arona to Orta, and from Verbania to Omegna.

Navigazione Lago d'Orta, © 0322 844 862, provides a **boat** service at least twice a day between the ports of Oria, Omegna, Punta di Crabbia, Pettenasco, L'Approdo, Orta, Isola San Giulio, Pella, San Filiberto and Lagna. The company also offers a midnight cruise from Orta, Pella and Pettenasco on Saturday and Sunday in July and August.

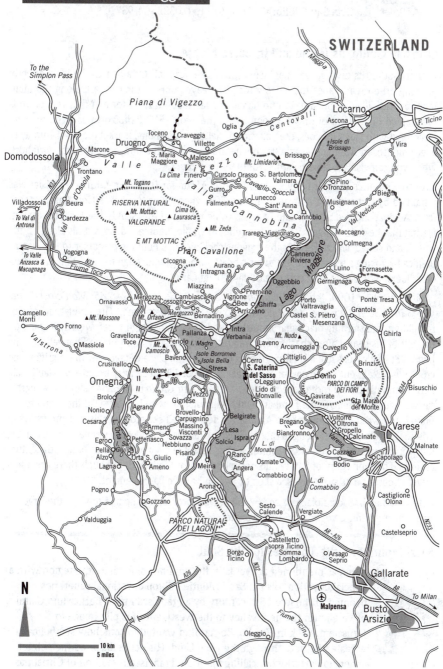

Lakes Orta and Maggiore

SWITZERLAND

To the
Simplon Pass

Piana di Vigezzo

Locarno

Ascona

F. Ticino

Vira

Centovalli

Toceno
Craveggia
Oglia
Villette

Druogno

Marone

S. Maria
Maggiore
Malesco

Brissago

Isole di
Brissago

Domodossola

Mt. Limidario

Pino
Tronzano

Biegno

Trontano

La Cima
Finero

Cursolo Orasso
Valmara

S. Bartolomeo

Val
d'Ossola

Valle
Vigezzo

Gurro

Cavaglio-Spoccia

Musignano

Villadossola

Beura

Mt. Togano

RISERVA NATURAL

Falmenta

Lunecco

Sant' Anna

Cannobio

Val Veddasca

To Val di
Antrona

Cardezza

Mt. Mottac

Cima di
Laurasca

Valle

Cannobina

Maccagno

VALGRANDE

Mt. Zeda

Trarego-Viggiona

Colmegna

To Valle
Anzasca &
Macugnaga

Vogogna

E MT MOTTAC

Pran Cavallone

Cannero
Riviera

Luino

Fornasette

Cicogna

Fiume Toce

Aurano
Intragna

Oggebbio

Germignaga

Cremenaga

Campello
Monti

Ornavasso

Forno

Mt. Massone

Mergozzo

Cossogno

Miazzina

Cambiasca

Vignone

Bee

Premeno

Ghiffa

Porto
Valtravaglia

Castel S. Pietro

Ponte Tresa

Grantola

N233

Massiola

Mt. Orfano

L. di
Mergozzo

Bernardino

Arizzano

Mesenzana

Ghirla

Valstrona

Crusinallo

Gravellona
Toce

Mt.
Camoscio

Pallanza

Feriolo

Baveno

I. Madre

Intra
Verbania

Isole Borromee
Isola Bella

Laveno

Mt. Nudo

Arcumeggia

Cuveglio

Cittiglio

Brinzio

Bisuschio

Omegna

Mottarone

Vezzo

Cerro
S. Caterina
del Sasso

Orino

PARCO DI CAMPO
DEI FIORI

Broglio

Gignese

Leggiuno

Lido di
Monvalle

Gavirate

Sta Maria
del Monte

Nonio

Agrano

Brovello
Carpugnino

Belgirate

Bregano

Voltorre

Oltrona

Varese

Cesara

Armeno

Massino
Visconti

Lesa

Biandronno

Gropello

Calcinate

Egro

Pettenasco

Sovazza

Ispra

Solcio

Cazzago

Capolago

Malnate

Pella

Alzo

Orta S. Giulio

Pisano

Ranco

L. di
Monate

Bodio

Lagna

Ameno

Meina

Osmate

Pogno

Angera

Comabbio

L. di
Comabbio

Castiglione
Olona

Valduggia

Arona

Castelseprio

Gozzano

Sesto
Calende

Vergiate

N233

PARCO NATURALE
DEI LAGONI

Castelletto
sopra Ticino
Somma
Lombardo

Arsago
Seprio

Gallarate

Borgo
Ticino

Malpensa

Busto
Arsizio

To Milan

Oleggio

Fiume Ticino

N

10 km

5 miles

131

Orta San Giulio: Via Olina 9/11, © 0322 911 937.

Orta San Giulio, its Island and its Sacro Monte

Blithely set on its own garden peninsula, the lake's 'capital' Orta San Giulio is a perfectly fetching little town. Lanes too narrow for cars (leave yours in the car park along the main road, by the Villa Crespi) all lead into handsome lakeside **Piazza Motta**, a cosy rendez-vous nicknamed the *salotto* or drawing room, with the bijou 1582 **Palazzotto** as a centrepiece. Decorated with faded frescoes, the Palazzotto shelters a bric-a-brac market the first Saturday of every month. In April and May, Orta opens the season with a flower festival, the Ortafiori, when you can visit the superb gardens of the Villa Motta.

Every 10 minutes or so, little boats leave Piazza Motta for **Isola San Giulio**. The islet was inhabited by serpents and monsters until AD 390 when Julius (Giulio), a Christian preacher from Aegina, showed up and calmly asked to be rowed to the island. The local fishermen, fearing that he would anger the dragons, refused; Giulio, undeterred, spread his cloak on the waters and surfed across. He sent the dragons packing, then built the precursor to the island's basilica by yoking a team of wolves to his ox cart—a feat good enough to make him the patron of builders, who gather here on his feast day, 31 January.

Around the year 1000, the **Basilica** (*open daily 9.30–12.15 and 2–6.45; Mon closed until 11; Sun 9.30–10.45 and 2–6.45*) was rebuilt for the first time. The chief relic of this rebuilding, the startling black marble **pulpit**, shows Giulio in high relief, wearily leaning on the hilt of his sword after chasing the dragons, along with symbols of the Evangelists—the Lion of St Mark looks like a sphinx grinning over a slice of pizza *al taglio*—while a griffon and crocodile duke it out in the corner. There are some good 15th-century frescoes by Gaudenzio Ferrari and his school (note especially the *Story of San Giulio* in the left aisle) and a marble sarcophagus belonging to the Lombard Duke Meinulphus, who had betrayed the island to the Franks and was beheaded by King Agilulf; his decapitated skeleton was duly found inside in 1697. The vertebrae belonging to one of Giulio's dragons are no longer visible in the sacristry, but you can see what's left of the saint in a glass casket and some fragments of his 4th-century church. The monastery of San Giulio occupies most of the island, although there are a few private houses on its silent lanes, a shop or two and a little bar-restaurant.

Orta is framed by sacred places; a road winds up the promontory behind town to the large car park under its holy acropolis or **Sacro Monte**.

Sacri Monti, or Little Theatres for the Soul

Orta, as mentioned above, is in the confines of Piedmont, a region with a special devotion to such Sacri Monti—hilltop devotional itineraries, invented in the late 15th century by a Franciscan friar, Bernardino Caimi of Varallo (in the next valley to the west), after his pilgrimage to Jerusalem. Back in Varallo, Bernardino wanted to somehow symbolically recreate his route through the Holy Land. His desire inspired the painter Gaudenzio Ferrari who, calling upon the Franciscan tradition of Christmas cribs and medieval passion plays, designed a series of tiny chapels, each containing life-sized statues representing a biblical scene, with the background frescoed in—the precursor of the 3D dioramas in natural history museums.

With the Counter-Reformation and its desire to make the faith more tangible, immediate and emotive, the idea of the Sacro Monte spread beyond Varallo, encouraged in particular by Counter-Reformation Grand Vizier Charles Borromeo (*see* p.142), although his enthusiasm was tempered by the insistence that the Church maintain strict control over every aspect of the work, to keep even the slightest tinge of heresy from infecting the desired response to each scene; Varallo's Sacro Monte, created in more innocent days, had to be completely reworked. Charles Borromeo also saw the Sacri Monti as a chance to promote the cults of Mary, the Rosary and the saints—the very aspects of Catholicism most beleaguered by the Protestants.

Orta's Sacro Monte, begun in 1591 and dedicated to Italy's patron St Francis, is one of the very best. Twenty numbered slate-roofed chapels in a wooded grove spiral to the top of the hill; in each, life-sized statues in 17th-century costume enact an important event in Francis' life—376 figures and 900 frescoes in all, contributed by various artists over the next two centuries. What sets Orta's Sacro Monte apart from the others is its delicious setting, with very distracting views over Isola San Giulio. By the 18th century, people began to come up on Sundays with picnics, and now there's a very pleasant bar and restaurant to make relaxing even easier. While dilly-dallying here, spare a thought for poor, shy, awkward Nietzsche who, beguiled by the nightingales of Sacro Monte, fell hopelessly head over heels for Lou Salomé, his Russian poet travelling companion. He boldly advanced; she, surprised, retreated. He never tried love again.

Where to Stay and Eating Out

Orta San Giulio ✉ 28016

Orta San Giulio is awash in lovely hotels, including one straight out of the *Arabian Nights*: ★★★★**Villa Crespi**, the lake's most luxurious, in a garden on top of town at Via C. Fava 8/10, ✆ 0322 911 902, ✉ 0322 911 919 (*very expensive*), a Moorish folly built in 1880 by Lombard cotton magnate Benigno Crespi and now painstakingly restored and furnished with period pieces. The eight suites and six bedrooms each have romantic canopied beds, marble baths and jacuzzis; the elegant dining room is equalled by the ravishing dishes prepared by top chef Natale Bacchetta: foie gras and *soncino* and pigeon stuffed with black truffles, for instance, accompanied by a wine and spirits list to die for: menus are surprisingly good value. *Closed Mon in winter.*

Down in Orta's historic centre, ★★★★**San Rocco**, Via Gippini 11, ✆ 0322 911 977, ✉ 0322 911 964 (*very expensive*) is located in a former 17th-century monastery with a pretty garden right on the water; in August it hosts a series of jazz and classical music concerts. Near Sacro Monte is the ★★★**Santa Caterina** (*moderate*), a peaceful hotel on the green hills overlooking the town. In Piazza Motta, brimming over with old-fashioned Italian character, ★★★**Orta**, ✆ 0322 90253, ✉ 0322 905 646 (*moderate*) has been run by the same family for over a century, with big rooms and bathrooms and a charming dining terrace directly on the lake. In 1882, Nietzsche and Lou Salomé spent their love-troubled week at the ★★★**Leon d'Oro**, Piazza Motta, ✆ 0322 911 991, 🖷 0322 90303 (*moderate*), and to this day the lake terrace and bar are especially amenable to such breaks from philosophy; rooms, recently remodelled, are small but immaculate. Set back on a quiet hill, ★★★**La Bussola**, Via Panoramica 24, ✆ 0322 911 913, 🖷 0322 911 934 (*moderate*) has 16 rooms and enjoys a magnificent panorama of the lake; there's a pretty garden with a swimming pool and a good restaurant. Central and simple ★**Taverna Antico Agnello**, Via Olina 18, ✆ 0322 90259 (*cheap*) offers warm, cosy rooms and a charming restaurant (*moderate*) with fish from the lake and more unusual fare such as smoked trout dressed with yoghurt and *torta di verdura*. A couple of steps further down, ★★**Olina**, ✆ 0322 905 656, 🖷 0322 905 645 (*cheap*) has very pleasant rooms and an elegant restaurant where the *risotto al saffrone* and *bonito al pomodoro* are particularly good; menus with *antipasti* for L45,000. **Venus** in Piazza Motta, ✆ 0322 90362, is always jam-packed for lunch: fill up on polenta with mushrooms, fish and Novara wine for L35,000. *Closed Mon.*

Around Lake Orta

It doesn't take long to drive around the 'grey pearl in a green casket' as Balzac called Lake Orta, and there's certainly no hurry. On the way you can delve into non-figurative art, and learn about saxophones and bathroom taps.

Tourist Information

Pettenasco: Piazza Unità d'Italia, ✆ 0323 89593. **Omegna**: Piazza XXIV Aprile 17, ✆ 0323 61930 (*both summer only*).

Pettenasco to Omegna

On the lake north of Orta, **Pettenasco** is a quiet little resort, a perfect place to meditate: in the past couple of years it has hosted hatha yoga courses out of Berkeley, California. Villas and vantage points are scattered in the hills above, along with **Armeno**, the town of cooks, with a fine Romanesque church. Armeno is the centre node of a network of mountain lanes and trails, including the road up to the top of Mottarone (*see* p.143), as well as to the **Santuario Bocciola** in **Vacciago di Armeno**, with lovely views over Orta. The painter Antonio Calderara (1903–78) lived in a 17th-century villa in Vacciago, surrounding himself with avant-garde paintings from the 1950s and 60s by 133 artists from all over the world, which he left as a museum, the **Collezione Calderara** (*open 15 May–15 Oct Tues–Sun 10–12 and 3–6; adm*). But his own paintings are the most memorable—still-life landscapes that capture the spirit of Lake Orta far better than any photograph.

At the southern point of Orta, **Gozzano** is overlooked by the **Torre di Buccione**, first built in the 4th century and rebuilt by the Lombards in the Dark Ages; its bells were loud enough to warn all the communities on the lake in times of trouble. Gozzano's **Villa Junker** has another fine garden and there are two tiny beaches under the main road. A bit up from Gozzano, on Orta's west shore, the church of the **Madonna di Luzzara** has 15th- and 16th-century frescoes. While here, consider how often you've ever pondered over your toothbrush on the secret inner workings of your bathroom tap, then find out the truth in **San Maurizio d'Opaglio**, where the **Museo de la Rubinetta**, ✆ 0322 969 325, is devoted to nothing else. Behind San Maurizio, a majestic rocky outcrop supports the **Santuario della Madonna del Sasso**, affording a grand view over the lake and the hamlets of Pella and Alzo near the shore.

On the northern tip of the lake, **Omegna** (Roman *Vomenia*) is the biggest town on the lake, where people make pots and pans, coffee pots and household appliances. The centre of town is pleasant enough, where the pretty Piazza del Municipio gives on to a bridge spanning the river that drains Orta, the **Nigoglia**—the only river in Italy to flow *towards* the Alps. The locals, who take some pride in being contrary themselves, like to say 'The Nigoglia flows up and we make the rules.'

From Omegna, a road curls up in ringlets through chestnut forests to the two hamlets called Quarna. **Quarna Sotto** (the lower one) has been manufacturing wind instruments for over 150 years; you can learn how they used to make clarinets, bassoons, oboes, saxophones, flutes and brass horns in the **Museo Etnografico e dello Strumento Musicale a Fiato** (*open July–14 Sep daily 10–12 and 3–7; otherwise ring the custodian,* ✆ *0323 826 368*). Downstairs, three traditional rooms from a farmhouse have been reconstructed filled with local crafts and costumes. The upper hamlet, **Quarna Sopra**, has spectacular views over Lake Orta. A second valley radiating from Omegna, the **Valstrona**, is less intensely spectacular, but **Forno** is a fine little place where dogs can sleep in the middle of the street, while the last hamlet in the valley, **Campello Monti**, is another Sunday-afternoon destination, where you can walk off too many *tortellini*.

Where to Stay and Eating Out

Pettenasco ✉ 28028

Right on Lake Orta, ★★★**Giardinetto**, Via Provinciale 1, ✆ 0323 89118, 🖷 0323 89219 (*moderate*) is a friendly family hotel with views of the Isola San Giulio. There are reduced rates for children, a swimming pool, private beach, and water sports facilities and an excellent restaurant serving locally cured meats, tortellini with goats' cheese and asparagus, and a soup of lake fish under a pastry crust. *Open April–Oct only.* A mile above the lake, **Osteria Madonna della Neve**, Pratolungo, ✆/🖷 0323 89122 (*cheap*) is a simple family-run guesthouse above a trattoria; all rooms have private bath. *Restaurant closed Wed.*

Pella ✉ 28010

If you want to stay on the quieter end of Lake Orta, ★**I Sorci Verdi**, Via Pietro Duro, ✆ 0322 969 282 (*cheap*) is simple, old-fashioned and sweet.

Omegna ✉ 28026

The family-run ★★**Vittoria**, Via Zanoia 37, ✆ 0323 62237 (*cheap*) has ten tidy rooms, all with bath and TV, and a reasonably priced restaurant. The ★★**Belvedere**, high up in Quarna Sopra, ✆ 0323 826 198, lives up to its name with enchanting bird's-eye views over Orta and has a garden and solarium. Up at Forno, in the Valstrona,

★Leone, ✆ 0323 885 112 (*cheap*) is peaceful and cosy. Book a table at **Da Libero** in nearby Fornero, ✆ 0323 87123 (*cheap*), a favourite rendezvous for its authentic, well-prepared trout, polenta, rice dishes and more, served on a lovely terrace in the summer. *Closed Tues and Jan.*

From Lake Orta to Domodossola: the Ossola Valleys

Unspoiled, and mostly unnoticed by visitors whizzing down the motorway to more Mediterranean delights, the Ossola valleys cut deep into the Alps, following the course of the River Toce and its tributaries on their way to Lake Orta. Napoleon drove the first road through here, from the Simplon Pass to Milan, but even the improved communications couldn't help the Fascists and Nazis when the inhabitants booted them out and formed an independent republic that lasted 40 days. Nowadays the valleys are visited for their forests, rustic hospitality and Alpine lakelets so blue they hurt.

Getting Around

Domodossola and the other towns along the Toce can be reached by **train** or **bus** from Milan, Lake Maggiore or Lake Orta; the other mountain valleys of the Ossola are served by bus from Domodossola. For Macugnaga, take the train to Piedimulera and the connecting Comazzi bus, ✆ 0324 240 333.

Tourist Information

Macugnaga: Piazza Municipio, ✆ 0324 65119.

Lake Mergozzo and the Valle Anzasca

North of Omega and Lake Orta, the road passes into the shadow of the mighty granite dome of Mount Orfano, which the locals are slowly whittling away to make flowerpots. Orfano in its turn guards an orphan lake, the small but deep **Lago Mergozzo**, which formed an arm of Lake Maggiore until the 9th century, when sediment from the Toce plugged it, a loss compensated by the fact that Mergozzo is now one of the cleanest lakes in Europe. Between the mountain and lake, the hamlet of **Montorfano** has a striking Romanesque church in the shape of a Latin cross, with a 5th-century baptismal font. The lake's attractive main town, also called **Mergozzo**, has been a quiet place ever since it lost its role as a transit centre with the construction of the Simplon road and tunnel. It has a 12th-century church made of Orfano granite, **San Giovanni** (usually locked); the small **Antiquarium** (usually locked, too) is said to contain local pre-Roman and Roman artefacts. The next town up the valley, **Candoglia**, is synonymous with the quarry which for six centuries has been worked for the pink and white marble to build the Duomo in Milan.

The first valley splitting off to the west, the enchanting **Valle Anzasca**, leads straight towards the tremendous east face of Monte Rosa. Among the woods and vineyards, look for **Cimamulera**, where one of the oldest horse chestnut trees in Italy grows next to the church (the old mule path from here to Piedimulera is especially lovely). The slate roofs of tiny **Colombetti** huddle under a lofty cliff; **Bannio-Anzino**, the 'capital' of the valley, has a 1st-century BC Gallo-Roman necropolis and in its parish church a 6ft-tall, 16th-century bronze Christ from Flanders. At **Ceppo Morelli** the vertiginous bridge over the Anza traditionally divides the valley's Latin population from the Walser—German-speaking Swiss settlers from the Valais who settled many of these valleys in the 13th century. Beyond Ceppo the road plunges through a gorge to the old Walser mining town of **Pestarena**. Mining in this case means gold; until recently the Valle Anzasca had Italy's largest gold deposits, extracted from galleries that extended for 40km.

The various hamlets that comprise **Macugnaga**, the Valle Anzasca's popular mountain resort, seem tiny under the tremendous 'cathedral of stone and ice', **Monte Rosa** (15,305ft). Macugnaga's Walser culture and traditions are recalled in the **Museo Casa Walser** in the hamlet of Borca (*open June and Sept Sat and Sun 3–5.30; July daily 3.30–6.30; Aug Mon–Fri 3–7, Sat and Sun 10.30–12; adm*); another museum, the **Museo della Miniera Aurifera** at Fornarelli (*open June–Sept 9–12 and 2–5.30; Oct–May Tues–Sun 1.30–5; adm*) is dedicated to gold-mining. Macugnaga has some 40km of ski runs; a dozen ski lifts; a chair lift that operates in the summer as well to the magnificent **Belvedere** which has views over the Macugnaga glacier, and a funivia to the **Passo Monte Moro** (9410ft), used by skiers in both the winter and spring seasons. From Macugnaga fearless alpinists attempt the steep, Himalayan-like east flank of Monte Rosa, one of the most dangerous ascents in the Alps; walkers can make a three-day trek over the mountains to Gressoney-St-Jean in the Valle d'Aosta (trail map essential).

North of the Valle Anzasca, the pretty wooded **Val d'Antrona** is famed for its trout fishing and old-fashioned ways: the older women still wear their traditional costumes every day and make Venetian lace. The valley begins at **Villadossola**, from where you can catch a bus to **Antronapiana**, a pleasant village lost in the trees, near the lovely lakelet of Antrona, created when a landslide buried half of Antronapiana in 1642. The north branch of the valley winds up to **Cheggio**, a wee resort with refuges, restaurants and another lake. If you're anywhere in the vicinity around the third week of July, don't miss the age-old *Autani dei Sete Fratelli*, a procession with Latin chants and beautiful traditional songs invoking protection for crops and animals; it runs for 25km along the Val d'Antrona and continues from the first crack of dawn until dusk.

Where to Stay and Eating Out

Mergozzo ☒ 28040

Near the lake, ★★★**Due Palme**, Via Pallanza 1, ✆ 0323 80112, ✉ 0323 80298 (*moderate*) has nice rooms and a pretty vine-clad terrace lorded over by a whistling parrot; the *gnocchi all'Ossalana* with pumpkin and chestnuts in the restaurant (*moderate*) are equally noteworthy.

Macugnaga ☒ 28030

The largest and most luxurious choice, ★★★**Zumstein**, Via Monte Rosa 63, ✆ 0324 65118, ✉ 0324 65490 (*moderate*) has attractive rooms near the centre of Staffa. *Closed May, Oct and Nov.* In the quiet *frazione* of Pecetto, ★★★**Nuova Pecetto**, ✆ 0324 65025, ✉ 0324 65891 (*moderate*) is charming and traditional with a garden and fine views of Monte Rosa. *Closed mid-Sept–Nov.* ★★**Chez Felice**, ✆ 0324 65229, ✉ 0324 65037 (*cheap*) is an unassuming villa with simple but charming rooms and the best restaurant in the valley (*moderate*), a haven of mountain *nuova cucina*, where you can sample salmon mousse with herbs, warm artichokes with a sauce of anchovies and capers, risotto with almonds, cheese and herb soufflé and many other delights; for afters, there's a magnificent array of local cheeses and exquisite desserts. *Closed Thurs; reserve if you're not staying at the hotel.*

Domodossola and the Upper Ossola Valleys

The capital of the Valle d'Ossola, Domodossola was a Roman settlement, and is perhaps best known in Italy these days as the largest town in the republic beginning with the letter D. After his victory at Marengo Napoleon, to make French meddling in Italy easier, built the first transalpine highway from Geneva to Domodossola through the Simplon Pass (Passo del Sempione), a major engineering feat completed in 1805. Exactly 100 years later the even more remarkable Simplon rail tunnel was completed—at the time the longest in the world at 19.8km.

Getting Around

A narrow-gauge electric railway, **La Vigezzina**, makes the picturesque journey between Domodossola and Locarno on Lake Maggiore through the Val Vigezzo in an hour and a half, serving all the villages on the way. From June to September, special circular tours are offered daily except Wed, travelling from Domodossola by train to Stresa, from Stresa to Locarno by boat, and then back to Domodossola by train. In Domodossola the station is at Via Mizzoccola 9, ✆ 0324 242 055. Comazzi buses to the valleys depart from the FS station, Piazza Matteotti: ✆ 0324 242 533 for trains; ✆ 0324 240 333 for buses.

Tourist Information

Domodossola: Corso Ferraris 49, ✆ 0324 481 308, ✉ 47974.
Santa Maria Maggiore: Piazza Risorgimento 5, ✆ 0324 95091.

Domodossola

Domodossola has a compact, car-swamped historic centre called the Motta. In the heart of the Motta, every Saturday for at least the past thousand years, a market has taken place in the pretty **Piazza Mercato**, lined with 15th-century porticoes. A few steps away, the old church of **SS. Gervasio e Protasio** was rebuilt in the 18th century, but conserving a baroque porch and a curious Romanesque architrave carved with the *Dream of Constantine*, informing the emperor that he would conquer under the sign of the cross.

Perhaps by the time you reach Domodossola its two museums will have reopened. Opposite SS. Gervasio e Protasio, the town's finest Renaissance building, the Palazzo Silva contains the **Museo Civico**, with Etruscan and Roman finds from the 3rd century AD necropolis in the Val Cannobina, Egyptian mummy bits and costumes. On the other end of Piazza Mercato, the Palazzo San Francesco contains the **Museo G.G. Galletti**, incorporating a medieval church and exhibiting something for every taste, from paintings to exhibits relating to natural history, the construction of the Simplon tunnel and the flight of the Peruvian Jorge Chavez, the first man to fly over the Alps (29 September 1910), only to die in a crash near Domodossola (he also has a monument in Piazza Liberazione). In 1944 the adjacent **Palazzo di Città** was the seat of the Repubblica Partigiana dell'Ossola for 40 days in one of the most significant acts of the Italian resistance.

From the centre, Via Mattarella leads up to the site of a ruined castle, where two Capuchin friars founded a **Sacro Monte** (*see* p.132; *open daily till dusk*) in 1656, with 15 baroque chapels dedicated to the Via Crucis. Unfortunately the first and best one exploded in 1830, when it was used to store powder—an accident that shouldn't happen again now that the Sacro Monte is part of a special reserve. Domodossola has its own ski station 10km away called **Domobianca**, and if pounds of polenta are weighing you down, the hot mineral springs at **Bognanco**, just up the next valley to the west, should put your digestion right (*open April–Oct*).

The Val Vigezzo

Just east of Domodossola begins the Val Vigezzo, a romantic beauty of woodlands, rolling hills and velvet pastures that has produced enough minor artists to earn the name 'the Valley of Painters'; one of the most charming features of the villages is the exterior frescoes they left behind. The Val Vigezzo had a knack for producing useful immigrants; one artist, Giuseppe Borgnis, ended up painting country homes in Buckinghamshire, where he died in 1761. In the 18th century two immigrants to Germany formulated and sold the first *acqua di colonia*, or cologne. Another family, the Mattei, who emigrated from **Druogno** to Holland in 1600, accidentally invented snuff when they bought a storm-wrecked cargo vessel and found that the casks of rum had soaked into the bales of tobacco; at first despondent, they later discovered that the rum had imparted a wonderful fragrance to the tobacco and sold it as a novelty that soon became the rage.

Druogno, now down to 1000 inhabitants, has pretty frescoed chapels scattered through its picturesque dry stone hamlets, crowned with stone roofs called *piode*. **Santa Maria Maggiore**, the Val Vigezzo's main town, is built around a little park and the 18th-century church, with a lovely *piode* roof; once Santa Maria had enough souls to fill its grand rococo interior, before they emigrated to become dockworkers in Livorno (the older people still speak with a slight Tuscan accent). Others became chimney sweeps, a hard trade honoured in the little **Museo dello Spazzocamino** (*open if someone's around*) in the park; every September Santa Maria hosts a chimney-sweep gathering and competition. The **Scuola di Belle Arti**, dedicated to local painters Carlo Fornara and Enrico Cavalli, hosts exhibits and runs summer painting courses. The tourist office has a map of walks and ski facilities including challenging treks through the new (1994) **Parco Nazionale della Val Grande**, one of the wildest places in Italy, stretching down to Lake Mergozzo; one of the entrances is at Scardi south of Santa Maria. Buses from Santa Maria go north up to **Toceno**, with pretty views and a Roman necropolis, and to **Craveggia**, birthplace of Giuseppe Borgnis, who left the valley's finest frescoes in the church.

Continuing up the Val Vigezzo, **Malesco** is a picturesque, higgledy-piggledy old village with narrow lanes, where you can turn off on a road that will keep you in second gear most of the way before winding down the Val Cannobina (*see* below, p.148) to Lake Maggiore. Further up the Val Vigezzo, **Re**, the last Italian *comune* before Switzerland, once had a church with a crude painting of the Madonna on the wall. In 1494 the village idiot threw a stone at it, striking the Virgin on the forehead, which immediately began to bleed profusely. The bleeding Madonna still has thousands of devotees: a ghastly neo-Gothic Byzantine **Santuario della Madonna del Sangue** was built in 1964, but it attracts enough pilgrims and is filled with sincere, home-made *ex votos*.

North of Domodossola

The **Val Divedro**, along the Simplon road, is as austere as the Val Vigezzo is gentle. Inhabited since the cows came home, in the Mesolithic era (7000 BC), it teems with legends of dragons and elves. But nature is the main attraction, especially the **Alpe Veglia**, a high alpine basin set amid little lakes—including the Lago delle Streghe, named for the witches who haunt it. Buses from Domodossola also plunge north towards the San Giacomo Pass, through the spectacular scenery of the **Valli Antigorio e Formazza**, valleys along the river Toce settled by the Walser in the 13th century. Their charming scattered villages are planted with vines and figs, and the valley's spa, **Crodo**, is famous in Italy for bottling a ludicrously chipper soft drink called Crodino, as well as iron-laced mineral water. Further north, **Baceno**'s parish church, **San Gaudenzio** (11th–16th century) is the best in the Valle d'Ossola; it has a fine front portal with sirens and a cartwheel window, 16th-century Swiss stained glass and a carved wooden altarpiece.

In **Premia** you can visit the **Orridi**, steep gorges sliced by the River Toce over the millennia. You can reach an evocatively empty old Walser settlement, **Salecchio**, by foot from Antillone; **Formazza**, further up, is a pretty, still lived-in Walser community, with its sturdy wooden houses. If you come on a Sunday or holiday between 9am and 5pm from June until September, or any day between 10 and 20 August, you can take in one of the most breathtaking waterfalls in all the Alps at the end of the road: the thundering 985ft veil of mist, the **Cascata del Toce**. At other times, like all of Italy's best waterfalls, its bounding splashing energy spins hydroelectric turbines.

Where to Stay and Eating Out

Domodossola ✉ 28037

The most stylish hotel in town, ★★★**Corona**, Via Marconi 8, ✆ 0324 242 114, 📠 0324 242 842 (*expensive*) has very comfortable rooms, and a garage. ★★★**Motel Europa**, 4km south on the N33, ✆ 0324 481 032, 📠 0324 481 011 (*moderate*) is comfortable enough; all rooms have private bath and TV. In the centre, **Trattoria Piemonte di Sciolla**, Piazza Convenzione 5, ✆ 0324 242 633 (*moderate*) comes highly recommended for its regional dishes such as polenta with milk and poppyseeds and its home-made desserts. *Closed Wed and late Aug.*

Druogno ✉ 28030

★★★**Stella Alpina**, Via Domodossola 13, ✆ 0324 93593, 📠 0324 93595 (*moderate*) is the most comfortable hotel in the village, but a bit close to the road; the piney, family-run ★★★**Boschetto**, by the ski slopes at Via Pasquaro, ✆ 0324 93554, 📠 0324 93559 (*moderate*) is more isolated, near the ski slope, with a playground for the kids.

Santa Maria Maggiore ✉ 28038

You can sleep and eat in style up near the station, at ★★★**Miramonti**, ✆ 0324 95013, 📠 0324 94283 (*moderate*), a cosy chalet with flowers flowing over the balconies. Also near the centre, the pleasant ★★**La Jazza**, Via Domodossola, ✆ 0324 94471, 📠 0324 94636 (*cheap*) has a garden and some cheaper rooms without bath. Next to the church, **Locarno**, ✆ 0324 95088, serves simple fare at lunchtime and good pizzas in the evening. *Closed Tues.*

Malesco ✉ 28030

The moderate-sized ★★★**Alpino**, in the quiet hamlet of Zornasco, ✆/📠 0324 95118 (*moderate*) has a pool and comfortable rooms; for something more basic but nice ★**Ramo Verde**, in the centre at Via Conte Mellerio 5, ✆ 0324 95012 (*cheap*); bathrooms are down the hall and there's a cheap menu in the restaurant.

Lake Maggiore

Have you not read in books how men when they
see even divine visions are terrified?
So as I looked at Lake Major in its halo
I also was afraid ...

Hilaire Belloc, *The Path to Rome*

Italy's second-largest lake after Garda, Lago Maggiore winds majestically for 65km between Piedmont and Lombardy, its northern corner lost in the snow-capped Swiss Alps. The Romans called it *Lacus Verbanus*, for the verbena that still grows luxuriantly on its shores: like Como and Garda, Maggiore is large enough to create its own warm, Mediterranean microclimate. The three jewel-like Borromean islands in its central Golfo Borromeo are what really set the lake apart from the others. They still belong to the Borromei of Milan, who also possess fishing rights over the entire lake—as they have since the 1500s.

The west shore of the lake, especially the triad of Stresa, Baveno and Verbania, are the most scenic places to aim for, with the best and most varied accommodation and festivals. Easter and July to September are the high seasons, when you should definitely reserve.

Getting Around

Trains from Milan's Stazione Centrale to Domodossola stop at Arona and Stresa; others from Milan's Porta Garibaldi station go to Luino on the east shore. A third option is the regional railway from Milano-Nord, which passes by way of Varese to Laveno. Trains from Turin and Novara go to Arona and Stresa; Stresa is also linked by train to Orta four times a day.

From Lake Orta, there are **buses** from Omegna to Verbania every 20 minutes. Buses that connect the two lakes also run from Stresa and Arona stations, while others serve all the villages along the west shore.

Navigazione Lago Maggiore, ✆ 0322 46651, runs **steamers** to all corners of the lake, with the most frequent services in the central lake area, between Stresa, Baveno,

Verbania, Pallanza, Laveno and the islands; **hydrofoils** buzz between the main Italian ports and Locarno (in Switzerland). Frequent services by steamer or hydrofoil from Stresa, Baveno and Pallanza sail to the Borromean Isles—a ticket for the furthest, Isola Madre, entitles you to visit all. **Car ferries** run year round between Intra and Laveno.

Tourist Information

Arona: Piazzale Duca d'Aosta, ✆/🖅 0322 243 601. **Stresa**: Principe Tommaso 70, ✆ 0323 30150, 🖅 32561. **Baveno**, Corso Garibaldi 16, ✆/🖅 0323 924 632.

Arona to Baveno

If you're approaching from the south, Lake Maggiore doesn't exactly make a striking first impression, dissolving into formless and reedy lagoons until you reach **Arona**, a rail junction and sprawling market town. There are views from Arona's lake promenade across to the Borromeo castle at Angera, and in the pretty cobbled Piazza del Popolo the 15th-century **Casa del Podestà** is distinguished with a portico of pointed arches. The old upper part of Arona has two churches to visit: Renaissance **Santa Maria**, where the Borromeo family chapel contains a lovely 1511 polyptych by Gaudenzio Ferrari, and **SS. Martiri**, with 16th-century stained-glass windows, a painting by Bergognone and another by the Venetian Palma Giovane.

A medieval fief of the Visconti, Arona passed to the Borromei in 1439. A few walls remain of their **Castle of Arona,** 2km up on top of the town; it was the birthplace of Charles Borromeo (1538–84), an event commemorated by his cousin and successor Cardinal Federico Borromeo with a church, three chapels of a Sacro Monte that was never finished and, in 1697, with **San Carlone** (St Big Chuck), a 115ft copper and bronze jug-eared colossus in the act of blessing the lake (*open April–Sept daily 8.30–12.30 and 2–6.30; Oct–Mar daily 9–12.30 and 2–5; adm*).

The World's Biggest Saint

Charles Borromeo, son of Count Gilbert Borromeo and a Medici mum, was the most influential churchman of his day, appointed 'Cardinal Nephew and Archbishop of Milan' at the age of 22 by his maternal uncle, Pope Pius IV. In Rome he was a powerful voice calling for disciplinary reform within the Church, and he instigated the Council of Trent, that decade-long Counter-Reformation strategy session in which he played a major role. There was one legendary point in Trent when the cardinals wanted to ban all church music, which by the 16th century had degenerated to the point of singing lewd love ballads to accompany the *Te Deum*. Charles and his committee, however, decided to let the musicians have one more chance, and asked Palestrina to compose three suitable Masses that reflected the dignity of the words of the service (and Charles reputedly told the composer that the cardinals expected him to fail). To their surprise, and to the everlasting benefit of Western culture, Palestrina succeeded, and sacred music was saved.

After the death of his uncle-pope, Charles went to live in his diocese of Milan, the first archbishop to do so in 80 years. Following the codex of the Council of Trent to the letter (that's the book under the statue's arm), he at once began reforming the once-cosy clergy to set the example for other bishops. The Milanese weren't exactly thrilled: Charles narrowly escaped an assassination attempt in the cathedral, when the bullet bounced off his heavy brocade vestments. He was a bitter enemy of original thought and not someone you would want to have over for dinner; if New York has a Statue of Liberty, Arona has a Statue of Tyranny. For a queer sensation walk up the steps through his hollow viscera (if the repairs are finished): his head can hold six people, who can peer out of his eyes, each a foot and a half wide. The plastic doodahs in the souvenir shop below are a trip in themselves.

From Arona to Stresa

Two roads link Arona to Stresa: the panoramic upper road through the villages of the **Colle Vergante** and the main route hugging the lakeshore. This lower road passes a number of villas before reaching **Meina**, the medieval Màdina, when it was the property of the Benedictines of Pavia. Meina has a sprinkling of neoclassical villas from the 18th century, when it first became fashionable, and is the base for visiting **Ghevio** and **Silvera**, charming villages immersed in the green of the hills of Vergante, and **Massino Visconti**, with its 13th-century castle and church. The lake road continues to **Lesa**, with the best-preserved Romanesque church on Maggiore, **S. Sebastiano** (1035); Alessandro Manzoni, better known for his links to Lecco on Lake Como (*see* p.186), spent his holidays here, in the Palazzo Stampa (now a bank). The lake really opens up at **Belgirate**, another small resort, with a pretty square, the 15th-century fres-coed church of **Santa Marta** and the Villa Carlotta, a favourite retreat of Italy's intellectuals in the 19th century, now a hotel.

Stresa, the 'Pearl of Verbano'

Beautifully positioned on the lake overlooking the Borromeo islands, under the majestic peak of Mottarone, Stresa is Maggiore's most beautiful town, bursting with flowers and sprinkled with fine old villas. A holiday resort since the last century, famous for its lush gardens and mild climate, it soared in popularity after the construction of the Simplon Tunnel in 1906; Hemingway used its **Grand Hôtel des Iles Borromées** as Frederick Henry's refuge from war in *A Farewell to Arms*. The little triangular Piazza Cadorna in the centre, shaded by age-old plane trees, is Stresa's social centre, its number of habitués swollen by participants in inter-national congresses and music lovers attending the *Settimane Musicali di Stresa*, featuring orchestras from around the world from the last week of August through September. Two of Stresa's lakeside villas are open to the public: **Villa Pallavicino** (1850) and its colourful gardens, where saucy parrots rule the roost, along with a small collection of other animals (*open mid-Mar–Oct daily 9–6; adm*) and the **Villa Ducale** (1771), once the property of Catholic philosopher Antonio Rosmini (*d.* 1855); besides the gardens, there's a small museum (*open daily 9–12 and 3–6; donation requested*).

From Stresa you can ascend **Monte Mottarone** (4920ft), via the cableway beginning at Stresa Lido (*8.10, then every 20mins 8.40–11.40 and 12.40–5.10; L18,000 round-trip adult,*

L10,000 ages 4–12). The views are famous, on a clear day taking in not only all seven major Italian lakes, but also glacier-crested peaks from Monte Viso (far west) and Monte Rosa over to the eastern ranges of Ortles and Adamello, as well as much of the Lombard plain. If you drive, walk or take the bus from Stresa, you can also stop and play golf at **Vezzo**; or visit the Alpine rock gardens of the **Giardino Alpinia** (*open April–15 Oct Tues–Sat 9–6, Sun and hols 9.30–6.30*), or **Gignese**, where the **Museo dell'Ombrello** (*open April–Sept Tues–Sun 10–12 and 3–6*) waits to tell you all about the history and making of umbrellas and parasols, a traditional industry in the Colle Vergante. Once you reach the confines of the **Parco del Mottarone** and the Strada Panoramica La Borromea, you'll have to pay the toll: the Borromei paved it, so you pay for it.

Baveno

Baveno is Stresa's quieter sister, connected by a beautiful, villa-lined road. Known for its quarries (source of the pink stone in Milan's Galleria Vittorio Emanuele and the Basilica of St Paul's in Rome, while the black and white was used for the Columbus monument in New York's Columbus Circle), it first made the society pages in 1879, when Queen Victoria spent a summer at the Villa Clara, now Castello Branca; Wagner spent a holiday here, and Umberto Giordano composed his opera *Fedora*—the only one that features bicycles on stage—in his Villa Fedora. In the centre of Baveno, the 11th-century church of **Santi Gervasio e Protasio** has retained its original plain square façade (note the Roman inscriptions on the ancient blocks reused in the front) even though the interior was redone in the 18th century; the charming little octagonal baptistry adjacent dates from the 5th century. A pretty road leads up **Monte Camoscio,** behind Baveno.

Where to Stay and Eating Out

Arona ✉ 28041

Arona has one of the finest restaurants on Lake Maggiore in its **Taverna del Pittore** in Piazza del Popolo, ✆ 0322 243 366 (*very expensive*); enjoy lovely views from the lake terrace while feasting on seafood lasagnette with saffron, fragrant ravioli with mushrooms, lamb in pastry, and exceptional hot or cold desserts. *Closed Mon, end Dec, last two weeks in June.* For half as much, the rather austere **Vecchia Arona**, Lungolago Marconi 17, ✆ 0322 242 469, serves a delicious L55,000 menu based on the market and the day's catch, and a L35,000 menu at lunchtime. *Closed Fri, two weeks June and two weeks Nov.*

Meina ✉ 28046

Right on the shore, ****Antico Albergo Verbano**, ✆/ 0322 660 229 (*cheap*) is charmingly old-fashioned, with a beach and garden; not all rooms have a bath, but the large windows provide a wonderful panoramic view of the lake. The speciality in the restaurant is lake fish, grilled and served with salad or vegetables.

Stresa ✉ 28049

Opened in 1863, *******Des Iles Borromées**, Corso Umberto I 67, ✆ 0323 30431, 32405 (*luxury*) is stylish in both its aristocratic *belle époque* furnishings and its modern conveniences. Overlooking the islands, and a lovely flower-decked, palm-shaded garden, the hotel has a pool, beach, tennis courts and a *Centro Benessere* ('well-being') where doctors are on hand to give you a check-up, exercises and improve your diet. There's even a heli-pad if you come by chopper. Some 40 years younger, ★★★★**Regina Palace**, Corso Umberto I, ✆ 0323 933 777, ✉ 0323 933 776 (*very expensive*) is a lovely, bow-shaped Liberty-style palace, tranquil in its large park. It has a heated pool, tennis courts, beach, and splendid views. *Open mid Mar–Oct.*

Another lake-front hotel, ★★★★**Milan au Lac**, Piazza Marconi, ✆ 0323 31190, ✉ 0323 32729 (*expensive*) has good-size rooms, many with balconies and, of course, wonderful views. *Open Mar–Oct.* ★★★**Primavera**, Via Cavour 39, ✆ 0323 31286, ✉ 0323 33458 (*moderate*) is a friendly hotel with a touch of style, and pretty balconies, but no restaurant. The ★★★**Moderno**, at Via Cavour 33, ✆ 0323 933 773, ✉ 0323 933 775 (*moderate*) has rooms set round an inner patio. All have TV and minibar, and there are also two very good restaurants. *Open Mar–Oct.*

★★★**Italia e Suisse**, Piazza Marconi, ✆ 0323 30540, ✉ 0323 32621 (*moderate*) is a good choice near the steamer landing. ★★★**Du Parc**, Via Gignous 1, ✆ 0323 30335, ✉ 0323 33596 (*moderate*) is a pleasant villa set in its own grounds right below the railway tracks. ★★**Elena**, Piazza Cadorna 15, ✆ 0323 31043, ✉ 0323 33339 (*cheap*) is a good budget option, with big modern rooms, most with balconies, all with satellite TV. It also has a garage. For even less, there's the simple, central ★**Fiorentino**, Via Anna Maria Bolongaro 9, ✆ 0323 30254, ✉ 0323 933 822 (*cheap*), and the nice family-run **Orsola**, Via Duchess di Genova 69, ✆ 0323 31087 (*cheap*).

Book for Stresa's elegant gourmet haven, **L'Emiliano**, on Corso Italia 52, ✆ 0323 31396 (*very expensive*), a temple of *nuova cucina* with a Bolognese touch and superb seafood specialities, local chicken baked with peppers, or salami with a tangy pear *mostarda*. The wine list includes sweet wines by the glass to go with excellent desserts. *Closed Tues, Wed lunch, Jan and Feb.* Find a table in the garden at **Piemontese**, Via Mazzini 25, ✆ 0323 30235 (*expensive*) to tuck into its divine spaghetti with melted onions, basil and pecorino and its excellent fish dishes. *Closed Mon, Jan and half of Feb.* The **Irish Bar**, Via Passeggiata Margherita 9, ✆ 0323 31054, has been an institution in Stresa for the past 25 years, run by the hospitable Giovanni and Brigid Zawetta. Equally lively is the **Red Baron Pub**, at the top of Via Roma, below the railway tracks, an English-run place serving draught beer, great sandwiches and imaginative salads.

Baveno ✉ 28042

Right by the lake, the modern ★★★★**Dino**, Via Garibaldi 20, ✆ 0323 922 201, ✉ 0323 924 515 (*very expensive*) offers a long list of extras, including a private beach. In the centre, a pretty old villa in a lush garden houses ★★★**Al Campanile**, Via Monte Grappa, ✆ 0323 922 377, ✉ 0323 925 409 (*moderate*); half-board only. On the north edge of town in Feriolo, ★★★**Carillon**, ✆ 0323 28115, ✉ 0323 28550 (*moderate*) is right on the beach; nice rooms but no restaurant. Just in back of the church, ★★**Villa Azalea**, Via Chiesa 2, ✆ 0323 925 068, ✉ 0323 924 300 (*cheap*) is simple and tranquil. The charming Monica and Marco run the bright ★**Elvezia**, up by the church at Via Monte Grappa 15, ☏ 0323 924 106 (*cheap*), with a little garden, tasty meals and a place to park. *Open April–Oct.* **Serenella**, Via 42 Martiri 5, in the hamlet of Feriolo, ☏ 0323 28112 (*moderate*) ,with a summer garden, serves delicious homemade pasta and risottos, and a good selection of fresh lake fish or meat *secondi*. *Closed Wed, Jan and Feb.*

The Borromean Islands

Lake Maggiore became a private fief of the Borromei in the 1470s, and to this day they own some of the finest bits, including the sumptuous gardens and villas of the Borromean Islands. There are frequent boats from Stresa, Baveno, Pallanza and Laveno, or you can hire a boat and row there under your own steam; the three main islands have restaurants if you want to make a day of it.

The closest island to Stresa, **Isola Bella** (*guided tours Mar–Sept daily 9–12 and 1.30–5.30; Oct daily 9.30–12.30 and 1.30–5; adm exp*) was a scattering of barren rocks until the 17th century, when Count Carlo III Borromeo decided to make it a garden in the form of a ship for his wife Isabella (hence the name Isola Bella). Architect Angelo Crivelli was put in charge of designing this pretty present, and arranged it in ten terraces to form a pyramid-shaped 'poop deck', to create the kind of architectural perspectives beloved by baroque theatre. The project was continued by Vitaliano VI Borromeo (*d.* 1670), who added the palace and grottoes but left it unfinished at his death. The Borromei completed the **palace** according to the original plans between 1948 and 1959 and left it a fine collection of art, with works by Annibale Carracci, Luca Giordano, Pannini, Zuccarelli, Cerano, Giambattista Tiepolo and a certain Pietro Mulier, or 'Il Tempesta' (*d.* 1701), who in spite of his stormy nickname was a long-time guest of the family. The room in which Napoleon slept in August 1797 is done up in the Directory style in his honour, while the music room, with its antique instruments, hosted the 1935 Stresa Conference, where Italy, Britain and France tried to decide what to do in the face of Hitler's rearmament—a sad sequel to the hopeful pact signed at Locarno ten years earlier—and ended up doing nothing, because France and Britain refused to recognize Mussolini's conquest of Ethiopia. A stair leads down to the six artificial grottoes right on the lake, covered all over with shells and pebbles—the effect is curiously confectionery—while the Tapestry Gallery has six 16th-century Flemish tapestries featuring the favourite Borromeo family emblem, the unicorn, who also holds pride of place in the gardens. Stendhal wrote that the panorama from the top is 'equal to the Bay of Naples, and speaks even more directly to the heart. It seems to me that these islands waken the emotions even more than St Peter's…'

The Borromei opened the delightful, larger **Isola Madre** (*hours and adm as Isola Bella*) to the public in 1978. Here they planted a colourful and luxuriant botanical garden, dominated by Europe's largest Kashmir cypress; its camellias begin to bloom in January (*be sure to pick up the free guide to the plants*). On its best days few places are more conducive to a state of perfect languor, at least until one of the isle's bold pheasants, peacocks or parrots tries to stare you out. The 16th-century villa has a collection of 18th- and 19th-century puppet theatres, marionettes, portraits and furnishings.

The third island, **Isola dei Pescatori**, is home to an almost too quaint and picturesque fishing village, and another private islet called **San Giovanni** is just off the shore at Pallanza, with a villa once owned by Toscanini.

Isole Borromei ✉ 28049

The lovely and quiet ★★★**Verbano**, Isola dei Pescatori, ✆ 0323 30408, ✉ 0323 33129 (*moderate*) offers the chance to see the island after the hordes return to the mainland, and has a restaurant, where romantic views compensate for brusque service and very average food. Expect more of the views than the food at the Borromeo's restaurants too: the **Delfino**, on Isola Bella, ✆ 0323 30473 and **La Piratera**, on Isola Madre ✆ 0323 31171 (*both moderate*).

Verbania and Maggiore's Northwest Shore

In 1994 the shore of Lake Maggiore, feeling rather neglected by the distant provincial capital Novara, became a province of its own, named for its capital, Verbania.

Tourist Information

Pallanza: Corso Zanitello 8, ✆ 0323 503 249, ✉ 0323 556 669.

Verbania: Pallanza and Intra

From Baveno the shore road circles over to the north side of the Borromean bay, with fine views of the islands all the way to **Pallanza**, a resort with a famously mild winter climate. In 1939 Pallanza was united with the neighbouring towns of Suna and Intra and christened Verbania as part of Mussolini's campaign to revive old Roman names. Each town, however, retains its own identity. Pallanza, the prettiest, has several man-made attractions, especially the Renaissance **Madonna di Campagna** on the edge of town up Viale Azari. Inspired by Bramante, the church has a curious gazebo-like arcaded drum and a Romanesque campanile, inherited from its predecessor; the lavishly decorated interior includes good 15th-century frescoes by Gerolamo Lanino (*St Bernardo*). In the centre of Pallanza the 16th-century Palazzo Dugnani houses the **Museo del Paesaggio**, Via Ruga 44 (*open April–Oct Tues–Sun 10–12 and 3–6; adm*) with a collection of 19th- and 20th-century landscapes of Lake Maggiore and vicinity: realistic and documentary, romantic, impressionistic, plus landscapes with a social conscience (*The Diggers* (1890) by Arnaldo Ferraguti). Other rooms contain plaster casts and sculptures by Giulio Branca from Cannobia, Paolo Troubetzkoy, born in Intra of noble Russian parents (*d.* 1938), and Arturo Martini (*d.* 1949).

The glory of greater Verbania is the **Villa Taranto**, built on the Castagnola promontory between Pallanza and Intra by a certain Count Orsetti in 1875. In 1931 the derelict villa was purchased by a Scots captain, Neil McEacharn, who had one of the world's greenest thumbs and pockets deep enough to afford to import exotic plants from the tropics to the tune of some 20,000 varieties, planted over 20 hectares. The aquatic plants, including giant Amazonian water lilies and lotus blossoms, the spring tulips and the autumn colour are exceptional, as are some of the rarer species—the handkerchief tree, bottle bush and copper-coloured Japanese maple. MacEacharn left his masterpiece to the Italian state; the villa is occasionally used by the Italian prime minister for special conferences (*if he's not in, open April–Oct daily 8.30–7.30; adm exp*).

Intra, Verbania's industrial and business quarter, has a large market each Saturday and a ferry across to Laveno; on the wall of the Casa di Comune note the almost unbelievable flood mark (3 Oct 1860). Buses from near the ferry landing serve the quiet, woodsy holiday towns in the hinterland: **Arizzano**, **Bèe** and most importantly **Premeno**, a mountain resort overlooking Maggiore and the Alps, with skiing in the winter and a beautiful golf course. In 1950 some 4th-century AD Roman tombs were discovered by Premeno's **Oratorio di San Salvatore**. The bus continues up to **Pian Cavallo** (1251m/4102ft), with views almost as good as those from Mottarone.

Back on the lake, north of Intra, **Ghiffa** is pleasant and quiet, with a waterside promenade and, up in its suburb of Ronco, the **Sacro Monte SS. Trinità**, another late 17th-century Counter-Reformation devotional trip (*see* pp.132–3) although here only three chapels were ever finished, dedicated to the Coronation of the Virgin, St John the Baptist and Abraham. Further north, **Cannero Riviera** is a quiet resort with a mild climate, set amid glossy green citrus groves. It faces two intensely picturesque islets, former strongholds of the five brothers Mazzarditi, fierce pirates defeated in 1414 by Filippo Maria Visconti. He razed the castles, and on their ruins Lodovico Borromeo built another tower and castle (1521). They seem to rise straight out of the water; in the twilight mists they could easily be the enchanted towers of the Lady of the Lake.

Cannobio and the Val Cannobina

Cannobio is an ancient town with steep, medieval streets, where every Sunday morning since anyone can remember the entire lake front has been given over to a bustling market. At other times you might find the monument honouring the local genius, Giovanni Branca (*d.* 1645), inventor of the steam turbine. Cannobio's churches adhere to the Milanese Ambrosian Rite, revived by Charles Borromeo in an effort to promote local pride. Much of this local religious fervour is concentrated by the lake in the Bramante-inspired **Santuario della Pietà**, built to house a miraculous painting on parchment of the *Dead Christ with the Virgin and St John*; the altarpiece by Gaudenzio Ferrari of *Christ meeting the Three Marys on the Road to Calvary* is one of his finest.

Buses from Cannobio plunge up the wild, sparsely populated **Val Cannobina**, which rises up to meet the Val Vigezzo and Domodossola. Just 2km from Cannobio you can hire a boat to visit the dramatic **Orrido di Sant'Anna**, a deep, narrow gorge carved by the Cannobio river and waterfall. Further up the valley lies a cluster of wee hamlets of stone houses, known collectively as **Cavaglio-Spoccia**, where the valley's first road, the Via Borromeo, crosses old mossy bridges. **Falmenta**, a tiny village on the other side of the valley, has among its quaint black stone houses a 1565 parish church with a rare wooden altarpiece, crowded with small figures, from the 1300s. The next village, **Gurro**, has retained its medieval centre and keeps alive its folk traditions, with a little **Museo Comunale** of local customs and produce (*open daily 8–8 excl Thurs and Sept; ask for the key at the Bar Scotch*). **Orasso** has a 13th-century Visitazione church, and another finely carved wooden altarpiece in the 15th-century parish church, San Materno.

Verbania-Pallanza ✉ 28052

Right on the lake, ★★★★**Majestic**, Via Vittorio Veneto 32, ✆ 0323 504 305, ✉ 0323 556 379 (*expensive*) is a comfortable grand old hotel, endowed with a good restaurant and plenty of amenities—indoor pool, tennis, park and private beach. *Open April–Oct.* ★★★**Belvedere**, Viale Magnolie 6, ✆ 0323 503 202, ✉ 0323 504 466 (*moderate*) is a good hotel for the price range, located near the steamer landing. ★★★**Pace**, Via Cietti 1, ✆ 0323 557 207, ✉ 0323 557 341 (*moderate*) offers excellent value, with modern rooms and old-style writing desks. *Open Mar–Oct.* ★**Villa Serena**, Via Crocetta 26, ✆ 0323 556 015 (*cheap*) enjoys a lovely position in a park near the lake.

The best place to eat in Pallanza, **Milano**, Corso Zanitello 2, ✆ 0323 556 816 (*expensive*) is located in a fine old lake-front villa, with dining out on the terrace for a very romantic evening. The food is some of the finest on Maggiore: wonderful *antipasti* and lake fish prepared in a number of delicious styles. *Closed Tues.* Also on the lake front the **Osteria dell'Angelo**, Piazza Garibaldi 35, ✆ 0323 556 362 (*moderate*) has lovely food—*crespelle* (little crepes) stuffed with *scamorza* cheese, and various risottos. *Closed Mon.* The recently opened **Boccon di Vino**, Via Troubetzkoy 86, ✆ 0323 504 039 (*cheap*) near the *imbarcadero* at Suno is a family-run place with great, good-value food and wine. Try the home-made pasta or roast and casseroled meats, or sample the local salami and cheeses. *Closed Sun, lunchtimes and Aug.* In Intra, the **Osteria del Castello,** Piazza Castello 9, ✆ 0323 516 579—a sociable meeting and drinking place to start (or indeed to end) the evening—Friday nights have no closing time. *Closed Sun in winter.*

Ghiffa ✉ 28055

The 15th-century ★★**Castello di Frino**, Via Cristoforo Colombo, ✆ 0323 59181, ✉ 0323 59783 (*moderate*) has 14 rooms with up-to-date comforts, a pool and tennis. The grand old ★**Park Paradiso**, Via G. Marconi, ✆ 0323 59548, ✉ 0323 59878 (*moderate*) has plenty of 19th-century character, and a pool too.

Cannero Riviera ✉ 28051

★★★**Cannero**, Lungolago 2, ✆ 0323 788 046, ✉ 0323 788 048 (*moderate*) has balconies overlooking the lake, a swimming pool, better than average food in the restaurant, and a garage. Minimum stay three days. *Open mid-Mar–Oct.* The much simpler ★**Miralago**, Via Dante, ✆ 0323 788 282, ✉ 0323 787 075 (*cheap*) has views, but the bathrooms are down the hall. *Open Mar–Oct.* Nearby on the Lungolago, **Europa** has a good L20,000 menu; get there early for a table right on the water. Overlooking the islets, **Ca' Bianca**, north of Cannero (*moderate*) is a fine place to linger over a plate of pasta and fish or a Sunday lunch.

Cannobio ✉ 28052

In the historic centre, ★★★**Pironi**, Via Marconi 35, ✆ 0323 70624, ✉ 0323 72184 (*moderate*) occupies a frescoed 15th-century palace shaped like the Flatiron building in New York; rooms have lake views and frigo bars. *Open Mar–Oct.* Under the porticoes by the lake, ★★★**Il Portico**, Piazza Santuario 2, ✆ 0323 71255, ✆ 0323 72289 (*moderate*) is another classy if more staid choice. ★★**Antica Stallera**, 50m from the lake in Via Paolo Zaccheo 7, ✆ 0323 71595, ✆ 0323 72201 (*cheap*) is quiet and comfortable, although the restaurant is a bit pricey. **Lo Scalo**, Piazza Lago 32, ✆ 0323 71480 (*moderate*) has a pretty terrace on the lake, and serves traditional Piedmontese recipes—tortellini with mountain cheeses, chicken stuffed with shrimp—on its ever-changing menu, along with more original dishes such as prawns stuffed with radicchio and a *sformatino* of rabbit with green peppercorns. *Closed Mon out of season.* **Osteria La Streccia**, in narrow Vicolo Merzagora, ✆ 0323 70575, has a good menu for L36,000. *Closed Mon.*

Del Lago, Via Nazionale 2, in Carmine, ✆ 0323 70595 (*expensive*) is one of the best restaurants in the area. Try the risotto with saffron, zucchini and mussels, turbot with caviar, or duck breast with honey-roasted sesame seeds. *Closed Tues and Wed lunch, and Nov–Mar.*

Swiss Lake Maggiore

The northern tip of the Big Lake is in the Italian-speaking Swiss canton of Ticino, where it is highly prized as the national suntrap.

Getting Around

Locarno is linked to Domodossola by the scenic narrow-gauge Vigezzina train (*see* p.138), while all the port towns are served by the Italian *Navigazione di Lago Maggiore* and clean and never smelly Swiss FART buses; ✆ 4191 751 0333.

Tourist Information

Ascona: Casa Serodine, ✆ 4191 791 0090. **Locarno**: Largo Zorzi 1, ✆ 4191 751 0333, ✆ 4191 751 9070. e-mail: *locarno@etlm.ch.*

Brissago and its Islands

Switzerland begins just north of Cannobio and the first place of any importance is bustling **Brissago**, a town that has rolled its own since 1846. The cigar factory is open for tours; other sights are a remarkable 600-year-old **cypress** growing next to the church of SS. Pietro e Paolo, and a beautiful Tuscan-Lombard church, the **Madonna di Ponte** (mid-1500s), with a porticoed dome, inspired by the designs of Bramantino. Fom **Porto Ronco** (the lowest town in Switzerland, a mere 643ft above sea level) boats sail to the **Isole Brissago**. The little one, Santa Apollinaire, has the ruins of a Romanesque church, while larger San Pancrazio is covered with a splendid exotic garden, the **Parco Botanico del Cantone Ticino** (*open April–15 Oct daily 9–6; adm*) with 1500 species of flora mostly from the southern hemisphere, created in 1883 by the Baroness Antoinette de Saint-Léger; the island's villa has a museum of African ethnography. Striking lake and mountain views continue along the shore: aim for **Ronco sopra Ascona**, 'the Balcony of Lake Maggiore'.

Ascona and the Mountain of Truth

On its sunny bay, **Ascona** rivals Stresa as Lake Maggiore's culture queen, counting the likes of Thomas Mann, Jung, Freud, Gropius, Klee and Kandinsky among its sojourners. Before the artists and literati it was favoured by the pope: Gregory XIII and Charles Borromeo founded a **Collegio Pontificio** here in 1584, in a fine building designed by Pelligrino Tibaldi (now a private school); the adjacent, older church, **Santa Maria della Misericordia**, has frescoes, a lovely painted casement ceiling and a polyptych of the *Madonna della Quercia* (1519) sent from Viterbo by the pope. The tourist office occupies the baroque **Casa Serodine** (1620), belonging to the Serodine family of painters. One, Giovanni Battista, contributed the elaborate stucco decorations, while the most famous, Giovanni Serodine, a pupil of Caravaggio, painted three fine canvases in **Santi Pietro e Paolo**. The **Museo Comunale d'Arte Moderna**, Via Borgo 34 (*open Tues–Sat 10–12 and 3–6, Sun 10–12; adm*) has frequent exhibits and a permanent collection of works by artists connected with Ascona (especially by the Russian Marianne von Werefkin, who died here, destitute) and others by Richter, Nicholson, Arp and Jawlensky to name a few.

In the late 19th century a group of artists, free thinkers, poets, anarchists, modern dancers, naturists and spiritualists, disillusioned with modern industrial society and longing to return to nature, founded a utopian vegetarian nudist commune on the promontory above Ascona that they called Monte Verità, 'the Mountain of Truth'. You can learn all about them and their 'air-light' wooden architecture in the **Percorso Museale del Monte Verità** (*open April–June and Sept–Oct 2.30–6; July–Aug 3–7; adm*), which includes the Casa Anatta (1902), 'Switzerland's most original wooden house'; the Casa Selma, a typical residence for members, inhabited until the 1940s; and, on the site of the original solarium, a round pavilion built in 1986 to house a vast circular *Chiaro Mondo dei Beati* (1923), the 'bright world of the blessed', a vision of the ideal world painted by member Elisar von Kupffer.

Locarno

Cross the River Maggio from Ascona and you're in Locarno, the town of camellias. Once part of the Lombard duchy of Angera, and ruled by the Visconti until 1513, the town earned its international cachet in 1925 with the Treaty of Locarno, that noble attempt to create a lasting peace in Europe by fixing borders, lightening the harsh terms imposed on Germany by the Treaty of Versailles and admitting Germany into the League of Nations. Since the end of the war that the treaty failed to prevent, Locarno has devoted itself to pleasure: open-air concerts and an international film festival (in August) take place in the city's big heart, the porticoed **Piazza Grande**; from here Largo Zorzi passes the **Casino-Kursaal** (*daily noon till 2am, Fri and Sat till 4am*) *en route* to the lake. The lake promenade, or Giardini di Muralto, is lined with beautiful rare trees, so many that the tourist office distributes a map to let you identify them as you stroll along.

Just up from Piazza Grande, the **Castello Visconteo** (*open April–Oct Tues–Sun 10–12 and 2–5; adm*) has well-preserved ceilings and frescoes from the 15th century. The castle houses the **Museo Civico e Archeologico**, with a collection of ancient Roman glass, ceramics from Magna Graecia and some good early medieval reliefs; on the second floor exhibits relate to the 1925 treaty. Admission includes the adjacent 16th-century palace, the ornately stuccoed

Casorella, with a fine loggia and court and an enormous 18th-century *Judgement of Paris* by local painter Giuseppe Orelli. Jean Arp donated many of his own works and those of his friends to the **Pinacoteca Comunale Casa Rusca**, Piazza S. Antonio (*open Tues–Sun 10–12 and 2–5; Thurs 2–9; adm*), site of frequent exhibitions in the summer. Near the train station for Basle in Locarno Muralto, the frescoed crypt of the 11th-century **San Vittore** has survived successive remodellings; look for the 15th-century relief of St Victor on horseback incorporated in the campanile.

From Locarno a rope railway ascends 1200ft to the **Santuario della Madonna del Sasso**, founded in 1497 after an apparition of the Virgin; walking up from town, however, allows you to visit the frescoed chapels of yet another 17th-century Sacro Monte. The sunflower-yellow sanctuary itself has the big art, however: a beautiful 14th-century *Pietà*, a *Flight into Egypt* by Bramantino and a *Removal of the Body of Christ*, by local painter Antonio Ciseri. A cablecar is currently under construction to carry you up to **Cimetta** (5600ft) for a fabulous view of the lake and Alps.

Continue east around Lake Maggiore for **Tenero**, a small resort (it has especially lovely camp sites, right on the lake) that claims the mildest climate in Switzerland, and makes a decent Merlot wine from its surrounding vineyards; one small cantine, the Fratelli Matasci, runs a little wine museum. South of Tenero the **Bolle di Magadino**, or River Ticino delta, is a favourite stopover for migratory birds; it forms part of the **Riviera del Gambarogno**, dotted with fishing villages down to the Italian frontier.

Where to Stay and Eating Out

Ascona ✉ CH6612, ✆ (004191–)

****Locanda Barbarossa**, Via Muraccio 142, ✆ 791 0202 (*very expensive*) is a splendid Relais & Châteaux hotel amid the vineyards and orchards; in the courtyard its restaurant, the Locanda, serves delicious food, including produce and poultry fresh from the farm. *Open mid-Mar–Oct.* One of the crenellated, vine-covered towers of the 13th-century Castle Ghiriglioni is now a hotel: ****Castello Seeschloss**, ✆ 791 0161, 🖷 791 1804 (*very expensive*) is central, with a lakeside garden with tall palms, pool and winebar. In the middle of the park, the restaurant of the **Monte Verità** hotel, one of the first modernist buildings in Switzerland, ✆ 791 4939 (*expensive*), reeks with atmosphere, and has fine view from its veranda; the food is good too. *Closed Sun out of season.*

Locarno ✉ CH6601, ✆ (004191–)

The signatories of the Treaty of Locarno stayed at the ****Grand Hotel**, Via Sempione 17, ✆ 743 0282, 🖷 743 3013 (*very expensive*), a lovely turn-of-the-century hotel, with a pool, tennis, pretty garden and every other amenity. ****Reber au Lac**, Viale Verbano 55, ✆ 743 0202 (*expensive*) is a very comfortable traditional hotel that welcomes children; it has a private beach, pool, tennis and an excellent restaurant. In Piazza Grand, the renovated ***Dell'Angelo**, ✆ 751 8175, 🖷 751 8256 (*moderate*) has comfortable rooms and pretty views from the roof terrace, and a decent restaurant pizzeria. Locarno boasts one of Switzerland's top gourmet shrines:

the ravishing, intimate **Centenario**, Lungolago Motta 17, ✆ 743 8222 (*very expensive*), where two chefs, Gerard Perriard and Giorgio Giner, buy the finest ingredients from across Europe and work culinary magic on everything they touch: lobster salad with mangoes, duckling in ginger, breast of pheasant in Dijon mustard seeds, Tuscan pigeon with Perigord truffles; sublime cheese trolley, desserts and wines; SF52 lunch menu makes it almost affordable, or celebrate a special day with a SF140 *gran menu degustazione* (*book a few days in advance; closed Sun and Mon, three weeks in Feb and two in July*).

Down the East Shore of Lake Maggiore

Recrossing the frontier into Italy at Maccagno and continuing down Maggiore's eastern, or Lombard, shore, cliffs hem in the lake and towns are fewer and more peaceful; the monastery of Santa Caterina del Sasso and Borromeo castle of Angera are the highlights.

Tourist Information

Maccagno: Via Garibaldi 1, ✆ 0332 562 009. **Luino**: Viale Dante Alighieri 6, ✆ 0332 530 019. **Laveno-Mombello**: Piazza Italia, ✆ 0332 666 666.

Maccagno to Laveno-Mombello

Maccagno is a quiet haven, with only a crenellated tower to recall its glory days, when it was the capital of an independent county, created in 962 by Emperor Otto I as a gift for the Mandelli brothers, who helped him in his war against King Berenguer II of Italy. The counts and their descendants remained staunchly faithful to the emperor and in return were given the right to mint their own coins; in 1542 Charles V gave them permission to hold a market on Wednesday (held to this day in nearby Luino). As time went by, however, competition with the big lords of the lake, the Borromei, made the county too expensive to maintain, and in 1692 the Mandellis finally gave in and sold it to their rivals. Maccagno is the base for visiting the wild, woody **Val Veddasca**, with venerable alpine villages accessible only on foot: **Curaglia** is a good one to aim for. Another road from Maccagno leads up to little **Lake Delio**, a pretty retreat; legend has it that a village was swallowed up by its waters after its miserly inhabitants refused hospitality to a stranger, and that on stormy nights you can hear the bells of its submerged campanile.

Five km south, where the River Tresa drains into Lake Maggiore from Lake Lugano, is the most important town on the Lombard shore, **Luino**, a pleasant town with plane trees along the lake. Luino is the presumed birthplace of Leonardo da Vinci's chief follower Bernadino Luini, who left a fresco up at the cemetery church, the **Oratorio di Santi Pietro e Paolo**. In 1848 Garibaldi was staying in an inn in Luini, ill with malaria, when a force of 1500 Austrians surprised him. Without even taking the time to dress, Garibaldi sprang out of bed and, holding up his drawers, took command of his troops and forced the Austrians to retreat. The mountain villages above Luino, such as **Dumenza** and **Agra**, are as unspoiled as they come; the latter enjoys a mighty view over Maggiore. The shore to the south is marked by a rocky pinnacle called **Sass Galet**, which looks like a praying nun or the Smog Monster, although it's supposed to be a chicken.

Laveno-Mombello, the ferry terminus from Intra, was known until 1980 for its ceramics, and the good old days of plates (i.e. 1895–1960) are remembered in the **Museo della Terraglia** in Cerro (*open Sep–June Tues–Thurs 2.30–5.30, Fri–Sun 10–12 and 2.30–5.30; July and Aug Tues–Sun 10–12 and 3.30–6.30; adm*). A dramatic cableway from Laveno and a 20-minute walk will take you to the top of the **Sasso di Ferro**, the 'Rock of Iron' just behind town, for fine panoramas over the middle of Maggiore. From Laveno it's 8km inland to **Casalzuigno**, where the 16th-century **Villa della Porta-Bozzolo** has rococo frescoes inside and a fine Italian baroque garden (*open Tues–Sun 10–1 and 2–5; adm*). Just beyond Casalzuigno, a winding road cuts up the wooded flank of Monte Nudo for **Arcumeggia**, an ancient hamlet where the stone houses are piled one atop the other and where, after the First World War, the locals decided to turn their home into a work of art by inviting famous Italian artists of the day to fresco the old stone walls, creating a curious outdoor 1950s time capsule. An easy path from Arcumeggia leads to **Sant'Antonio**, with splendid views over the lake.

Santa Caterina del Sasso

Hanging—literally—on the sheer cliffs of the Sasso Ballaro between Cerro and Reno is the deserted Carmelite convent of Santa Caterina del Sasso (*open 8.30–12 and 2–6*). Visible only from the lake, it is visited by boats between April and September; if you're driving, follow the signs from the shore road and take the steps down from the car park.

According to legend, in the 12th century a wealthy merchant and usurer named Alberto Besozzi was sailing on the lake when his boat sank. In deadly peril he prayed to St Catherine of Alexandria, who saved him from the waves and cast him upon this rock-bound shore. Impressed, Alberto repented of his usury and lived as a hermit in a cave, becoming famous for his piety. When his prayers brought an end to a local plague, he asked that as an *ex voto* the people construct a church to St Catherine. Over the centuries, a convent was added next to the cave of 'Beato Alberto' and it became a popular pilgrimage destination, especially after a huge boulder fell on the roof, only to be miraculously wedged just above the altar, directly over the head of the priest saying Mass. The boulder finally crashed through in 1910, without harming anyone, because nobody was there; the convent had been suppressed in 1770 by Joseph II of Austria. In 1986, a 15-year long restoration of Santa Caterina was completed, revealing medieval fresco fragments (note the one in the Sala Capitolare of armed men from the 13th century). Don't miss the 16th-century fresco of the Danse Macabre, high up in the loggia of the Gothic convent.

South of Santa Caterina, the surprisingly suburban bungalow estates of **Ispra** and **Ranco** house the employees of EURATOM, a 'peaceful' European atomic study centre. For lower tech, follow the signs in Ranco for the **Museo Europeo dei Trasporti** (*open Tues–Sun 10–12 and 3–5*), the fruit of the passion of a lawyer named Francesco Ogliari (author of a 66-volume *History of Transportation*), who created the museum with the motto of 'Two Centuries in Two Hours': among the trains, buses, ski lifts and metros note the Ferrovia Eolica (1858), a quirky wind-propelled rail line that ran for a few years out of Sesto Calende. The costumed mannequins going for rides add a certain flair; there's even a wax priest in a chapel, with some food for thought over the door: 'The world of transport exists by the measure of time. Here time has no measure. Eternity redeems time.'

Angera and its Castle

Angera, just south, lies in the shadow of the **Rocca di Angera** (*open April–Oct daily 9.30–12.30 and 2–6; adm*), a castle that commands the entire south half of the lake. Built in the 11th century by the Della Torre, it passed to the Visconti in 1314, then was ceded by Milan to the Borromei in 1449. Don't miss their 17th-century wine press right by the castle entrance, so huge that only San Carlone, standing across the lake in Arona, could possibly work it (it would be nice to imagine him hopping down from his pedestal and doing something useful). Since 1988 the occupants have been on a smaller scale: Lilliputians made of porcelain, wood, celluloid and plastic, all members of the **Museo della Bambola** or Doll Museum, one of the best collections in Europe. Barbie and Ken's ancestors from the 17th century on are beautifully displayed, along with their often staggeringly detailed little households and accessories; there are even nun and priest dolls and play-Hosts for children who want to grow up to be saints. The cumulative effect of gazing at so many smiling human simulacra is surreal; expect to end up as glassy-eyed as the dolls. Other rooms contain children's clothing from the last three centuries.

There's more, especially 15th-century frescoes from the Borromeo palace in Milan, or at least the bits that survived the bombs in 1943: the ghostly *Pomegranate pickers* by Giovanni da Vaprio, peacocks and Aesop's fables by Michelino da Besozzo, Borromeo family portraits and mythologies, and an *Atalanta e Ippomene* by Guido Reni. Archaeological finds litter the courtyard, includings bits of a Mithraeum discovered in 1917 in a cave under the castle. Best of all is the vast **Sala della Giustizia**, which the proud Visconti had frescoed with astrological fancies and scenes of battling bishop Ottone Visconti's victory over the Della Torre in 1277. If you don't mind the creaky old wooden steps and signs disclaiming all responsibility for your safety, you can continue up the tower from here for commanding views over the lake and the castle's vineyards.

Where to Stay and Eating Out

Maccagno ✉ 21010

The simple but enchanting **Al Pozzo**, ✆ 0332 560 145, on the mountain road leading up to Lake Delio, enjoys a spectacular view and offers a basic but cheap menu—*cansonsei*, tagliatelle with porcini. *Open daily.*

Luino ✉ 21016

Old-fashioned ★★★★**Camin**, Viale Dante 35, ✆ 0332 530 118, 🖃 0332 537 226 (*expensive*) has big rooms, plush fittings and heavy wooden furniture, combined with the modern: TV (and in some rooms, video), hydro-massage baths and twin basins in marble. Opposite the station in Piazza Marconi, ★★**Internazionale**, ✆ 0332 530 193, 🖃 0332 537 882 (*cheap*) has a smart modern interior, with fully equipped and good-size rooms, and parking facilities. In Piazza Libertà, ★★★**Ancora**, ✆/🖃 0332 530 451 (*cheap*) is a bit basic, but enjoys fine views. ★★**Del Pesce**, Via del Porto 16, ✆ 0332 532 579 (*cheap*) doesn't look like much from the outside, but has comfortable rooms and a good lake fish restaurant. Just down from the station ★**Elvezia**, Via XXV Aprile 107, ✆ 0332 531 219, 🖃 0332 535 800 (*cheap*) is neat, clean and convenient; it's towards the top of this price range, but still good value.

Laveno-Mombello ✉ 21014

★★★**Il Porticciolo**, Via Fortino 40, ✆ 0332 667 257, 🖃 0332 666 753 (*moderate*) has the ten nicest rooms in town and the best restaurant, serving a delicious risotto with scampi and watercress and plenty of lake fish, accompanied by an excellent wine list. *Closed Tues, and Wed lunch*. For a spectacular view of Lake Maggiore, there's ★★**Funivia**, at the top of the cableway in Poggio S. Elsa, ✆ 0332 604 200 (*cheap*); it's a 2-hour walk from the town (for those wishing to build up an appetite for lunch in the restaurant). *Open in winter at weekends only*.

Ranco ✉ 21020

Surrounded by gardens, ★★★★**Il Sole**, Piazza Venezia 5, ✆ 0331 976 507, 🖃 0331 976 620 (*very expensive*) is a superb retreat from the cares of the world, a lovely old inn with a charming terrace and one of the finest restaurants on the lake. The exquisitely and imaginatively prepared lake fish and crayfish are worth the journey; they're complemented by a magnificent wine list and delicate desserts. *Closed Mon and Tues, Dec and Jan*.

Between Lakes Maggiore and Lugano: the Varesotto

The triangle formed by Lakes Maggiore, Lugano and the Swiss border is called the Varesotto, not exactly a destination you'll see in a Thomas Cook poster. Obscure, yes, but dull, no: besides ten small and hygienic lakes and the Campo dei Fiori natural park, the Varesotto is richly endowed with frescoes, ranging in date from the 8th century to last year, including exquisite works by that Tuscan charmer, Masolino, in Castiglione Olona. If you're driving, take a good map: the road sign network is a masterpiece of obfuscation.

Getting Around

Varese, the main town between the lakes, is served by the FS and Milano-Nord **trains** from Milan—the stations in Varese are next to each other. There's also a station at Castiglione Olona. **Buses** from Varese go to Castiglione, Arsago, Castelséprio, Lake Varese and the Campo dei Fiori.

Varese: Via Carrobbio 2, ✆ 0332 283 604.

Varese and the Campo dei Fiori

Varese, city of gardens, city of shoes and increasingly bedroom suburb of Milan, spills over a plateau between Lake Maggiore and the Olana river. Although it was founded by the Celts it has managed to avoid history for most of its career. Maria Theresa gave it briefly to the Duke of Modena, Francesco III d'Este (1765–80), whose main contribution was to build himself a vast spread in the centre of town, the **Palazzo Estense**, now the Municipio; its gaudiest room, the Salone Estense, is open by request. The duke's park, modelled on the Schönbrunn gardens in Vienna, and the adjacent English garden of the eclectic **Villa Mirabello** are now a city park; the Villa Mirabello houses the **Musei Civici** (*open Tues–Sat 9.30–12.30 and 2–5.30, Sun 9.30–12.30; adm*), with a hodgepodge of paintings, local archaeology and the butterfly collection of the great tenor Tamagno.

The central square in Varese, Piazza Monte Grappa, received a stern Mussolini facelift; stylish, perhaps, but not exactly cosy. Just beyond it, Varese's landmark, the garlic-domed 17th-century **Campanile del Bernascone**, rings the chimes for the **Basilica di San Vittore**, an ancient foundation rebuilt by Pellegrino Tibaldi with a neoclassical façade pasted on; inside the most important paintings are by Il Morazzone. The austere 12th-century **Baptistry** contains some original frescoes.

City bus C from the station goes up 8km to Varese's **Sacro Monte** (*see* pp.132–3), with 14 chapels filled with frescoes and stuccoes on the Mystery of the Rosary, built between 1604 and 1684. By foot it's a 2km walk up beginning at the Prima Cappella; the most artistic one, the seventh (*The Flagellation*) was frescoed by Il Morazzone. The devotional tour climaxes at **Santuario di Santa Maria del Monte**, founded in the 5th century by St Ambrose in gratitude for Lombardy's safe deliverance from the Arian heresy. Rebuilt in 1473 and later lavishly baroqued, it houses a ballistically ornate marble altar, a much revered 14th-century 'Black Virgin' attributed to St Luke and *trecento* frescoes in the crypt. The nearby **Museo Baroffio** (*open by request; adm*) houses works of art donated to the sanctuary, and the **Museo Pogliaghi** (*closed for restoration*) contains Egyptian, Greek and Roman antiquities, paintings, and works by the villa's former owner Ludovico Pogliaghi, including a full-size plaster cast of his Milan cathedral door.

From the sanctuary, continue 5km up to the karst massif of the **Parco Naturale di Campo dei Fiori** (4050ft) for lovely views over the lakes and mountains. Near the grand abandoned Liberty-style **Albergo Campo dei Fiori** (1912) stone steps lead up to the Monte Tre Croci, the 'Balcony of Lombardy', with views as far as Monte Rosa.

Lake Varese

Just under Varese lies its lake, an 8½km-long sheet of water set in its low rolling hills, the big, gentle, sleepy head of the Varesotto's 'minor lakes'. There's a Renaissance vision of it just outside the centre of Varese, along the road to Gavirate, in the **Castello di Masnago** (*open*

Tues–Sun 3–6; adm), where in 1938 two sets of 15th-century secular frescoes were discovered under the whitewash: an elegant courtly scene by the lake and, upstairs, female vices and virtues, including Vanity, preening her elaborate muffin of hair. Lake Varese's main settlement, **Gavirate**, is famous for its hand-carved pipes, and has a collection from around the world in its **Museo della Pipa** (*ring ahead,* © *0332 743 334*). For carvings of a different nature go to Voltorre (just south of Gavirate), where the 11th-century Cluniac monastery of **San Michele** (now a cultural centre) has a cloister with beautifully sculpted capitals, attributed to the Comacino master Lanfranco. The campanile has one of the oldest bells in Italy, and sounds like it too.

Catch the little boat from **Biandronno** on Lake Varese's west shore for **Isolino Virginia**, a wee wooded islet inhabited three millennia ago by people who built their homes on pile dwellings just off shore. The islet's **Museo Preistorico di Villa Ponti** (*open June–Oct Sat and Sun 2.30–6.30*) chronicles the settlement, which endured into Roman times. Isolino Virginia is a good spot for a picnic, or you can lunch in the little island restaurant. To the southwest the lake dissolves into marshlands, not as much fun for humans as for waterfowl; the same holds true for the reed beds in Lake Varese's twin baby sisters to the west, **Lago di Monate** and **Lago di Comabbio**.

Arsago Séprio to Castiglione Olona

South of the lakelets and Lake Maggiore, the River Ticino divides Piedmont from Lombardy. This area is now a Natural Park, although you may not immediately notice it around Milan's Malpensa airport and industrial centres such as **Somma Lombardo**. Somma was defended by the large **Castello Visconti** (*guided tours April–Sept Sat and Sun 10–11.30 and 2.30–6.30; adm*); rebuilt in the 1400s, it expanded into a residence over the centuries. Much of its family furnishings are intact, along with monumental fireplaces, a canopied royal bed with a Visconti viper on top and a huge collection of barber's dishes. The enormous spreading cedar in the garden is as old as the castle.

North of Somma, a cemetery in **Golasecca** gave its name to the local Iron Age culture (9th–6th century BC); in the same vicinity, you can visit the cromlechs of the **Necropoli del Monsurino**, some of the oldest monumental tombs in Italy (find the Golasecca Centro Orizzonte/Parco Ticino, and follow the path from there). Celtic, Roman and Lombard finds from the area are housed in the **Museo Civico** (*closed*) in **Arsago Séprio**, 2km east of Somma Lombardo. The Lombards were responsible for Arsago's 9th-century gem of a church, the **Basilica di San Vittore**, with a lovely façade, three apses, a 9th-century campanile that has bells looped on top and aisles of Roman columns. In the 11th century, a hexagonal **baptistry** was added, crowned with a round drum dressed in blind arches; the serene interior has traces of the original frescoes.

Castiglione Olona

The little Renaissance nugget of **Castiglione Olona**, southeast of the lake 8km from Varese, is known as an islet of Tuscany in Lombardy, but it's an islet wrapped in a huge lake of suburban sprawl around an aeronautics plant, with nary a sign to point the way; locate the ghastly new church and take the steep winding road down to the bottom of the valley to find the Borgo— the Castiglione Olona you want. It owes its quattrocento Tuscan charm to Cardinal Branda

Castiglioni (1350–1443), a son of the local nobility who went on to serve as a bishop in Hungary and briefly in Florence, where he was so enchanted by the blossoming Renaissance that he brought Masolino da Pancale (after his famous collaboration with Masaccio in Florence's Brancacci Chapel), Lorenzo di Pietro (Il Vecchietta) and other Florentine artists home with him to do up Castiglione, and incidentally introduce the first glimpse of new humanism into Lombardy.

The Borgo, the Cardinal's 'ideal citadel', is essentially unchanged since the 15th century. In tiny central Piazza Garibaldi, the **Chiesa di Villa** was inspired by Brunelleschi, a cube surmounted by an octagonal drum, its exterior decoration limited to framing bands of grey and two giant statues on either side of the door, of St Christopher and St Anthony Abbot. Inside, nearly all the art dates from the 1400s: the Annunciation, the tomb of Guido Castiglioni by the school of Amadeo, and the four terracotta Doctors of the Church. Opposite, the cardinal's **Palazzo Branda Castiglioni** is now a museum (*open Tues–Sat 9–12 and 2.30–5.30, Sun 3–6*). The cardinal's bedroom has charming frescoes of children playing under the fruit trees by an unknown Lombard painter, while below are various emblems and sayings—mnemonic devices?—probably designed by the scholarly cardinal himself. Il Vecchietta frescoed the palace chapel (1437); in the study, Masolino painted a scene of Veszprem, Hungary, as described by the cardinal from memory.

Ancient plane trees line the steep Via Cardinal Branda that leads up to the Gothic **Collegiata** (*open Oct–Mar Tues–Sun 10–12 and 2.30–5; April–Sept Tues–Sun 10–12 and 3–7; adm*), built in 1421 over the Castiglioni castle (the gate still survives). The brick church contains beautiful frescoes, especially Masolino's *Life of the Virgin* in the vault, while Il Vecchietta painted the *Life of St Stephen* and Paolo Schiavo frescoed the *Life of St Lawrence*; the *Crucifixion* in the apse is attributed to yet another Tuscan master, Neri di Bicci. In 1435 Masolino frescoed the entire **Baptistry** (once the castle tower), a work commonly considered his life's masterpiece, the culmination of his evocatively lyrical and refined style.

The Olana valleys hold a pair of other surprises 700 years older than Castiglione. The **Monastero di Torba,** set in the woods just off the road in **Gornate Olana** (*open Oct–Dec 10–1 and 2–5; Feb–Sept till 6; closed last 2 weeks of Dec, and Jan; adm*) was founded in the 5th century as a Lombard defence tower, but three centuries later it found a new use as a monastery. Acquired by the Fondo per l'Ambiente Italiano (the Italian National Trust), the 8th-century frescoes in the tower have been restored, along with the original crypt and tombs. The tower defended **Castelséprio** to the south, a Lombard *castrum* designed on the Roman model. Destroyed in the 13th century, ruins of the walls, churches and castle moulder under the trees 1.5km from the centre, but the main reason to stop is little **Santa Maria Foris Portas**: its unique 8th-century frescoes in an Eastern Hellenistic style were discovered during the Second World War by a partisan hiding here (*all part of a Zona Archeologica; open April–Sept Tues–Sat 9–6, Sun 9–4.45; Oct–Mar Tues–Sun 9–6*).

From Varese to Lugano

From Varese there are two valley routes to Lake Lugano. The prettiest, N233, cuts through the Valganna to Ponte Tresa, a route that takes in a Liberty-style brewery at Grotte, the **Birreria Liberty Poretti**; the 11th-century **Badia di San Gemolo** at Ganna; and little **Lake Ghirla** beside a village of the same name. The second route, from Varese to Porto Ceresio, passes near **Bisuschio**, site of the magnificent Renaissance **Villa Cicogna Mozzoni** (*on the SS244, just north of Arcisate; open Sun and public hols April–Oct 9.30–12 and 2.30–7; open every afternoon in Aug; adm*). Built in 1400 as a hunting lodge, enlarged in 1500 as a permanent residence, and still owned by the Counts Cicogna Mozzoni, the villa has delightful frescoes by the Campi brothers of Cremona and their school, forgotten for centuries under layers of white-wash (applied in the hope of 'sterilizing' the villa against the plague in the 1600s). The porticoes open out into a Renaissance garden of box hedges and fountains with a lofty water staircase, laid out in the 1560s. **Viggiù**, just to the east, is a little resort and belvedere, and was the birthplace of early baroque architect Martino Longhi, who worked mainly in Rome.

Where to Stay and Eating Out

Varese ✉ 21100

An elegant villa of 1821, the ★★★★**Villa Castiglioni**, Via Castiglioni 1, in Induno Olona (8km north), ✆ 0332 200 201, ✉ 0332 201 269 (*very expensive*) has hosted the likes of Garibaldi and Mazzini and, as you stroll the shady park, swim, play tennis, or doze in one of the canopy beds, you can easily forget that this is a hotel (until you come to pay the bill!).

Lago Maggiore, Via Carrobio 19, ✆ 0332 231 183 (*expensive*) has been one of Varese's best restaurants for decades, using top-notch ingredients in regional and more exotic dishes; the cheeseboard alone may revolutionize your ideas about Italian cooking. *Closed Sun eve, Mon lunch, and July.*

Lugano, Como and the Valtellina

The two lakes north of Milan, Lugano and Como, are very beautiful and very accessible from the Lombard capital in less than an hour on the *autostrada*. Lake Lugano is two-thirds Swiss, which lends it a different flavour: there's more money floating around, more modern and contemporary art, more organization. Lake Como is thoroughly Italian, a prestigious retreat since Roman times; a surprising number of Lombard foundations and very early Romanesque churches dot its shores and the hills of La Brianza, the region just south of its straddling legs. The dramatic Grigna mountains over the Lecco branch of the lake haunted Leonardo da Vinci, while in the 19th century the romantic villas and gardens on the west shore were a favourite haven of opera composers and their divas, on leave from rehearsals at La Scala.

This chapter also includes Lombardy's northernmost, alpine province of Sondrio. This follows the valley of the River Adda, the Valtellina (a name you'll hear far more often than Sondrio), all the way from Lake Como to Stelvio National Park and the skiers' paradise at Bormio, offering stunning mountain scenery, unspoiled valleys, an excellent network of trails and refuges, distinctive wines and good cheer along the way.

Lake Lugano

Zigzagged Lake Lugano with its steep, fjorded shores is a striking sight, especially in the centre where its curious shape and narrow span closed in by mountains give it a rare intimacy and benign climate. In a few places, especially around the city of Lugano, the lake has become a victim of its own attractiveness; other shores, too steep for building, still darken the waters with emerald green and white reflections of the wooded cliffs.

Lugano's extremities are Italian, but its heart has been part of the Canton Ticino ever since the Swiss snatched the province from French-occupied Milan back in 1512. Two centuries later, when Ticino had a chance to return to Italy, it stalwartly refused: as part of its punishment, the Italians insist on calling Lake Lugano by its Latin name, Ceresio. Another punishment is to have a border rimmed with petrol stations. And a crumb of Italian territory, Campione d'Italia, survives in the middle of the lake, which is just big enough to support a casino that more than welcomes Swiss francs. If you can't beat them, soak them.

Getting Around

Lugano's **airport** is served by Crossair, linked up to Swissair flights from London, Paris, Nice, Rome, Florence and Venice as well as the major Swiss airports. From Varese, **trains** go as far as Porto Ceresio on the west end of Lugano; from Milan trains to Como continue to Lugano by way of Chiasso, while Lugano itself is linked by a local train line (the FLP) to points west as far as Ponte Tresa. Porlezza, on the east end of the lake, is linked by **buses** to Como or Menaggio; buses from Lugano or Como go directly to Campione d'Italia. All the lakeside towns are served by **steamers** on the *Società Navigazione Lago di*

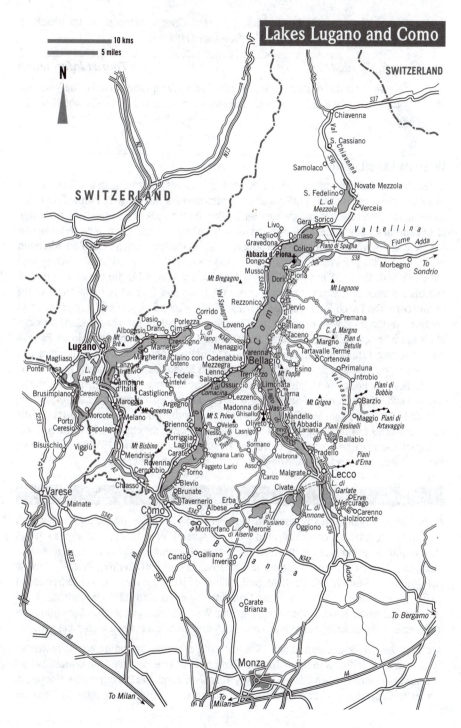

Lakes Lugano and Como

SWITZERLAND

Chiavenna

S. Cassiano

Val Chiavenna

S37

Samolaco

S36

Novate Mezzola

S. Fedelino

L. di Mezzola

Verceia

Valtellina

Livo

Gera

Sorico

Fiume Adda

Peglio

Domaso

Piano di Spagna

Gravedona

Colico

S38

Abbazia di Piona

Dongo

Morbegno

To Sondrio

Musso

Piona

Mt Bregagno

Dorio

Mt Legnone

Rezzonico

Dervio

Val Sanagra

Premana

Corrido

C. d. Margno

Loveno

Bellano

Pian d. Betulle

Dasio

Porlezza

Menaggio

Taceno

Margno

Albogasio

Drano

Cima

L. di Piano

Cressogno

Tartavalle Terme

Cortenova

Oria

Mamete

Varenna

Primaluna

Lugano

Mt Brè

Margherita

Claino con Osteno

Cadenabbia

Mezzegra

Bellagio

Introbio

Magliaso

Lanzo d'Intelvi

Lenno

Esino

Mt Foppe

Ponte Tresa

S. Fedele Intelvi

Salano

Tremezzo

Limonta

Piani di Bobbio

L. Lugano

Campione d'Italia

Ossuccio

Comacina

Lierna

Mt Grigna

Barzio

Brusimpiano

Ceresio

Castiglione

Lezzeno

Maggio

Piani di Artavaggio

Maroggia

Argegno

Madonna di Ghisallo

Vassena

Porto Ceresio

Morcote

Mt Generoso

Melano

Brienno

Mt S. Primo

Veleso

Oliveto

Mandello Lariana

Piani Resinelli

Abbadia

Capolago

Nesso

Piano di Tivano

Lasnigo

Ballabio

Bisuschio

Viggiù

Mt Bisbino

Torriggia

Laglio

Sormano

Pradello

Piani d'Erna

Mendrisio

Carate

Pognana Lario

Valbrona

Lecco

Ravenna

Torno

Faggeto Lario

Asso

Malgrate

L. di Garlate

Cernobbio

Chiasso

Blevio

Canzo

Civate

Erve

Vercurago

Varese

Brunate

Erba

L. di Annone

Carenno

Malnate

Tavernerio

Albese

Calolziocorte

Como

S342

Montorfano

L. di Alserio

L. di Pusiano

Merone

Oggiono

S36

A9

Cantù

Galliano

Inverigo

Adda

N342

Carate Brianza

To Bergamo

Monza

A4

To Milan

To Milan

SWITZERLAND

N13

N2

Valsassina

Brianza

A8

N33

S233

A2

S335

S342

163

Lugano line, run with the precision of Swiss clockwork, except when the wind's up
(© (004191) 971 5223; a variety of passes are available).

Lugano © (004191–)   ***Tourist Information***

Caslano: Piazza Lago, © 606 2986. **Campione d'Italia**: Via Volta 16,
© 649 8182, 🖂 68505. **Lugano**: Riva Albertolli 5, © 921 4664, 🖂 922
7653.

Western Lake Lugano

Lugano slowly drains its rather polluted waters into Lake Maggiore through the Tresa, a river
that forms the border between the Italian and Swiss halves of the village of **Ponte Tresa**. Just
above all the petrol stations and the steamer landing, on the nook of a promontory, the village
of **Laveno** has a pretty medieval core. If you're travelling with children, however, make for
the Swiss shore, where the Alprose chocolate company in **Caslano** runs a **Chocolate Museum**
on Europe's 200-year-old love affair with the brown stuff; top it off with a factory tour
(*Mon–Fri 9–6, Sat and Sun 9–5*). Nearby at Magliaso the **Zoo al Maglio** has over a hundred
animals and birds from around the world (*open 10–5; summer 9–7; adm*). In the pretty village
of **Morcote**, the **Parco Scherrer** (*open daily 15 Mar–Oct 10–5; July and Aug 10–6; adm*)
opens on to the lake, with exotic statues, in a setting of palms, camphor, cedars, Mexican
pines and other exotic flora. Morcote's Romanesque **Cappella di Sant'Antonio da Padova**
has interesting 13th-century frescoes (including an unusual one of dead souls squirming in a
net); above, on a panoramic terrace, **Santa Maria del Sasso** has others from the Renaissance.
North, near the bridge at Melide, **Carona** has a number of mansions painted with exterior
frescoes and, in the church of **San Giorgio**, a rare copy of Michelangelo's *Last Judgement*,
painted in 1585 by Domenico Pezzi. Copying was something of a fad in these parts (artistic
copyrights obviously didn't apply once Ticino became Swiss); the church at **Capriasco** north
of Lugano has an earnest copy of Leonardo's *Last Supper*, painted before 1550 by an unknown
hand. It hardly measures up to the original, but it's certainly in better nick.

Lugano

Warm, palmy Lugano is an arty resort city piled between Monte Brè and Monte San Salvatore,
a lovely setting that has been compared to Rio de Janeiro; in Switzerland at any rate it's as
close as you can get to Paradise (its residential suburb, 10 minutes west by bus). To go with its
sumptuous lake views, it has a sumptuous Renaissance gem, in waterfront Piazza Luini: the
plain church of **Santa Maria degli Angioli**, built in 1510 by the Franciscans and frescoed in
1529 with an enormous, nearly life-sized *Crucifixion* by Bernardino Luini: his masterpiece, full
of colour and detail. Ruskin, who wrote that Luini was 'ten times greater than Leonardo', saw
it and gushed, 'Every touch he lays is ethereal; every thought he conceives is beauty and purity…'

Art from the late Gothic period and 19th and 20th centuries, including works by Renoir,
Degas and Klee, is displayed in the **Museo Cantonale d'Arte**, in three 15th-century *palazzi*
in Piazza Manzoni 7 (*open Wed–Sun 10–6, Tues 2–6; adm*). On the other side of town, in
Via Pietro Cappelli, the **Villa Favorita** (*open Easter–Oct Fri–Sun 10–6; adm exp*) was the

home of Baron Heinrich von Thyssen-Bornemisza's fabulous collection of the Old Masters, now on loan in Madrid and Barcelona (thanks to the Baroness, a former Miss Spain), although the villa retains the Thyssen collection of European and American modern art, with a special emphasis on the Luminists and Hudson River School. Further along the lake, along Via Cortivo (take bus 2 from Piazza Manzoni to S. Domenico and walk 5 minutes), the neoclassical Villa Heleneum is now the **Museo delle Culture Extraeuropee** (*open Wed–Sun 10–5; adm*), containing a fascinating collection of wooden figures and cult objects from Oceania, Africa and Asia donated by Surrealist artists Serge and Graziella Brignoni.

As ever, one of the big thrills is going up to look back down again: a funicular runs up to the summit on **Monte Brè** (3150ft), 'Switzerland's sunniest mountain' (*take bus no.1 from the centre of Lugano to the station; departures every 30mins until 6.15, © 004191 971 3171*); there's a restaurant on top and the little village of Brè to explore. Another funicular ascends from Lugano's suburb of Paradiso to **Monte San Salvatore** (915m/3000ft), with more fine views over the lake and Alps, a restaurant and nature trails (*Mar–mid Nov every 30mins, in summer till 11pm*). For even bigger views, catch the steamer down the south arm of the lake to **Capolago** and take the rack railway for 40 minutes up to the summit of **Monte Generoso** (1714m/5623ft), call © 004191 649 7722 for schedules. Lastly, boats from Lugano call at **Gandria** for visits to the **Museo Doganale Swizzero** (*open Palm Sun–end Oct daily 1.30–5.30*), dedicated to a subject that has been many a traveller's nightmare—Swiss customs. Learn about all the cracks and crevices they've found in cars, false passports, counterfeit goods and more: children like the night-vision tunnel and catch-the-smuggler computer games.

Campione d'Italia

Campione has been a little enclave ever since its Lombard owner Totone bequeathed it to the church of Sant'Ambrogio in Milan in 777, and to this day its church follows the Ambrosian rites and prolonged carnival. In the Middle Ages Campione was celebrated for its master builders, the Maestri Campionesi, symbolized by the big snail on the fief's coat of arms. The Maestri Campionesi had a hand in most of Italy's great Romanesque cathedrals—Milan's Sant'Ambrogio, Cremona, Monza (by Matteo da Campione, one of the rare masters to leave his name), Verona and Modena—and such was their reputation that when Hagia Sophia in Constantinople began to sag, the Emperor of Byzantium hired them to prop it up. Rather disappointingly, in Campione itself they left only a small sample of their handiwork: ancient San Zenone (thoroughly mutilated in the 17th century), **San Pietro** (1326) and the baroque-encased church of the **Madonna dei Ghirli** (Our Lady of the Swallows—i.e. the masons who periodically returned home), with a lively, personalized *Last Judgement* (1400) by Lanfranco and Filippolo De Veris under the portico, and inside 13th-century frescoes and the monochrome *Labours of the Months*.

Although part of Italy since Napoleon passed through in 1797, Campione is best known these days as the Las Vegas of Lombardy. The **Casinò Municipale** was founded in 1917 in bizarre circumstances: Italian naval intelligence, hoping to capture the displacement plans of the imperial fleet in the Adriatic, which were locked in the safe of the Austro-Hungarian ambassador in Bern, opened a casino to draw in foreign diplomats; the games tables were operated by Italian spies and safecrackers released from prison to serve their country. These days the profits go for public works in the province of Como; the bandits are all one-armed and open from 1.45pm to 3am, the game tables from 3.30pm to 2.30am.

Where to Stay and Eating Out

Lugano ☑ CH6900, ✆ (004191–)

If money's no object, the 19th-century Relais & Châteaux ★★★★★**Villa Principe Leopoldo**, Via Montablano 5, ✆ 985 8855, ✆ 985 8825 (*luxury*), in a beautiful hillside park overlooking the city, will keep you in the style you'd like to be accustomed to, complete with a health centre. Near the lake in the city centre, ★★★**International au Lac**, Via Nassa 68, ✆ 922 7541, ✆ 922 7544 (*expensive*) is more than comfortable, with the added amenities of a pool, garden terrace and underground parking; if you're driving, the traditional, family-run ★★★**Washington**, Via San Gottardo 55, ✆ 966 4136, ✆ 967 5067 (*moderate*), surrounded by gardens, is tranquil and charming and boasts a good restaurant. Smack on the lake far from the traffic, ★★**Fisher's Seehotel**, Sentiero di Gandria 10, ✆ 971 5571, ✆ 970 1577 (*moderate*) is simple and pleasant; ★**Montarina**, a villa set in a palm garden not far from the station at Via Montarina 1, ✆ 966 7272, ✆ 966 1213 (*cheap*) has pretty views over the lake and free parking.

Lugano is chock-full of top-notch restaurants where you can seriously strain your overdraft facilities, but lunch at some of these temples of cuisine can be quite reasonable. Fashionable **Parco Saroli**, Via Stefano Franscini 6, ✆ 923 5314, serves excellent and unusual homemade pasta dishes, seafood, a wide choice of superb breads, cheeses, desserts and an award-winning wine list: for SF37.50 you can choose a pasta course, main course and dessert, and get a half-bottle of wine into the bargain; the *menu desgustazione* with 6 courses is SF65. *Closed Sun*. A delightful experience if you remember to book a day or two in advance, the intimate, utterly simple **Antica Osteria Gerso**, Piazzetta Solaro 24 at Massagno, ✆ 966 1915, serves a limited but discriminating menu: favourite dishes include onion soup with tangy pecorino cheese, *tortelli di zucca alle mandorle* and duck with oranges, all accompanied by a fair wine choice from the adjacent *enoteca*; menu SF30. *Closed Sun and Mon*.

Campione d'Italia ☑ 22060, ✆ (004191–)

★**Bellevue**, ✆ 649 7566 (*cheap*) has the local hotel monopoly, with 7 simple rooms, but after winning big at the tables, or perhaps as consolation, punters congregate at **La Taverna**, Via Roma 2, ✆ 649 4797 (*expensive*) for delicious truffle and mushroom dishes. *Closed Wed and Thurs lunch*.

Back in Italy: Eastern Lake Lugano

East of Lugano, the lake enters the Italian province of Como. The hamlets on the north shore all belong to the *comune* of **Valsolda**, among them pretty **San Mamete**, a steamer landing with an arcaded piazza by a lake, and picturesque **Oria**, site of Antonio Fogazzaro's famous (in Italy, at any rate) novel, *Piccolo Mondo Antico*. **Porlezza**, a pleasant if rather Swissified town on the far east end of the lake, was the Roman *Portus Retiae* (gate to the Rhaetic tribes) and the cradle of the Della Porta sculptors (including Guglielmo, Michelangelo's pupil). Buses from Porlezza cross over to Menaggio on Lake Como, passing on the way the tiny, enchanting **Lago di Piano**, a bit of Lake Lugano that got away in a landslide; a new road from here leads up to **Cavargna** (3534ft) in the Lepontine Alps, a region so remote it was once called 'Little Tibet'; its traditional crafts and characters (the Blacksmith, the Carpenter, the Smuggler) are recalled in the **Museo della Valle** (*open Sun 2–5, or ask at the Trattoria Butti, © 0344 63261*).

Lake Lugano to Lake Como: the Val d'Intelvi

An alternative, longer, meandering route between the lakes runs through the Val d'Intelvi. In the Middle Ages (when it was called the Val Antelami) the valley produced dynasties of masons and master builders—most importantly the inimitable Benedetto Antelami, 12th-century architect and sculptor of Parma's baptistry. These cousins of the Campionese masters reached the peak of their fame in the 18th century, when the courts of Naples, Spain, Austria and Russia kept them busily employed on a hundred projects.

The Val d'Intelvi follows the stream Telo, which flows into Lake Lugano at **Osteno**, west of Porlezza; you can make a boat excursion up the watery ravine and take in the marble *Madonna and Child* (1464) in the parish church, carved by Osteno native Andrea Bregno. From Osteno the road winds up to **Lanzo d'Intelvi**, the most important resort in the valley, with a golf course and nearby ski runs up at Pellio and San Fedele. If you don't have a car, you can get there from Lake Lugano by way of a funicular from the steamer landing of **Santa Margherita**, which deposits you at the panoramic **Belvedere**, 2km under Lanzo. Yet another funicular near Lanzo connects Monte Sighignola (4271ft) to Campione d'Italia.

The valley's builders left a number of churches in the Intelvi, many decorated with sculpture and stuccoes, another local speciality: you'll find especially good examples at **Laino** (16th-century San Lorenzo) and **Scaria** (13th-century Santi Nazaro e Celso). Scaria also has a museum dedicated to the Val Intelvi, the **Museo della Valle** (*open Aug 4–6; all other times call Maria Grazia Carroni, © 031 839 772*) with works salvaged from its churches, including a Byzantine cross. Clutches of medieval houses remain at unspoiled **Ponna Superiore** and **Ponna Inferiore**, both set in some of the Intelvi's prettiest landscapes; also **Pellio Superiore**, **Castiglione d'Intelvi** (at Montronio) and **Dizzasco**. The church at **Casasco d'Intelvi** has a fresco attributed to Luini while **Pigra** has another famous viewpoint, this time overlooking Lake Como.

Where to Stay and Eating Out

San Mamete (Valsolda) ✉ 22010

***Stella d'Italia**, © 0344 68139, ℱ 0344 68729 (*moderate*), is a lovely lakeside hotel with a lido, garden, good restaurant and waterside terraces. Each room has a balcony, and you can borrow the hotel's boat for outings. *Open April–Oct.* Also on the lake, in nearby Oria, **Riviera**, ©/ℱ 0344 68156 (*cheap*) also has a pretty lido and an excellent restaurant (*moderate*), with plenty of fish and a flair for flambéeing. *Closed Wed.*

Porlezza ✉ 22018

Try the inexpensive **★★Rosen-Garden**, ✆/🖶 0344 61974, which has ten comfortable rooms, all with bath, near the lake, or **★★Regina**, ✆/🖶 0344 61228 (*moderate*) with quiet and simple rooms on the lake, all with bath. The fine restaurant features good homemade pasta, excellent fish and specialities such as breast of duck with grapes. *Closed Mon.*

Lanzo d'Intelvi ✉ 22024

★★★★ Belvedere, by the funicular station, ✆031 841 461, 🖶 031 840 122 (*expensive*) has long been Lanzo's finest, with a garden and superb views. Set off on its own amid the trees, **Locanda del Dosso**, Via alla Fonte, ✆ 031 840401 (*expensive*) serves delicious trout and mushroom dishes, *fagottini di manzo intelvese* and homemade desserts. *Closed Tues.*

Lake Como

Sapphire Lake Como has been Italy's prestige romantic lake ever since the early days of the Roman empire, when it was called Lario and the Plinys wrote of the luxuriant beauty surrounding their villas on its shores. It was just the sort of beauty that enraptured the children of the romantic era, inspiring some of the best works of Verdi, Rossini, Bellini and Liszt, as well as enough good and bad English verse to fill an anthology. And it is still there, the Lake Como of the Shelleys and Wordsworths, the grand villas and lush gardens, the mountains and beloved irregular shore of wooded promontories. But there are times when the lake can seem schizophrenic, its nostalgic romance and mellowed dignity challenged by demands that it serve as Milan's weekend Riviera playground. Even so, Como is large and varied enough to offer retreats where, to paraphrase Longfellow's ode to the lake, no sound of Alfa Romeo or high heel breaks the silence of the summer day.

Third largest of the Italian lakes, 50km long but only 4.4km at its widest point, Como is one of the deepest in Europe, plunging down 1345ft near Argegno. It forks in the middle like a pair of legs: the prettiest region of Tremezzo, Bellagio, and Varenna hangs like a belt on its waist; the mountain-bound east branch is known as the Lago di Lecco. The seven excellent golf courses on the lake are a legacy of the English, while the waters around Domaso are excellent for windsurfing. As a rule, the further you go from the city of Como, the cleaner the water, and the more likely you are to find wooden racks of fat twaite shad, drying in the sun—Como's famous *missultit* (or *missoltini*), served lightly grilled with oil and vinegar and slices of polenta. The winds change according to the time of day; the *breva* blows northwards from noon to sunset, while the *tivà* blows south during the night.

Getting Around

 There are frequent FS **trains** from Milan's Centrale or Porta Garibaldi stations, taking you in some 40 minutes to Como's main San Giovanni station (information ✆ 031 261 494). Slower trains run on the regional Milano-Nord line to the lakeside station of Como-Lago. From Como, trains to Lugano and Lecco all depart from San Giovanni. **Buses** from Como run to nearly every town on the lake.

A **steamer** (the 1926 *Concordia*), **motor boats** and **hydrofoils** are operated by *Navigazione Lago di Como*, based in Como at Piazza Cavour, ✆ 031 304 060, and in Lecco at Lungolario C. Battisti, ✆ 0341 364 036, where you can pick up schedules and tourist passes. The most frequent connections are between Como, Tremezzo, Menaggio, Bellagio, Varenna and Cólico, with additional services in the central lake, and at least one boat a day to Lecco. Note that hydrofoil tickets cost about half as much again as the more leisurely steamers. **Car ferries** run between Bellagio, Menaggio, Varenna and Cadenábbia. Some services stop altogether in the winter.

Tourist Information

In **Como** there are tourist offices at Piazza Cavour 17, ✆ 031 269 712, 🖷 031 261 152, and in the San Giovanni railway station, ✆ 031 267 214.

The City of Como

Magnificently located at the southern tip of the lake's left leg, Como is a lively little city that has long had a bent for science, silk and architecture. In AD 23 it was the birthplace of Pliny the Elder, compiler of antiquity's greatest work of hearsay, the *Natural History*, and later it produced his nephew and heir Pliny the Younger, whose letters are one of our main sources for information on the cultured Roman life of the period. From *c.* 1050 to 1335, when Como enjoyed a period as an independent *comune*, it produced a school of master builders, known generally as the Maestri Comacini, rivals to Lugano's Maestri Campionese.

Como's historic centre, its street plan almost unchanged since Roman times, opens up to the lake at **Piazza Cavour**, with its cafés, hotels, steamer landing and pretty views. Two land-marks in the public gardens just to the west offer an introduction to Como's more recent scientists and architects. The first, the circular **Tempio Voltiano** (*open April–Sept, Tues–Sun 10–12 and 3–6; Oct–Mar, Tues–Sun 10–12 and 2–4; adm*), was built in 1927 to house the manuscripts, instruments and inventions of Como's electrifying native son, the self-taught physicist Alessandro Volta (1745–1827), who lent his name to volts in a hundred languages. A bit further on, the striking **Monumento ai Caduti**—a memorial to the fallen of the First World War—was designed by the young Futurist architect Antonio Sant'Elia of Como (1888–1916), who himself died in action on the Front; his plans and drawings in particular have established him as one of the most important visionary planners of the 20th century. The monument was actually built by Giuseppe Terragni (1904–34), a native of Como province and the most inspired Italian architect to work during the Fascist period. His buildings are spread throughout Como (the 1927 Hotel Metropole Suisse in Piazza Cavour is one) and the tourist office offers a special Terragni town plan if you care to hunt them out. One ends up wishing that he, like Sant'Elia, had lived a little longer.

The Historic Centre

From Piazza Cavour, Via Plinio leads back to Como's elegant salon, the Piazza Duomo. Unusually, the chief monuments are all attached: the **Torre del Comune** to the charming white, grey and red marble striped town hall or **Broletto** (both built in 1215), one of the rare Romanesque (and not Gothic) symbols of civic might in the north; and this in turn to the magnificent **Duomo** (1396), the whole now looking spanking new thanks to a thorough cleaning for its 700th birthday. The Duomo is Italy's most harmonious example of transitional architecture, although Gothic dominates in the façade and lovely rose window and pinnacles. The sculpture and reliefs are mainly by the Rodari family (late 15th–early 16th century) who also sculpted the lateral doors (the most ornate one, facing the Broletto, is called the Frog Door, although half the frog was chopped away by vandals). Perhaps even more unexpected than frogs are the two statues flanking the central door, under delicate stone canopies: Pliny the Elder (on the left) and Pliny the Younger. And just what are such famous pagans doing on a cathedral? Although Pliny the Younger did write a letter to Trajan on the subject of Christians, praising their hard work and suggesting that they be left in peace, the fact is that Renaissance humanists regarded all noble figures of antiquity as honorary saints, especially if they were hometown boys.

Inside, the three Gothic aisles combine happily with a Renaissance choir and transept, crowned by a dome designed by the great late baroque master Filippo Juvarra in 1744. Nine 16th-century tapestries hang along the nave, lending an air of palatial elegance; a pair of Romanesque lions near the entrance are survivors from the cathedral's 11th-century predecessor. But most of the art is from the Renaissance: in the right aisle six reliefs with scenes from the Passion by Tommaso Rodari, and fine canvases by two of Leonardo's followers, Gaudenzio Ferrari (*Flight into Egypt*) and Luini (*Adoration of the Magi*); the latter's famous *Madonna with Child and four saints* adorns the high altar. The left aisle has more by the same trio: Rodari's *Deposition* on the fourth altar, Ferrari's *Marriage of the Virgin* and Luini's *Nativity*, as well as a 13th-century sarcophagus.

For a contrast, go behind the Duomo and across the train tracks to the Piazza del Popolo, where Giuseppe Terragni's ex-Casa del Fascio, now the **Palazzo Terragni**, stands out in all its functional, luminous beauty. Built in 1931 but completely unlike the typically ponderous travertine buildings constructed under Mussolini, the Palazzo Terragni is 50 years ahead of its time, practically transparent, an essay in light and harmony, the masterpiece of the only coherent architectural style Italy has produced in the 20th century. Its present occupants, the Guardia di Finanza, will let you in to visit the ground floor.

From the cathedral, main Via Vittorio Emanuele leads to Como's old cathedral, **San Fedele**, first built in 914. It has a unique pentagonal apse and a doorway carved with chubby archaic figures and a griffon; the interior is lavishly decorated with 18th-century frescoes and stuccoes. Further up the street, in the Piazza Medaglie d'Oro Comasche, the two sections of the **Museo Civico** (*open Tues–Sat 9.30–12.30 and 2–6; Sun 10–1; adm*) is the city's attic of artefacts, dating from the Neolithic era up until the Second World War, with some interesting Roman finds and detached frescoes along the way. From the Piazza Medaglie d'Oro Comasche, continue down Via Giovio to the **Porta Vittoria**, a striking skyscraper of a gate from 1192, its immaculate tiers of arches rising 72ft.

Near here, Como's small **Pinacoteca**, Via Diaz 84 (*same hours as the Museo Civico*) contains carved capitals and wonderful medieval paintings from the old monastery of Santa Margherita del Broletto. Two anonymous paintings are particularly notable: a placid *St Sebastian* shot through with arrows, and the poignant *Youth and Death*. Best of all, a short walk away from the Porta Vittoria, at the beginning of the Via della Regina (the road built by Lombard queen Theodolinda around Lake Como), is Como's Romanesque gem **Sant'Abbondio**, consecrated by Pope Urban II in 1095. The façade is discreet, and the twin campaniles are believed to be of Norman inspiration, while the interior, with its lofty vaults and forest of columns forming five aisles, offers a kind of preview of coming great events in Italian architecture. Its clean, unadorned majesty is relieved by the incredibly rich bands of reliefs around the windows of the nave and apse, imitating the intricate patterns of damasks from the Near East. The elegant apse is decorated with 14th-century frescoes: note the knights in armour coming to arrest Christ in Gethsemane.

If you've brought your walking shoes or car, continue 3km south up to the **Castel Baradello**, built by Emperor Barbarossa in 1158. In 1277 it became the military headquarters of the Archbishop of Milan, Ottone Visconti, exiled by Milan's arrogant Guelph boss Napo della Torre. Napo marched out to capture the archbishop, but so carelessly disdained his opponent that he was captured instead, spending the last 19 months of his life suspended in a metal cage from its 112ft tower; you can enjoy the same view that tormented Napo (*open Thurs, Sat and Sun 10–12 and 2.30–5, but check at the tourist office*).

Around Como: Watersports, Silk and Lace

Como is framed by beaches. One is on the west end of town in Via Cantoni, by the neoclassical **Villa dell'Olmo** (1782), named for an enormous elm on the grounds, which the Comaschi claim was planted by the younger Pliny. The villa and garden are used for special exhibitions and concerts; the top floor preserves architectural drawings by Antonio Sant'Elia (*open 8–6; closed Sun and hols*). The other lido, on the east end of town, is by the **Villa Genio**, with another park and a geyser fountain spouting high over the lake. Close by, in Piazza De Gasperi, funiculars wind up to **Brunate**, a mountain village with famous views across the lake and Alps as far as Monte Rosa (*every 15–30 minutes; call © 031 303 608 for exact times*). If you drive up to Brunate you can take in one of the quainter contemporary works of Italian piety at Garzola: the reinforced concrete **Tempio Sacrario degli Sports Nautici** (*open Sun 2.30–6, or call © 031 305 958*), 'a spiritual clubhouse for all who practise watersports', built by a speedboating parish priest, its shipshape walls and sea-crib altar covered with seashells; showcases are packed with watersport memorabilia. Lastly, architecture buffs can seek out the Villa Elisi in **San Maurizio** (the village next to Brunate), the only work Sant'Elia actually built in his abbreviated life.

When Como lost its independence to Milan in the 14th century, it gained a major market for its textiles. In 1510 it turned to silk in a big way and has been Italy's leading producer ever since. Although the mulberry-munching worms are no longer raised by the lake, Chinese thread is woven and dyed here to the specifications of the Milanese fashion industry. In 1990 the Silkmakers' School set up the **Museo Didattico della Seta**, south of central Como at Via Valleggio 3 (*open Tues–Sat 9–12 and 3–6; adm*) to display their work; shops in town sell it by the yard, but not at any noticeable discounts.

If Como supplies Milan's silk, the industrious town of **Cantù**, a short hop away on the Lecco train or SPT bus, provides its handmade lace as well as some of its furniture. Cantù's landmark is the tall, minaret-like Romanesque campanile of its parish church, but the main point of interest, the 10th-century **Basilica di San Vicenzo** and **Battistero de S. Giovanni**, is a kilometre to the east of the station in the neighbouring hamlet of Galliano. Isolated in the pines, the basilica is decorated with a remarkable fresco cycle painted just after the first millennium; the baptistry with its little cupola is one of the oldest in Lombardy (*contact the keyholder, Signora Carla Panzeri, before setting out, © 031 706 148*).

Sports and Activities

Como has a full 18-hole golf course, the Circolo Villa d'Este, 4km away in Monteforno, © 031 200 200. To hire a sailboat, contact the Circolo della Vela, Viale Puecher 8, ©/® 031 574 725; horses can be hired up in Grandate in the Frazione Barella, © 031 450 235. The tourist office has maps for walkers published by the Italian Alpine Club, and an exceptionally pretty trek runs from Como to Bellagio.

Como ✉ 22100   ## Where to Stay

For character, charm and history, ★★★★**Le Due Corti**, Piazza Vittoria 15, © 031 328 111, ® 031 328 800 (*expensive*) is *the* place to stay in Como. Converted from a monastery into a post house, it reopened in 1992 as a hotel. Rooms are arranged around the former cloister and all are individual, preserving much of their original architecture and decorated with local fabrics, antique furniture and old prints. Concessions to modernity include air-conditioning, satellite TV, minibar and jacuzzis in some bathrooms. On the lake, the luxurious ★★★★**Palace Hotel**, Lungo Lario Trieste 16, © 031 303 303, ® 031 303 170 (*expensive*) partly occupies the former palace of the Archbishop. Its rooms are big and modern, and some have fax machines. On Piazza Cavour, overlooking the lake, the grand old ★★★★**Barchetta Excelsior**, © 031 3221, ® 031 302622 (*expensive*) has many rooms boasting balconies over the lake. *Open all year.* Right in the heart of town is the elegant, recently reopened 1902 ★★★★**Albergo Terminus**, Lungo Lario Trieste 14, © 031 329 111, ® 031 302 550 (*expensive*), with a panoramic terrace on the lake. Just outside Como on the west shore, the 19th-century ★★★★**Villa Flori**, Via Cernobbio 12, © 031 573 105, ® 031 570 379 (*expensive*) is classy and romantic and has Como's finest restaurant to boot; *see below*.

Near the lake, ★★★**Park Hotel**, Viale Fratelli Rosselli 20, © 031 572 615, ® 031 574 302, (*moderate*) is medium-sized and welcoming, but without a restaurant. Another good choice, ★★★**Marco's**, Via Coloniola 43, © 031 303 628, ® 031 302 342 (*moderate*) has 11 small rooms, all with TV, phone and balcony. You can dream about the glories of the corporate state at the ★★**Posta**, Via Garibaldi 2, © 031 266 012, ® 031 266 398 (*cheap*), a hotel designed in 1930 by Terragni. Little ★**Sole**, Via Borgovico 89/91, ©/® 031 573 382 (*cheap*) is a good budget choice, but bring your earplugs if you want to sleep in past 7am. There's also a youth hostel in Villa Olmo park, **Ostello dell'Olmo**, Via Bellinzona 6, © 031 573 800.

Eating Out

Como is one of those towns where the restaurants tend to process clients with slipshod food and service, especially in summer. One that doesn't is the **Terrazzo**

Perlasca, Piazza de'Gasperi 8, ℰ 031 300 263 (*expensive*), run by four brothers, two in the kitchen and two out front. The menu changes almost every day and features typical dishes like *filetto di laverello* and *fettuccine e funghi*, a peerless pasta with local mushrooms, all accompanied by wonderful views over the lake. *Closed Mon.* **Sant'Ana**, Via Filippo Turati 1/3, ℰ 031 505 266 (*expensive*) is also a good family establishment dating back to 1907, more frequented by toilers in the silk trade than tourists, featuring well-prepared if unadventurous Lombard specialities: good risotto with radicchio and trout with almonds. *Closed Fri and Sat lunch, and late July–late Aug.* For an elegant splurge, join Como society at the aforementioned hotel **Villa Flori's Ristorante Raimondi**, ℰ 031 573 105 (*expensive*) where exquisite renditions of classic Italian and Lombard cuisine are served on the lakeside terrace or in the luminous dining room. *Closed Mon.* Another winner, the **Locanda dell'Oca Bianca**, Via Canturina 252 (on the road to Cantù) ℰ 031 525 605 (*expensive– moderate*) serves sit-up-and-take-note dishes from a variety of Italian regions out on its summer terrace. *Closed Mon out of season.* **Villa Olmo Parco**, Via Cantoni 1, ℰ 031 572 321 (*moderate*) serves well-prepared food with fine wines near the beach. *Closed Tues.* Or try the **Ristorante Teatro Sociale**, near the cathedral flank at Via Maestri Comacini, ℰ 031 264 042, serving a good L30,000 tourist menu with wine.

The West Shore to Cadenábbia

This stretch of Lake Como, famous for its mild climate and azalea gardens, was the aristocratic high-rent district in the 19th century. The main lake road, Via Regina, is named after the queen who laid it out: 7th-century Theodolinda of the Lombards.

Tourist Information

Cernobbio: Via Regina 33b, ℰ/✉ 031 510 198. **Tremezzo**: Via Regina 3, ℰ 0344 40493.

Cernobbio to Argegno

Only a few minutes from Como, at the foot of green Monte Bisbino, **Cernobbio** (which sounds disconcertingly like 'Chernobyl' if you're not listening closely) dates its status as an aristocratic enclave back to 1816–17, when Queen Caroline of England held her wild parties in what is now the fabulous Hotel Villa d'Este; these days politicians love to book it for somewhat more discreet conferences at Italian taxpayers' expense (*see* below). Cernobbio has a few old lanes off its lakeside square, and superb views across the Alps from atop **Bisbino** (4836ft), a dizzy 17km drive up from the centre.

Moltrasio, the next resort to the north, clings to the slopes of Bisbino on either side of a deep ravine. Here the **Villa Passalacqua** has a lovely Italianate garden decorated with ceramics, while a plaque on the nearby **Villa Salterio** commemorates Vincenzo Bellini, who stayed here in 1831, in love with its owner Giuditta Turina Cantù, while he composed his operas *La Straniera* and much of *La Sonnambula*. In **Carate-Urio**, next to the north, at the summit of a chapel-lined Via Crucis (1752), the panoramic **Santuario de Santa Marta** dates from *c*. 1000 but was much rebuilt in the 12th century (the date of its campanile), while inside are charming provincial frescoes from the 1400s.

North, the road passes the hamlet of **Torriggia**, where prehistoric cave bears once looked out of their lairs over the narrowest stretch of Lake Como (650m). The waters lick many of the houses in **Brienno**, further north, where the parish church claims to possess the relics of Barbarossa, 'canonized' by the Comaschi for razing hated Milan to the ground (flying in the face of the fact that the emperor drowned in six inches of water in a Turkish river and that every German knows he sleeps under Köningsberg, ready to return in the hour of Germany's greatest need). At **Argegno**, north of Brienno, a little monument stands to Pietro Vassena who in 1948 went down 1352ft in his bathysphere—then the world record. Argegno enjoys a privileged position, overlooking the snow-clad mountains to the north and marking the Como end of the **Val d'Intelvi** (*see* p.167).

Isola Comacina

Up the shore from Argegno, **Sala Comacina** and **Ossuccio** have irresistibly romantic views over Como's only island, **Isola Comacina**, sheltered in the arm of the long Lavedo peninsula. This intimate nook of Como, once the independent Pieve dell'Isola Comacina, is sometimes called the *zoca dell'oli* or 'oil hollow' for the olive trees that once made it rich. First inhabited by the Romans, it prospered to the extent that Isola Comacina was nicknamed *Chrysopolis*, the city of gold. By the 12th century it was a fierce rival of Como, joining Milan to crush their mutual enemy in 1128; in 1190 Como, back in favour with Barbarossa, sent raiders to decimate the little island state, burning it to the ground and forbidding its inhabitants ever to return. By some twist of fate in the 19th century the island came to be owned by the King of the Belgians, who donated it as a retreat for Milanese artists; their cottages share the island with a good restaurant (*see* below), the 16th-century church of **San Giovanni** and the ruins of five ancient churches, including a 6th-century baptistry. Isola Comacina comes blazingly alive on the Saturday or Sunday nearest St John's Day, illuminated by hundreds upon hundreds of *lumaghitti*—snail shells made into tiny oil lamps; this is accompanied by an immense show of fireworks and a Sunday parade of boats decked with flowers and islanders in 18th-century garb.

On the mainland, Sala's **Villa Beccaria** was a favourite retreat of Cesare Beccaria when the Church drove him crazy (*see* p.56); the parish church has Romanesque frescoes. Boats from Sala transport visitors to the gardens of the famous **Villa del Balbianello** (or Arconati Visconti) at Punta Balbianello, the very tip of the Laveno peninsula. Built by Cardinal Duini in the early 18th century over the ruins of a medieval monastery, its enchanting garden spilling down to the stone arches of its boat entrance is the distilled quintessence of Italian lake romanticism: don't miss it (*open 1st and last Sun of month 10–12.30 and 3–6.30; gardens generally open, but only accessible by boat; adm*). The main road passes next to Ossuccio's landmark, the delightful brick and terracotta Gothic campanile on the 11th-century church of **Santa Maria Maddalena**, but you'll have to get out of the car to walk to the panoramic **Santuario della Madonna del Soccorso** (early 1500s). In the 17th century, the pious locals gave it a home-made **Sacro Monte** (*see* pp.132–3) of 14 little chapels, each filled with earnest sculptures and frescoes.

The Tremezzina

North of Ossuccio at **Lenno** the lake opens up again to become the 'mirror of Venus' in the sheltered district of the Tremezzina, where carpets of azaleas, agaves, camellias, rhododendrons and magnolias bloom under the towering cypresses and palms. Lenno was the site of Pliny the Younger's Villa Comedia; in one of his letters he describes how he could fish from his bedroom window. The Museo Civico in Como houses two columns of the villa found near the church **Santo Stefano**, where ruins of Pliny's baths were found under the floor. The church's crypt dates from the 11th century, as does its sturdy octagonal **Battistero San Giovanni**, a classic example of the Lombard style of its day, and restored to its original appearance. In nearby **Giulino di Mezzegra** Mussolini and his mistress Claretta Petacci spent their last night in a room at Via Riale 4 after local partisans captured them as they attempted to flee in a German truck to Switzerland. A plaque in nearby Via XXIV Maggio marks the spot where they were executed 28 April 1945; Claretta was killed trying to shield the Duce from the bullets.

Beautiful villas are chock-a-block along the shore at **Tremezzo**, including two of the finest on Como: the early 18th-century **Villa La Quiete** with its stone balustrades at Bolvedro and, from the same period, the celebrated **Villa Carlotta** (*open Mar and Oct daily 9–11.30 and 2–4.30; April–Sept daily 9–6; adm exp*) on the north end of Tremezzo. Originally built in 1747 as the Villa Clerici, the villa took its name from Princess Carlotta of the Netherlands, who received it as a wedding gift from her mother upon her marriage to the Duke of Saxony-Meiningen in the 1850s. But most of what you see was the work of the former owners, the Counts Sommariva, who laid out the magnificent gardens and park, where in April and May the thousands of azaleas, camellias and rhododendrons put on a dazzling display of colour. But no matter when you come you can also take in the neoclassical interior, filled with cool, virtuoso, insufferable neoclassical statuary that the Sommarivas couldn't get enough of: a copy of Antonio Canova's *Cupid and Psyche* (the original is in St Petersburg), *Venus and Paris*, *Mary Magdalene* and *Palmedes* (rebuilt by Canova after someone understandably smashed it) and in the drawing room Icelander Bertel Thorvaldsen's marble frieze of *Alexander's Triumphant Entrance of Babylon*, commissioned by Napoleon but completed after Waterloo for the Sommarivas.

After the Villa Carlotta, look for 'the leafy colonnade' of trees described by Longfellow marking the entrance to **Cadenábbia**, still served by an Anglican church built in the 19th century when the English came here in droves; Verdi composed *La Traviata* at the **Villa Margherita-Ricordi** at Maiolica and Konrad Adenauer spent his well-earned holidays at the **Villa Rosa**. Other sumptuous villas and a core of old houses fill **Griante**, a village just above Cadenábbia, and above Grianta the isolated 16th-century church of **San Martino** offers an incomparable view over the Bellagio headland.

Where to Stay and Eating Out

Cernobbio ✉ 22012

The fabulous ★★★★★**Grand Hotel Villa d'Este**, ✆ 031 3481, 🖷 031 348 844 (*luxury*) is Lake Como's most glittering showcase. It was built in 1557 by Pelligini for Cardinal Tolomeo Gallio, the son of a Como fisherman who went on to become one of the most powerful men in the

Vatican—besides this villa, he had seven along the road to Rome so he never had to spend a night 'away from home'. Queen Caroline was not the only crowned head to make use of the cardinal's old digs, and since 1873 it has been a hotel. Each room is individual, furnished with antiques or fine reproductions, the public rooms are regal, the food is superb, prepared by a battalion of 40 chefs; the glorious gardens are in themselves a reason to stay. Add a floating swimming pool, another indoor pool, a fine golf course, squash, tennis, sailing, nightclub and more. Be warned that the rooms cost a king's ransom too, at L800,000 or more for a double; non-guests are welcome at the restaurant, where the average bill is L150,000. *Open April–Oct.* If you haven't inherited a million bucks, there's the ★★★★**Asnigo**, Piazza S. Stefano, ✆ 031 510 062 ✆ 031 510 249 (*expensive*), a stunning hotel built in 1914 with a beautiful terrace overlooking Cernobbio and Como and pretty rooms, friendly service and a good restaurant with a L33,000 daily menu. *Open all year.* ★★**Terzo Crotto**, Via Volta 1, ✆ 031 512 304 (*moderate*) has nine rooms, all with bath, and an excellent restaurant (*dinners for around L50,000*). *Closed Mon and Tues lunch.* The rustic **Trattoria Gatto Nero**, Via Monte Santo 69, ✆ 031 512 042 (*expensive*), has lovely lake views and delicious food. *Closed Mon and Tues lunch.*

Moltrasio ✉ 22010

On the left of the main road as you enter Moltrasio from Como, the cosy ★★★**Posta**, ✆ 031 290 444, ✆ 031 290 657 (*moderate*) occupies a former posthouse; the restaurant offers mouthwatering trout and decent wine on the small shady terrace.

Ossuccio ✉ 22018

The Isola Comacina is deserted except for a restaurant, the 50-year-old **Locanda dell'Isola Comacina**, ✆ 0344 55083. For one fixed price (L50,000) you are picked up in a boat at Cala Comacina or Ossuccio, and regaled with a set meal of *antipasti* followed by grilled trout, fried chicken, wine and dessert, a rendition of poetry and a return trip to the mainland. *Open April–Nov; closed Tues.*

Tremezzo ✉ 22019

Next door to Villa Carlotta, the ★★★★**Grand Hotel Tremezzo Palace**, ✆ 0344 40446, ✆ 0344 40201 (*expensive*) offers the generous comforts of a large 19th-century hotel, with a garden, tennis, pool, lakeside restaurant and big rooms with good views on all sides. *Open Mar–mid-Nov.* Overlooking the lake and a shady garden, ★★**Villa Marie**, ✆ 0344 40427 (*moderate*) is an intimately Victorian hotel with 15 pleasant rooms. *Open April–Oct.*

Cadenábbia ✉ 22011

Right on the lake and charmingly old-fashioned, ★★★★**Bellevue**, ✆ 0344 40418, ✆ 41466 (*moderate*) is a large but very pleasant place to stay, with plenty of sun terraces, garden and pool. *Open mid-Mar–mid-Oct.* A cosy old hotel in Cadenábbia's piazza overlooking the lake, ★★★**Britannia Excelsior**, ✆ 0344 40413, ✆ 0344 42068 (*moderate*) has lots of rooms with balconies, including inexpensive ones without bathrooms. *Open April–Oct.*

Lenno ✉ 22016

On the market square, **Santo Stefano**, Piazza XI Febbraio 3, ✆ 0344 55434 (*moderate*) serves delicious, reasonably priced lunches and dinners. Try the olive *ascolonane*—deep-fried olives stuffed with a mild fish pâté—marvellous golden ravioli stuffed with ricotta and asparagus, caramelly grilled courgettes and grilled lake fish, and wind up with apple cake or an apple and calvados sorbet. Ask to sit outside. *Closed Mon.*

The Central Lake: Bellagio and the Larian Triangle

If time or inclination limit you to one destination on Lake Como, make it Bellagio, spectacularly set at the tip of the mountainous Triangolo Lariano that divides Como in two. From Cadenábbia the ferry crosses over to Bellagio, and buses make the journey as well, but to really see it all walk the easy two-day, 30km *Dorsale del Triangolo Lariano* trail along the ridge; pick up the free brochure at the Como tourist office.

Tourist Information

Bellagio: Piazza della Chiesa,14 ✆ 031 950 204; *closed Tues and Sun.*

Como to Bellagio

Just around Cape Geno from Como, the road winds around the mountain to **Blevio**, a collection of hamlets and villas that attracted all the prima donnas and ballerinas in the 19th century: Adelaide Risotri, Maria Taglioni and the great soprano Giuditta Pasta, who is buried in the parish church. **Torno** (ancient Roman Turnum) once had a population of 5000 and rivalled Como until 1522, when the bigger town squashed it for good. Torno has some fine old houses; its church of **San Giovanni** has a marble door by the Rodaris, a wooden roof of 1469, old frescoes on the pillars and a 6th-century tombstone. The north end of town is occupied by the grounds of the 16th-century **Villa Pliniana**, rising straight from the lake. The villa must holds the local record for hosting literati, among them Byron, Ugo Foscolo, Stendhal and Bellini; Rossini composed *Tancredi* in a record six days during his stay and Shelley loved it so much that he tried to buy it.

Its name comes from its peculiar intermittent 240ft waterfall, described by Pliny in his *Natural History* (II, 232) and in a letter of Pliny the Younger; you can only see it from the lake or the villa.

Villa Pliniana

Waterfalls are almost run of the mill here: there's another one at **Molina** and another to the north at **Nesso**, a picturesque place, where the water splashes into the lake under a quaint stone bridge. At Nesso a road zigzags up to the **Triangolo Lariano**, that wedge of karst that makes Como do the splits. Aeons of dripping water have bored long caverns in its very intestines—one cave at **Zelbio** meanders for 9km and has yet to be explored to its end. A number of paths, best in the spring and autumn, crisscross the **Piano del Tivano** basin, where rain off the surrounding 4000ft mountains is sucked into a natural drain called the Buco della Niccolina.

After Nesso the shore road passes through the long-drawn-out *comune* of **Lezzeno**, which has its own version of Capri's Blue Grotto, although it would probably attract more tourists if it weren't named **Buco dei Carpi** (Carp Hole); the reflections are best in the afternoon. After Lezzano cliffs plummet into the lake all the way to **San Giovanni** on the outskirts of Bellagio, where its baroque church has an explosively ornate 18th-century high altar by Valtellina sculptors, an *Ascension* by Gaudenzio Ferrari and an *Immaculata* by Bernini's school.

Bella Bella Bellagio

Enjoying one of the most beautiful sites in all Italy, spilling over the promontory in the very centre of Lake Como, Bellagio (from the Latin *bi-lacus*, or between the lakes) is as charming as its setting: steep, stepped lanes of handsome old houses, ornate balconies spilling over with flowers and an endlessly fascinating waterfront, where you can linger all day watching the waltz of the ferries gliding to and fro over the mountain-bound lake.

Although Bellagio was fortified and fought over by Como and Milan, its first mention in history appropriately has to do with pleasure, referring to Pliny the Younger's Villa Tragedia. The villa sat rather higher over the lake than his Villa Comedia in Lenno, and got its name not only because tragedy was considered a 'loftier' art than comedy but because in his day tragic actors wore high heels. Most scholars place Pliny's old digs in the spectacular grounds of the **Villa Serbelloni**, extending to the summit of the Punta Bellagio. The villa is now the Study and Conference Centre of the Rockefeller Foundation, but there are two daily guided tours of the grounds run between April and October (*Tues–Sun at 11 and 4; tickets are available from the tourist office up to 10mins beforehand; in season beware that the morning tour is often solidly booked by groups*). While up at the top of Bellagio, take in Romanesque **San Giacomo**, built by the Como masters between 1075 and 1125 near a tower from Bellagio's fortifications. The Evangelists on the pulpit are from the 11th century, and the *Madonna delle Grazie* in the sacristry is by Foppa.

A second villa in Bellagio is open for visits: the white neoclassical **Villa Melzi** (*open late Mar–Oct daily 9–6.30; adm*), built in 1808 for one of Napoleon's henchmen, the Duke of Lodi, Francesco Melzi d'Enril. Topped with a score of pointy little chimneys, the villa has immaculate lawns, banks of flowers, a rare Montezuma pine and a water-lily pond, all decorated with Egyptian, Roman and Hellenistic sculpture, and a little Moorish temple where in 1837 Liszt composed his sonata dedicated to Dante and Beatrice.

Other Roads from Bellagio

The narrow corniche road from Bellagio to Lecco is wilder and lonelier, with stunning views over the jagged Grigne range. **Oliveto Lario**, the main *comune* here, encompasses

Limonata, a pretty place with a tiny port which until the advent of Napoleon in 1796 was a tiny independent state. Alternatively, for a big dose of lake and mountain scenery, take the high road from Bellagio towards the Valsassina, to Erba in La Brianza (*see* p.190); there are famous views over the entire lake from the summit of **Monte San Primo** (5630ft, a 2-hour walk from the refuge at Guello). Cyclists pedal up to pay their respects to their patroness, the **Madonna di Ghisallo**, to whom the great Italian champions have dedicated their bikes, shirts and trophies. Further south, the hamlet of **Lasnigo** has a fine 11th-century church, **Sant' Alessandro**, with a slender bell tower and bright 16th-century frescoes by Andrea de Passeris, a local painter from Torno.

Where to Stay and Eating Out

Torno ✉ 22020

A beautiful hotel tucked away in Torno, ★★★**Villa Flora**, ✆ 031 419 222, 📠 031 418 318 (*moderate*) is just the ticket for peaceful atmosphere, swimming pool and friendly hosts: look for great *antipasti*, fine cuisine and a choice list of wines served in the restaurant overlooking the lake. *Open Mar–Dec.*

Bellagio ✉ 22021

Romantic Bellagio has several fine hotels, among them the magnificent, ornate ★★★★★**Grand Hotel Villa Serbelloni**, Via Roma 1, ✆ 031 950 216, 📠 031 951 529 (*luxury*), set in a flower-filled garden at the very tip of the headland. The frescoed public rooms are glittering and palatial, and there's a heated pool and private beach, tennis, gym, boating and water-skiing, and dancing in the evening to the hotel orchestra. You can also swim in the lake and bask on an anchored raft. *Open April–Oct.* The genial, family-run ★★★**Hotel Du Lac**, Piazza Mazzini, ✆ 031 950 320, 📠 031 951 624, *dulac@mbox.vol.it* (*expensive–moderate*) occupies a 16th-century building near the centre, with fine views from the rooftop terrace and a traditional restaurant. The bar under the arcades is one of the nicest in town. Ask for one of the rooms with wonderful lake views. ★★★**Firenze**, Piazza Mazzini 42, ✆ 031 950 342, 📠 031 951 722, *hotflore@mbox.vol.it* (*expensive*) is located in a 19th-century villa right next to Bellagio's harbour, owned by the same family for over a century. The terraces and many of the rooms have lake views, there's a cosy lobby with heavy beams and a Florentine fireplace, and a restaurant under an arbour just by the lake. *Open April–Oct.*

Other choices include the lake-front ★★★**Excelsior Splendide**, ✆ 031 950 225, 📠 031 951 224 (*moderate*), with a touching, faded Liberty-style charm, big old rooms (most with a view, though be sure to ask), a pool and its own garden. The ★★★**Nuovo Hotel Metropole**, ✆ 031 950 409, 📠 031 951 534 (*moderate*) also has lake views, but slightly smaller rooms, and less character. *Open Mar–Oct.* A few kilometres from the centre in Loppia, the family-run ★★**Silvio**, Via Carcano 12, ✆ 031 950 322, 📠 031 950 912 (*moderate*) is an absolute must for good value accommodation, friendly service, peaceful surroundings and excellent home cooking. Fresh fish, caught daily by father and son, and homemade pasta and very good *tiramisù* have already been approved by Pavarotti, Chancellor Kohl and Robert de Niro. ***Roma**, Salita Grandi 1, ✆ 031 950 424, 📠 031 951 966 (*cheap*) is just up from the lake, with views and large balconies on the top floor. *Open April–Oct.* **La Pergola**, Piazza del Porto, ✆ 031 950 263 (*cheap*), in the tiny fishing harbour of Pescallo, is a small, charming olde-worlde place with rooms overlooking the lake and a waterside restaurant. *Closed Tues out of season.*

One of the nicest places to dine in the centre of Bellagio is **Bilacus**, Salita Serbelloni 9, ✆ 031 95080 (*moderate*), where you sit on a romantic terrace, feasting on excellent, intense *spaghetti alle vongole*, saffrony mushroom risotto or simple grilled fish. *Closed in winter.* In the hamlet of San Giovanni, a pleasant half-hour walk through the Villa Melzi and beyond, is **Mella**, Via J. Rezia, ✆ 031 950 205 (*moderate*), *the* place to go for a feast of fish—starve yourself first—order the mixed fish *antipasto*, the mixed grilled fish and a bottle of lemony Soave. *Closed Tues and winter.*

Como's Upper West Shore and the Alto Lario

The last really stylish address for villas and hotels on the west shore, Menaggio (linked by ferries to Bellagio and Varenna) was a favourite of Venice's Cardinal Roncalli (later Pope John XXIII) and Churchill, who came here to sketch. It has always been one of Como's more important trading towns, thanks to its position at the head of two valleys: the Val Menaggio, an easy route to Lake Lugano (*see* p.162) and the Val Sanagra. To the north in the Alto Lario (Upper Como) the shores are more rugged and decidedly less visited.

Tourist Information

Menaggio: Piazza Garibaldi, ✆ 0344 32924. In **Dongo**, a cooperative called IMAGO, ✆ 0344 82572, offers guided walking tours in the summer.

Menaggio to Musso

Although flowerbeds and lindens line the lake and lido, pink and ochre Menaggio's main vocation is as a base for sport. Just above town there's a lovely 18-hole golf course (✆ 0344 32103), and the tourist office has good detailed information in English on the many well-marked walks in the area, ranging from the expert-only Alta Via Lario to easier targets, reached from the panoramic Rifugio Menaggio atop Monte Grona (5729ft); from here you can make one of the finest ascents from the lake, up **Monte Bregagno** (6910ft).

After Menaggio, the Via Regina road plunges through tunnels *en route* to the waterside hamlets of **Santa Maria Rezzonico** (where the parish church has a fresco of the Battle of Lepanto) and **Rezzonico**, cradle of the family of Venetian patricians who built one of the grandest palaces on the Grand Canal and produced Pope Clement XIII. Further up, a 19th-century spinning mill in **Pianello del Lario** houses a rich collection of 160 traditional boats from Lake Como, the **Raccolta della Barca Lariana**, ✆ 0344 87294 (*open Easter–Nov; guided tours Sat 2.30–6.30, Sun 10.30–12.30; closed Thurs; July–Sept daily 2.30–6.30; adm*). The old photos of the lake traffic in the last century are especially winsome; it would be fun to bring them back.

Continuing up the coast, **Musso** is gathered under the Sasso di Musso, the lofty, almost inaccessible rocky abutment dominating the Via Regina, the source of the marble in Como cathedral and other buildings around the lake. Its castle was the stronghold of Lake Como's notorious pirate Gian Giacomo de' Medici, nicknamed Il Medeghino. Born during the Medici exile from Florence in 1498, he was given the castle by Francesco II Duke of Milan in 1523 for helping to remove the French from Milan and assassinating the duke's best friend for him. Il Medeghino made it the base for a fleet of armed ships that terrorized the lake and extorted levies from towns and traders for a decade, until the same Duke Francesco II, with help from the Swiss, managed to dislodge him and demolish his citadel. As a consolation prize the old pirate (brother of Pope Pius IV and uncle of Charles Borromeo) was made Marquis of Marignano by Charles V, and in return he helped the emperor win Siena and oppress the burghers of Ghent. The site of the castle, by the little church of Santa Eufemia, was made into an eclectic **Giardino di Merlo** in the 1850s, which is soon to be opened to the public.

Dongo, Gravedona and Sorico

To the north, Como's shapely figure spreads; the shore loses its clear definition amid reedy shallows and camp grounds full of German families. Things were livelier in the Middle Ages, when the three towns of **Dongo**, **Gravedona** and **Sorico** formed the independent republic of the Tre Pievi or Three Parishes. In the 12th and 13th centuries, the Tre Pievi was a hotbed of Paternene (or Cathar) heresy, and scores of citizens were sent to the stake by the inquisitor Peter of Verona for doubting, among other things, that the pope was Christ's representative on earth. In 1252 Peter was waylaid and murdered for his trouble—earning himself an express canonization the very next year from the pope as St Peter Martyr; he's the saint who figures in so much Dominican art, standing about nonchalantly with a hatchet sticking out of his tonsure. Dongo was also the end of the road for Mussolini and his mistress, who were caught here while trying to escape to Switzerland.

Gravedona was and still is the most important town of the three. By its parish church of San Vicenzo (with an intact 5th-century crypt), the tall 12th-century grey and white striped Santa Maria del Tiglio was founded as a detached baptistry, and rebuilt reusing Palaeo-Christian carvings (the centaur pursuing a deer is Early Christian symbolism, representing the persecution of the Church); the solemn interior, lined with two lofty galleries, has damaged frescoes and a stark 13th-century crucifix over the altar. Just above Gravedona, **Santa Maria delle Grazie** (1467) contains frescoes by local painters, the De Donatis, a few invoking divine aid against the plague and the funniest one called *Cifulett dul cunvent* of the Virgin walloping the devil. In **Peglio**, just above Gravedona, Sant' Eusebio (*open Sat and Sun during Mass*) is a model Counter-Reformation church, its frescoes (1611–25) the masterpiece of Como painter Giovan Mauro della Rovere, better known as the Fiammenghino or 'little Fleming'. He was granted asylum here after murdering a man, a fact that inspired him to take special care over the torments of hell in his *Last Judgement*. He left his own portrait, elegantly dressed, listening to the *Sermon of St John* in the Cappella di San Carlo, next to the local woman he loved and their children. The fishing village **Sorico**, the northernmost of the three parishes, has a tower that guarded the entrance to Lake Como from the north and a church dedicated to San Mirus, a 14th-century hermit and local rain god who floated to Sorico on his cloak, inspired by a similar feat perfomed by St Giulio at Orta; *ex votos* attest to his control over precipitation.

In Roman times Lake Como encompassed shallow **Lake Mezzola**, an important breeding ground for swans. On the west shore of the lake, accessible only by boat or path from Albonico, the square 10th-century **Oratorio di San Fedelino** is a minor jewel, with a fresco of Christ and the Apostles from the year 1000. Across the lake from San Fedelino, **Novate Mezzola** is the base for walks into the enchanting and unspoiled **Val Codera**, which is just as inaccessible to cars. The track up passes a granite quarry lost in the woods, as well as two tiny granite hamlets, **San Giorgio di Cola** and, beyond the chasm of the Gola della Val Ladrongo, **Codera** (2 hours), where the **Museo Storico del Val Codera** in Piazza della Chiesa, © 0343 44145 (*open June–Sept daily 10–12 and 3–6; Oct–May, weekends only*) has exhibits on the valley's history, customs and natural environment.

Where to Stay and Eating Out

Menaggio ✉ 22017

The ★★★★**Grand Hotel Victoria**, © 0344 32003, 🖶 0344 32992 (*expensive*) was built in 1806 next to the lake; during recent renovation its original décor was carefully preserved and complemented with creature comforts like designer bathrooms, TVs and minibars. The public rooms are elegant and there's a pool in the garden. *Open all year.*

The more modern ★★★★**Grand Hotel Menaggio**, © 0344 30640, 🖶 0344 30619 (*very expensive–expensive*) also stands in its own grounds on the lake. Rooms are fully equipped, most of them with a stunning view, and there's a pool. *Open Mar–Oct.* ★★★**Bellavista**, © 0344 32136, 🖶 0344 31793 (*expensive–moderate*) is right on the lake and also has nice rooms. *Open Mar–Dec.* Near the centre ★★**Corona,** © 0344 32006, 🖶 0344 30564 (*moderate*) has lake views and some inexpensive rooms without bath.

Menaggio's very fine youth hostel, **Ostello La Primula**, Via IV Novembre 38, © 0344 32356 (*cheap*) has a restaurant serving some of the best cheap meals in the area. *Open Mar–Oct.* For a friendly low-key restaurant with great pizzas and pasta at affordable prices, try **Alpino Ristorante Pizzeria**, Via Lago 13, © 0344 32082, both calmer and better than the obvious tourist havens by the lake. *Closed Wed.*

Sorico ✉ 22010

Sorico is a good place to stop for a meal, either for the full works at the **Al Beccaccino**, Via Boschetto, © 0344 84241 (*moderate; closed Tues*) or at one of the long tables at **Spluga**, on main Via V. Emanuele 12, © 0344 84124 (*cheap*) to tuck into a good pizza (evenings only) or hearty trattoria favourite. *Closed Mon.*

Como's East Shore: Colico to Lecco

The mountains are even more dramatic on Como's east shore, and with the exception of charming Varenna the villas and hotels are scarcer—there's scarcely any room to build them. Northern Lake Como and the Lago di Lecco are favourite destination for windsurfers and are rich in *agoni* (freshwater shad), one of the tastiest of lake fish.

Varenna: in the centre, © 0341 362 360.

The Pian di Spagna and the Abbazia di Piona

The vaguely eerie grassy marshland between the Lago di Mezzola and river Adda has been known as the Pian di Spagna ever since 1603, when the Spanish governor of Milan built a massive fort on a hillock at Fuentes Montecchio. The fort was the furthermost outpost of Spain in Italy, guarding the strategic entrance to the Valtellina (*see* p.193), the principal warpath between Milan to Austria; today horses and waterfowl share the wetlands with Telespazio's futuristic parabolic aerials.

South of **Cólico**, Como's northernmost steamer landing, the road passes the peculiar green waters of the Lago di Piona, a basin of fossils and garnet notched into the side of Como. On the lick of land enclosing the basin, monks from Cluny took over the ruined apse of a 7th-century church in 1138 and established the **Abbazia di Piona**, adding a pretty cloister of 1257 with animals and faces on some the columns. The church, Lombard Romanesque with a crown of arches, has a single nave, where you'll find the marble lions that once guarded the porch and remains of 13th-century frescoes. It was restored by the Cistercians of Casamari (in Frosinone), whose brothers distil a potent herb liqueur called *gocce imperiali* ('imperial drops'), for fire-safety reasons best taken in small doses.

Dervio and a Detour up the Val Varrone

To the south the lake road climbs to tiny **Corenno Plinio**, where plane trees shade the cobbles by the church of **San Tomasso à Becket** (1356), a popular saint in medieval Italy (he was on the pope's side, after all). Behind it are three ruined tombs (late 1200s and 1371) by the Maestri Campionesi, and inside are 14th-century frescoes and a 16th-century Tuscan *Annunciation*. Next to the church are two embattled towers of the **Castello Andreani**. Corenno Plinio belongs to Dervio, with some of Como's widest beaches; steps lead up to the old Castello district, marked by a massive stump of a tower.

From Dervio a road leads up into the Val Varrone, dotted with old settlements like **Treménico** and **Introzzo**, where the church of **San Martino** (1583) has a pulpit carved by rococo master Antonio Fantoni and a campanile with an excellently preserved clock of 1707. At the top of the valley, **Premana** is a large ironworking village with a picturesque main street, where some older women continue to wear their traditional costumes. Premana specializes in scissors, although in the past it rather more romantically produced the iron beaks of gondolas, some of which are in the **Museo Etnografico Comunale** in Via Roma (*open April, July, Sept and Oct Sat and Sun 3–6; Aug daily 4–6; at other times call Antonio Codega,* © *0341 980 175, to book; adm*).

Bellano

South again, **Bellano** lies at the bottom of the steep gorge or **Orrido** of the Pioverna torrent, where a series of steps and gangways threads through the rocky chasm and its bulging walls, offering remarkable views of the thundering water just below. Once the walkway has been repaired it should open from March to September; to find out its current status, ring Filippo Vinciguerra, © 0341 821 101. Bellano has a fine Lombard church, **Santi Nazzaro e Celso**

(1348), built by the Campionese and Intelvi masters (*open most days for religious services*) with a rose window in majolica and a fine 16th-century painting of the Madonna and Child, inspired by Luini. From Bellano you can head up the Valsassina (*see* p.188); only 8km up there are more watery thrills at the **Tomba di Taìno**, a cascade in a 98ft abyss, located by Cosmasìra, near **Vendrogno**.

Varenna and its River of Milk

Wedged on a promontory under the mountains, picturesque Varenna has been the most important village on Como's east shore since the Middle Ages; as the ferry port for Bellagio, Cadenábbia and Menaggio it makes a fine base for visiting the entire lake. But Varenna itself is well worth exploring: its 10th-century **Oratorio di San Giovanni**, with later frescoes inside, is one of the oldest surviving churches on the lake, while the larger, Romanesque **San Giorgio** (1313) is marked by a lofty campanile and an exterior fresco of St Christopher (giant-sized, the better to bring luck to passing travellers); inside are 14th-and 15th-century frescoes and polyptychs by Como-based artists. Varenna's proudest lakeside villas are now used as congress centres, although their gardens are open to the public. The oldest, **Villa Monastero**, was built on the site of a 13th-century convent suppressed by Charles Borromeo in 1567 for the scandalous and luxurious behaviour of its nuns; the garden, with statues and bas-reliefs, is famed for its citrus trees (*open May–Oct 10–12 and 2–6.30; winter Sat and Sun only; adm*). The nearby **Villa Cipressi**, built between 1400 and 1800, also has a fine garden under its towering cypresses (*open Mar–Oct daily 9–6.30*). Varenna's museum is for the birds, literally: the **Museo Ornitologico** (*open June–Sept Tues, Thurs and Sat 3–6, Sun 10–12; other times Sun only 10–12*) houses 700 species that frequent Como's shores.

Varenna's other attractions are higher up, especially the partially ruined **Castello Vezio** (*to visit call © 0341 830 611 at meal times*), founded in the 7th century by Lombard Queen Theodolinda; you can drive or walk up (in about 20 minutes) for the fantastic view over the Bellagio headland. South of Varenna, the scenic path to the cemetery continues up in 15 minutes to the headspring of Lake Como's most curious natural wonder, the **Fiumelatte** ('river of milk'), Italy's shortest river, lasting only 820ft before blasting down in creamy foam into the lake. Not even Leonardo da Vinci, who delved deep into the cavern from which it flows, could discover its source, or why it abruptly begins to flow in the last days of March and just as abruptly ceases at the end of October; a stair and iron bridge allow you to get quite close to the source. From the headspring (the Sorgente) another path descends to the river's mouth in the hamlet of Fiumelatte; a third path branching off from the walk to the source leads to another lovely viewpoint over the lake, the cypress-fringed **Baluardo**.

Behind Varenna stretch the northernmost peaks of the saw-toothed Grigna massif. Only a few minutes up in Perledo, the 14th-century **Castello di Vézio** still guards the central lake. Further up, the little resort of **Esino Lario** is the site of the **Museo delle Grigne** (*open July and Aug daily 4–7; June and Sept call © 0341 860 111*) housing local Gallic and Roman finds, minerals and fossils. For beautiful views continue up from Esino to the plateau of **Ortanella**, a natural balcony over the lake and site of the 1000-year-old church of **San Pietro**; another road from Esino leads up to **Cainallo** and Vó di Moncòdeno, near the centre of the North Grigna range and a favourite place to begin daring walks. The main road from Esino continues up through grand scenery to Cortenova in the Valsassina (*see* p.188).

The Lago di Lecco

South of Varenna, the shores close in around the Lago di Lecco, a brooding fjord where mountains plunge down steeply into the water, entwined in rushing streams and waterfalls and carved with shadowy abysses—landscapes that so enchanted Leonardo da Vinci when he visited Lecco to plan canals and water schemes for Lodovico Sforza in Milan that he used them as backgrounds in his *Virgin of the Rocks* and *The Virgin and St Anne*. The mountains of the east shore—Resegone and the Grigna range—are wild and sharp dolomitic peaks of limestone shot through with fossils from a primordial sea—including those of Lake Como's very own dinosaur, the Lariosaurus.

For all that, the last two towns on the lake are known for their industries. **Mandello del Lario** rolls out Guzzi motorcycles, manufactured here since 1921; you can learn all about them at the **Museo del Motociclo**, Via E. Parodi 57 (*free guided tours Mon–Fri at 3pm*). Further south, on a spur over the lake, the 15th-century church of **San Giorgio** has an interior like an illuminated manuscript, decorated with wall-to-wall frescoes on everything from heaven to hell. The old silk town of **Abbadia Lariana** offers demonstrations at its **Civico Museo Setifico** in the 1917 Monti throwing-mill, with an impressive round throwing machine of 432 spools from the 1850s (*ring ahead, © 0341 731 241; closed Sun and Mon*).

Where to Stay and Eat

Varenna ✉ 22050

Right on the lakeside, ★★★★**Hotel du Lac**, © 0341 830 238, ● 0341 831 081 (*expensive*) has rooms and bathrooms that are very small though fully equipped, and its views are marvellous. There's also a good if very pricey restaurant at lake level. If it's not booked up for an event, you can stay in the ★★★**Villa Cipressi**, Via IV Novembre 18, © 0341 830 113, ● 0341 830 401 (*expensive*) with its gorgeous garden and lake terraces.

Varenna has two excellent small, family-run hotels on the lake: ★★**Olivedo**, Piazza Martiri 4, near the steamer terminal, ©/● 0341 830 115 (*moderate*) is run by the friendly Colombo family (the daughter speaks English), and meals, served on the terrace if the weather's nice, are excellent.

★★★**Albergo Milano**, Via XX Settembre 29, ©/● 0341 830 298 (*moderate*) enjoys an exquisite setting in the village, with eight rooms with balconies and wonderful views. The ones to request (months in advance) are numbers 1 or 2 with their large terraces, ideal for couples and incurable romantics. Central ★**Del Sole**, Piazza S. Giorgio 21, © 0341 830 206 (*cheap*) has six clean and quiet double rooms and a pizzeria.

For gastronomic joy book a table at the **Vecchia Varenna** , Via Scoscesa 10, © 0341 830 793 (*moderate*), where the sumptuous views are matched by dishes prepared with the finest ingredients from France and Italy: the lake fish is exquisite. *Closed Mon, also closed Tues in winter.*

Lecco

A sombre industrial city, magnificently positioned at the foot of jagged Mount Resegone, Lecco grew up where the River Adda leaves Lake Como to continue its journey south to the Po (a typical entry in Pliny's *Natural History* records how the Adda passes pristinely through the lake without mingling its waters). After a rocky history of wars and plagues and emigration, Lecco found its feet under the Austrians, who improved transportation with the Paderno d'Adda canal—an idea first proposed by the Duke of Milan's hydraulic engineer, Leonardo da Vinci, in 1498—and opened up the city for growth and industry (most notably in iron) by demolishing its tight girdle of walls. Feeling neglected by its old rival Como, Lecco split away and became a provincial capital in its own right in 1994, taking the east shore of the lake, the Grigna mountains and La Brianza with it.

Desperately Seeking Lucia and Renzo

What most Italians want from Lecco, however, is Manzoniana. For the city, as it will gently remind you wherever you turn, was the childhood home of Alessandro Manzoni (born in Milan 1785, died 1873) and provided the setting of his I Promessi Sposi (The Betrothed), Italy's 19th-century fictional classic. Revolutionary in its day, the Sposi was the first to look at Italy's history through the eyes of the common man, and it sparked pro-unification sentiments in the breast of every Italian who read it. The novel was also a sensation for its language: a new popular national Italian that everyone could understand—no small achievement in a country of a hundred dialects where the literary language had remained unchanged since Dante. Even now the perils of young Lucia and Renzo's union remain required reading for every schoolchild, a sacred cow breathlessly milked by every denizen of Italian culture—but confessedly something of a hard slog for the uninitiated.

Getting Around

Lecco is connected by rail with Milan, Como, Bergamo and Cólico (Lecco rail information ✆ 0341 420 364. SAL buses from Via Pergola 2, ✆ 0341 363 148, serve most of the towns in the provinces.

Tourist Information

Via Nazario Sauro 6, ✆ 0341 362 360, ✉ 286 231.
Lecco On Line: *http://www.vol.it./pvlecco.*

A Walk Around Lecco

Although Lecco's charm is mostly concentrated in its spectacular surroundings, there are a few things to see as well. When Leonardo da Vinci passed through town, he liked to stand on the

11-arch **Ponte Azzone Visconti**, built over the Adda in 1336 as part of Azzone's defensive line from Lecco to Milan, and watch what he called 'the great gathering of waters' as the river, flowing from the lake, swells to form the Lago di Garlate. Once bristling with towers, the bridge isn't quite as Leonardo saw it. From the bridge Via Azzone Visconti leads to Piazza Manzoni with its large **Monument to Manzoni**, the author sitting pensively over a base covered with scenes from the *Sposi*. From here Via Roma leads to the old centre of town, Piazza XX Settembre, where a market has been held every Wednesday and Saturday since 1149. Its landmark, the **Torre Viscontea**, is all that survives of the towers and walls that Azzone built around Lecco; there are plans to make it into a museum of the mountains.

From Piazza XX Settembre, Via G. Bovara and Corso Matteotti lead to the **Castello** quarter of 18th-century mansions, among them the **Palazzo Belgioso** at Corso Matteotti 32 (*closed for restoration*) with an old-fashioned natural history collection, archaeological finds and a section on Lecco's metallurgy. Literary pilgrims flock to the museum in Manzoni's boyhood home, the **Villa Manzoni**, now lost amid the urban sprawl at Via Guanella 7 (*from Piazza Manzoni, walk up Viale Dante; open Tues–Sun 9.30–2; adm*); here you can inspect the great man's cradle, tobacco boxes and nightcap, although the house itself, little changed since the 18th century, forms the main attraction. The upper floor is now a gallery of 16th–20th-century paintings by local artists.

Want more? The tourist office distributes a special Manzoni brochure that pinpoints the various scenes and buildings from *I Promessi Sposi*, most of which (Lucia's house, Don Rodrigo's castle, the marriage church) are in **Olate**, the neighbourhood just east of Castello. Another scene from the novel took place at Padre Cristoforo's convent (now ruined) at **Pescarenico**, an old fishing village just south of the Ponte Visconti; the village's quirky, triangular campanile, erected in the 1700s, survives in better condition and has been listed as a national monument. Pescarenico is one of the last true fishing villages on the lake, where the fishermen still use their traditional narrow, thin-bowed boats and nets.

Just east of Lecco towers **Monte Resegone** ('Big Saw'), a jaggedy, bumpety Dolomite that got away; on weekends it becomes a major Milanese escape route, especially for rock climbers. Those not up to grappling on crusty cliffs can take the funivia 4360ft up Resegone's flank to the woods and meadows of the **Piani d'Erna** (bus 5 from the city centre will take you to the station, for information © 0341 497 337) but mind that it's a clear day, when the view is quite extraordinary.

Lecco ✉ *22053*   **Where to Stay**

Lecco doesn't exactly brim over with hotels, but just a kilometre away at Malgrate ★★★★**Il Griso** Via Provinciale 51, © 0341 202 040, ✉ 0341 202 248 (*expensive*) is a moderate-sized but elegant hotel with fine views of the lake from its wide terrace. There's a pool in the garden, and one of the region's best gourmet restaurants. *Reservations are essential*. In town the ★★★**Moderno**, Piazza Diaz 5, © 0341 286 519, ✉ 0341 362 177 (*moderate*) doesn't have much character but the rooms are adequate with all mod cons. Up the funicular at the Pian d'Erna, little ★**Marchett**, © 0341 505 019 (*cheap*) has simple rooms with views.

You can pick your fish from the tanks at **Al Porticciolo**, Via Valesecchi 5, ✆ 0341 498 103 (*expensive*), Lecco's best restaurant, where the chef concentrates on bringing out the natural flavours of the seafood. *Closed Mon and Aug.*

Just outside town, on the road to the Pian d'Erni funivia, is the **Taverna ai Poggi**, Via ai Poggi 14, ✆ 0341 497 126 (*cheap*), serving regional specialities such as local salami and lake fish, as well as good sandwiches and soup, at extremely reasonable prices. You can sit outside in summer. *Closed Mon.*

Around Lecco: the Grigna Range and the Valsassina

The magnificent pale peaks of the Grigna mountains attract skiers in the winter and walkers and rock climbers in the summer. The range is divided into two distinct groups: the southern **Grigna Meridionale** (7142ft) may be approached from Lecco by way of **Ballabio Inferiore**, where a long and winding road leads up to the green saddle of **Piani Resinelli** and its Rifugio Porta. Here begins a spectacular trail (suitable for experienced trekkers) called the *Direttissima* which heads north to Rifugio Rosalba, passing the fantastic pinnacles over the Val Tesa.

The more massive northern group, **Grigna Settentrionale** (7903ft), runs between Lake Como and the **Valsassina**, the lofty valley on either side of the torrent Pioverna. The road north of Ballabio Inferiore reaches it by way of a gloomy gorge and **Colle di Balisio**, another green saddle (with access to the popular ski resorts of **Barzio, Cremeno** and **Moggio**) then continues up to **Pasturo**, the market town of the Valsassina, famous for its soft cheeses. Further up, the valley's medieval capital **Introbio** is still defended by its stalwart medieval **Arrigoni Tower**; the environs are full of abandoned silver, lead and iron mines. Introbio looks east to the mighty **Piazzo dei Tre Signori** (8380ft) that once marked the border between Milan, Venice and Switzerland.

The next village in the Valsassina, **Vimogno**, has a lovely waterfall, the **Cascata del Troggia**, while **Primaluna**, further up, was the cradle of the Della Torre family, who ruled Milan from 1240 until the Visconti came along and snuffed them out. Some of the small palace-fortresses in town still bear their coat of arms; the church, **San Pietro**, has paintings in the manner of Titian and the beautiful golden 15th-century Torriani Cross, of Tuscan manufacture. Neighbouring **Cortabbio** was the first feudal court of the archbishop of Milan; here the oldest Christian tombstone in Lombardy (AD 425) was discovered. At **Cortenova** the road forks, and a hard choice it is because both routes, one to Varenna (*see* p.184) and the other to Bellano and the Val Varrone (*see* pp.183–4), take in spectacular mountain scenery.

Between Lecco and Como: La Brianza

South of the mountainous Triangolo Lariano, La Brianza is a gentle region of little lakes that span the legs of Lake Como like blue footprints. Its villages spun the silk that was woven in Como and Lecco, and Milanese nobles erected summer villas on their shores in the 18th and

19th centuries. Today La Brianza, close to the big-name designers in Milan, is the most important furniture-making region in all Italy.

The lake just south of Lecco, the **Lago di Garlate**, was closely associated with the silk industry. In 1950 the Abegg silk mill, on the SS30 in the town of Garlate, was converted into the **Museo Civico della Seta** (*open Sun 10–12 and 2–6, or by request © 0341 681 306; adm*), where you can find out more about one of the nicest things ever made by worms; exhibits include some 500 tools and machines, most impressive of which are the 19th-century throwing-machines, capable of 10,000 revolutions a minute .

Civate: Churches from the First Millennium

Lake Annone, the next lake to the west, is the biggest and most striking in La Brianza, its waters nearly split in two to the north by a long narrow promontory and islet. Near here stands **Civate**, a major pilgrimage destination in the Dark Ages thanks to its abbey of **San Calocero**, founded in 705 to house the relics of the Roman martyr Calogerus and the keys of St Peter—a spare set, one hopes, or perhaps Peter eventually descended from heaven's gate to collect them, because they're long gone. In the 1080s the abbey led the post-Patariane reformation in Lombardy, and in the 1590s, after one of its cardinal owners became Pope Gregory XIV, it became an Olivetan monastery until its suppression in 1803. During restorations of the basilica in 1983, 11th-century frescoes (including a *Judgement of Solomon*) were discovered behind the 17th-century vaulting and in the Romanesque crypt. The beautiful cloister and abbey buildings are now a rest home for the blind.

Best of all, a lovely hour and a half's walk up from Civate to Monte Cornizzolo (2095ft) will take you to the even older **San Pietro al Monte** (*open Sun after 8am, or contact Mario Canali, Via Monsignor Gilardi 3, © 0341 551 576*), founded by Desiderius, the last king of the Lombards, taking its final form in the 11th century, with a pair of choirs, a door like a giant's oven and a great round gallery. The twin apses have remarkable Byzantine-style frescoes and stuccoes inspired by the Apocalypse, of the four rivers of the New Jerusalem, St Michael slaying the dragon (unusually, with plenty of help from the saints, transfixing the beast with their spears) and the Christ of the Second Coming liberating Lady Church. The high altar has a rare *baldacchino* from the 1050s, decorated with vivid reliefs of imaginary animals and a Tree of Life; the ancient crypt, unusually enough, also has beautiful if damaged stuccoes. The adjacent centrally planned **Oratorio di San Benedetto** has an unusual 12th-century painted altar.

Stendhal often took refuge at Lake Annone, retreating there whenever Milan, much as he loved it, got on his nerves; his farm in **Oggiono** on the south shore is now a hotel and restaurant. Oggiono was the home town of one of Leonardo's pupils, Marco d'Oggiono, who left a fine polyptych of *S. Maria Assunta and Saints* in the parish church of **Santa Eufemia**, which still retains its Romanesque bell tower (in spite of a cyclone in 1898) and an octagonal 11th-century baptistry.

South of Lake Annone, the **Monte di Brianza** is one of the most unspoiled corners of the region; south of Castello stand the romantic ruins of the **Campanone della Brianza**, a tower built by Lombard Queen Theodolinda; south of Campanone the regional **Parco delle Valle del Curone** (near Missaglia and Montevecchia) offers pretty walks through chestnut and birch woods. The big attraction in these parts is **Merate**, where the gentle hills are scattered with noble Milanese villas, mostly from the 1700s: the beautiful **Villa Belgioso** has a superb garden. Two kilometres from the centre, the **Osservatorio Astronomico** was founded in 1927 and remains today one of the most important in Italy (*open for guided tours the first Friday of each month, at 9.30, 10.30, 2.30 and 3.30; ☏ 039 999 111*).

Erba and Around

The central lakes of La Brianza, Pusino, Segrino and Alserio are less compelling although they have their interest, mostly concentrated in and around **Erba**, the most important town between Lecco and Como. Erba's environs were another favourite place for planting villas; one, in the suburb of Crevenna, holds the **Museo Civico Archeologico**, Via Foscolo, ☏ 031 615 282 (*open Tues–Fri 9.30–12, Sat 3–7*). In another suburb, Incino, **Santa Eufemia** has a magnificent 11th-century Romanesque campanile. To the west above Erba the **Buco del Piombo**, 'Lead Hole', is a spectacular chasm-cave with sheer 330ft walls threaded by a stream. Near here Napoleon's viceroy Eugène de Beauharnais planted a double row of pine trees leading up to the pastures of the panoramic **Alpe del Vicerè**, still a popular outing for summer picnics. From Erba a scenic road heads north through the Valsassina to Bellagio (*see* p.178).

Where to Stay and Eating Out

Oggiono Brianza ✉ 22048

You can sleep in a quiet room in Stendhal's farmhouse, the ★★★**Fattorie di Stendhal**, Via Dante 16, ☏ 0341 576 561, ☏ 0341 260 106 (*moderate*), which also has a good restaurant, or try **Pizzeria Country**, Via Dante 25, ☏ 0341 576 166. *Closed Mon.* Both have lovely views over Lake Annone.

The tiny village of Viganò Brianza, 9km south of Lake Annone, is worth a special trip for its restaurant **Pierino Penati**, Via XXIV Maggio 36, ☏ 039 956 020, (*very expensive*). Delicious regional specialities and a superb wine list complement the chef's own innovations (gnocchetti in a saffron-scented prawn bisque, for instance), followed by an excellent choice of cheeses and desserts. *Closed Sun eve and Mon, Aug and Oct–Jan.*

Erba ✉ 22036

The 12th-century ★★★★**Castello di Pomerio** Via Como 5, ☏ 031 627 516, ☏ 031 628 245 (*very expensive*) has been converted into a lovely hotel. The interior has been meticulously restored, right down to the frescoes. Many rooms have fireplaces and massive wooden beds (but modern bathrooms); the public rooms are furnished with antiques.

In Lurago d'Erba, south of Lago di Alserio, **La Corte**, Via Mazzini 20, ☏ 031 699 690 (*expensive*), is a charming restaurant known for its superb regional dishes, from the homemade breadsticks to pâtés to exquisite artistic desserts. *Closed Sun eve, Wed, and two weeks in August.* It also has several (*moderate*) rooms with bath.

Beyond Como: the Valchiavenna and Valtellina

North and east of Lake Como lies the majestic mountain-bound wine-growing province of Sondrio, sandwiched between the Orobie Alps and Switzerland. It occupies a watershed in central Europe; its glacier-fed rivers flow into Como and the Mediterranean, but also into the Danube and the Black Sea and through the Rhine into the North Sea. Only four roads link Sondrio's two main valleys, the Valchiavenna and the Valtellina, with the rest of Italy. Both valleys are among the least-exploited regions in the Alps, offering plenty of opportunities to see more of the mountains and fewer of your fellow creatures.

The Valtellina has always clung to its own hard-working cultural traditions, while politically it often played the part of a football between Milan and the Swiss Grison dynasty. Milan had it in the 14th century, but when the Spanish took Milan the Valtellina, with its many Protestants, joined the Grisons. Years of war followed; in 1620 the Spanish in Milan instigated the Valtellina's Catholics to perform the 'Holy Butchery' of 400 of their Protestant neighbours, a move that backfired in 1639 when the Grisons regained the province. The Valtellina rejoined Italy only in the Napoleonic partition of 1797.

One place where the old Valtellina has not only survived but thrived is at the table, most famously in its wines (*see* p.195) but in every course of the meal. Buckwheat is the staff of life, in the Valtellina's grey *polenta taragna* (mixed with butter and cheese), *sciatt* (buckwheat pancakes with cheese) and buckwheat tagliatelle or *pizzoccheri*; there are delicious cheeses like *bitto* (cow's milk mixed with a maximum 20% goat's milk, becoming stronger with age) and mild *casera*, the low-fat *matûsh*, *scimudin* and *Valtellina d'Alpe*. Mushrooms abound, and the local chestnut-fed pork, hams, salami and *bresaola* (thin slices of beef or venison cured in salt, spices and wine, and then left to dry) are excellent. Desserts are based on walnuts, chestnuts and honey; try *fiurett*, a cake flavoured with fennel seeds, sambuco and aniseed, or *bisciöla*, a rich chewy cake shot through with raisins, walnuts and figs, served with cream.

The Valchiavenna

The Valchiavenna stretches from Novate Mezzola north of Lake Como to the Spluga and Maloja passes, threading through the Lepontine and Rhaetic Alps. Many of the towns here started as stations along the Roman road and prospered thanks to thick veins of the pot-stone in the mountains—turned on a lathe and carved into cooking pots (*laveggi*), or sculpted into decorations, especially on windows and portals.

Getting Around

At Cólico the **railway** from Milan and Lecco forks, one line heading north as far as Chiavenna. Buses from there link up to Madesimo and other valley towns.

Tourist Information

Chiavenna: Piazza Stazione, ✆/🖷 0343 36384. **Madesimo**, Via Carducci 27, ✆ 0343 53015, 🖷 0343 53782.

Chiavenna

Chiavenna, the valley metropolis, is a pleasant town along the Mera river. Its distinctive natural rock cellars, the **Crotti**, maintain a steady year-round temperature of 6–8°C and have long been used for ripening local cheeses and hams; some have been converted into popular wine cellars, celebrated in mid-September at the annual *Sagra dei Crotti*. Chiavenna's most important church, **San Lorenzo**, was begun in the 11th century and contains a treasure including a 12th-century golden gem-studded 'Pax' cover for the Gospels (in a bank vault at the time of writing, however); also note in the Romanesque baptistry the octagonal font (1156) carved from a single chunk of pot-stone. Above the 15th-century Palazzo Baliani you can walk up to the **Parco Botanico Archeologico Paradiso** (*open Tues–Sat 2–6, Sun 10.30–12.30 and 2–6; winter Tues–Fri 2–5, Sat and Sun 10–12 and 2–5; adm*), an ancient pot-stone quarry where workers once cut out pots and stones for architectural details. Further up, the **Parco Marmitte dei Giganti**, 'the giants' kettles', is named for its remarkable round glacial potholes, the finest collection in Europe. The path up to the park passes *crotti* under the horse chestnuts and charming meadows; beyond the potholes a sign directs the way to the *incisioni rupestri*—etchings in the boulders left by centuries of passers-by (but you can bet the guards don't want you to add your two cents' worth).

East of Chiavenna on the St Moritz road in the Val Bregaglia, a magnificent waterfall, the **Cascate dell'Acqua Fraggia**, is just above **Borgonuovo**; 2000 leg-aching steps lead up past *crotti* to the ancient hamlet of Savogno atop the waterfall. In 1618 a landslide off Monte Conto buried the town of **Piuro**, next to Borgonuovo; you can visit the excavations of this humble 17th-century Pompeii, once an important pot-stone quarrying town, and finds are displayed in the church of **Sant'Abbondio** in Borgonuovo (*Sun only 3–5*). Before it was buried Piuro had fine mansions like the 16th-century **Palazzo Vertemate Franchi** in nearby **Prosto di Piuro** (*open Mar–Oct; guided tours only, Tues–Fri 10, 11, 2, 3 and 4, Sat and Sun 10, 11, 3, 4 and 5; adm*), its rooms decorated throughout with beautiful carved ceilings and lush mythological frescoes by the Campi brothers of Cremona. At Santa Croce di Piuro, the church of **San Martino in Aurogo** has 11th-century frescoes.

North of Chiavenna, the **Valle San Giacomo** becomes increasingly rugged and steep, with dramatic landslides, glaciers and waterfalls. The village of **Campodolcino**, with a Roman bridge and a church with florid rococo altars, shares the 45km 'Skirama' ski slopes with Madesimo, watched over by a 43ft gilt statue of the **Madonna d'Europa**. **Madesimo**, further up, is a high-rise, high-altitude international summer/winter resort (skiing, cross-country skiing, ice skating, trekking and riding)—before the 6948ft **Splügen Pass**, generally closed six months of the year.

Where to Stay and Eating Out

Chiavenna ✉ 23022

Al Cenacolo, Via Pedretti 16, ✆ 0343 32123 (*moderate*) serves a mix of regional dishes and innovative cuisine, based on local seasonal ingredients (including game dishes in season) while Valtellina wines fill the cellar. *Closed Tues eve, Wed and June.* Equally good, the family-run **Passerini** in the 17th-century Palazzo Salis, Via Dolzino 128, ✆ 0343

36166 (*moderate*) offers a good-value L26,000 lunch menu; *à la carte* don't miss the ravioli filled with sea bass or the spaghetti with scampi and chilli. *Closed Mon and July.* Best of all, 10km west in Villa di Chiavenna, the family-run **La Lanterna Verde**, Via S. Barnaba 7, ✆ 0343 38588 (*moderate*) is a place to taste the regional cuisine elevated to a gourmet level, accompanied with exquisite cheeses, desserts and enormous wine list: be sure to book. *Closed Wed, Thurs lunch, half of June and Nov.*

Madesimo ✉ 23024

Madesimo has most of the accommodation in the Valchiavenna, with the large **★★★Cascata e Cristallo**, Via Carducci 2, ✆ 0343 53108, ✎ 0343 54470 (*expensive–moderate*) at the top of the list with its pool and health centre. *Open all year.* **Osteria Vegia**, Via Cascata 7, ✆ 0343 53335 (*moderate*) has been the place to go for *pizzoccheri* and other local treats for 280 years; another good place, 'the big cellar' **Il Cantinone**, Via De Giacomi 37, ✆ 0343 56120 (*moderate*) has not only wines but rather unusual dishes to go with them: *pennette* in a vension sauce and barley-based *orzotto ai finferli*. *Closed Wed except in July and Aug.*

The Valtellina

East of Cólico and Lake Como the thoroughly unpleasant, traffic-swollen SS38 enters the Valtellina, giving a false first impression: the rest of the great valley of the Adda, where villages and vineyards hang precariously on the faces of the mountains, is as pure and unadulterated and fresh as any, a great alpine playground only a couple of hours from smoggy Milan. Recently the mountains south of the Adda, the Orobie Alps, have been set aside as the Parco Regionale delle Orobie Valtellinesi to protect, among other things, an endangered species of wood grouse.

Getting Around

FS **trains** from Milan and Lecco serve the valley as far east as Tirano, where you can pick up the '*trenino rosso del Bernina*' for St Moritz, 70km away, ✆ 0342 701 353. A network of **buses**, connecting with the trains, serves the villages and points east, and there are direct coach connections to Sondrio from Milan, as well as direct summer and winter services to Bormio and Stelvio National Park from Milan, Varese and Como.

Tourist Information

Morbegno: Piazza Bossi, ✆ 0342 610 015. **Sondrio**: Via C. Battisti 12, ✆ 0342 512 500, ✎ 0342 212 590, with a horde of information on walking, climbing, mountain biking, riding, and skiing. **Chiesa in Valmalenco**: Piazza SS. Giacomo e Filippo 1, ✆ 0342 451 150, ✎ 452 505.

To Sondrio: the Costiera dei Cèch

To enter the lower valley from Colico is to enter the territory of the Cèch, a people whose origin is as mysterious as their name. Located just above and north of the Adda, the nine old vine-wrapped villages of the Costiera dei Cèch are veritable suntraps and make for pretty, not too demanding walks; there's also an 18th-century wine press and museum, the **Torchio de Cerido** (*open Thurs and Sun 3–6;* © *0342 611 342*). The Cèchs' busy and pleasant main town, **Morbegno**, is just over the river, where you'll find a pair of interesting churches: 14th-century **Sant'Antonio** with a Rodari *Pietà* and a fresco by Gaudenzio Ferrari on the façade and another within, and **San Giovanni Battista**, frescoed in the 18th century by local rococo master Gianpaolo Ligari. Natural history predominates in the **Museo Civico** in the Palazzo Gaulteroni, in Via Cortivacci (*open Tues, Thurs, Sat and Sun 2.30–5.30*). You can also visit the **Museo dell'Homo Salvadego** in Cosio just to the west: a country house, frescoed in 1464 with the hairy, club-wielding 'Wild Man' of the Alps, the local incarnation of the Green Man, the spirit of nature (*open Tues–Sat 9–12 and 2–5; there's a resident caretaker,* © *0342 617 056*).

From Morbegno buses make excursions towards the south into two scenic valleys, the **Valli del Bitto**, with iron ore deposits that made them a prize for the Venetians for two centuries, and the rural **Val Tartano**, a 'lost paradise', dotted with alpine cottages, woods and pastures, its declining population still farming as their ancestors did. The road through the valley was finished only in 1971, though many hamlets even today are accessible only by foot or mule. A third valley running to the north, the wild granite **Val Másino**, is the beginning of the magnificent six-day path, the 'Sentiero Roma' to the Valchiavenna, laid out in the 1920s. It begins at the little 15th-century spa **Bagni di Masino**, although other paths from Bagni can be walked in a single day, especially up to the meadows and torrents of the Piano Porcellizzo. The Val Másino also serves as the base for the ascent of **Monte Disgrazia** (12,074m), one of the highest peaks in the region, first climbed in 1862 by Leslie Stephen, father of Virginia Woolf. According to legend, Disgrazia is haunted by the huge and hairy Gigiat, a kind of monster goat—the yeti of the Valtellina. **Val di Mello**, a little branch valley to the east, is equally tempting for its crystal streams and waterfalls and granite bulwarks, reminiscent of Yosemite, cut and carved by local granite workers, and scaled by rock climbers, who also like to pit themselves against the biggest monolith in Europe: the granite **Sasso Remenno**, near the village of Cataéggio.

Sondrio

The provincial capital Sondrio (from *sundrium*, the land Lombard lords gave to their peasants) is a mostly modern town, built on either side of the flood-prone Torrente Mallero which devastated the city in 1987. Many of Sondrio's surviving old mansions have been put to new uses: in the 18th-century Palazzo Sassi De' Lavizzari, the new **Museo Valtellinese di Storia e Arte**, Via M. Quadrio 27 (*open Tues–Sat 10–12 and 3–6;* © *0342 526 270*) has statues, gold work and frescoes salvaged from churches, and an exceptional collection of rococo drawings, etchings and oils by the 18th-century Ligari family. At Via del Gesù 6, the Palazzo Sertoli (with a fancypants *trompe l'œil* ballroom) houses the **Collezione Fulvio Grazioli** (*open Tues–Sat 9–10 and 2–3*), one of Italy's most important collections of rocks and minerals, nearly all from the Valmalenco (*see* below). Opposite the Palazzo Sertoli, Via Scarpaletti leads up into the old Sondrio, dominated by the oft-remodelled **Castello Masegra**, dating from 1041. On the other side of the Torrente Mallero the **Palazzo Carbonera** (1533) is Sondrio's finest, with a beautiful courtyard. But most of all, Sondrio is known for wine.

Valtellina in a Bottle

Valtolina, as it's called, a valley surrounded by tall and fearsome mountains, makes wines that are heady and strong...

Leonardo da Vinci, *Codex Atlanticus 214*

People have been making wine in the Valtellina since the days of the ancient Ligurians and Etruscans. They soon found that while the easy, deep, rich soil in the valley yielded a fresh light red wine—as it does to this day (DOC Valtellina)—body and alcohol content improved dramatically with altitude. The thirst for a wine that aged well led generations to build drystone terraces like tiny shelves in the mountains, some wide enough for only two or three rows of knotty vines, then to laboriously carry up soil in woven baskets on their backs. Their efforts in the upper valley or Valtellina Superior (which continue today—of necessity everything has to be done by hand) have been awarded DOC status since 1968.

Red, with a distinctive rich, almost pungent character, capable of ageing ten years or longer, Valetellina Superior is made from a minimum of 95% chiavennasca (the local name for nebbiolo, the same noble grape that goes in Barolo) and aged for a minimum of two years in oak. The DOC area is divided into four subzones, each with a different climate and growing conditions. Sassella, just west of Sondrio, is the sunniest and most inaccessible area, named for its pretty frescoed church of the Madonna di Sassella (1521); the ruby wines are elegant, made with 5% rossola, for fragrance. Grumello, northeast of Sondrio, produces a warm garnet, almond-scented win. Inferno, named for the extra heat and sun the vines receive in a pocket micro-climate just east of Sondrio, yields exceptionally warm, powerful wines. Valgello, 10km northeast of Sondrio (between Chiuro and Téglio), the largest subzone, produces lighter, but dry, savoury wines with a toasted almond aftertaste. Another DOC wine from the Valtellina, Sforzato (or Sfursat), is partly made from grapes left to dry on the vine, producing a rich, powerful, velvety soft wine at 15°, perfect with strong cheeses or for sitting by the fireside after dinner on a cold winter's eve.

You can visit the cellars of some of the best firms: Pellizzatti Perego, Via Buon Consiglio 4, © 0342 380 167 and Fondazione Fojanini, Via Valeriana 32, © 0342 512 954, both in Sondrio, and to the east in Chiuro, one of the most venerable firms, the excellent Nino Negri, Via Ghibellini 3, in Chiuro, © 0342 482 521.

North of Sondrio: The Val Malenco

The lovely Val Malenco, with its deep chestnut forests and pretty glacier lakes, is a top destination in the lower Valtellina and a paradise for rock hounds. No valley in all the Alps comes close to matching the 260 different minerals that have been found here, including the commercially mined serpentine (green marble) and pot-stone. **Chiesa in Valmalenco** and **Caspoggio** are the main towns and ski resorts in the valley; Caspoggio has stables for riding tours of the region, while the former has a small **Museo Storico della Valmalenco** (*to visit call the tourist office in Chiesa in Valmalenco, ✆ 0342 451 150*), containing various stone objects found in the valley, from Roman times to the present day.

The high road or **Alta Via della Val Malenco** offers a 7-day trekking excursion around the rim of the valley, beginning at Torre di Santa Maria, south of Chiesa; the less ambitious can drive most of the way from San Giuseppe (north of Chiesa) up to the Rifugio Scarscen-Entova, for one of the most spectacular mountain views in the area. Another fine (and easy) excursion is up to the rugged lakes of **Campo Moro**, on the east branch of the valley; a white road will take you as far as the Rifugio Zóia, and from here it's an easy three-hour hike up to the glacier-blasted peaks around the Rifugio Marinelli.

Where to Stay and Eating Out

Morbegno ✉ 23017

★★★**Margna**, Via Margna 24, ✆ 0342 610 377, ✆ 0342 615 114 (*moderate*) has been in business since 1886, but was completely remodelled and modernized; the excellent restaurant features the likes of crêpes filled with *bitto* cheese, risotto with wild mushrooms, and venison cutlets in juniper.

Tartano ✉ 23010

★★★**La Gran Baita**, Via Castino 7, ✆/✆ 0342 645 043 (*cheap*), a comfortable hotel offering rooms with bath. *Closed Feb and Mar.* A modern little chalet, the family-run ★**Vallunga**, Via Roma 12, ✆ 0342 645 100 (*cheap*) has rooms with bath and a good restaurant; the *risotto ai funghi porcini* is excellent.

Sondrio ✉ 23100

Garibaldi is only one of the illustrious guests to have slept at ★★★★**Della Posta**, Piazza Garibaldi 19, ✆ 0342 510 404, ✆ 0342 510 210 (*expensive*). Formerly the old stage post, this grand old hotel offers big rooms with lots of charm, as well as amenities like TV, phone and minibar. It also has a cosy reading room and an excellent restaurant.

Alternatively, park your bags in Albosaggia, 5km south of Sondrio at ★★★**Campelli**, Via Moia 6, ✆ 0342 510 662, ✆ 0342 213 101 (*moderate*) a pretty family-run hotel; the cooking offers a lighter, updated version of Valtellina's somewhat rich delights, with excellent wines. *Closed Sun eve and Mon lunch, and most of Aug.*

In a 16th-century tower, high up on a hill a couple of kilometres outside Sondrio, the wonderful **Torre della Sassella**, ✆ 0342 218 500 (*expensive*) serves fine cured fish, risotto and meats, and excellent wines, in three elegant yet rustic dining rooms, each set on a different level. Reserve in advance, especially on Saturdays when it often fills up with wedding feasts. *Closed Tues eve and Wed.*

Near Piazza Campello, **Cima 11**, Via Pelosi 5, ✆ 0342 515 040 (*moderate*) is a traditional old inn, complete with long tables and benches, where diners feast on hearty old-style Valtellina cooking. *Closed Sun.* **Eden**, Via Nazario Sauro 40, ✆ 0342 214

038 (*cheap*) offers excellent value for money for its *sciatt* and *picatta* (slices of veal) cooked in Inferno wine (*see* p.195). *Closed Sun and Aug.* The **Amici Vecchie Cantine**, Via Parravicini 6, ✆ 0342 512 590, is a wine bar serving excellent locally cured meats, cheeses and vegetables in oil. *Closed Sun.*

Chiesa in Valmalenco ✉ 23023

★★★★**Tremoggia**, Via Bernina 6, ✆ 0342 451 106, ✉ 0342 451 718 (*moderate*) is a welcoming place where rooms come with TVs and minibars, and the restaurant serves good cheesy *sciatt* and beef marinated in juniper. *Closed Wed and Nov.*

In a peaceful setting, ★★★**Chalet Rezia**, Via Marconi 27, ✆/✉ 0342 451 271 (*moderate–cheap*) is a lovely little place with a covered pool, recommended by readers. The local cuisine is good, too, at the **Taverna Valtellinese**, Via Rusca, ✆ 0342 451 200 (*moderate*) with delicious *pizzoccheri* and an extensive wine list. *Closed Mon.*

The Middle Valtellina

East of Sondrio the SS38 rises relentlessly, but if you're not in a hurry take the scenic 'Castel road' running through the vineyards north of the highway, beginning at Tresivio and the melancholy ruins of Grumello castle.

Tourist Information

Aprica, Corso Roma 150, ✆ 0342 746 113, ✉ 747 732. **Tirano**: Viale Italia 183, ✆/✉ 0342 703 211.

Ponte in Valtellina to Aprica

The old patrician town of **Ponte in Valtellina** is mostly visited for its parish church of **San Maurizio**, with an unusual bronze *cimborio* or lantern (1578), and frescoes by Bernardino Luini. In 1746 it was the birthplace of astronomer Giuseppe Piazzi who, as a monk in Palermo, had such a passion for observing the heavens that he inspired the Viceroy of Naples to send him to England to study astronomy, and to finance the manufacture of a lens twice the size of the one in Greenwich observatory. He brought it back to Palermo to discover Ceres, the first asteroid, on New Year's Day 1801.

Further east, charming **Teglio** gave its name to the entire valley (from Tellina Vallis). The stumpy tower of its castle still stands guard above, while the Renaissance **Palazzo Besta** is the finest in the region (*guided tours May–Sept 9, 10, 11, 12, 2.30, 3.30 and 4.30; closed 2nd and 4th Sun and 1st and 3rd Mon of the month; in winter call the tourist office at Aprica for details; adm*). Built in 1539, the arcaded courtyard is embellished with fine *chiaroscuro* frescoes from the *Aeneid* and *Orlando Furioso*; inside, the Sala della Creazione has a world map dated 1549. Downstairs, the **Antiquarium Tellinum** (*same ticket*) houses the Stele di Caven, known as the Mother Goddess, an exceptional example of the prehistoric rock incisions common in these parts, which the locals once believed were made by the claws of witches. Among the old lanes in the centre, look for 11th-century **San Pietro**, with geometric decorations, a fine campanile and a Byzantine-style fresco of Christ Pantocrator in the apse;

the **Oratorio dei Bianchi**, its exterior frescoed with a ruined 15th-century *danse macabre*; and the **Ca' del Boia** with blackened arcades, once the home of a particularly adept and sought-after executioner. These days Teglio takes special pride not only in its wines but in its *pizzoccheri*, 'narcotic grey noodles with butter and vegetables', served up at the annual autumn *Sagra dei Pizzoccheri*.

East of Teglio, the road splits: the SS38 heads north to Tirano, while SS39 runs east to **Aprica** (3897ft), a winter and summer resort with a covered pool, roller rink, riding school, tennis, 40km of ski runs and three ski schools, including one for international competitors. You can escape the crowds at **Corteno Golgi**, where you can hire a horse to explore two remote valleys, the **Val Brandet** and **Val Camovecchio**, both part of a little-known park of firs, rhododendrons, tiny lakes, wooden bridges and old stone alpine huts. Or you can continue towards Edolo and the Valle Camonica (*see* p.221).

Tirano to Sondalo

The vines begin to give way to lush apple orchards as you approach **Tirano**, a historic cross-roads: mule trains from Venice and Brescia would pass up the Valle Camonica and at Tirano either turn west to trade in the Valtellina or continue north into Switzerland and Germany. Today the town is the terminus of the FS trains from Milan, as well as the narrow-gauge **Trenino rosso del Bernina** that plunges and twists 70km through dramatic gorges to St Moritz; in July and August special open cars make it even easier to drink in the stupendous scenery. Once the site of a major annual Swiss-Italian fair, Tirano has a fine clutch of 16th- and 17th-century buildings in its centre, but its most famous, the **Santuario della Madonna di Tirano** (1505), is a kilometre away, marking the spot where the Virgin made one of her appearances, in September 1504. It became the focal point of Catholicism during the Counter-Reformation, and was exuberantly baroqued, painted and stuccoed and given an impressive wood-inlaid organ to keep the faithful dazzled when the Valtellina was quickly sliding away into the Protestant camp. Just above the basilica, the little 10th-century church of **Santa Perpetua** has rare frescoes from the same period, discovered in 1987; arrange to get inside with the Tirano tourist office.

The Stelvio road continues up to **Grosotto**, with another major church to the Madonna, the 17th-century **Santuario della Beata Vergine delle Grazie**, with an even better 18th-century organ and, in the sacristy, a painting by Michelangelo's friend Marcello Venusti. The large old village of **Grosio**, another 2km on, was long the fief of the Visconti Venosta family, whose ruined castle sits on top of town. Just below the castle, however, is evidence that Grosio was important long before their arrival, in the curious stick-man engravings (2200–1000 BC) on the whaleback rock of its **Parco delle Incisioni Rupestri**. Art in Grosio took another step forward in the 16th century with the birth of Cipriano Valorsa, the 'Raphael of the Valtellina', who in Grosio frescoed **San Giorgio** and his own house, the **Casa di Cipriano Valorsa**. The early 20th-century Villa Visconti Venosta contains the **Museo Civico** (*open summer Tues–Sun 10–12 and 2–5; winter Tues–Sat 10–12 and 2–4*); among the exhibits are Venetian-inspired costumes, with bright kerchiefs and colourful, Burano-embroidered aprons that the older women in Grosio still wear. **Sóndalo**, the next town, has courtly 16th-century frescoes by another local painter, Giovannino da Sondalo, in its 12th-century church of Santa Marta.

Ponte in Valtellina ✉ 23026

One the region's best restaurants, occupying a 17th-century palace, **Cerere**, Via Guicciardi 7, ✆ 0342 482 284 (*moderate*) has long set the standard of classic Valtellina cuisine with dishes like *sciatt*, *pizoccheri* and tagliatelle in a hearty sausage sauce; the wine list includes the valley's finest. *Closed Wed, Jan and July.*

Teglio ✉ 23036

Down in San Giacomo di Teglio, **La Corna**, ✆ 0342 786 105 (*moderate*) has a beautiful dining room with polished wooden floors and elegant round tables, creating a warm atmosphere that complements the home-made pastas, local specialities and excellent wines produced by the owners themselves. *Closed Mon and July.*

Aprica ✉ 23031

Nothing too special here: try ★★★**Villa Maria**, Via Europa 8, ✆ 0342 746 054, ✆ 0342 747 286 (*cheap*), a typical, moderate-sized establishment with a garden, or the older ★★**Serenella**, Via Europa 110, ✆/✆ 0342 746 066, with even cheaper rooms without bath.

If you enjoy hearty mountain food, the cosy **Baita le Lische**, ✆ 0342 746 401 (*cheap*) will fill you up with huge portions of deliciously warm *pasticceria* covered with melting Gruyère cheese, followed by *polpette* or *bocconiani* and mouth-watering desserts—the *pannacotta* is a must. Book ahead. *Closed Tues.*

La Stua, Via Valtellina 11, ✆ 0342 747 776 (*moderate*) is named for its pretty ceramic stove; the various risotti are superb, and the game dishes are served with an imaginative flair. *Closed Wed.*

Tirano ✉ 23037

Opposite the *trenino rosso* station, ★★**Bernina**, Via Roma 24, ✆ 0342 701 302, ✆ 0342 701 430 (*cheap*) has been run by the Cioccarelli family for over a hundred years; most rooms have bath. The restaurant (*moderate*) with a pretty summer terrace offers a *menu del giorno* and a Valtellina menu; on Wednesdays you can feast on something rare in the Alps: fish. *Closed Mon out of season, Nov and Jan.*

Grosio ✉ 23022

A fine old hotel and restaurant, ★★★**Sassella**, ✆ 0342 847 272, ✆ 0342 847 550 (*moderate*) where all the rooms are fitted with private bath and TV. The restaurant (run by Pini Jim, the chef who feeds the Italian ski team) serves a refined version of local specialities like *bresaola condita* (served with olive oil, lemon and herbs), crêpes with mushrooms and local cheese, smoked trout and Valtellina wines; excellent inexpensive menu. *Closed Mon in winter.*

Another good place to go wine tasting is the **Enoteca Valtellinese**, 'Al bun vin', near the centre of the village.

The Upper Valtellina: Stelvio National Park

The east end of Sondrio province, where the mountains kiss the sky, was an ancient county not unjustifiably called the Magnifica Terra. Today much of the Magnifica Terra is in Stelvio National Park, Italy's most majestic; it also has some of the best skiing in Europe.

Tourist Information

Bormio: Via Stelvio 10, ℘ 0342 903 300, ℘ 904 696. **Livigno**: Via Gesa 55, ℘ 0342 996 379, ℘ 996 881, *aptminfo@.livnet.it.*

Bormio

Bormio, the seat of the Magnifica Terra, is splendidly situated in a mountain basin 4019ft up. The occasional host of the World Alpine Ski Championships, Bormio keeps visitors coming year round with an indoor sports complex, ice palace, golf courses, tennis courts and a new congress centre. But along with all of its sporty infrastructure, Bormio is also a picturesque old town of narrow medieval lanes and frescoed palaces, recalling the days of prosperity when Venice's Swiss trade passed through its busy Via Roma. One rare survival is the 13th-century council chamber or **Kuerc**, from where the Magnifica Terra was administered. The 18th-century **Palazzo De Simoni**, Via Buon Consiglio 12, now houses the **Museo Civico** (*call ℘ 0342 912 201 or ℘ 0342 904 141 for opening times as they change regularly*); the Romanesque **San Vitale** is frescoed in and out, while outside the centre at Combo the **Chiesa del Crocifisso** contains good 15th-century frescoes. Bormio is also known for its waters, either distilled into Braulio, an Alpine herbal tonic made since 1875, or in the **Bagni di Bormio**, first mentioned by Pliny the Elder, where the water steams out of the rocks at 40°C and is good for everything from acne to vaginitis.

Bormio is the western gateway to the **Parco Nazionale delle Stelvio**, Italy's largest national park, founded in 1935 around the grand alpine massif of Ortles-Cevedale and linked to Switzerland's Engadin National Park. A tenth of Stelvio is permanently covered with a hundred glaciers, including one of Europe's largest, the *Ghiacciaio dei Forni*. The peaks offer many exciting climbs, especially **Grand Zebrù** (12,631ft), **Ortles** (12,811ft) and **Cevedale** (12,395ft). The park includes Europe's second-highest pass, the **Passo di Stelvio** (9048ft) where you can ski all summer and continue into the South Tyrol between the months of June and October. Building the road here was such an engineering feat that its mastermind has a small museum in the pass, the **Museo Carlo Donegani** (*open June–Oct 9–12.30 and 2–5*).

Some 14km east of Bormio, in the confines of the park, is 'the skier's last white paradise', perhaps better known as **Santa Caterina Valfurva**, a typical alpine village and cradle of ski champions—most recently Olympic gold medallist Deborah Compagnoni—who learn to ski as soon as they can toddle on snow that lasts from early autumn to late spring.

Into Little Tibet and Livigno

From Bormio a white road winds up along the Valle di Fraele, towards the source of the River Adda, into a landscape called 'Italy's Little Tibet', as much for its quantity of snow as for its rugged mountains. Two towers, the stark 16th-century **Torri di Fraele**, guard the mule road, the old German Via Imperiale; a more modest route diverging to the west is known as the *sentiero dei Contrabbandieri* or smugglers' path. The steep gorge of the Adda survives, although the river does not, diverted by a hydroelectric plant to feed the industries of Milan; the source of the Adda is now dammed back to form the artificial lakes of Cancano and San Giacomo di Fraele.

From Bormio the N301 follows the **Valdidentro**, another ski haven, west into the **Valle di Livigno**. Before reaching **Livigno** proper, however, you must first pass through Customs—for this old paradise for smugglers has been Europe's highest duty-free zone since 1805, thanks to Napoleon, a status confirmed in 1960 by the EC. Besides being a favourite weekend destination for Bavarians who barrel down through the Drossa tunnel to replenish their tobacco or hooch supplies, Livigno preserves many of its old wooden houses or *baits*, and has excellent skiing, with snow most of the year; its outer hamlet of **Trepalle** claims to be the highest settlement in Europe inhabited year-round.

Sports and Activities

Stelvio National Park is administered by the provinces of Sondrio, Trentino and Bolzano, all of which have **park visitor's centres**. Bormio's is at Via Monte Braulio 56, © 0342 910 100 (*open July–10 Sept daily 9–12 and 3–6*); they can tell you where to find the 1500km of marked trails at all levels of ability, or the best place to watch for the park's chamois, the not very shy marmots, golden eagles, lammergeyers and other wildlife, including the ibex, reintroduced in 1968. The last bear in these mountains was bagged in 1908, but hunting is now illegal, at least in the Lombard section of the park.

Above the visitor's centre, the **Giardino Botanico Alpino Rezia** (*same hours*) contains many of the 1800 species of plants and flowers that grow in Stelvio.

Where to Stay and Eating Out

Bormio ✉ 23032

In the centre of Bormio, ★★★★**Rezia**, Via Milano 9, © 0342 904 721, 🖅 0342 905 197 (*very expensive–expensive*) is one of the town'scosiest hotels, furnished throughout with locally handcrafted furniture; the restaurant (*moderate*) is especially good, serving up delicious mushroom dishes in season, as well as solid Valtellina homecooking. *Closed Mon.*

Modern and upmarket, the ★★★★**Palace**, Via Milano 54, © 0342 903 131, 🖅 0342 903 366 (*very expensive*) offers tennis, swimming pool and very comfortable rooms, all with bath and TV. *Closed in May.*

★★★★**Baita dei Pini**, Via Don Peccedi 15, © 0342 904 346, 🖅 0342 904 700 (*expensive*) is central and pleasant, with very good rooms, all with bath. *Open Dec–April, 15 June–Sept.* ★★**Everest**,Via S. Barbara 11 ©0342 901 291, 🖅 0342 901 713 (*cheap*) has a garden and pleasant rooms, all with baths. *Closed Oct, Nov.*

Kuerc, in the heart of old Bormio on Piazza Cavour 8, ✆ 0342 904 738 (*moderate*), named after the ancient council of Bormio, is a good place to try local dishes in an attractive setting.

Livigno ✉ 23030

With 97 hotels and 800 holiday flats, you'll probably find a place to sleep in Livigno. One of the best is the family-run ★★★**Alpina**, Via Bondi 3, ✆ 0342 996 007, ✆ 0342 996 350 (*moderate*), in business for over a century, with a woodsy elegance; its excellent restaurant (*moderate*) is usually packed with hungry diners feasting on game and mushroom dishes, tasty local cheeses and excellent Valtellina wines. *Closed May and Nov.* Another atmospheric choice, ★★**Camana Veglia**, Via Ostaria 107, ✆ 0342 996 310, ✆ 0342 996 904 (*moderate*) occupies a historic building near the centre and also has a first-rate, cosy restaurant serving dishes based on the finest local ingredients. *Closed Tues; hotel closed May and Nov.*

The East: Bergamo to Lake Garda

The eastern lakes, Iseo and Garda, and the great art cities of Bergamo and Brescia are markedly different from the rest of Lombardy, thanks mostly to Venice, which ruled here from the early 1400s until the advent of Napoleon, the Serenissima's *numero uno* party-pooper. If the medieval Venetians got very mixed reviews from the Greeks and their other subject states in the eastern Mediterranean, they had, by the time they acquired their *terra ferma* real estate in Italy, learned to rule with a light hand, in part by making a visual statement of their dominion. This was achieved not only by fixing a marble relief of the lion of St Mark to every gate and tower, but by reflecting graceful bits of Venice in the architecture, in the art in the churches and in exceptional paintings that now fill the galleries in both Bergamo and Brescia.

Lake Iseo, between Bergamo and Brescia, is one of the best-kept secrets in this book—a perfectly charming little lake rimmed by the mellow vine-clad hills of the Franciacorta to the southeast and the Valle Camonica to the north, with fascinating prehistoric rock incisions spanning thousands of years. Lake Garda, the largest lake in Italy, is stunning, with colourful towns and olive groves and vineyards and too many tourists in the summer; of all the lakes it is the most whole-heartedly devoted to sheer fun, with its watersports, discos and amusement parks.

Bergamo

At the end of *A Midsummer's Night Dream*, Bottom and his mechanic pals who played in 'Pyramus and Thisbe' dance a bergamask to celebrate the happy ending. Bergamo itself has the same happy, stomping magnificent spirit as its great peasant dance, a city that mixes a rugged edge with the most delicate refinement: it has given the world not only a dance but the maestro of *bel canto*, Gaetano Donizetti, the Renaissance painter of beautiful women, Palma Vecchio, and the great master of the portrait, Gian Battista Moroni.

Piled on a promontory on the edge of the Alps, the city started out on a different foot, founded by mountain Celts who named it 'Bergheim' or hill town. To this day the Bergamasques speak a dialect that puzzles even their fellow Lombards; their language, courage and blunt up-front character are all a part of the essential *bergheimidad* that sets them apart. Although old Bergamo owes many of its grace notes to the long rule of Venice (1428–1797), it was by no means a one-way traffic of culture from Lagoon Land to hill peasants: Bergamo contributed not only artists, but the Serenissima's most brilliant and honourable *condottiere*, Bartolomeo Colleoni (1400–75), as well as many of Venice's servants, porters and stock comic characters. The city prospered to the extent that in the 16th century another Bergamo, Bergamo Bassa, grew up on the plain below; the two cities, high and low, contributed so many men to Garibaldi in its enthusiasm for the Risorgimento that it received the proud title 'City of the Thousand'.

Getting To and From Bergamo

Bergamo is an hour's **train** ride from Milan, and also has frequent connections to Brescia, but only a few trains a day to Cremona and Lecco; for information, call ✆ 035 247 624. Bergamo's **airport** has connections to Rome and Ancona.

There are regular **bus** services (✆ 035 387 547) to Lake Iseo, as well as to Milan, Como, Lecco, Lake Garda, the Bergamasque valleys and Boario in the Val Camonica. Both train and bus stations are located near each other at the end of Viale Papa Giovanni XXIII. If you're **driving**, try to leave your car elsewhere. Bergamo is purgatory to navigate, hell at rush hours (which is nearly always), and once you reach your destination you may as well be in limbo with no place to park.

Tourist Information

Bergamo has two tourist offices, one by the train station (walk out of the station, turn left and look for the little 'I'), ✆ 035 242 226, ✆ 035 242 994; another, open summer only in the Città Alta, is at Vicolo Aquila Nera 3, ✆ 035 232 730.

Bergamo Bassa

The heart of Bergamo's pleasant Città Bassa was laid out in the 1920s by Marcello Piacentini, wide and stately, lined with trees and always full of cars. Viale Giovanni XXIII goes up from the station to the elongated **Piazza Matteotti**, where a wide leafy pedestrian-refuge called the Sentierone, the 'Big Path', is flanked by cafés, the 18th-century **Teatro Donizetti**, with five tiers of boxes, and the church of **San Bartolomeo**, housing a 1516 altarpiece of the *Madonna* by the Venetian Lorenzo Lotto, who spent 15 years working around Bergamo. The north extension of Piazza Matteotti, arcaded Piazza Vittorio Veneto, was graced by Marcello Piacentini with one of the more elegant Fascisti bell towers anywhere. Further up Viale Vittorio Emanuele II, don't miss the Liberty-style Banco d'Italia and the Art Deco post office just behind it off Via Zelasco.

The oldest part of Bergamo Bassa lies a few blocks east: **Via Pignolo**, lined with 16th-century palazzi built for the local cloth merchants, and their three churches, each containing paintings by Lotto: Renaissance **Santo Spirito** on the corner of Via Torquato Tasso, with paintings by Bergamo natives Previtali and Bergognone; **San Bernardino in Pignolo** on the corner of Via S. Giovanni, with a superb *Pala of the Madonna and Saints* (1521) by Lotto; and near pretty Piazzetta del Delfino **Sant'Alessandro della Croce**, with a *Trinity* by Lotto and excellent works by Costa and Previtali, all a preview to the Accademia Carrara, just up Via S. Tomaso.

The Accademia Carrara

Open daily 9.30–12.30 and 2.30–5.30; adm; free Sun.

This is nothing less than one of the top provincial art museums in Italy, and certainly one of the oldest, founded in 1796 by Count Giacomo Carrara and housed in this neoclassical palace since 1810. It has exquisite portraits—Botticelli's haughty *Giuliano de' Medici*, Pisanello's refined *Lionello d'Este*, Gentile Bellini's *Portrait of a Man*, Lotto's *Portrait of Lucina Brembati*

Accademia
Carrara

Galleria d'Arte Moderna
e Contemporanea

Santo
Spirito

San Bernardino
in Pignolo

Sant'Alessandro
della Croce

Porta Sant'
Agostino

VIA C. BATTISTI

VIA SAN GIOVANNI

VIA T. FRIZZONI

VIA DELLA NOCA

VIA SAN TOMASO

VIA PIGNOLO

VIA TORQUATO TASSO

VIA PIGNOLO

Piazzale
del Delfino

VIA S. ELISABETTA

VIA DEL PRADELLO

VIA GIUSEPPE VERDI

VIA MASONE

Convento di
Sant'Agostino

Venetian Walls

Piazzale
Sant'Agostino

San Michele al
Pozzo Bianco

Sant'Andrea

VIALE VITTORIO EMANUELE II

VIALE DELLE MURA

PORTA DIPINTA

VIA MONTE ORTIGARA

Post
Office

VIA ZELASCO

VIA LOCATELLI

VIA ANTONIO

Piazza della
Repubblica

VIA DELLA FARA

Rocca

VIA SOLATA

VIA MIRIA

VIALE VITTORIO EMANUELE II

VIALE DELLE

Funicular

VIA MAIRONI DA PONTE

VIA BOCCOLA

SAN LORENZO

VIA GOMBITO

VM. LUPO

VIA SANT' ALESSANDRO

Biblioteca Civica

Luogo Pio

Piazza
Vecchia

Piazza
Duomo

Duomo

Battistero

Santa Maria
Maggiore

Cappella Colleoni

CITTÀ
ALTA

VIA DELLA BOCCOLA

VIA VAGINE

VIA B. COLLEONI

Palazzo
della
Ragione

VIA ARENA

Piazza
Mascheroni

Museo
Donizettiano

VIA TRE ARMI

Cittadella

VIALE DELLE MURA

VIA MILANO

Giardino
Botanico

Casa Natale
di Donizetti

VIA BORGO CANALE

Funicular

VIA DELLO STATUTO

To S.Vigilio &
Castello

N

300 metres
250 yards

Bergamo

with a vicious weasel under her arm and a sickly moon overhead, and another strange painting of uncertain origin, believed to be of Cesare Borgia, with an uncannily desolate background. Other portraits (especially the *Young Girl*, one of the most beautiful portraits of a child ever painted) are by Bergamo's Giovan Battista Moroni (1520–78), the master to whom Titian sent the *Rectors of Venice*, with the advice that only Moroni could 'make them natural'. There are beautiful *Madonnas* by the Venetians, three superlative ones by Giovanni Bellini, others by Mantegna (who couldn't do children), Fra Angelico, Landi and Crivelli (with his cucumber signature). The anti-plague saint Sebastian is portrayed by three contemporaries from remark-ably different aspects—naked and pierced with arrows before a silent city, by Giovanni Bellini; well-dressed and rather sweetly contemplating an arrow, by Raphael; and sitting at a table, clad in a fur-trimmed coat, by Dürer, who also painted the eerie black and silver *Calvary*. Other paintings are by Bergognone, Cariani, Fra Galgario, Palma Vecchio and Prevetali (all from Bergamo), the Venetians Carpaccio, Vivarini, Titian, Veronese, Tintoretto, Tiepolo and Guardi; also Cosmè Tura, Foppa, Luini, Savoldo, Moretto, Clouet, Van Dyck and Bruegel.

Opposite, in Via S. Tommaso 53, the **Galleria d'Arte Moderna e Contemporanea** was opened in 1991 for temporary exhibitions, mostly of 20th-century art (*open Mon, Wed–Fri 9.30–12.30 and 3–7, Thurs till 10.30, Sat and Sun 10–7*). Follow Via della Noca up to Piazzale Sant'Agostino, where the 16th-century **Porta Sant'Agostino**, bearing the Lion of St Mark, is the main gate to the Città Alta. From just inside the gate, the Viale delle Mura circles the top of the mighty **Venetian walls**, built between 1561 and 1591; the impressive under-ground passage in one of the ramparts, the **Cannoniera di San Michele**, has recently been restored (*open June–Sept for limited periods; contact the tourist office*).

The Città Alta: Piazza Vecchia

The view of the Città Alta, its domes and towers rising boldly on the hill against a background of mountains, is one of the most arresting urban views in Italy. City bus no.1 from the station stops at the **funicular**, built in 1888 to rise to the heart of the Città Alta, only a short walk from the beautiful **Piazza Vecchia**. Architects as diverse as Frank Lloyd Wright and Le Corbusier have heaped praise on this square, encased in a magnificent ensemble of medieval and Renaissance buildings, overlooking a low, dignified fountain with marble lions donated by the Contarini of Venice in 1780. At the lower end of the piazza, the white **Biblioteca Civica** was begun in 1594 on a design by Palladio's student Vincenzo Scamozzi, modelled after Sansovino's famous library in Venice; one treasure inside is Donizetti's autograph score of *Lucia di Lammermoor*. An ancient covered stair leads up to the 12th-century **Torre Civica**, with a 15th-century clock and curfew bell that still vainly orders the Bergamasques to bed at 10pm; there is a lift to take visitors up for the fine views over Bergamo (*open April–Sept daily 9–12 and 2–8, Fri and Sat till 11pm; Oct and Mar daily 10–12 and 2–6; Nov–Feb weekends only 10–12 and 2–4; adm*). Closing the square, the 12th-century **Palazzo della Ragione** has some interesting capitals and a relief of the Lion of St Mark, recently added to commemorate Bergamo's golden days under Venice.

In the 15th century, the ground-floor walls of the Palazzo della Ragione were removed to allow glimpses through the dark, tunnel arches that remain into a second square, **Piazza Duomo**, and what appears to be a jewel box. The jewel box reveals itself as the sumptuous façade of the 1476 **Colleoni Chapel** (*open daily 9–12 and 2–6.30; Nov–Mar till 5.30; closed*

Mon) designed by Giovanni Antonio Amadeo, moonlighting while he was working on the Certosa at Pavia. Colleoni, whose coat of arms features a pair of testicles or *coglioni* (a play on his name—but there's Bergamasque humour for you), was born just around the corner. At the height of his fame as a *condottiere*, he was given complete control of Venice's armies—a unique act of trust from a republic that never trusted any individual—and when he died he received the equally unique honour of an equestrian statue in Venice, which as a rule never erected personal monuments (it helped that Colleoni left the Republic a fortune in exchange). Somehow there were enough ducats left over to demolish the sacristy of Santa Maria Maggiore and build a dashing tomb in its place, a project the old soldier directed from his retirement castle at Malpaga (*see* below).

The Colleoni Chapel is even more ornate and out of temper with the times than Amadeo's Certosa, a crazy quilt of medieval motifs and flourishes that spits in the face of the usual Renaissance aims of proportion and serenity. Amadeo also sculpted the tombs within, a double-decker model for Colleoni and his wife (his remains, in a silk gown and red hat, were found intact in 1969, but Mrs Colleoni was buried elsewhere). On top, a golden equestrian statue by Sixtus of Nuremburg makes the *condottiere* look like a wimp compared to Verrocchio's haughty Klaus Kinski version in Venice—neither, however, was carved from life. Another wall has the calmer tomb of Colleoni's young daughter Medea, brought here in the 19th century from another church. The fine paintings under the dome were done by G.B. Tiepolo in 1733, and on the altar there's a *Holy Family* by Goethe's constant companion in Rome, the Swiss painter Angelica Kauffmann.

Flanking the chapel are two works by Giovanni, a master from Campione: the octagonal **Baptistry** of 1340 (*open by appointment only,* © *035 210 223*) in white and red marble from Verona, and the colourful porch (1353) of the **Basilica of Santa Maria Maggiore**, with lions and an equestrian statue of St Alexander. Giovanni da Campione also built the basilica's second door, to the left, tucked up the steps in the corner of the transept and decorated with reliefs of the *Nativity of Mary* (1367). The basilica itself dates from 1137 and is one of the finest Romanesque churches in Lombardy, although much has been hidden by other buildings; the fine apse and drum are just about visible from the east end, blocked by the new sacristy; up the steps around back, past the campanile, is another excellent door by Giovanni and the tiny 11th-century church of Santa Croce.

Once past the door, however, the palatial late 16th-century interior hits you like a gust of old lilac perfume. Sumptuous tapestries hang from the walls: nine are scenes from the *Life of the Virgin* by Alessandro Allori, woven in Florence and Flanders in the 1580s, while the others are more secular—one shows a deer hunt, another the Triumph of Emperor Vespasian. Donizetti's tomb with mourning putti and his spirit hovering over the keyboard is tucked in the back of the church, and there's a florid confessional by Fantoni, but the best art is up in the chancel and choir, where Lorenzo Lotto designed a series of 33 Old Testament scenes, beautifully executed in intarsia in 1552 by Capodiferro ('Ironhead') di Lovere. Only the four along the chancel rail, *Crossing the Red Sea, David and Goliath, Judith beheading Holofernes* and *Noah's Ark*) are generally visible, and then only on Sunday or by special arrangement with the sacristan; at other times their locked wooden covers are in themselves food for thought, their subjects unfathomable allegories and abstractions, a veritable fad at the time, as in Isabella d'Este's mysterious suite in Mantua.

Piazza Vecchia is also the address of the **Duomo**, which has stood on this site since the 6th century. The present cathedral, designed by Florentine humanist Filarete in 1459, was remodelled by Carlo Fontana two hundred years later and given a pseudo-but-pleasing late baroque façade in 1886. Inside there's a statue of the 'Good Pope' John XXIII, born in nearby Sotto del Monte, the *Martyrdom of St John* by Tiepolo by the main altar, a boxwood bishop's throne by Fantoni, *SS. Fermo, Rustico and Procolo* by Sebastiano Ricci (all from the 1700s) and Cariani's early 16th-century *Madonna of the Turtle Doves*.

Around the Città Alta

The Visconti, who ruled Bergamo until the Venetians snatched it in 1428, built the 14th-century **Rocca** at the highest point in the Città Alta; now ruined, it has been closed for years. Below it, Via Porta Dipinta curves around to the Porta S. Agostino (*see* above), passing two churches on the way: neoclassical **Sant'Andrea**, housing a superb altarpiece of the Madonna and saints by Moretto; and Romanesque **San Michele al Pozzo Bianco**, rebuilt in the 1400s, its solemn interior illuminated with frescoes from the 1200s and 1500s and paintings by Lotto. By the car park, the **Convento di Sant'Agostino** with its elegant Gothic façade was Bergamo's cultural centre in the 13th century; inside are more frescoes, from the 14th and 15th century, including some by Vicenzo Foppa.

Bartolomeo Colleoni lived at Via B. Colleoni 9/11, where he founded the **Luogo Pio** charity; among the frescoes there's a portrait of the *condottiere* (*to visit © 035 217185*). Via Colleoni continues to the west end of the Città Alta, closed off by Piazza Mascheroni and the 14th-century **Cittadella**, former residence of the Venetian captains, and now of the **Museo di Scienze Naturale** (*open Tues–Sun 9–12.30 and 2.30–7.30; until 5.30 in winter*) with stuffed animals and birds, and the **Museo Civico Archeologico** (*open Tues–Sun 9–12.30 and 2.30–6*), with finds from Bronze Age to the Lombards. The **Giardino Botanico** nearby, at the top of the Scaletta Colle Aperta, is planted with 600 species of mostly medicinal plants (*open Mar–Oct 9–12 and 2–5*). Near the Cittadella, Bergamo's second funicular rises to **San Vigilio** where there's another fortress, the **Castello**, with superb views, especially over the green Parco dei Colli, dotted with old farmhouses and villas.

Near the lower funicular station, picturesque Via Borgo Canale is the address of the **Casa Natale di Donizetti** (*open Sat and Sun 11–6.30, or ring © 035 320 472*), where the composer was born. From the Cittadella, quiet medieval Via Arena leads around to the back of the cathedral, passing by way of the elegant 17th-century Palazzo Scotti, now the **Museo Donizettiano** (*open Tues–Sat 9.30–12.30 and 2.30–5, Sun 10–12 and 2–4*).

A Bitter End for a Sweet Composer

Gaetano Donizetti (1787–1848), son of the doorkeeper of Bergamo's pawnshop, composed 65 of the most lyrical operas of all time—grand old chestnuts of the bel canto repertoire such as Lucia di Lammermoor, L'Elisir d'Amore and La Favorita as well as a score of one-act pieces, down to the much-scoffed-at (by English singers anyway) Emilia di Liverpool. By 1843 he was the toast of Europe, when all of a sudden the syphilis he had contracted in his bachelor days manifested itself during the Paris rehearsals of his Dom Sébastien, when the composer, usually as affable and charming as his own music, burst forth in fits of uncontrollable anger. His creeping madness alternated with bouts of helpless despair. When the Paris sanatorium could do no more for him, he was packed off to Bergamo to die, where his friends tried to cheer his last days in the Palazzo Scotti with arias from his most famous operas; Donizetti, reduced to a vegetable state, could no longer respond. The palazzo, now the town conservatory, has a few wistful sticks of furniture, his little piano, and portraits and daguerreotypes that recall happier days.

Bergamo ✉ *24100*   **Where to Stay**

A few minutes from the funicular, ★★★★**Excelsior San Marco**, Piazzale della Repubblica 6, ✆ 035 366 111, ⊜ 035 223 201 (*very expensive*) is the city's most comfortable hotel, with air-conditioned, modern rooms, and an excellent restaurant. ★★★★**Capello d'Oro e del Moro**, Viale Giovanni XXIII 12, ✆ 035 232 503, ⊜ 035 242 946 (*expensive*) offers well-equipped modern rooms with satellite TV, lovely bathrooms, and a very good restaurant. The ★★★**San Vigilio**, Via S. Vigilio 15, ✆ 035 253 179, up beyond the Città Alta—reached by the S. Vigilio cable car— was built earlier this century by a local bank for its employees' holidays. It has just 7 rooms—5 with magnificent views—and a nice olde-worlde atmosphere. The most atmospheric hotel in the Città Alta, ★★**Agnello d'Oro**, Via Gombito 22, ✆ 035 249 883, ⊜ 035 235 612 (*moderate*) was built in 1600, although rooms are modern, all with bath and TV; the restaurant, a clutter of copper pots and masks, is excellent. Nearby, ★★**Sole**, Via Rivola 2, ✆ 035 218 238, ⊜ 035 240 011 (*moderate*), on the corner of the Piazza Vecchia, is a shade noisier but homey, with baths in all the rooms; the restaurant specializes in fish.

★**Caironi**, Via Toretta 6, ✆ 035 243 083 (*cheap*) is a good cheaper option in Bergamo Bassa, but involves a 20min walk from the station or a ride on bus nos.5, 7 or 8. ★**Quarenghi**, Via Quarenghi 33, ✆ 035 320 331, ⊜ 035 319 914 (*cheap*) is basic, with bathrooms down the hall, but it has parking—rare in Bergamo Bassa. ★**San Giorgio**, near the station at Via S. Giorgio 10, ✆ 035 212 043, ⊜ 035 310 072 has quiet rooms in spite of its location, with private bath, TVs and other comforts. Bergamo's new **youth hostel**, Via G. Ferraris 1, ✆/⊜ 035 361 724, is 2km from the station (take bus no.14); L25,000 a head with breakfast.

Eating Out

Bergamo prides itself on its cooking: look for *casoncelli* (ravioli filled with tangy sausage-meat, in a sauce of melted butter, bacon and sage), *polenta taragna* (with butter and cheese), risotto with wild mushrooms. Many restaurants, surprisingly, feature seafood—Bergamo is a major inland fish market. In August, however, you might have to resort to a picnic. The classic for fish, **Da Vittorio**, Viale Papa Giovanni XXIII 21, ✆/⊜ 035 218 060 (*expensive*) specializes in seafood prepared in a number of exquisite ways, as well as a wide variety of meat dishes, polenta, risotto and pasta. *Closed Wed, and three weeks in Aug*. The celebrated **Taverna del Colleoni** on the Piazza Vecchia,

☎ 035 232 596, ✆ 035 231 991 (*expensive*) features exquisite classical Italian cuisine, including superb, delicate dishes such as ravioli filled with leek and potato in a toasted pine nut pesto. *Closed Mon and one week in Aug*.

Da Ornella, Via Gombito 3, ☎ 035 232 736, is the place to come for hearty rib-sticking winter dishes such as *polenta taragna* with rabbit, roast veal and *casoncelli*. Near Donizetti's birthplace **La Colombina**, Borgo Canale 12, ☎ 035 261402 (*cheap*) is almost the perfect restaurant, with stunning views from its dappled terrace, and a pretty Liberty-style dining room. Try the salad of local *taleggio* cheese with slivers of pear, a plate of cured meats, and the best *casoncelli* in town. Leave room for a slice of deep, dark caramelized apple cake. *Closed Mon and Aug*. Another nice spot is the **Bar Donizetti**, Via Gombito 17a, ☎ 035 242 661, which has tables inside the arcaded market, a wine bar serving gourmet snacks—*crostini* with gorgonzola, honey and truffle—as well as hot dishes. *Closed Fri, and mid-Oct–mid-Nov*. For ice cream, head for **Marianna**, by the Porta S. Alessandra, where you can sit on the shady terrace gorging on fig, apricot, rose petal or peach flavours. *Closed Mon in winter*.

Around Bergamo

The year after Bartolomeo Colleoni was appointed Captain General of Venice, he purchased the ruined **Castello di Malpaga** in **Cavernago**, 8km southeast of Bergamo, which he had restored for his old age; his heirs added a series of frescoes by Romanino or someone like him, commemorating a visit by Christian I of Denmark in 1474, portraying Colleoni hosting the *de rigueur* splendid banquets, jousts, hunts and pageants of Renaissance hospitality (☎ *030 840 003; should reopen in 1999 after restoration*).

At **Trescore Balneario**, 14km east of Bergamo on the road to Lovere, the chapel of the **Villa Suardi** (*call ☎ 035 943 376 to arrange a visit*) has an utterly charming fresco cycle by Lorenzo Lotto, painted in 1524 during his 15-year stint in Bergamo, when he was driven from his home in Venice by the merciless 'Triumvirate' of Titian, Sansovino and the poison-pen Aretino. The subject of the frescoes is the story of St Barbara, patroness of artillerymen, architects and gravediggers. Her apocryphal life reads like a fairy-tale—her pagan father locked her in a tower, and after various adventures had her martyred for being a Christian, although he paid for his wickedness by being struck down by a bolt of lightning—and Lotto gave it just the treatment it deserved.

Southwest of Bergamo, **Caravaggio** was the birthplace of Michelangelo Merisi da Caravaggio, who left not a smear of oil paint behind, not even in the popular pilgrimage shrine of the **Santuario della Madonna del Fonte**, designed in a cool Renaissance style by Pellegrino Tibaldi (1575) on the site of a 1432 apparition of the Virgin. **Treviglio**, a large, rather dull town nearby, has an exquisite 15th-century polyptych in the Gothic church of San Martino. In **Capriate San Gervasio**, off the *autostrada* towards Milan, the **Parco Minitalia** (*open Mar–Oct daily 9–6; check winter opening hours with tourist office; adm*) cuts Italy down to size—1310ft from tip to toe, with mountains, seas, cities and monuments all arranged in their proper place. Even a miniature train is on hand to take visitors up and down the boot. Due east of Bergamo, **Sotto del Monte** was the birthplace of the beloved Pope John XXIII, and is an increasingly popular pilgrimage destination; there's a **Museo Papa Giovanni** near his birthplace, filled with memorabilia (*open Tues–Sun 8.30–11.30 and 2.30–6.30*).

Towards the Orobie Alps: Bergamasque Valleys

North of Bergamo the two Bergamasque valleys plunge into the stony heart of the Orobie Alps, the mighty wall of mountains that isolates the Valtellina further north. The western one, the Val Brembana, was the main route for Venetian caravans transporting minerals from the Valtellina; the eastern Valle Seriana is Bergamo's favourite summer retreat.

Tourist Information

San Pellegrino Terme: Viale Papa Giovanni XXIII 106, ✆ 0345 21020. **Clusone**: Piazza dell'Orologio, ✆ 0346 21113. **Castione della Presolana**: Piazza Roma, ✆ 0346 60039, or ✆ 0346 31146.

The Val Brembana: Sparkling Water and the Birthplace of Harlequin

A clutch of old villages guards the entrance to the valley, where any merchant passing up the 'Via Mercatorum' had to pay a toll in Clanezzo, 13km from Bergamo, before continuing up to **Almenno San Bartolomeo**. Here, isolated just off the main road, the tiny, late 11th-century church of **San Tomè** (*open Sun and hols only 2–4; summer till 6*) is a jewel of Lombard Romanesque, built by the Comaschi masters. Composed of three cylinders, stacked one atop the other, the interior has sturdy pillars and arches circled by a matriorum (the space set apart for women), and lovely capitals. **Zogno**, further up the valley, is the site of the **Museo della Valle Brembana** (*open Tues–Sun 9–12 and 2–5; adm*), with artefacts from the valley's history. Next up the valley, **San Pellegrino Terme** is synonymous with delicious mineral water and still makes some claim as Lombardy's most fashionable spa, especially recommended for recuperating heart-attack patients. Hoping to attract the crowned heads of Europe, San Pellegrino splashed out in 1907 for a fabulously ornate Grand Hotel, casino and Palazzo del Fonte bathhouse in the most florid *stilo Liberty*.

According to legend, the humorously frescoed **Casa dell'Arlecchino** at Oneta in **San Giovanni Bianco** was the birthplace of Harlequin (*see* p.60). The role was said to have been invented by a *commedia dell'arte* actor named Ganassa who lived there, though more likely it is just a reminder of the many men and women who, like Harlequin, chose to forsake their poor hills to become servants in Venice or Bergamo. There are any number of lovely, forgotten hamlets like Oneta in these mountains; many of them lie in a mini-region called the Val Taleggio, on the other side of the spectacular gorge of the **Torrente Enna**. The road from San Giovanni Bianco was completed only recently.

The next town north, medieval **Cornello dei Tasso**, may be down to 30 inhabitants, but it preserves as if in aspic its appearance as a relay station on the merchants' road, with an arcaded lane to protect the mule caravans. In the 13th century much of the business of expediting merchandise here was in the hands of the Tasso family, whose destiny, however, was far bigger than Cornello. One branch went on to run the post between Venice and Rome; another moved to Germany in the 1500s to organize for Emperors Maximilian I and Charles V the first European postal service. Their network of postal relay stations was still in use into the 19th century. Another branch of the family operating out of Sorrento produced the loony, melancholy Renaissance poet Torquato Tasso. As well as the muleteers' arcades, Cornello preserves the ruins of the Tasso ancestral home and frescoes in the 15th-century church.

Beyond **Piazza Brembana** the road branches out into several mountain valleys. The most important and developed resort is **Foppolo**; besides winter sports it offers an easy ascent up the **Corno Stella**, with marvellous views to the north and east. Other ski resorts include **Piazzatorre** and **San Simone** near Branzi; **Carona** is a good base for summer excursions into the mountains and alpine lakes.

East of Piazza Brembana, a lovely road rises to **Roncobello**; from here your car can continue as far as the Baite di Mezzeno, the base for a bracing 3-hour walk up to the **Laghi Gemelli**. From here experienced hikers can pick up the beautiful **Sentiero delle Orobie**, a 6-day trail that begins at Valcanale to the east in the Valle Seriana and ends in the Passo della Presolana. Another important village on the Via Mercantum, **Averara**, was the last station before the Passo San Marco into the Valtellina; its covered arcade for the caravans survives, as do buildings decorated with exterior frescoes from the 1500s.

Valle Seriana

Bergamo's eastern **Valle Seriana**, industrial in its lower half and ruggedly alpine in the north, is known for the whirling baroque wood sculptures and carvings by the Fantoni and Caniana families. You can see one of their finest works, a fabulously ornate pulpit, every inch covered with reliefs and soaring cherubs, in the **Basilica di San Martino** 8km from Bergamo in **Alzano Lombardo**; the basilica also has fine 17th-century inlaid and intarsia work, cupboards and other precious woodwork in its three sacristies.

Gandino is another town to aim for, just off the main Valle Seriana road at the bottom of its own valley. In the Middle Ages Gandino was the chief producer of a heavy, inexpensive cloth of wool and goat hair called bergamot, and the picturesque centre of town has changed little since. The 17th-century **Basilica di Santa Maria Assunta**, with its garlic-domed campanile, has confessionals and other works by the Fantoni and Caniana, and an octagonal wooden '*tempietto*' of 1500 inside the modern baptistry. The rarely opened basilica museum houses portraits and relics of the old textile industry. Another church, the 15th-century **Santuario della Trinità**, contains a dramatic fresco of the *Last Judgement*.

Clusone, in the middle of the valley, is the prettiest town and capital of the Valle Seriana. In central Piazza dell' Orologio, the 11th-century **Palazzo Comunale** is covered with secular frescoes—the most joyfully decorated building in Lombardy—and bears a beautiful astronomical clock called the **Orologio Planetario Fanzago** (1583); come on a Monday when the market in the piazza overflows with cheeses and sausages. Near the clock, the **Oratorio del Disciplini** is adorned with an eerie 1485 fresco of the *Danse Macabre* and the *Triumph of Death*, where one skeleton mows down the nobility and clergy with arrows, while another blasts them with a blunderbuss. There are more frescoes inside from the same period, especially a superb *Crucifixion*; the *Deposition* is another work by the Fantoni, who also contributed works in the late 17th-century **Santa Maria Assunta**. But it's the exterior frescoes and porticoes that lend Clusone so much of its charm; in the 1980s others were reclaimed from under the grimy stucco, including one glorious, grinning Venetian lion. Just east, **Rovetta**, the cradle of the Fantoni, remembers them in the **Casa Museo Fantoni**, Via A. Fantoni 1 (*closed for restoration*), with special focus on the swirling, curling extroverted rococo works of Antonio.

Further up, **Castione della Presolana** is the biggest resort in the Valle Seriana, surrounded by striking dolomitic mountain scenery: the population in August goes from 3000 to 30,000. The pulpit in the parish church was sculpted by the Fantoni workshop. One of the biggest attractions is the lovely **Passo della Presolana** (1125m/3691ft) near sheer dolomite walls and Monte Pora, a ski resort, with tremendous views over Lake Iseo.

Where to Stay and Eating Out

San Pellegrino Terme ✉ 24016

The Grand Hotel has been closed for years, but the ★★★★**Terme**, right by the baths, ✆ 0345 21125, ✆ 0345 23497 (*just barely expensive*) with its garden and pool preserves some of the tone of bygone days. *Open late May–mid-Oct*. The central ★★★**Villa Emilia**, Via Tasso 15, ✆ 0345 21101, ✆ 0345 21384 (*moderate*), is comfortable and has a small garden.

Castione della Presolana ✉ 24020

★★★★**Milano,** at Bratto, ✆ 0346 31211, ✆ 0346 36236 (*expensive in season, otherwise moderate*) is a large complex in a park designed for families, complete with two restaurants (the Caminone is especially good) and an *enoteca. Closed Oct and Nov.* The older ★★★**Prealpi**, also at Bratto, ✆/✆ 0346 311 380 *(cheap)* has rooms with and without bath, and disabled access; the restaurant serves regional specialities. *Closed mid-Sept to mid-Oct.*

Lake Iseo, Franciacorta and the Valle Camonica

Lake Iseo (the Roman *Lacus Sebinus*) is only the fifth in size but one of the first in charm, well endowed with what it takes to get under your skin; even back in the 1750s it was the preferred resort of Italophile Lady Montagu, who disdained the English that 'herd together' by the larger lakes. The southeast shore borders on the lovely wine-growing region of Franciacorta; the lake's main source, the river Oglio, runs through the lovely Valle Camonica, the rocky palette for some of the world's most intriguing prehistoric art.

Getting Around

Buses run frequently from Bergamo to the lake towns of Tavèrnola and Lovere. For a special treat, on summer Sundays and holidays, FS **trains** run from Bergamo to Palazzolo sul Oglio to link up to the little steam train Ferrovia del Basso Sebino to Saronico, with direction connections on to the lake steamers; ✆ 035 910 900 for information. Iseo town is served by frequent buses from Brescia, and a regional railway, the FNME, runs along the entire east shore of Lake Iseo from Brescia or the FS rail junction at Rovato, between Bergamo and Brescia. From Pisogne at the north end of the lake several FNME trains a day continue up the Valle Camonica as far as Edolo. **Steamers** run by **Navigazione Lago d'Iseo**, Via Nazionale 16, Bergamo, ✆ 035 971 483, ply the lake between Lovere and Sàrnico, calling at 15 ports and Monte Isola. Timetables are posted by the quays.

Iseo: Lungolago Marconi 2, ✆ 030 980 209, 🖷 030 981 361.

Up Lake Iseo's West Shore: Sárnico to Lovere

The west shore of Iseo is the quieter one, much of it being too steep for building. The road from Bergamo meets the lake at **Sárnico**, a pleasant town with a 15th-century church of **San Paolo** at the top and a sprinkling of Liberty-style villas, most notably the two **Villas Faccanoni**, built by Milanese architect Giuseppe Sommaruga on the west end of town, along the Predore road. **Predore** itself was a fierce bone of contention between Guelphs and Ghibellines in the Middle Ages, and has a small historical museum recalling the feud in its Romanesque church. North of Predore, cliffs force the road through a tunnel and it turns sharply north for **Tavèrnola Bergamasca**, its Monte Saresano scarred by lime quarries and cement works. There are some good 15th-century frescoes in the church, and a fine panorama over the lake from **Santuario di Dosso**, a kilometre up from the village. Until 1910 the road stopped at Tavèrnola, and even today the rugged scenery around **Riva di Solto** is best seen from the little lake steamers; the view of its coves, rugged rocks, ravines and formidable Adamello mountains in the distance is said to have caught the fancy of Leonardo da Vinci, who used it as the background for his *Mona Lisa*: the black marble columns of St Mark's in Venice were quarried here.

Just north of Riva di Solto a scenic road zigzags up to the Val Cavallina and Lake Iseo's baby sister, the long, narrow **Lago di Endine**, which because of its currents freezes in bizarre shapes and patterns each winter. There are a pair of medieval villages on its shores: **Endine Gaiano** to the north and **Monasterolo del Castello** to the south, and an exceptionally well-preserved 13th-century **Castello di Suardi** up in Bianzano.

From Endine Gaiano the main road rejoins Lake Iseo at **Lovere**. The largest town of the west shore, it has a medieval core dating from its days as a Venetian textile centre. In 1630 it shifted from cloth to steel, and to this day Lovere mixes grit with art. There are 16th-century frescoes in the baroqued interior of **Santa Maria in Valvendra** (*due to re-open in 1999 after restoration*), a *Martyrdom of St George* by Palma il Giovane on the altar of **San Giorgio**, a church partly built into a medieval tower; and best of all, twenty rooms of fine paintings in the **Galleria dell'Accademia Tadini** in a neoclassical palace (*open late April–Oct Mon–Sat 3–6, Sun 10–12 and 3–6*), including works by Tiepolo, Lorenzo Veneziano, Strozzi, Piazza, Parmigianino, Bordone, and a lovely *Madonna* by Jacopo Bellini.

Down the East Shore: Pisogne to Clusane

From Lovere, the road circles the north lake and reaches the sprawling village of **Pisogne**; you can see traces of walls and gates around its medieval core, arcaded Piazza del Mercato. The main reason to stop, however, is north of the centre: the 15th-century church of **Santa Maria della Neve**, covered between 1532 and 1543 with frescoes of the *Passion*, and *Prophets* and *Sibyls* by Romanino (*open Tues–Sun 10–12 and 3–6; if the church is closed you can get the key from the bar next door*). South, beyond the tunnels, **Marone** overlooks the cute private Isolina di Loreto and stands at the crossroads of the little **Val Valeriana**, a fascinating detour through uncanny scenery: here glaciers deposited their debris aeons ago atop the dolomitic rock, to be eroded into striking spiky 'earth pyramids', many balancing boulders on top like something out of

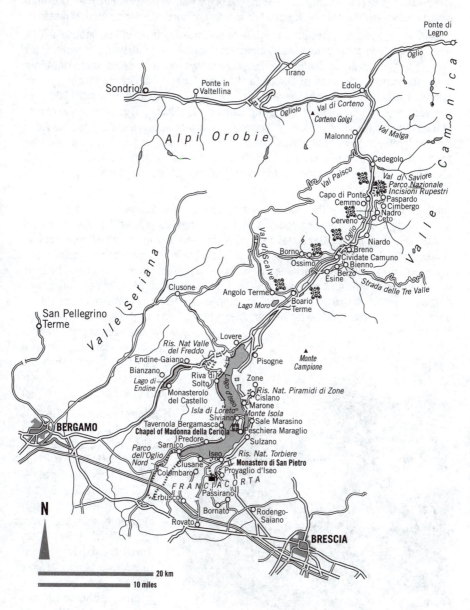

Ponte di Legno

Oglio

Tirano

Sondrio

Ponte in Valtellina

Edolo

Ogliolo

Val di Corteno

▲ Corteno Golgi

Malonno

Val Malga

Alpi Orobie

Cedegolo

Val Paisco

Val di Saviore

Parco Nazionale *Incisioni Rupestri*

Capo di Ponte
Cemmo

Paspardo

Cimbergo

Nadro

Cerveno

Ceto

Val di Scalve

Niardo

Breno

Borno

Cividate Camuno

Ossimo

Bienno

Berzo

Clusone

Esine

Strada delle Tre Valle

Angolo Terme

Boario Terme

Lago Moro

San Pellegrino Terme

Valle Seriana

Lovere

Ris. Nat Valle del Freddo

▲ Monte Campione

Pisogne

Endine-Gaiano

Bianzano

Lago di Endine

Riva di Solto

Zone

Monasterolo del Castello

Ris. Nat. Piramidi di Zone

Cislano

Marone

Isla di Loreto

Tavernola Bergamasca

Siviano

Monte Isola

Sale Marasino

BERGAMO

Chapel of Madonna della Ceriola

Peschiera Maraglio

Predore

Sulzano

Parco dell'Oglio Nord

Sarnico

Iseo

Ris. Nat. Torbiere

Clusane

Monastero di San Pietro

Colombaro

Provaglio d'Iseo

F R A N C I A C O R T A

Erbusco

Passirano

Bornato

Rodengo-Saiano

Rovato

BRESCIA

N

20 km

10 miles

= Rock engravings (*incisioni rupestri*)

a *Road Runner* cartoon. There's a famous view of the pyramids—locally known as 'the fairies'— at **Cislano** (where the church has an exterior fresco of St George) on the way to **Zone** (678m/2224ft), an old-fashioned village at the end of the road, where the church **San Giovanni Battista** houses an 18th-century life-sized *Entombment of Christ* sculpted by Antonio Fantoni.

Back on the lake, olive groves surround **Sale Marasino**, a little resort built around a 16th-century town, one of the prettier and warmer spots on the lake; **Sulzano**, just south, is the closest point and main port for the Arcadian, car-less (but well motorbiked) island of **Monte Isola**, the largest lake island in Europe, a fair-sized copy of Gibraltar soaking in its own bathtub. It was once a hunting reserve of the local nobles and Visconti; now some 200 souls live year round in its genteelly decaying hamlets. The locals, especially in **Peschiera Maraglio** where the steamer docks, still catch fish, but their talent for making nets has led to the more profitable weaving of professional tennis and basketball nets. Stroll through the olive groves to Sensole to the west, and up to **Siviano**, the main village, and perhaps through ancient chestnut groves as far as the chapel of the **Madonna della Ceriola**—over 300m/1000ft above the lake.

South of Sulzano, **Iseo** is the lake's endearing, low-key and thoroughly fetching 'capital' where flowers spill out of every window and the narrow alleys have kept their medieval names. In central **Piazza Garibaldi** a statue of the hero, looking tired and philosophical, contemplates the comings and goings and the Friday market from the top of a great mossy lump; here the small **Santa Maria del Mercato** has some late medieval frescoes. The 11th-century **Pieve di Sant'Andrea** has an air of benign neglect, its façade unfinished, with a tomb of the old town boss Giacomo Oldofredi stuck on as an afterthought. A sign on the church door asks that visitors please enter without their bicycles. The long, curved lake promenade, shaded with ancient plane trees, is the perfect place to laze on a summer's day and watch the sailboats and little steamers dart to and fro.

Lago Iseo

Clusane, south of Iseo, is crowned by an abandoned Castello di Carmagnola—it briefly belonged to the famous Venetian captain— and has a fishing fleet of white-, blue- and pink-rimmed boats called *naêcc* in the local dialect. They spend the day bagging the ingredients of *tinca al forno* (baked lake tench with polenta), a dish based on a recipe invented in 1800, and served in 20 restaurants, seating 4000—in a village with a population of 1500!

Sarnico ✉ 24067

The best seafood in town is prepared in a variety of ways at **Al Desco del Vicolo Scaletta**, Piazza XX Settembre, ✆ 035 910 740 (*moderate*): the fresh tagliatelle with shrimp and scampi is a treat. *Closed Mon.* For a pizza or a glass of wine with *bruschetta* or a sandwich, try the garden of the **Taverna L'Angolo Antigo Lantieri**, Via Lantieri 5, ✆ 035 913 331.

Lovere ✉ 24065

Right on Lovere's main Piazza 13 Martire, ★★★**S. Antonio**, ✆/📠 035 961 523, has modern, soundproofed rooms and a scenic 5th-floor restaurant and terrace overlooking the lake.

Sale Marasino ✉ 25057

By the lake, the ★★★★**Villa Kinzica**, ✆ 030 982 0975, 📠 030 982 0990 (*expensive*) opened in July 1996 with every comfort, although there's a busy road just in front. An excellent bargain, ★★★**Rotelli**, ✆ 030 986 115, 📠 030 986 241 (*moderate*) has magnificent views, a pool, tennis, sauna and gym and well-sized, modern rooms.

Iseo ✉ 25049

The top choice, ★★★★**I Due Roccoli**, in the hills above the town in Fraz. Invino, ✆ 030 982 2977, 📠 030 982 2980 (*expensive*) occupies part of an old hunting lodge, amid its own large gardens. The suites, rooms and bathrooms are beautifully designed and have either garden views or breathtaking views of the lake. There's a sun terrace, pool and an intimate dining room with an open log fire, where the service is impeccable and much of the superb food is freshly harvested from the hotel's own farm. Favourite dishes include an *antipasto* of salad and truffles, a delicious green pasta with mushrooms known as *pappardelle verdi con funghi porcini* and, for dessert, a *mousse di cioccolato bianco* that's one of the best in the country. *Closed Oct–Mar; restaurant open to non-residents Thurs–Mon only.* Other choices include ★★★**Ambra**, Piazza G. Rosa, ✆ 030 980 130, 📠 030 982 1361 (*moderate*) on the lake and near the town centre. All its rooms have modern fittings, and most have bathrooms and balconies, though there's no restaurant. ★★★**Moselli**, in Pilzone, just outside Iseo, ✆ 030 980 001, 📠 030 980 231 (*cheap*) is near the beach, in a garden. ★★**Milano**, Lungolago Marconi 4, ✆ 030 980 449, 📠 030 982 1903 (*cheap*) offers smaller old-fashioned rooms, many with lake views, and a small restaurant and bar. Dine at **Il Volto**, Via Mirolte 33, ✆ 030 981 462 (*moderate*) an old-fashioned inn, naturally featuring lake fish (excellent with tagliolini) but also tasty land dishes such as roast pigeon in a mustardy cream sauce. *Closed Wed and Thurs lunch, and 2 weeks in July.*

Monte Isola ✉ 25050

There are two wonderful inexpensive places in Siviano: at ★★**Bellavista**, ✆ 030 988 6106, rooms are comfortable, small and simple with outstanding views, and there's a nice little restaurant too; the quiet, romantic ★★**Canogola**, ✆ 030 982 5310 (*cheap*) has only seven rooms in the trees by the lake, all with bath.

Clusane ✉ 24023

When it's time to tuck into a steaming plate of *tinca al forno* or a long list of other lake specialities (pike terrine, marinated bleak—*aole in capione*—grilled sardines, fish stew), washed down with a fine wine from the nearby Franciacorta, you won't go wrong at **Al Porto**, ✆ 030 989 014 (the oldest), *closed Wed eve*, or **Gallo**, ✆ 030 982 9200, *closed Tues*, or **Sole**, ✆ 030 989 013, *closed Mon*, or **Punta dell'Esta**, ✆ 030 989 060, which also has inexpensive rooms.

The Franciacorta

The triangle formed by Lake Iseo, Brescia and the A4 is a sweet and mellow corner of old Lombardy. Originally the *corte franca*, 'free court', it was wild and poverty-stricken in the Middle Ages, then colonized and reclaimed by monastic courts, an effort encouraged by tax-free concessions. Once the monks had done all the hard work, the lack of taxes endeared the Franciacorta to the patricians of Lombardy, who built castles and villas and planted the vineyards, producing an excellent champagne-method wine, Franciacorta Spumante DOC (Ca' del Bosco makes one of the best) as well as a fragrant white wine from pinot bianco and/or chardonnay, and a ruby herbaceous red with an unusually mixed pedigree: cabernet, barbera, nebbiolo and merlot.

The initial project in the Franciacorta was the reclamation of the swamps in **Provaglio** just in from Iseo town, when monks from Cluny founded **San Pietro in Lamosa** in 1083. Part of their project, an emerald bog called **Le Torbiere**, has remained defiantly wet, and after a century of peat extraction is now a protected area; in late spring it becomes an aquatic garden of pink and white water-lilies, navigable by row boats on hire. Cluny also founded the abbey of San Nicola at **Rodengo Saiano**, with three cloisters now occupied by Olivetan monks; there are frescoes by Romanino and Moretto in the church and a **Museo del Ferro** (*open daily 9–12 and 3–6; donations*) dedicated to iron.

The Franciacorta is filled with 16th–18th-century villas, castles and parks. There's a well preserved 14th-century castle with swallowtail battlements in **Passirano**; in nearby **Bornato** a Roman fortress was expanded in the 13th century by a faithful follower of Charles d'Anjou into the **Castello di Bornato** (*open Easter–Sept Sun 10–12 and 2.30–6; Oct Sun 10–12 and 2.30–5; adm*). Dante slept here, and over the years an Italian garden and vineyards were added; there are fine frescoed rooms from the 16th–18th centuries with Olympian gods and landscapes; the wine is good too. Bornato is surrounded by 18th-century villas, including **Villa Rossa** with its lovely garden, stair and belvedere. **Villa Lana da Terzo** in **Colombaro** has Italy's oldest cedar of Lebanon in its garden. **Erbusco** has the fine 17th-century Villa Lechi and a 13th-century church of Santa Maria, and another excellent Franciacorta vineyard that welcomes visitors (Longhi-De Carli, Via Verdi 4, ✆ 030 776 0280).

Where to Stay and Eating Out

Colombara ✉ 25040

New in 1996, the ★★★★**La Colombara**, Via Lana 7, ✆ 030 982 6461 (*very expensive*) occupies a lovely old villa by a wine estate; the trattoria, opened several years previously, serves excellent meals. *Closed Mon eve and Tues.*

Erbusco ✉ 25030

> ****L'Albereta**, ✆ 030 776 0550, 🖷 030 776 0573 (*very expensive*) is an old, entirely renovated villa containing 39 rooms and suites, all individual and all beautifully designed. There's every possible attention to detail, with wall paintings by Jacques Margerin, open log fires, jacuzzis in the bathrooms and a swimming pool, sauna, tennis and garage. The (*very expensive*) restaurant has a rather patchy reputation nowadays. *Closed Sun evening, Mon, and most of Jan.*

Rovato ✉ 25038

> In Rovato, on the edge of the Franciacorta, **Antica Cucina de Biagi**, Via Bonvincino 6, ✆ 030 772 1450 (*cheap*) serves meaty, hearty food including such dishes as pasta in duck sauce; *agnoli* filled with hare; stuffed pheasant, guinea fowl or pigeon. *Closed lunch and Sun eve.*

North of Lake Iseo: the Valle Camonica, or History on the Rocks

From Pisogne the road and railway continue northeast of Lake Iseo into the fertile Valle Camonica. Its name is derived from a Rhaetian tribe, the Camuni, whose ancestors used the valley's smooth, glacier-seared Permian sandstone as tablets to engrave their enigmatic solar discs and labyrinths, mysterious figures and geometric designs, animals, weapons and people. What is especially remarkable is the continual span of creativity: the oldest engravings have been dated to the 9th millennium BC and the last date from 16 BC, the year the Romans conquered the valley—a period enabling scholars to trace intriguing prehistoric stylistic evolutions, from the random scratched symbols of the Palaeolithic era to the finely drawn narrative figures of the Bronze and Iron Ages. Although one can only hazard guesses at the significance these etchings had for their makers, their magic must have been extraordinary: in the valley some 180,000 examples have been discovered so far. Some are beautiful, some ungainly and peculiar, some utterly mystifying; a few fuel crackpot theories. UNESCO has shortlisted them as part of the artistic patrimony of humanity.

Tourist Information

Boario Terme: Piazza Einaudi 2, ✆ 0364 531 609, 🖷 0364 532 280; **Capo di Ponte**, by the highway, ✆ 0364 42080; **Edolo**: Piazza Martiri della Libertà 2, ✆/🖷 0364 71065; **Ponte di Legno**: Corso Milano 41, ✆ 0364 91122.

Boario Terme to Breno

Liver playing you up? Consider a cure at **Boario Terme**, 12km north of Pisogne, where the medicinal springs are protected by a pretty Liberty-style cupola, set in a lavish garden. Boario bottles a popular mineral water, but the allure of the source is being soaked, sprayed, massaged in therapeutic mud, and hosing out every orifice with jets of the stuff. The first inhabitants, however, were into rocks: in the **Parco delle Luine**, 1.5km up from the spa, they scratched the oldest incisions yet discovered in the Valle Camonica (8000 BC) and others from the Bronze Age (*c.* 1500 BC)—men on horses, with shields and weapons, and a labyrinth—while some distance apart, at Corni Freschi, they carved nine halberds like the heads of swans. Unfortunately, the rock has weathered here more than at other sites and the graffiti—there are some 10,000 drawings in all—can be hard to decipher. A favourite excursion from Boario is up the Val di Scalve to a smaller spa, **Angolo Terme**, near pretty little sapphire **Lago Moro**, then continuing into the wild and narrow **Dezzo Ravine**. You can learn to hang-glide at the national school in **Montecampione**, to the south, or come back in the winter to enjoy 'Europe's largest computerized snowfields.'

Heading up the Valle Camonica from Boario Terme, you can make a brief but scenic detour east into the Vallata della Grigna, where the villages found the wherewithal to have their churches adorned with some surprisingly good art: **Santa Maria Assunta** at **Ésine** is a national monument, with its trecento campanile and charming, brightly coloured frescoes by the valley's own Giovan Pietro Da Cemmo (1493), who also contributed to the church of San Lorenzo in **Berzo Inferiore,** and to the 15th-century Santa Maria Annunziata in **Bienno**; the latter also contains frescoes by Romanino and an altarpiece by Fiamminghino. Bienno has a pretty medieval core, and a **Museo Etnografico del Ferro,** Via Artigiani 13 (*open Mon–Sat 9–12 and 2.30–5.30*) tracing the history of ironworking in the valley. Here, too, the rather difficult **Strada delle Tre Valle** rises through 18km of pure mountain scenery to the **Passo di Croce Dómini** (1904m/6244ft), where you can pick up roads to the Val Trompia or Lake Idro: fill up the tank before you go.

Below Bienno, **Breno** is the modern capital of the Valle Camonica, under the towers of an imposing 14th-century castle, with a spooky dungeon you can explore. The keys are at the town hall in Piazza Ghislandi, along with the **Museo Civico Camuno** (*open Mon–Fri 8–12; adm*), housing an ethnographic collection and paintings from the valley. The church of **Sant'Antonio** has a pretty Renaissance door and excellent frescoes (1535) by Romanino. Four km south of Breno, and guarded by a stout medieval tower of its own, **Cividate Camuno** was Civitas Camunnorum, the Romans' administrative centre in the valley; its small **Museo** (*open Tues–Sun 9–2*) remembers their passing with mosaics, tombstones and other finds. West of Cividate, **Óssimo Inferiore**'s 15th-century **Convento dell'Annunciata** has a pretty pair of cloisters and frescoes on the *Life of Mary* (1475) by Da Cemmo, while in upper Óssimo, a group of statue-stelae carved with the valley's first representations of carts and metal tools and weapons suggest a Bronze Age holy site. Similar stelae were found at **Borno**, further up the valley, amid lovely high meadows.

Capo di Ponte and its National Park

In the centre of the Valle Camonica, within a 6km radius of Capo di Ponte, are the most extensive and best-preserved prehistoric engravings: pick up a map in the tourist office. The most notable and accessible are in the **Parco Nazionale delle Incisioni Rupestri Preistoriche** (*open Tues–Sun 9–1hr before sunset; adm L8000*), where the enormous **Naquane rock** attracted artists from the Neolithic to Etruscan periods. Over a thousand figures, often superimposed, are etched into the rock: labyrinths, dogs, hunters and deer; enigmatic processions, armed warriors and horsemen, priests, a funeral; looms, carts, huts, even an Iron Age smithy. Certain symbols are repeated so often as to suggest a code: 'blades', slashes and four-petalled, dotted 'Camuna roses'.

Capo di Ponte's **Centro Studi Preistorici** has a small museum, with plans of Camuni sites among other explanatory items (*open Mon–Fri 9–4*), while just up beyond a car park two great lumps of sandstone, the **Massi di Cemmo**, once formed part of a much longer megalithic alignment, covered with engravings of deer, oxen, other animals and human figures, all dating from the 3rd millennium BC. A bit further up, **Archeodromo** (*open daily 8.30–12.30 and 1.30–6.30; adm*), the 'Centre of Experimental Archaeology', has a reconstruction of an Iron Age Camuni village; above this, a path leads to the lovely 11th-century Romanesque **San Siro**, its three tall apses rising over the River Oglio (*to visit call Pro Loco at Capo di Ponte, © 0364 42080*). Across the river, the equally beautiful Cluniac church of **San Salvatore** was built in the late 11th century in the Burgundian style, its monastic grounds still protected by walls (*to visit, call © 0364 42389*).

A few kilometres south, another great concentration of engravings was discovered in 1975 in what is now the **Riserva Regionale Incisioni Rupestri Ceto-Cimbergo-Paspardo** (*open Mon–Sun 9–12 and 2–6; adm*). The main entrance is in tiny **Nardo**, where from the small museum a path leads up to Foppe di Nardo, dotted with rocks etched from Neolithic to Etruscan times: scenes of solar worship, five-pointed stars, weapons, a village, footprints and what looks like a god by praying figures. The reserve also encompasses the rocks of Campanine, just under the ruined castle and village of **Cimbergo**, where Iron Age graffiti mingle with a Latin dedication to Jove and early Christian symbols, and Iron Age etchings in three different sites in **Paspardo**. Down on the main Valle Camonica road below Ceto is the crossroads for **Cerveno**, up in the hills to the west, where the Sacro Monte-style chapels of the **Santuario della Via Crucis-San Martino** contain 198 life-sized figures carved and painted in the 18th century, acting out the Passion of Christ.

North of Capo di Ponte

Further up the Valle Camonica the mountain scenery becomes grander as the Adamello Dolomites (3577m/11,733ft) loom up to the right. Beautiful excursions into the range are possible from **Cedegolo**, into the lovely **Val di Saviore** with its mountain lakes Arno and Salarno. Further north, from **Malonno**, you can drive or walk along a scenic road through the chestnut woods of the **Valle Malga**, with more pretty lakes and easy ascents.

Surrounded by majestic mountains, **Edolo**, where the railway ends, is a busy market town at the crossroads of the Valle Camonica and the Valtellina (*see* p.193) and the Passo di Tonale. To the west are the ski stations of the **Valle di Corteno** (Corteno Golgi, the main centre, is named for Dr Camillo Golgi, a native who won the 1906 Nobel prize in medicine) and to the north those of **Ponte di Legno**, an old town that has grown to become the most developed resort in the region, with 80km of pistes. From Ponte di Legno a daring stretch of Italian road engineering rises north through Stelvio National Park to Bormio (*see* p.200), while the main road continues up to the **Passo di Tonale**, with more skiing: **Passo Paradiso** (8366ft), reached by the cableway, has snow and skiing year round. From the Passo di Tonale the road continues east into Trentino's lovely Val di Sole.

Where to Stay and Eating Out

Boario Terme ✉ 25041

****Rizzi**, Via Carducci 5, © 0364 531 617, ✆ 0364 536 135 (*moderate*) has the most comfortable rooms in town, all with TV, phone, safe etc. It has its own garden, with an outside veranda and a very nice restaurant featuring local dishes. *Open May–Oct.* Opposite the Terme, ★★★**Diana**, Via Manifattura 12, ✆/✉ 0364 531 403 (*moderate*) is stylish and modern, with good-sized rooms with all mod cons, large bathrooms and wonderful views of the mountains, as well as a restaurant and garden.The slightly old-fashioned ★★★**Brescia**, Via Zanardelli 6, ✆ 0364 531 409, ✉ 0364 532 969 (*moderate*) has fully equipped rooms, and a very stylish dining room and a pub/disco downstairs. ★★★**Armonia**, Via Manifattura 11, ✆ 0364 531 816, ✉ 0364 535 144 (*low moderate*) has simple rooms, all with TV and bath, and perhaps the most generous see-how-much-you-can-eat lunches and dinners in all Italy. A good budget option, in the station forecourt, ★★**Ariston**, ✆/✉ 0364 531 532 (*cheap*) offers small, clean rooms with modern fittings and old-fashioned hospitality.

Capo di Ponte ✉ 25044

Two simple, *cheap* choices here: ★★**Graffiti**, Via Sebastiano Briscioli 42, ✆/✉ 0364 42013, with en suite baths, and the slightly cheaper ★**Cumli**, Via Italia 27, ✆ 0364 42034 without; both have restaurants.

Ponte di Legno ✉ 25056

Sleek and modern ★★★★**Mirella**, Via Roma 21, ✆ 0364 900 500, ✉ 0364 900 530 (*expensive*) is the top choice, with a pool and tennis courts among its facilities. The less glamorous ★★★**Dolomiti**, up at the Passo del Tonale, ✆ 0364 900 260, ✉ 0364 900 251 (*moderate*) is still a quite adequate choice. Dine at **Al Maniero**, ✆ 0364 900 490 (*moderate*), which features hearty local cuisine in a cosy, happy atmosphere.

Brescia

Lombardy's second city, Brescia is a busy and prosperous place but somehow it's no one's favourite town, even though it has a full day's supply of fine art, architecture and historic attractions: Brescia's Roman and Lombard relics are among the best preserved in northern Italy. Perhaps it's the vaguely sinister aura of having been Italy's chief manufacturer of arms for the last 400 years. Perhaps it's because the local Fascists saw fit to punch out the heart of the old city and replace it with a piazza as frosty and heavy as an iceberg. The Brescians seem to detest it, but it's hard to avoid; they would do well to raze it. Give them credit, however, for preserving the rest of their historic centre by spawning Brescia Due, a mini-version of Paris's La Défense, to quarantine all its new gangly office buildings.

History

Brescia was founded by the Gauls, an origin remembered only in its name Brixia, from the Celtic *brik* ('hill'). Brixia saw the inevitability of Rome early on, became a willing ally, and in 26 BC achieved the favoured status of a *Colonia Civica Augusta*, when it was embellished with splendid monuments. By the 8th century Brescia had recovered enough from the barbarian invasions to become the seat of a Lombard duchy under King Desiderius, whose daughter Ermengarda was wed by Charlemagne—the condition imposed by the Italians before they crowned him emperor. He later repudiated her, and the forlorn Ermengarda returned to Brescia to die in the Abbey of San Salvatore.

When Brescia joined the Lombard League against Frederick Barbarossa, its opposition had a voice: that of a Benedictine monk, Arnold of Brescia, who studied under Peter Abelard in Paris and went to Rome, preaching eloquently against the tyranny of the emperor and the corrupt, worldly materialism of the Church. In 1155, Barbarossa, in collusion with Adrian IV, arrested the troublesome monk and handed him over to the pope, who burned Arnold alive at the stake in front of Castel Sant'Angelo.

Brescia itself was too tempting a prize to be left in peace. Firmly in the Guelph camp, for the freedom of cities against imperial pretensions, it held tight when Frederick II besieged it for 68 days, then suffered under his lieutenant, the unspeakable Ezzelino da Romano, in 1258; in 1421, when the detested Visconti horned in, the weary Brescians turned to Venice for relief and asked to be adopted. The Venetians didn't have to be asked twice; Brescia meant access to the unusually pure iron deposits in the valleys to the north. By the 16th century Brescia had become Italy's major producer of firearms, and the Republic imposed severe emigration restrictions to keep skilled workers from wandering.

Venice not only brought peace and prosperity, but initiated an artistic flowering as well. The Brescian Vincenzo Foppa (1485–1566) was a key figure in the Lombard Renaissance; his monumental paintings were among the first to depict a single, coherent atmosphere. The individualistic linear style of Girolamo Romanino (1485–1566) may stand somewhat apart, but Romanino's contemporary Alessandro Bonvincino (better known as 'the little Moor' or Moretto; 1498–1554), an ardent student of Titian, contributed the first Italian full-length portrait and taught Giovanni Battista Moroni of Bergamo. His contemporary Giovanni Girolamo Savoldo, a Brescian who later worked in Venice, was neglected in his day but is now recognized for his lyricism, especially in his use of light. Recently Giacomo Antonio Ceruti (1698–1767) has been the centre of interest for his realist, un-romanticized genre paintings of Brescia's humble, demented and down-and-out—a unique subject for the time. His nickname was Il Pitocchetto ('the little skinflint').

Getting Around

Brescia is on the main Milan–Venice **rail** line, 55 minutes from Milan, an hour from Verona, and less to Desenzano del Garda, the main station on Lake Garda. There are also frequent services to Bergamo (1 hour) and Lecco (2 hours); to Cremona (just over an hour); and to Parma via Piadena (2 hours). For FS rail information, call ✆ 030 37961. The regional FNME railway line wends its way north along the east shore of Lake Iseo and up the Valle Camonica to Edolo (2½ hours).

There is an even more extensive **bus** network, with frequent links to the towns of Lakes Garda and Iseo and less frequently to Idro; also to Turin and Milan, Padua and the Euganean Hills, Marostica, Bassano del Grappa and Belluno; to Trento via Riva and to the resorts of Pinzolo and Madonna di Campiglio in Trentino, as well as to all points within the province. For information, call ✆ 030 44061.

The **bus** and **railway stations** are located next to each other just south of the city centre on Viale Stazione. Bus C connects them to the centre, or you can walk there in 10 minutes up the Corso Martiri della Libertà.

Porta
Trento

VIA DEL CASTELLO

CONTRADA DEL CARMINE

VIA DELLE BATTAGLIE

VIA SAN FAUSTINO

S. Maria del
Carmine

VIA CALATAFIMI

VIA

S. Maria
delle Grazie

CAPRIOLO

VIA DEL CASTELLO

Piazzale
Garibaldi

CORSO GARIBALDI

S. Giovanni
Evangelista

S. Faustino
in Riposo

CORSO MAMELI

VIA PACE

VIA DEI MILLE

Torre della
Pallata

Loggia

Piazza
della
Loggia

Broletto

VIA CAIROLI

VIA DANTE

Duomo

Piazza
Paolo
VI

VIA CATTANEO

Queriniana

Rotonda

VIA TRIESTE

FRATELLI PORCELLAGA

Piazza
della
Vittoria

S. Francesco

CORSO

Piazza
del Mercato

S. Maria d. Miracoli

PALESTRO

CORSO MARTIRI DELLA LIBERTÀ

CAVALLETTO

CORSO

Teatro
Grande

VIA TOSIO

S. S. Nazzaro
e Celso

VIA GRAMSCI

ZANARDELLIA

CORSO

VIA MORETTO

i

VIA MORETTO

DELLA BATTAGLIA

CORSO

S. Alessandro

VIA

VIA S. MARTINO

CORSO CAVOUR

Piazzale della
Repubblica

VIA

VITTORIO

CAVALCAVIA KENNEDY

EMANUELE

Bus Station

VIA

XX

SETTEMBRE

SOLFERINO

Railway
Station

N

Brescia

300 metres
300 yards

Cydnean Hill

Museo delle Armi

Museo del Risorgimento

Castello

S. Pietro in Oliveto

VIA DEL CASTELLO

VIA G. PIAMARTA

VIA BRIGIDA AVOGADRO

Tempio Capitolino

Teatro Romano

Monastero S. Giulia

Museo della Città

Museo Romano

VIA DEI MUSEI

Piazza del Foro

Curia

VIA CATTANEO

Piazza Tebaldo Brusato

VIA GALLO

VIA TRIESTE

VIA CRISPI

VIA TOSIO

Piazzale Arnaldo

Porta Venezia

CORSO MAGENTA

VIA BRIGIDA AVOGADRO

Pinacoteca Tosio-Martinengo

VIA CALLEGARI

Piazza Moretto

S. Angela Merci

VIA SPALTO SAN MARCO

Museo Arte e Spiritualità

VIA CRISPI

VIA CALLEGARI

VIA SPALTO SAN MARCO

Corso Zanardelli 38, ✆ 030 45052, near the central Piazza del Duomo.

The Central Squares

Hurry, as the Brescians do, through the deathly pale **Piazza della Vittoria**, designed in 1932 by Marcello Piacentini; that frigid, Fascist square that melts each May, when it acts as the starting gate for the famous *Mille Miglia* vintage car race across Italy. Duck behind the post office to enter into a far more elegant display of power, the closed, Venetian-style **Piazza della Loggia**, named for the **Palazzo della Loggia**, Brescia's town hall, a neo-Roman confection begun in 1492 and designed in part by Venice's top architects, Sansovino and Palladio; its great white roof swells over the old city like Moby Dick on the prowl. Opposite the Palazzo della Loggia, the **Torre dell'Orologio** is a copy of the clock tower in St Mark's Square, complete with two bell-ringing figures on top. The Brescians must have been hopeless spendthrifts: the other chief buildings on the square are the old and new municipal pawn shops, the **Monte di Pietà Vecchia** (1489) and the **Monte di Pietà Nuova** (1590s); the Roman inscriptions embedded in the façade of the former constitute Italy's very first lapidary collection.

Looming up behind the clock tower rises the third-highest dome in Italy, the green-lead-roofed crown of the **Duomo**, built in 1602 by Gianbattista Lantana. From the **Piazza Paolo VI** itself, however, the dome is hidden by a high marble front—a Lombard 'wind-breaker' façade. Over the door a bust of Brescia's great Cardinal Querini 'winks mischievously, as if inviting the faithful to enter'. You should take him up on it, not so much for the few paintings by Romanino (by the bishop's throne) and Moretto that try to warm the cold interior, as to visit the adjacent **Duomo Vecchio** or La Rotonda (*open April–Oct Wed–Mon 9–12 and 3–7; Nov–Mar Sat and Sun only, 9–12 and 3–6*). Built in the 11th century over the ruins of the Basilica of San Filastrio and the ancient Roman baths, this singular old cathedral is the only one in Italy designed in the shape of a top hat, low and rotund, with a massive cylindrical tower rising from its centre, supported by eight pillars, the light diffused through its upper windows. Inside, its simple form is broken only by a 15th-century raised choir; the altar-piece, an *Assumption* by Moretto, is one his greatest works. The crypt of San Filastrio, a survival of the ancient basilica, contains a mixed bag of Roman and early medieval columns, and mosaics from the Roman baths. Several medieval bishops are entombed around the walls, most impressively Bishop Mernardo Maggi in his sarcophagus of 1308; the treasury holds two precious relics—the 16th-century *Stauroteca* containing a bit of the True Cross, and the 11th-century banner once borne on the *carroccio* (sacred ox cart) of the Brescian armies.

On the other side of the new Duomo, the 12th-century **Broletto** was the civic centre of Brescia prior to the construction of the

Palazzo della Loggia which later became the seat of the Venetian governor; its formidable tower, the **Pegol**, predates it by a century. Just behind the new cathedral, on Via Mazzini 1, the 18th-century **Biblioteca Queriniana** (*no longer open to the public*) contains 300,000 rare books and manuscripts, including the 6th-century 'Purple Evangeliary' with silver letters, from San Salvatore, and Eusebius' 11th-century Concordances of the Gospels; Cardinal Querini, the library's founder, enriched his own collection at the expense of the Vatican library.

Roman and Lombard Brixia

Flanking the Broletto, the ancient *Decumanus Maximus*, now the Via dei Musei, leads to the heart of Roman Brixia. Its forum, now the narrow **Piazza del Foro**, lies under the mighty columns of the **Capitoline Temple**, erected by the Emperor Vespasian in AD 73 and preserved for posterity by a medieval mud-slide that covered it until its rediscovery in 1823. In 1955 an earlier, Republican-era Capitoline temple was discovered beneath Vespasian's, with unusual mosaics of natural stone. The Temple is divided into three *cellae*, which were probably dedicated to the three principal Roman deities—Jupiter, Juno and Minerva. They are now filled with the tombstones and mosaics of the **Civico Museo Romano** (*open Tues–Sun 9–12.30 and 3–5, summer 10–12.30 and 3–6; adm*), a considerable collection thanks to the foresight of the 1485 municipal council, which forbade the sale of antiquities outside Brescia. The museum's best treasures are upstairs: six gilded bronze busts of emperors and a 6ft bronze Winged Victory, all found in the temple; the Victory, bereft of the object she once held, seems to be snapping her fingers in a dance. There's a gilt bronze figurine of a Gaulish prisoner, believed to be Vercingetorix, a beautiful Greek amphora from the 6th century BC and a facsimile of the 25ft-long Peutringer Map of Vienna, itself a 12th-century copy of a Roman road map.

Next to the temple is the unexcavated *cavea* of the **Roman Theatre**, while down Via Carlo Cattaneo, in Piazza Labus, you can make out the columns and lintels of the third building of the forum: the **Curia**, or senate, imprinted like a fossil in the wall of a house.

From Piazza del Foro, Via dei Musei continues to the **Monastero di San Salvatore- Santa Giulia** (*open Tues–Sun 10–5; adm*), founded in the 700s by the wife of the Lombard king Desiderius, and disbanded at the end of the 18th century. Its **Museo della Città**, in the process of being rearranged, partly reopened in February 1996; during the work, a large Roman *domus* was uncovered under one of the three cloisters. The heart of the complex, the 8th-century **Basilica of San Salvatore**, was modelled on the 6th-century churches of Ravenna. In the nave, the capitals are either ancient Roman or made of stucco, an art at which the Lombards excelled. Some Carolingian frescoes remain under the arcades; others were painted by Girolamo Romanino in 1530. The semi-circular crypt, where the relics of St Giulia were laid in 762, was enlarged in the 12th century, with vigorous capitals sculpted by the school of Antelami: the one on the life of Giulia is a serene masterpiece. The same century saw the addition of another church, sturdy **Santa Maria in Solario**, crowned with an octagonal dome or tiburium, its lower vaults supported on an ancient Roman altar, its upper level frescoed by Floriano Ferramola (1480–1528). In the 16th century a third church, **Santa Giulia**, was built; the nuns' choir has more bright frescoes by Ferramola.

The museum contains two exceptional pieces. One is the 8th-century golden Lombard *Cross of Desiderius*, studded with 212 gems and cameos, including one from the 4th century of a Roman woman with her two children, peering warily into the approaching Dark Ages; the

Brescians like to believe it is the great Galla Placidia of Ravenna. The other is a 4th-century ivory coffer called the *Lipsanoteca*, adorned with beautiful bas-reliefs of scriptural scenes. One of the superb 5th-century ivory diptychs originally belonged to the father of the philosopher Boethius. Lombard jewellery, medieval art and Renaissance medals round out the collection.

The Cydnean Hill

The poet Catullus, who considered Brixia the mother of his native Verona, was the first to mention the Cydnean hill that rises behind the Via dei Musei. Named after the Ligurian king Cidno, the legendary founder of Brixia, the site has been inhabited since the Bronze Age. It was the core of Gaulish and early Roman Brixia—along Via Piamarta are the ruins of the city's last surviving **Roman gate**, as well as the attractive 1510 **San Pietro in Oliveto**, named after the ancient silvery olive grove that surrounds the church.

Up on top an imposing Venetian gate in Istrian marble, still guarded by the Lion of St Mark, is the entrance to the **Castello**, with its round 14th-century Mirabella Tower, sitting on a Roman foundation. Built in 1443, during the brief reign of the Visconti, the donjon houses the **Museo Civico delle Armi Antiche Luigi Marzoli** (*open June–Sept Tues–Sun 10–5; Oct–May 9.30–1 and 2.30–5; adm*), one of Italy's most extensive collections of Brescia's bread-and-butter industry, with a special collection of 15th–18th-century firearms. The castle's Venetian granary now houses the **Museo del Risorgimento** (*same hours*) with paintings, uniforms, decrees and weapons, with special honours going to Brescia's Ten Day revolt in 1849, bloodily suppressed by Austria. The gardens around the castle are a favourite refuge from the car-filled city below.

The Pinacoteca and Around

From the Capitoline Temple, Via Crispi descends to Piazza Moretto, site of the **Pinacoteca Civica Tosio-Martinengo** (*open June–Sept Tues–Sun 10–5; Oct–May 9.30–1 and 2.30–5; adm*), housed in a 16th-century patrician palace. It showcases Brescia's local talent, including Foppa (*Madonna and Saints*), Savoldo, Moretto (his *Salome* is a portrait of the great Roman courtesan-poetess Tullia d'Aragona), Romanino, Moroni and Ceruti; there's also a lovely *Adoration of the Magi* by Lorenzo Lotto, a *Senator* by Tintoretto, a *Portrait of Henri III* by Clouet and two early works by Raphael—a not altogether wholesome, beardless *Redeemer* and a lovely *Angel*, and an anonymous golden fairytale picture of *St George and the Princess*, painted around 1460.

South on Via Crispi, there's more art in little 16th-century **Santa Angela Merci** (by Tintoretto and Francesco Bassano) and at Via Monti 9, in the Istituto Paolo VI's **Museo Arte e Spiritualità** (*open Thurs–Sun 4–7*), devoted to contemporary religious art, something that Pope Paul VI sincerely believed wasn't an oxymoron. **Sant'Alessandro**, in Via Moretto, contains a pretty *Annunciation* by Jacopo Bellini; further north, in elegant, porticoed Corso Zanardelli, the **Teatro Grande** with its luscious foyer and five tiers of boxes is one of the most lavish theatres in Lombardy; here in 1904 Puccini's *Madam Butterfly* was wholeheartedly vindicated by the public after its disastrous premiere.

West Side Churches

The piquant quarters west of the Piazza della Loggia are rich in interesting old churches. Just west of Via S. Faustino (off Piazza della Loggia) there are two strikingly unusual ones—**San**

Faustino in Riposo, a cylindrical, steep-roofed drum of a church from the 12th century (near the intersection with Via dei Musei) and, further up, on Contrada Carmine, the 14th-century **Santa Maria del Carmine**, crowned with a set of Mongol-like brick pinnacles; it contains frescoes by Foppa, among his finest work, and a 15th-century terracotta *Deposition* by Mazzoni (*open Tues–Sun 4–7*).

Just off Corso G. Mameli, Renaissance **San Giovanni Evangelista** has good works by Moretto, Romanino and the Bolognese painter Francia. Further along the Corso stands the giant **Torre della Pallata**, a survivor from the rough-and-tumble 13th century, with a travesty of a 16th-century fountain like a bunion on its foot. From here Via della Pace heads south to the venerable **San Francesco** (1265) with its cloister in red Verona marble and frescoes (a few by Romanino and Moretto), and the nearby **Santa Maria dei Miracoli** with a lovely 15th-century Lombard Renaissance marble façade that survived even though the interior was blown to smithereens in the last war. Further south, on Corso Matteotti, the 18th-century **Santi Nazzaro e Celso** houses the Averoldi polyptych (1522), considered the masterpiece of Titian's youth, with a gravity-defying, virtuoso *Risen Christ* in the centre that soars overboard into the numbing bathos of spiritual banality. The chapels hold works by Moretto (*to get in, contact Signor Federici at nearby S. Maria dei Miracoli*).

Brescia ✉ 25100   **Where to Stay**

Brescia caters mainly to business clients, and its best hotels are comfortable if not inspiring. The city's premier hotel, ★★★★★**Vittoria**, Via X Giornate 20, ✆ 030 280 061, 🖷 030280 065 (*very expensive*) has everything it should—large, sumptuous rooms, palatial bathrooms of French *Rosa* marble, banqueting suites, and liberal use of marble and chandeliers throughout. But the severe Fascist-era architecture is a bit soulless.
Near the centre by the castle, ★★★★**Master**, Via L. Apollonio 72, ✆ 030 399 037, 🖷 030 370 1331 (*expensive*) has some of the best rooms in town.

A bit further out of the centre, ★★★★**Ambasciatori**, Via Crocifissa di Rosa 92, ✆ 030 399 114, 🖷 030 381 883 (*moderate*) is very modern, with a garage; it also has very good, air-conditioned rooms, all with private bath and TV. ★★★**Cristallo**, Viale Stazione 12, ✆ 030 377 2468, 🖷 377 2615 (*moderate*) is an adequate albeit nondescript place near the station; ★★**Astron**, Via Togni 14, ✆/🖷 030 48220 (*cheap*) has clean, simple rooms.

Eating Out

Brescians are rather stolid conservatives at table: kid, stews, risotti, meat on a skewer and polenta have been in vogue since the Renaissance. You'll find them at the elegant **La Sosta**, Via San Martino della Battaglia 20, ✆ 030 295 603 (*expensive*), set in a 17th-century stable that has been stripped and completely overhauled; a second menu features prestige fish and Italian classics. *Closed Mon, Sun eve, and Aug*. In the same price range, the lovely medieval **Castello Malvezzi**, just north of the centre at Via Colle San Giuseppe 1, ✆ 030 200 4224, serves delicious food, cooked by a French and an Italian chef, to go with a superb selection of wines. *Open evenings only, closed Mon, Sun eve, and most of Aug.*

The freshest of seafood with a Tuscan touch holds pride of place at **I Templari**, Via Matteotti 19, ℗ 030 52234 (*expensive*). *Closed Sat lunch and Sun*. Near the Duomo Vecchio, the intimate **Circolo delle Arti**, Via Trieste 3, ℗ 030 43008 (*moderate*) serves excellent southern Italian dishes; try the reasonably priced lunch menu. *Closed Tues*. **Bersagliera**, Corso Magenta 38 (*cheap*) is a good, popular pizzeria. At **La Vineria**, Via X Giornate 4, ℗ 030 280 477 (*cheap*) you can feast on excellent cured meats and salami, herby risotto, *casoncelli* and home-made tarts. *Closed Mon.*

North of Brescia: Lake Idro

Although Iseo and the Valle Camonica attract most of the visitors, two green valleys north of Brescia have their quiet virtues. Due north of Brescia, the **Val Trompia** is named for the ancient Ligurian tribe, the Triumplini. Pope Paul VI's birthplace at **Concesio**, 9km from Brescia, is marked with a plaque, and there's a painting by Palma Giovane in the parish church. But what the lower valley is really known for is guns: **Lumezzane** makes excellent reproductions of ancient firearms, while the handguns produced since the 1500s by **Gardone Val Trompia** were so valuable that the town enjoyed the special protection of Venice; it still makes hand-crafted sports rifles. North of Gardone the road climbs to two popular summer and winter resorts, **Bovegno** and **Collio**. Beyond Collio a new road continues up to the scenic **Passo del Maniva** (1662m/5453ft) and over to the Passo di Croce Dómini (*see* p.222); in summer, you can also drive east to Lake Idro.

In the next valley east, the Val Sabbia, the River Chiese widens to form a fjord in the mountains known as **Lake Idro** (the ancient Eeidio). Long, narrow, surrounded by a corniche of steep dark mountains, it is the highest of the larger Lombard lakes (1214ft), and one of the best for trout fishing. A scattered collection of hamlets form **Idro**, at the south tip of the lake; in one, Castel Antinco, you can visit the ruins of a 1st-century BC village. **Anfo**, on the west bank, has a 15th-century castle built by the Venetians, where Garibaldi set up his headquarters briefly in 1866 during the battle of Monte Suello, just to the north. Although 8km up the Val Sabbia from the lake on the trout-filled River Caffaro, picturesque **Bagolino** with its medieval streets is Idro's most important town, where the most traditional carnival in Lombardy takes place, with the bizarre dances of the *ballerini*. The 18th-century parish church that dominates Bagolino has minor paintings attributed to Titian and Tintoretto; 15th-century **San Rocco**, on the edge of the village, was frescoed in 1486 by Giovan Pietro Da Cemmo.

Eating Out

When Brescians have a hankering for something special, they drive up to Concesio's celebrated **Miramonti L'Altro**, Via Crosetta 34, ℗ 030 275 1063 (*expensive*). You won't find better traditional Brescian maccheroni, risotti, kid, duck, game and rabbit dishes anywhere, especially when wild mushrooms are in season; in addition, every year Mauro Piscini invents new tempting delicacies. For afters, there's a fine array of cheeses, or one of Miramonti's great desserts. The enormous cellar features French and Italian wines. *Closed Mon.*

Lake Garda

Kennst du das Land wo die Citronen blühn?

Goethe

The Italian lakes culminate in Garda, the largest (48km long, 16km across at its widest point) and most dramatic, its 'Madonna blue' waters, as Winston Churchill described them, lapping at the feet of the Dolomites. Shaped like the profile of a tall-hatted witch, its Latin name *Benacus* is of Celtic origin, a word similar to the Irish *bennach*, 'horned one', for its many headlands. If memories of the two Plinys mingle in the waters of Lake Como, Garda's shores recall two of Italy's greatest poets of pure passion: ancient, tragic, lovelorn Catullus and that 20th-century Italian fire hazard, Gabriele D'Annunzio.

The other lakes are warm but Garda, Venice's 'little sea', has a genuine Mediterranean climate. Open to the south and blocked off from the cold winds of the north by the Dolomites, Garda's great volume (its average depth is 445ft) make it a giant solar battery, heating the surrounding hills throughout the winter and keeping deadly frosts and clammy mists at bay. For Goethe and generations of chilblained travellers from Middle Europe, its olives, vines, citrus groves and palm trees have long signalled the beginning of their dream Italy. No tourist office could concoct a more scintillating oasis to stimulate what the Icelanders call 'a longing for figs', that urge to go south.

Perhaps it's because Lake Garda seems more 'Italian' that it has traditionally been less stuffy and status-conscious than its sister lakes. It attracts more families (thanks to Gardaland), party-goers (at Desenzano), beach bums (the water's very clean) and older package tourists (especially German and Austrian). Sailors and windsurfers come to test their mettle on the winds, first mentioned by Virgil: the *sover* which blows from the north from midnight and through the morning, and the *ora*, which puffs from the south in the afternoon and evening. White caps and storms are not uncommon, but on the other hand the breezes are delightfully cool in the summer. Although services drop to a minimum, winter is a good time to visit, when the jagged peaks shimmer with snow and you can better take in the voluptuous charms that brought visitors to Garda in the first place.

Getting Around

There are two **train stations** at the southern end of Lake Garda, at Desenzano and Peschiera, both of which are also landings for the lake's **hydrofoils** (*aliscafi*) and **steamers**. **Buses** from Brescia, Trento and Verona go to their respective shores; Desenzano, the gateway to Lake Garda, is served by buses from Brescia, Verona and Mantua. Frequent buses connect Sirmione to Desenzano and Peschiera.

Other local bus lines run up and down the road that winds around the lake shores—a marvel of Italian engineering, called *La Gardesana*, Occidentale (SS45) on the west and Orientale (SS249) on the east. In summer, however, their scenic splendour sometimes pales before the sheer volume of holiday traffic.

All **boat services** on the lake are operated by *Navigazione sul Lago di Garda*, Piazza Matteotti 2, Desenzano, © 030 9141 9511, where you can pick up a timetable; the tourist offices have them as well. The one **car ferry** crosses from Maderno to Torri; between Desenzano and Riva there are several hydrofoils a day, calling at various ports (2 hours the full trip), as well as the more frequent and leisurely steamers (4½ hours). Services are considerably reduced from October to March. Full fare on the 4-hour sail from Desenzano to Riva on the steamer is L15,400, and on the hydrofoil L20,700. Lunch on board costs L25,000.

Tourist Information

Desenzano del Garda: Via Porto Vecchio 27, ✆ 030 914 1510, ✉ 914 4209.

Garda's South Shore: Desenzano

Lively, colourful and thoroughly pleasant **Desenzano del Garda**, on a wide gulf dotted with beaches, is Garda's largest town, built up in the 15th and 16th centuries (if you arrive by train, a bus will take you to the centre). Life centres around its busy portside cafés, presided over by a statue of Sant'Angela, foundress of the Ursuline Order, who seems appalled at all the carryings-on; another statue on the lake front, the whooshing **High Speed Monument**, celebrates an air speed record (709km per hour) set here in 1934 by Francesco Agello. On the lower end of the technological scale, Desenzano's Bronze Age (2200–1200 BC) inhabitants lived in pile dwellings, recently discovered in the peat bogs southwest of town and yielding the contents of the new **Museo Archeologico Rambotti** in the cloister of Santa Maria de Senioribus, Via Anelli 7 (*open Tues, Fri, Sat, Sun and hols 3–7*). There are models of houses and, amongst the ornaments, little 'pearls' of amber: Desenzano was on the ancient trade route between the amber-rich Baltic and the Mediterranean, which endured until the end of the Roman period.

Desenzano, also on the Bergamo–Verona Via Gallica, became a popular resort (read refuge) of the Romans towards the end of the empire, when the rich and powerful retreated from the growing anarchy to their country estates. Incorporating vast agricultural lands, maintained by hundreds of slaves and retainers, these estates were the origins of feudalism. One of the most important was Desenzano's **Villa Romana**, just in from the Lunglago at Via Crocifisso 22 (*open Mar–Oct Tues–Fri 8.30–7, Sun 9–5.30; Oct–Feb Tues–Fri 8.30–4.30, Sun 9–4.30; adm*). Although begun in the 1st century BC, the villa was given its present form in the 4th century, fitted with sumptuous heated baths, a triclinium (dining hall) with three apses, and other rooms covered with the most extensive mosaic floors in northern Italy; pick up the free archaeological itinerary pamphlet in English. Nearby, along Via Roma, **Santa Maria Maddalena** has 27 huge canvases by a transplanted Venetian, Andrea Celesti (*d. 1712*), and a strikingly different *Last Supper* by Gian Domenico Tiepolo.

Wine, Wine, and More Wine

One secret of Desenzano's success through the ages lies in a bottle, or rather bottles: a bewildering number of wines are grown on all sides of town. The south shore of Garda is the restricted growing area of a prestigious white wine, dry, fresh, straw-coloured Lugana DOC, both still and spumante, produced from Trebbiano di Lugana grapes. When they weren't guzzling out of fresh skulls, Lugana was a favourite tipple of the

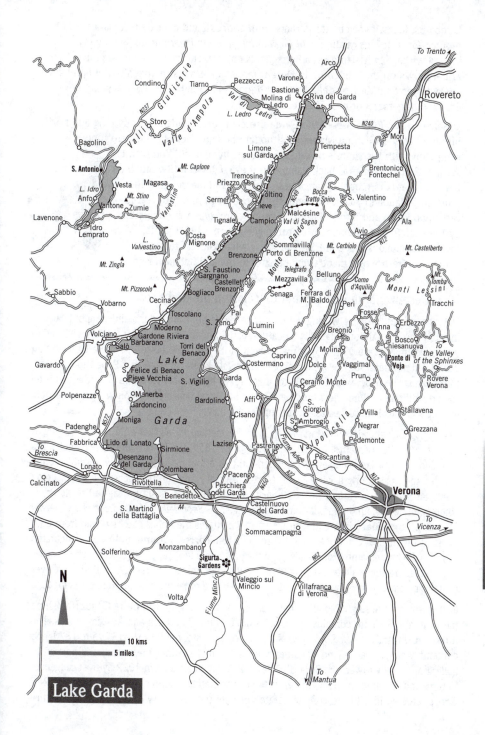

Lake Garda

Lombards; today it goes better perhaps with *antipasti* and delicate fish dishes, and is reputed for its joyous quality: '*Ubi Lugana ibi gaudium magnum*' or so they say. A second white, San Martino della Battaglia, is made exclusively from tocai grapes from Friuli, grown on the hills south of Desenzano, and has a distinctive bitter almond after-taste; golden San Martino della Battaglia liquoroso is a floral, fruity 16% wine, best drunk with desserts or blue cheeses.

Desenzano also forms part of the Garda Bresciano area, which extends west and north into the Valtenesi behind Manerba, although the vines here have a hard time competing with the shore's new-found interest in olive oil. You won't see any Garda Brescianos back home, but they go down well enough on the spot. A mix of gropello, sangiovese, barbera and marzemino (the same grape lauded by Don Giovanni in the opera) go into ruby Garda Bresciano Rosso and into Chiaretto, a young claret-type wine invented by Venetian Senator Pompeo Molenti in Moniga in 1896. Gentle, savoury Gropello is made of 85% you guess what; Garda Bresciano Bianco is a fresh white made from a mix of Rhine and Italian rieslings.

Near Desenzano: the Risorgimento Hills and the Red Cross

Desenzano is the base for visiting not only Lake Garda but the low, morainic amphitheatre of hills to the south. Although famous for battles, perhaps more important for western civilization was the combat averted in 425, at the twilight of the Roman empire. Attila the Hun, having devastated northeast Italy, was marching to annihilate Rome when he met Pope Leo I south of Desenzano. The pope, with Saints Peter and Paul as his translators, informed Attila that if he should continue to Rome he would be stricken by a fatal nosebleed, upon which the terrible but superstitious Hun turned aside, sparing central Italy.

Move the clock ahead 1400 years, when Italy, fragmented for all that time, was beginning to reunite in the Risorgimento. In a single day, 24 June 1859, the Italians and their French allies pounded the Austrian occupier twice, when King Vittorio Emanuele II and his Sardinian army crushed the Austrian right wing at San Martino, while Napoleon III defeated Emperor Franz Joseph at Solferino, 11km to the southwest. At **San Martino della Battaglia** the victory is commemorated by a monumental complex (*open April–Sept daily 9–12 and 2–6.30; Oct–Mar till 5.30*). An **ossuary** in a 13th-century chapel contains the bones of 2619 dead from both sides. At the highest point of the hill the round 213ft **Torre Monumentale** was inaugurated in 1893; a winding ramp inside leads up to the panoramic terrace, passing rooms with frescoes and statues on the events and heroes of the Risorgimento. A **museum** behind the tower contains portraits, photos, weapons, uniforms, letters and other mementoes from the campaign.

Solferino saw the single bloodiest battle in the whole war; the **Cappella Ossuaria** behind the church of S. Pietro contains the remains of 7000 mostly French and Austrian troops. The **museum** (*same hours as S. Martino; adm*) traces the history of Italy from 1796 to 1870, and contains weapons, arms and documents from the battle: other memorabilia is housed in Solferino's mighty tower, the **Spia d'Italia** ('Italy's spy') first built in 1022 by the Scaligers of Verona and restored in the 17th century. Nearby stands a simple **Memorial to the Red Cross**, erected in 1959 to commemorate not only the centenary of the battle, but Henry

Dunant's founding of what was first known as the Committee to Aid the Wounded in War. You can learn more about it in the **Museo della Croce Rossa**, Via Garibaldi 50 in **Castiglione delle Stiviere** (*open Oct–Mar 9–12 and 2–5.30; April–Sept 9–12 and 3–7; closed Mon; donation*).

Organizing Compassion: the Invention of the Red Cross

Henry Dunant of Geneva was trying to get to Napoleon III to present a petition requesting concessions in Algeria when he heard of the battles and stopped to spend the night of 24 June 1859 in Castiglione, 8km west of Solferino. Over the next few days, some 6000 wounded from both sides were brought into temporary hospitals thrown up overnight in Castiglione's churches, convents, homes, streets and squares. The villagers—outnumbered by the wounded—pitched in to help and supply what food, blankets and clothing they could, while Dunant worked at their sides, deeply impressed not only by the horrors wrought by war but by Castiglione's selfless dedication, although few of the inhabitants could even understand French or German. Inevitably, in spite of the good intentions, confusion reigned.

A week later, as he returned to Geneva, Dunant formed the idea of setting up a permanent, trained committee of partial volunteers to succour the battle-wounded. In 1862 he published the *Souvenir de Solferino* at his own expense, a book that brought many across Europe over to his point of view. In 1863, what became the International Committee of the Red Cross was founded by Dunant in Geneva. The museum, founded in 1959, contains early ambulances, medical kits and portable field hospital beds as well as photos and videos on current Red Cross work around the world and the first Nobel peace prize, awarded to the tireless Dunant in 1901, as well as the three others presented to the Red Cross over the years.

Before inspiring the creation of the Red Cross, Castiglione delle Stiviere witnessed the birth of St Luigi Gonzaga (every great Italian family managed to churn out a saint or two) and built a big baroque basilica in his honour. His life is chronicled in the **Museo Storico Aloisiano**, Via Perati 6 (*open 9–11 and 3–6; donations*), in the early 17th-convent of the Vergini di Gesù. The museum also holds a ripe bounty of mostly religious baroque paintings (by F. Bassano, Barocci, Piazza and Guardi), a beautiful, functioning clock of 1567 called the Orologio de San Luigi and an important pewterware collection.

Lastly, if it's a weekend, stop in **Lonato**, north of Castiglione and only 4km from Desenzano, to visit the **Fondazione Ugo Da Como** (*open Sat and Sun 10–12 and 2.30–7, winter until sunset; other times by appointment*). Ugo Da Como was a Brescian scholar and humanist who, when he died in 1941, left his house, furnishings and priceless library of parchments, codices and manuscripts to a foundation for scholars; the house-museum, with its rich, eclectic collection of ancient sculpture, antiques, detached frescoes, Renaissance and Mannerist paintings, ceramics, antique pewter and more, is impressive to stroll through; it becomes even more so when you learn that Da Como bought the house, the 15th-century residence of the Venetian Podestà, in a public auction in 1906 for L1000!

Desenzano del Garda ✉ 25015

Small, white ★★★★**Tripoli**, Piazza Matteotti 18, ✆ 030 914 1305, 🖅 030 914 4333 (*moderate*) has renovated, well-equipped-rooms in the centre of action and a garage, although ★★★**Il Veliero**, Via T. da Molin 33, ✆ 030 914 1318, 🖅 030 914 0322 (*moderate*) with its own beach and pier is only a short walk. Nearby, with its own olive grove, the ★★★**Piccola Vela**, Via T. dal Molin 36, ✆/🖅 030 991 4666 (*moderate*) has views over the lake from its balconies.

The venerable ★★★**Mayer e Splendid**, right by the quay at Via U. Papa 10, ✆ 030 914 2253, 🖅 030 914 1409 (*cheap*) allows you to tumble out of bed and on to a steamer; not all rooms have bath, but there is parking. *Open Mar–Nov.*

Desenzano has a larger selection of good restaurants than any town on the lake. For an unforgettable feast, book a table at **Cavallino**, Via Murachette 21, ✆ 030 912 0217, where the chef creates imaginative, seasonal dishes based on lake fish and seafood, duck, pigeon (the pigeon stuffed with foie gras is superb) and offal, followed by an excellent cheeseboard and desserts (*menu degustazione* L60,000 and L80,000). *Closed Mon and Tues lunch.*

The equally delightful if rather formal **Esplanade**, Via Lario 10, ✆ 030 914 3361, has a lovely lakeside terrace, where clients tuck into the likes of a delicate lasagne with seafood fused with wine, or zucchini flowers stuffed with goats' cheese; excellent wine list and desserts; topnotch L70,000 *menu degustazione*, more *à la carte.* *Closed Wed.*

Good home cooking is the draw at the picturesque **Trattoria Bicocca**, squeezed in a tight corner at Vic. Molini 6, ✆ 030 914 3658 (*moderate*) and offering a wide variety of lake fish—salmon trout, *coregone*, perch, sole, pike and gilt head, prepared with fresh herbs. *Closed Tues.*

Lonato ✉ 25017

Stylish **Da Oscar**, Via Barcuzzi 16, ✆ 030 913 0409 (*moderate*) serves ambitious dishes that score high on the palate and sometimes come up trumps: folks drive from far and wide for fresh potato, asparagus and pea soup, and lamb cutlets with thyme. *Closed Mon and Tues lunch; open evenings only in the summer, also closed two weeks in Jan and Nov.*

Entertainment and Nightlife

On summer nights, Desenzano becomes the vortex of one of the hottest scenes in north Italy. A Liberty villa at Via Da Molin 99 houses the **Stesso Senso Club**, where posing with Italian TV celebs is part of the fun; different theme nights from Wednesday to Sunday. Just south of the A4 in Lonato you can bop the night away (*except on Mondays and Wednesdays*) at the 'Greatest Disco in the World,' the **Nuovo Genux** on four dance floors, with 1,000,000 watts of light and sound and 150 computer-controlled fountains.

Czech beer, spaghetti and live music heat up the vast **Rising Sun Pub** opposite the Genux (*open 8pm–3am; closed Mon*). Less than 1km from the A4's Casello di Sirmione exit, two other discos attract punters from as far away as Milan and Venice: on Friday nights for the experimental/ progressive **Mazoom** 'the Moment of Impact!' and on Saturday nights for underground and garage sounds at **Le Paisir** 'Sound Sitting Room!' You've been warned.

South Lake Garda: Sirmione and Around

> *Sweet Sirmio! thou, the very eye*
> *Of all peninsulas and isles,*
> *That in our lakes of silver lie,*
> *Or sleep enwreathed by Neptune's smiles*

Catullus

Few towns enjoy the dramatic position of Sirmione, strung out along the narrow 4km-long peninsula that pierces Lake Garda's broad bottom like a pin. Lake views and a lush growth of palms, cypresses and parasol pines keep the medieval core from ever feeling claustrophic, even when it's heaving with people, as it tends to be in season: to find fewer daytrippers and more of the atmosphere that inspired Catullus, Dante, Goethe, Byron, and later Pound and Joyce, who met here, come before June or after September.

Tourist Information

Sirmione, Viale Marconi 2, ✆ 030 916 114, ✉ 030 916 222. **Peschiera del Garda**, Piazza Bettelloni, ✆ 045 755 0381.

The Rocca Scaligera to the Grotte di Catullo

Large car parks signal the entrance into the historic centre; only the vehicles of residents and hotel guests are permitted into town over the bridge of the fairy-tale castle, the **Rocca Scaligera**. Built by Mastino I della Scala, *signore* of Verona in the 13th century, it is entirely surrounded by a moat where mallards and swans bob and float (*open April–Oct 9–6 (may change summer 1999), Nov–Mar 9–12.30; adm*). Palms fill the courtyard; Dante slept here, but there's not much to see inside, though the views of lake and town from its swallowtail battlements and lofty tower are lovely. A second set of battlements protect the 15th-century church of **Santa Maria Maggiore**, overlooking a slender beach; note the reused Roman capital on the porticoed façade and the unusual pastel brick ceiling. Nearby begins the *passeggiata panoramica* that skirts the peninsula's east shore.

Rome's greatest lyric poet, Catullus, was born in Verona in 84 BC, only to die some 30 years later in the fever of a broken heart. In between passionate bouts in the Palatine home of his fickle mistress, 'Lesbia', he would cool his heels at the family villa at Sirmione. But chances are the great late 1st-century BC villa at the very tip of the rocky promontory known as the **Grotte di Catullo** wasn't it—only a millionaire could have afforded such an opulent pleasure dome. The superb site (*open daily Mar–Oct Tues–Sat 8.30–7, Sun 9–6; Nov–Feb Tues–Sat 8.30–4.30, Sun 9–4.30; adm exp*) is romantic with a capital R, set among ancient olives and rosemary hedges. Rigidly rectangular, symmetrical and vast (550ft by 310ft), the villa was flanked by porticoes on the east and west (as well as a long underground cryptoporticus on the west), while a belvedere on the north end overlooked the lake. Of this only the supporting hall called the Aula dei Giganti survives, strewn with enormous chunks; some of the ceilings here once stood over 55ft high. Olive trees trace the villa's main residential section which collapsed in the 4th century. A huge cistern, 141ft long, fed the large bath complex and heated pool. A small **museum** on the site contains fragments of vases, lamps, spearheads and other bits salvaged from the ruins.

Near the Grotte di Catullo, standing alone on the peninsula's highest point, the Romanesque **San Pietro in Mavino** was built of scavenged Roman bricks; inside are frescoes from the 13th–16th centuries by the school of Verona. Also near here is the thermal **Stablimento Termale Catullo**, where a pipe brings up steaming sulphuric water from the bottom of the lake, just the thing for respiratory ailments. The medieval lanes in the very centre have been given over to boutiques, bars and pizzerias; if you want to escape, there are good places to swim off the rocks along the west shore.

Peschiera del Garda, Gardaland and the Sigurtà Gardens

East of Sirmione, Peschiera is an old military town, near the mouth of the River Mincio that drains Lake Garda. Its strategic position has caused it to be fortified since Roman times, though the imposing walls that you see today are actually 16th-century Venetian, reinforced by the Austrians when Peschiera was one of the corners of the empire's 'Quadrilateral'. Today Peschiera is mainly a transit point to the lake from the Veneto but its massive purifying plant, the ultimate destination of what goes down every drain in every lakeside town (thanks to an underwater pipeline) still helps it to fulfil its ancient role as a defender, this time of the lake's status as the cleanest in all Europe.

Here, too, you can treat the children—at **Gardaland**, ✆ 045 644 9777, Italy's largest, and most massively popular, Disney-clone theme park with a green dinosaur named Prezzemolo or 'Parsley' as official mascot (*open late Mar–June and Sept–Oct daily 9.30–6.30; July–mid-Sept daily 9am–midnight; adm; children under a metre high free*). Attractions include the Magic Mountain roller coaster, Colorado boat ride, the Valley of the Kings, an African safari, some fairly scary space rides, a pirate ship, robots, a dolphin show and 'The World Of Barbie' (Her Sublime Plasticity continues to exert a subliminal effect on Italian womanhood: every little Italian girl owns at least ten Barbies).

The region south of Peschiera is known for its flavourful dry white wine, Bianco di Custoza, and for the pretty gardens and groves that line the Mincio all the way to the lakes of Mantua. The most amazing of these, the **Sigurtà Gardens**, 8km from Peschiera (*open Mar–Nov daily 9–6; adm)* were the 40-year project of Dr Count Carlo Sigurtà, 'Italy's Capability Brown'—who, granted water rights from the Mincio, used them to transform a barren waste of hills into 500,000 square metres of Anglo-Italian gardens along 7km of lanes; 13 parking areas have been provided on the route so you can get out and walk as much as you like. The Sigurtà Gardens are near **Valeggio sul Mincio**, an attractive town in its own right, with a castle and a bridge built by the Visconti, and a pair of competing water fun parks that stay open until midnight.

Sirmione ✉ 25019

If you're driving, have the confirmation of your reservation handy to get past the castle guards.

A neoclassical villa built by an Austrian general and converted into a hotel in 1954, ★★★★★**Villa Cortine**, Via Grotte 12, ✆ 030 990 5890, 📠 030 916 390 (*very expensive*) offers an immersion in romance, and perhaps the rarest amenity in the town—tranquillity. Its century-old garden occupies almost a third of the entire peninsula, with exotic flora, venerable trees, statues and fountains running down to the water's edge. Inside, all is plush and elegant under frescoed ceilings and perhaps a bit too exclusive, but it's ideal for a break from the real world, with private beach and dock, pool and tennis court. *Open April–Oct*. Another top choice, ★★★★★**Grand Hotel Terme**, Viale Marconi 7, ✆ 030 916 261, 📠 030 916 568 (*very expensive*) has a private beach, pool, gym and a full health and beauty programme, as well as a lovely lakeside restaurant. *Open April–Oct*.

In the heart of the old town, ★★★**Catullo**, Piazza Flaminia 7, ✆ 030 990 5811, 📠 030 916 444 (*expensive*) was refurbished in 1991, offering good-sized rooms with beautiful views and all modern amenities. *Open April–Nov*. Also in the centre, in a medieval building, ★★★★ **Eden**, Piazza Carducci 18, ✆ 030 916 481, 📠 030 916 483 (*moderate*) has been beautifully remodelled with fine marbles, and co-ordinated bedrooms with princely bathrooms, TV and air-conditioning. Unusually, it does not have a restaurant. *Open Mar–Oct*.

Near the castle, **★★Grifone**, Via Bocchio 4, ✆ 030 916 014, 📠 030 916 548 (*cheap*) is more attractive on the outside than in the rooms, but has a great location. *Open April–Oct.* **★★Speranza**, Via Casello 6, ✆ 030 916 116, 📠 030 916 403 (*cheap*) has all the fittings of a three-star hotel, including air-conditioning and marble bathrooms, but at significantly lower prices. *Open Mar–Nov.*

One of Garda's finest restaurants is near the base of Sirmione's peninsula: the classy **Vecchia Lugana**, Via Verona 71, ✆ 030 919 012 (*expensive*). The menu changes to adapt with the seasons and the food, based very much on lake fish, is exquisite, prepared with a light and wise touch—try the divine asparagus tagliatelle in a ragoût of lake fish, or the mixed grill of fish and meat; menus at L60,000 and L80,000 (*closed Mon eve and Tues*).

Near the Scaliger castle **La Rucola**, Via Strentelle 7, ✆ 916 326 (*expensive*) has a great atmosphere to go with its particularly flavoursome specialities, many dishes judiciously prepared with fruit. *Closed Thurs.* **Marboré**, Via Vittorio Emanuele 71, ✆ 030 916 409 (*cheap*) serves tasty pizzas and simple L24,000 menus in a pretty garden by the lake. *Closed Mon.*

Lake Garda: Up the West Shore

The west or Lombard shore of Garda is its most prestigious, with the oldest villas (one, belonging to Gabriele d'Annunzio, is the lake's biggest attraction after Gardaland) and grandest hotels. The climate is especially benign between Gardone Riviera and Limone.

Tourist Information

Salò: Lungolago Zanardelli 39, ✆ 0365 21423.
Gardone Riviera: Corso Repubblica, ✆ 0365 20347.
Gargnano: Piazza Feltrinelli 2, ✆ 0365 712 224.

The Valtenesi and Salò

Six km north of Desenzano, **Padenghe** marks the beginning of a peaceful olive- and wine-growing and white-truffle-finding corner of gently rolling hills called the Valtenesi. The old Valtenesi villages—Padenghe, but especially **Moniga**—preserve tracts of their walls going back to the 10th century. The Valtenesi's fortress, the **Rocca di Manerba**, sits high on the headland that extends into the lake like a great wolf's muzzle; under the big rock the shore, with Mediterranean flora and beaches, is now a natural park. The Rocca looks out over the **Isola di Garda**, the lake's largest island. When its monastery, visited by St Francis in his peregrinations, fell into ruins in the 19th century, it provided the foundations for a white confectionery neo-Venetian-Gothic-style palace, owned by the Borghese; one scion of the family, Scipione, won the famous race from Peking to Paris in the early days of the automobile. With its green trees trailing over the water, the island is as tantalizing as it is off limits, unless you can wheedle an invite from the Count.

On the north edge of the Valtenesi, **Salò** (the Roman *Salodium*) is traditionally Garda's 'capital', the seat of the Venetian magistrates. It enjoys a privileged location, set on a deep bay with a grand promenade, lit by street lamps that resemble Minoan sacral horns. In 1901 an earthquake shook it hard, but architecturally at least it was an auspicious moment for a disaster, and when Saló was rebuilt it was with a Liberty-style flourish. Some fine older buildings survived the quake, including a late Gothic **cathedral** with a Renaissance portal of 1509 stuck in its unfinished façade; among the paintings by Romanino and Moretto there's a golden polyptych by Paolo Veneziano kept securely (but hard to see properly) under glass.

The Venetian-style Loggia della Magnifica Patria at Lungolago Zanardelli 55 contains the tourist office and a small **Museo Civico Archeologico**, with items found in Salodium's necropolis; **L'Ateneo**, in the Renaissance Palazzo Fantoni, contains a collection of 13th-century manuscripts and early printed books. At Via Fantoni 49, the **Museo del Nastro Azzuro** (*open Easter–Sept daily 5–7, Sun 10–1; closed Thurs*) is dedicated to 'blue-ribboned' Italian military figures from 1797 to 1945: a collection of uniforms, weapons and portraits, and a room on the Fascist period and the 'Republic of Salò' (or Italian Social Republic) of 1943–5.

Götterdämmerung, Italian-style

Italy's period of paralysis and confusion after the Allied landings in July 1943 was one of the tragedies of the war. The King and the Fascist Grand Council had deposed and arrested Mussolini, and not long after signed an armistice with the Allies. But they did nothing to defend Italy from the inevitable, and while the political and military leaders dithered and blundered in Rome, German divisions poured over the Alps to seize control of the country. The Italians found themselves caught in the middle, and their soldiers were faced with a choice of joining the Nazis, a risky desertion, or prison and forced labour.

Mussolini didn't proclaim the Italian Social Republic; the order to do it came from Hitler's field headquarters in East Prussia. Hitler sent an SS commando team in a tiny plane to rescue the *Duce* from the ski hotel in the Abruzzo where the Rome government had stashed him. (They might have just sent a car, so poorly was he guarded, but Hitler had just at that time decided on a major propaganda campaign to glorify the SS, and the business was built up into a heroic exploit.) The Nazis cleaned Mussolini up and got him a shiny new uniform; they took him up north to meet Hitler and trotted him past the newsreel cameras, and then found a nice lakeside villa for him in Salò, which they had decided upon for the capital of the new puppet republic. In the next villa over lived the German ambassador.

Salò was a place where the war seemed far away. Wealthy Milanese came whenever they could; their sons, who had somehow managed to avoid conscription, played tennis and lounged in the cafés in their white jackets. Some of the Republic's ministries were occupying other villas around the lake, but there was little work for them to do; the Germans were running everything. The SS had a strong presence around Milan and the lakes, busying themselves in earnest with the round-up of Jews that began in October 1943; when there wasn't enough room on the train they simply shot those left over and threw the bodies into Lake Maggiore.

For the fortunates back in Salò, life before 5pm meant a dreary, unavoidable bit of attention to business. At one meeting, Mussolini and his men demanded aid for the thousands of Italians in the north who had been injured or made homeless by the war; the German ambassador looked at the figures and politely noted that there were more casualties, due to the bombings, in his own city. After 5pm, all could retreat into a dream-world of pleasure; the Germans held noisy, drug-fuelled orgies, with car-loads of girls brought in from Milan, while the Italian officials conducted more discreet liaisons with their mistresses in their villas. Mussolini met Clara Petacci every day at five o'clock in a room of his villa called the Sala dello Zodiaco, with constellations painted on the ceiling. The *Duce* told somebody that she was a pain, always bothering him about jobs or favours for her family. Occasionally there would be spectacles to relieve the routine and feed the newsreel cameras: carefully staged rallies, or parades of Germans and die-hard Fascist 'Black Brigades', singing as they passed the reviewing stand the hit tune of the day, 'Auf Wiedersehen'.

Towards the end, in 1945, the atmosphere crossed over into the truly surreal. Mussolini was losing his grip, and babbled to his few confidants about the secret weapons the Nazis were getting ready—an atomic bomb, and V-rockets numbered all the way up to V-9 and V-10; Hitler had told him all about them. The Italians would do even better; Marconi had invented an electronic Death Ray before he died, Mussolini said, and he had the plans in his pocket. And if the worst happened there was the Fascists' last redoubt, up in the mountainous Valtellina, where he would lead 30,000 true believers in a fight to the death, the memory of which would live forever (such a project was actually started, but most of the men in the Valtellina eventually got tired of waiting for the *Duce* and went home). In January 1945 Mussolini gave his last public speech at the Teatro Lirico in Milan. He spoke gravely of the challenges facing the 'revolution', and at the end received tumultuous applause when he promised a steadfast determination that would surely lead to final victory. Cheering crowds thronged the streets outside to see him off.

By that time, there were some 300,000 *partigiani* operating in the north, and many rural areas were already free. On 25 April, Mussolini arranged a meeting with resistance leaders at the archbishop's palace in Milan. He wanted to cut a deal; they offered him a fair trial. The *Duce*'s bags were already packed, but he hesitated long enough near the Swiss border for the resistance to win over the border guards. On 28 April, he wrapped himself in a discarded Luftwaffe overcoat and marched off, Clara by his side, with a column of retreating Germans on the road towards Austria; the *partigiani* caught up with him and shot him and Clara near Dongo, on Lake Como, and then took him back to Milan for his final public appearance, dangling upside down from the roof of a petrol station on Piazzale Loreto.

Where to Stay and Eating Out

Manerba ✉ 25080

Capriccio, Piazza S Bernardo 6, ✆ 0365 551 124 (*expensive*) is a beautiful family-run restaurant with a terrace looking out on to soft rolling hills, where you can tuck into a novel variety of dishes—sturgeon in a tartare of coriander to start, or the mouthwatering *sachertorte* with strawberries for dessert. *Open for lunch by appointment only; closed Tues in winter.*

Salò ✉ 25087

One of loveliest places to stay on the lakes, ★★★★**Laurin**, Viale Landi 9, ✆ 0365 22022, ✆ 0365 22382 (*expensive*) is an enchanting Liberty-style villa converted into a hotel in the 1960s, retaining the elegant period décor in the public rooms.The charming grounds include a swimming pool and beach access. *Closed Jan.*

At the ★★★★**Duomo**, Lungolago Zanardelli 63, ✆ 0365 21026, ✆ 0365 21028 (*expensive*) the first-floor rooms are the ones to request—all lead out to a huge geranium-laden balcony overlooking the lake. Rooms are big and modern, and there's a fine restaurant. Similar if less exalted accommodation is available at the lakefront

★★★**Benaco**, Lungolago Zanardelli 44, ✆ 0365 20308, ✆ 0365 20724 (*moderate*), which also boasts a good restaurant. ★★★**Vigna**, Lungolango Zanardelli 62, ✆ 0365 520144, ✆ 0365 520516 (*moderate*) has rooms that are none too individual, but comfortable and modern, and views that really steal the show. For a good, reasonably priced and traditional meal try the **Trattoria alla Campagnola**, Via Brunati 11, ✆ 0365 22153 (*moderate*). Garden-fresh vegetables are served with every dish, the pasta is homemade, and they make great use of wild mushrooms in season.

Another extremely good value place is the **Osteria dell'Orologio**, Via Butterini 26, ✆ 0365 290 158 (*cheap*), an old, beautifully restored inn where you can indulge in local dishes such as '*tonno del Garda*' (pork cooked in wine and spices), lake fish and skewered wild birds. *Closed Wed.*

The same family run the slightly more expensive **Antica Trattoria delle Rose**, Via Gasparo da Salò 33, ✆ 0365 43220 (*moderate*). Go for *pasta e fagioli*, or lake fish with fresh pasta. *Closed Wed.*

Gardone Riviera and D'Annunzio's Folly

North of Salò, sumptuous old villas, gardens and hotels line the lovely promenade at **Gardone Riviera**. Gardone became the most fashionable resort on Lake Garda in 1880, when a German scientist noted the almost uncanny consistency of its climate. One place that profits most from this mildness is the **Giardino Botanico Hruska** (*open Mar–Oct daily 9–6.30; adm*), a botanical garden with 8000 exotic blooms and plants growing between imported tufa cliffs and artificial streams.

Above the garden waits **Il Vittoriale degli Italiani**, the home of Gabriele D'Annunzio (1863–1938). This luxurious Liberty-style villa in an incomparable setting, designed for a German family by Giancarlo Maroni, was presented to the extravagant writer by Mussolini in 1925, ostensibly as a reward from a grateful nation for his patriotism and heroism during the First World War, but also as a sop to keep the volatile, unpredictable poet out of politics. D'Annunzio immediately dubbed his new home 'Il Vittoriale' after Italy's victory over Austria in 1918; with Maroni's help he recreated it in his own image, leaving posterity a remarkable mix of eccentric beauty and self-aggrandizing kitsch.

More Italian than Any Other Italian

 Born Gaetano Rapagnetta into a very modest family in the Abruzzo, the self-styled angel Gabriel of the Annunciation (one wonders what he would have thought of Madonna!) went on to become the greatest Italian poet of his generation, a leading figure in the fin-de-siècle Decadent school who managed to have nearly all of his works placed on the pope's Index. But Gabriele D'Annunzio scoffed at the idea that the pen is mightier than the sword. A fervent right-wing nationalist, he clamoured for Italy to enter the First World War, and when it was over he was so furious that Fiume (Rijeka), a town promised as a prize to Italy, was actually to be ceded by the Allies to Yugoslavia that he took matters into his own hands and invaded Fiume with a band of volunteers (September 1919). In Italy D'Annunzio was proclaimed a hero, stirring up a diplomatic furore before being forced to withdraw in January 1921.

Luigi Barzini has described D'Annunzio as 'perhaps more Italian than any other Italian' for his love of gesture, spectacle, and theatre—what can you say about a man who would boast that he had once dined on roast baby? Yet for the Italians of his generation, no matter what their politics, he exerted a powerful influence in thought and fashion; he seemed a breath of fresh air, a new kind of 'superman', hard and passionate yet capable of writing exquisite, intoxicating verse; the spiritual father of the technology-infatuated Futurists, ready to destroy the old bourgeois *Italia vile* of museum curators and parish priests and create in its stead a great modern power, the 'New Italy'.

He lived a life of total exhibitionism—extravagantly, decadently and beyond his means, at every moment the trend-setting, aristocratic aesthete, with his borzois and melodramatic affairs, with the actress 'the Divine' Eleanora Duse and innumerable other loves (preferably duchesses). Apparently he thought the New Italians should all be as flamboyant and clever, and he disdained the corporate state of the Fascists. For Mussolini, the still-popular old nationalist was a loose cannon and an acute embarrassment, and he decided to pension him off into gilded retirement on Lake Garda, correctly calculating that the gift of the villa would appeal to his delusions of grandeur.

The Tour

Open Oct–Mar Tues–Sun 9–12.30 (ticket office closes an hour earlier) and 2–6.30, Sat and Sun only until 6; April–Sept 8.30am–8pm; adm exp; you can buy a cheaper ticket for the museum and grounds only; expect queues.

D'Annunzio made the Vittoriale his personal monument, suspecting (correctly) that one day crowds would come tramping through the estate to marvel at his cleverness and taste, if not sheer acquisitiveness: the villa is a pack rat's paradise, its every nook and cranny filled with quirky, desirable and hilarious junk, more or less all left as it was in 1938, when a sudden brain haemorrhage put an abrupt end to the poet's hoarding.

Once past the entrance gate to the Vittoriale, note the double arch, a copy of the bridge pier on the Piave, where the Italians held the line against the Central Powers in 1917–18. Like many a jerk, D'Annunzio loved fast cars and two of his favourites are parked near the courtyard—one is the the 1913 Fiat he drove in triumph to Fiume. The tour begins with the 'cool reception' room for guests D'Annunzio disliked—it's austere and formal, compared to the comfy one reserved for favourites. When Mussolini came to call he was entertained in the former; D'Annunzio escorted the dictator over to the mirror and made him read the inscription he had placed above: 'Remember that you are of glass and I of steel'. Perhaps you can make it out if your eyes have had time to adjust to the gloom. Like Aubrey Beardsley and movie characters usually played by Vincent Price, D'Annunzio hated the daylight and had the windows painted over, preferring low-watt electric lamps.

The ornate organs in the music room and library were played by his young American wife, who gave up a promising musical career to play for his ears alone. His bathroom, in spite of 2000 pieces of bric-a-brac, somehow manages to find space for the tub. In his bedroom, the Stanza della Leda, he kept a cast of Michelangelo's slave, the naughty bits veiled by a skirt. In his spare bedroom, adorned with leopard skins, there's a coffin he liked to lie in to think cosmic thoughts. He designed the entrance to his study low so that visitors would have to bow as they entered; here he kept a bust of Duse, but covered, to prevent her memory from distracting his genius. The dining room, with its bright movie-palace sheen, is one of the more delightful rooms; but D'Annunzio didn't care much for it and left his guests here to dine on their own with his pet tortoise, which he had had embalmed in bronze after it expired from indigestion, to remind his visitors of the dangers of overeating.

In the **museum**, located in the Art Deco Casa Schifamondo ('escape the world') that D'Annunzio built but never moved into, you can ponder his death bed and death mask, more casts of Michelangelo's sculptures, paintings and biographical memorabilia. In the adjacent auditorium hangs the biplane our hero used to fly over Vienna to drop propaganda leaflets in the War. The recently opened **private garden** occupies an 18th-century lemon terrace, where a magnolia grove contains D'Annunzio's war memorial, with a throne and stone

Il Vittoriale

benches for nationalist legionary ceremonies, which must have been a hoot. The open-air theatre, designed by Maroni after the ancient Greek theatre in Taormina, has a magnificent view from the top seats, stretching from Monte Baldo to Sirmione; in July and August it hosts D'Annunzio's plays. There's a nice surreal touch nearby: the prow of the battleship *Puglia* from the Fiume adventure, jutting out mast and all through a copse of cypresses. Walk above this to the **mausoleum**, the poet's last ego trip, a perverse wedding cake in glaring white travertine. Within three concentric stone circles, the sarcophagi of the Fiume legionnaires pay court to the plain tomb of D'A himself, raised up on columns high above the others like a pagan sun-king, closer to his dark star than anyone else, the whole in hellish contrast to the mausoleum's enchanting setting.

Toscolano-Maderno and Gargnano

The double-barrelled *comune* of Toscolano-Maderno has one of the finest beaches on Lake Garda, a 9-hole golf course and the car ferry to Torri. Toscolano traces its origins to the Etruscans, and Maderno was the site of *Benacum*, the main Roman town on the lake. In the 12th century, many of Maderno's Roman bits were incorporated into the extremely elegant **Sant'Andrea**, a Romanesque beauty benignly restored in the 16th century by St Charles Borromeo; inside, the capitals, some retaining their original paint, are sculpted with fighting animals. The 18th-century parish church has a *Sant'Ercolano* by Paolo Veronese and a *Martyrdom of St Andrew* by Palma Giovane. Toscolano was the chief manufacturer of nails for Venice's galleys and had a famous printing press in the 15th century; to this day the Cartiera di Toscolano papermill is Garda's largest industry. The cool, green **Valle delle Cartiere**—the valley of the papermills—is a favourite excursion.

To the north, **Gargnano**, the last town before the towering cliffs, means sailing. Since 1950 it has hosted the colourful Centomiglia regatta the second week of September, attracting yachts from as far away as the US, New Zealand and Australia. The Franciscans were among the first to live here in the 13th century; their church has been baroqued inside and the cloister's capitals have carvings of lemons and oranges, a reminder of the tradition that the Franciscans were the first to cultivate citrus in Europe. In the 14th century Gargnano was the capital of the villages in the hinterland proudly known as the Magnifica Patria, and in 1866 an Austrian flotilla sailed up and fired cannons at the port; if you look closely you can see the scars. After the Borghese ranch on Isola di Garda, the largest villa on the lake is just south of Gargnano: the enormous 18th-century **Villa Bettoni** in Bogliaco, used as a set in a dozen films. In another villa, built for the publisher Feltrinelli (whose chain of bookstores is a blessing to the English-speaking traveller in Italy), the University of Milan runs summer courses for foreign students; a second Villa Feltrinelli was Mussolini's home during the Republic of Salò.

Where to Stay and Eating Out

Gardone Riviera ✉ 25083

Gardone Riviera and its suburb Fasano Riviera have competing Grand Hotels, both attract old pleasure domes. In Gardone, the ★★★★**Grand Hotel**, Via Zanardelli 72, ✆ 0365 290 220, ✉ 0365 290 221 (*very expensive*) with its 180 rooms was one of the largest resort hotels in Europe when built in 1881. It is still recognized as a landmark, and its countless chandeliers glitter as brightly as when Churchill stayed there in the late 1940s. Almost all the palatial air-conditioned rooms look on to the lake, where guests can luxuriate on the garden terraces, or swim in the heated outdoor pool or off the private sandy beach. The dining room and delicious food match the quality of the rooms. *Open mid-April–mid-Oct.*

Fasano's alternative, ★★★★**Fasano Grand Hotel**, ✆ 0365 20261, 🖷 0365 22695 (*very expensive*) was built in the early 19th century as a Habsburg hunting palace and converted into a hotel around 1900. Surrounded by a large park, it's furnished with *belle époque* fittings; there are tennis courts, a heated pool and private beach, and the restaurant is one of Lake Garda's best. *Open May–Oct.*

Another excellent choice, Fasano's ★★★★**Villa del Sogno**, Via Zanardelli 107, ✆ 0365 290 181, 🖷 0365 290 230 (*very expensive*) was its creator's neo-Renaissance 'Dream Villa' of the 1920s. Immersed in trees, there's a private beach 5 minutes' walk away and a pool in its flower-filled garden. *Open April–Oct.* A Liberty-style palace set in luxuriant gardens directly on the lake, ★★★**Villa Fiordaliso**, Corso Zanardelli 132, ✆ 365 20158, 🖷 0365 290 011 (*very expensive*) has only seven rooms, all finely equipped. You can request (for a price) the suite where Mussolini and his mistress Clara Petacci spent their last few weeks. Located in a serene park, with a private beach and pier, it also boasts an elegant restaurant, the best in Gardone, featuring classic Lombard dishes; the *menu degustazione* goes for L65,000 and 90,000. *Closed Nov, Mon.*

Less pricey choices include lakeside ★★★**Monte Baldo**, Via Zanardelli 104, ✆ 0365 20951, 🖷 0365 20952 (*moderate*), where a well-aged outer appearance hides a fully refurbished and modern stylish interior. The hotel also has a pool. *Open April–Oct.* Above the main road overlooking the lake, with a garden sheltering it from the traffic, ★★★**Bellevue**, Via Zanardelli ✆ 0365 20235, 🖷 0365 290 088 (*moderate*) offers modernized rooms, all with private bath. (*Open April–Oct*).

Halfway up to Il Vittoriale, ★**Hohl**, Via dei Colli 4, ✆ 0365 20160 (*moderate–cheap*) is another atmospheric 19th-century villa in a pleasant garden. None of the rooms has a bath, but they're quiet. In Fasano the modern ★★**Touring**, Via Zanardelli 147, ✆ 0365 21031 (*cheap*) is a solid year-round budget choice, all rooms with bath.

Gargnano ✉ 25084

In Villa, just outside Gargnano, ★★★**Baia d'Oro**, Via Gamberera 13, ✆ 0365 71171, 🖷 0365 72568 (*expensive*) is a small but charming old place on the lake front with an artistic inn atmosphere. It has a private beach and picturesque terrace; all rooms have baths. *Open mid-Mar–Oct.* ★★**Du Lac**, smack on the water at Via Colletta 21 in Villa, ✆ 0365 71107, 🖷 0365 72594 (*moderate*) is a salmon-tinted charmer: all rooms with bath and satellite TV. *Open April–mid Oct.* Near the port **La Tortuga**, Via XXIV Maggio 5, ✆ 71251 (*expensive*) is a celebrated gourmet haven, specializing in delicate dishes based on seasonal ingredients and lake fish, perfectly prepared; there are also delicious vegetable soufflés, innovative meat courses, mouth-watering desserts and fresh fruit sherbets, and an excellent wine and spirits cellar; menus at L65,000 to L95,000. *Closed Mon eve, Tues and mid Jan–Feb.*

Northern Lake Garda: Limone, Riva and Malcésine

The highest mountains embrace northern Lake Garda, and the consistent gusts of wind and air currents make the triangle between Limone, Riva and Malcésine the stuff that windsurfing dreams are made of; World Championship meets take place here on a regular basis, and the shores are well supplied with rentals and schools if you're inspired to give it a whirl. Expect to hear a lot of German as sunstarved Austrians, Swiss and Germans pour down here for ersatz Mediterranean weekends among the bougainvillaea and olives.

Tourist Information

Limone sul Garda, Piazzale A. De Gaspari, ✆ 0365 954 070, 🖷 0365 954 355; **Riva del Garda**, Giardini di Porta Orientale 8, ✆ 0464 554 444, 🖷 0464 520 308; **Arco**, Viale delle Palme 1, ✆ 0464 532 155, 🖷 0464 532 353.

Limone sul Garda

North of Gargnano the lake narrows, the cliffs plunge sheer into the water and the Gardesana road pierces tunnel after tunnel like a needle. In the morning, when the wind's up, windsurfers flit across the waves like a swarm of crazed one-winged butterflies. On weekends their cars are parked all along the road around **Campione**, a tiny hamlet huddled under the cliffs. For tremendous views, take one of the several turnings inland that wind precipitously up to the cliffs: to peaceful **Tignale**, with its church perched on the edge of a spectacular viewpoint, and **Tremósine**, atop a 1000ft precipice that dives down sheer into the blue waters below, looking across the lake to mighty Monte Baldo.

The inland route from Tremósine rejoins the lake and La Gardesana shore road at **Limone sul Garda**, a popular resort town with a teeny tiny port and a beach over 3km long. Its name comes from the Latin *limen* (border), although by happy coincidence Limone was one of the main citrus-producing towns on Lake Garda, and to this day its lemon terraces with their white square pillars are a striking feature of the landscape: D.H. Lawrence, who lived south of Limone for a spell, liked to see them as the ruins of ancient temples.

Of Lemons and Apolipoproteins

 Citrus fruit reached Italy from the subtropics of Asia by the first century AD, but it wasn't until the 13th century that Garda's first trees were introduced by the Franciscan monastery in Gargnano. Over the years, lemons and citrons became Garda's cash crops (citrons, lemons' close cousins, play an important ritual role in the Jewish Feast of the Tabernacle), but they die when the temperature goes below −3°C, as it does some 20 times a year around Garda. To keep the trees alive the south-facing, square-pillared lemon terraces evolved, their openings covered with wooden supports and glass between November and February. Even then gardeners had to keep a constant vigil, ready to light wood stoves when the mercury dropped. In the spring the trees were kept in a penumbra to delay the maturation of the fruit until summer, when demand was highest.

Lemon cultivation began to decline in the mid-19th century, with the unification of Italy (Sicily is the world's top producer of lemons) and the building of railways that transported the cheaper fruit to Garda's old continental markets. Nearly all of the lemon terraces that have survived are in Limone, Gargnano and Torri del Benaco, but only a few are kept up as a hobby; most are abandoned, or converted into vineyards or vegetable gardens. The citron distillery at Salò continues to produce brandy (*acqua di cedro*) but imports the citrons from the south.

Limone may no longer make lemonade, but in 1979 its inhabitants were discovered to make something even rarer and potentially more benefical for humanity—a protein in their blood known as Apolipoprotein A-1 Milano gene Limone. This protein miraculously purges fat from arteries, keeping the incidence of arteriosclerosis and heart disease to practically nil. Centuries of isolation, prior to the construction of the Gardesena road, helped to develop the protein in a limited gene pool. The discovery took the medical world by storm. Since 1979 Limone has hosted four congresses on its Apolipoprotein, as researchers seek to duplicate the town's magic protein into a serum for all.

Riva del Garda and Around

North of Limone the lake enters into the Trentino region, where the charming town of Riva sits snug beneath an amphitheatre formed by Monte Brione. An important commercial port for the bishops of Trento beginning in 1027, it was much sought and fought after through the centuries, ruled at various times by Verona, Milan and Venice before it was handed back to the bishop-princes of Trent in 1521. In 1703, during the War of the Spanish Succession, the French General Vendôme sacked it and all the surroundings, leaving only a ghost of the former town to be inherited by Napoleon in 1796.

With its long beaches and refreshing summer breezes, Riva revived as a resort during the days of Austrian rule (1813–1918) as the 'Southern Pearl on the Austro-Hungarian Riviera', a pearl especially prized by writers: Stendhal, Thomas Mann, D.H. Lawrence and Kafka were among its habitués. The centre of town, Piazza III Novembre, has a plain **Torre Apponale** (1220), where salt and grain were stored (*adm with the same ticket as the Museo Civico*) and the **Palazzo Pretorio**, built by Verona's Cansignorio della Scala in 1376, while the lake front was defended by the sombre grey bulk of the 12th-century castle, the **Rocca**, surrounded by a swan-filled moat. This now houses Riva's **Museo Civico** (*open Tues–Sun 9.30–6.30; July and Aug 9.30am–10.30pm, but hours change frequently*) with finds from the Bronze Age settlement at Lake Ledro, and six statue-stelae with human features from the 4th–3rd millennia BC, recently discovered; and from Roman Riva, as well as paintings, detached frescoes and sculpture gleaned from the surroundings. Riva's best church, the **Inviolata** (1603), was commissioned by the princely Madruzzo family of Trento from an unknown but imaginative Portuguese architect, who was given a free hand with the gilt and stucco inside; it also has paintings by Palma Giovane.

Only 3km north, a dramatic 287ft waterfall, the **Cascata del Varone**, crashes down a tight grotto-like gorge by the village of Varone; walkways allow visitors to become mistily intimate with thundering water (*opening times according to season; adm*). From the west side of Riva the exciting Ponale Road (N240) rises to **Lake Ledro**, noted not only for its scenery but also for the remains of a Bronze Age settlement (*c.* 2000 BC) of pile dwellings, discovered in 1929. One has been reconstructed near the ancient piles around **Molina di Ledro**, where the

Museo delle Palafitte houses the pottery, axes, daggers and amber jewellery recovered from the site (*open June–Sept daily 9–1 and 2–6; Oct and Nov, Tues–Sun 9–1 and 2–5; Dec Sat and Sun only 9–12 and 2–5; Mar–May, Tues–Sun 9–1 and 2–5*); the visit includes the new prehistoric botanical garden, dedicated to the plants cultivated by northern Italian farmers in the Bronze Age. From here you can continue to Lake Idro, through the shadowy gorge of the **Valle d'Ampola.**

One of the most dramatic sights on Garda is just behind Riva, in a natural balcony of hills overlooking the lake: the jagged crag and **Castello d'Arco**, dramatically crowned with ancient, dagger-sharp cypresses and the swallowtail crenellations. Built to defend the Valle di Sarca, the main funnel of northern armies into Italy, it was controlled by the cultured Counts of Arco, who tugged their forelocks at various stages to Verona, Milan and Trento. The path up is lovely if a bit tiring on a hot day and, despite the damage wrought by Vêndome's troops, there are a few frescoes left, including one of a courtly game of chess.

Arco itself, once heavily fortified and moated (the only surviving gate has a drawbridge) became, like Riva, a popular Austro-Hungarian resort in the 1800s, prized for its climate. In the centre, a baroque fountain dedicated to Moses splashes before the Palladian-inspired **Collegiata dell'Assunta** (1613): another Madruzzo project, this time by Trentino architect Giovanni Maria Filippi, who went onto become court architect of Emperor Rudolph II in Prague. There's a pretty public garden full of Mediterranean plants, near the equally pretty 19th-century **Casino**, while on the edge of town, off Via Lomego, the park laid out at the end of the 19th century by the Habsburg Archduke Albrecht has recently been restored and opened as an **Arboretum** (*open winter 9–4, summer 8–7; free*).

Dro, up the Sarca valley, is near the small lakes of Cavedine and Toblino, and **Le Sarche**, where an ancient glacier deposited the *marocche*, a remarkable field of enormous boulders. Olive trees as well as enormous chestnuts grow around **Drena**, at the bottom of Val Cavedine. The landmark here is the stark **Castello**, its keep rising up like a finger accusing heaven. Built by the Counts of Arco in 1175 and ruined by Vêndome in 1703, the lists, where knightly tournaments once took place, have been restored to host congresses and theatrical performances; the keep has splendid views, taking in the mighty *marocche*, and contains a museum of local artefacts, dating from the 18th century BC to the Renaissance (*open Nov–Mar, Sat, Sun 10–6; Apr–Oct daily exc Mon 10–6; adm*).

Torbole

Back on Garda's northeast shore, **Monte Baldo** looms over **Torbole** and the mouth of the Sarca, the most important river feeding the lake. An old fishing village and a pleasant resort, Torbole is famous in the annals of naval history. In 1437, during a war with the Visconti, the Venetians were faced with the difficulty of getting supplies to Brescia past the southern reaches of Lake Garda, then controlled by Milan. A Greek sailor made the suggestion that the Venetians sail a fleet of provision-packed warships up the Adige to its furthest navigable point, then transport the vessels over Monte Baldo on to Lake Garda. Anyone who has seen Herzog's film *Fitzcarraldo* will appreciate the difficulties involved, and the amazing fact that, with the aid of 2000 oxen, the 26 ships were launched at Torbole only 15 days after leaving the Adige. But after all that trouble, the supplies never reached Brescia. The same trick, however, perhaps even suggested by the same Greek, enabled Mohammed II to bring the Ottoman fleet into the upper harbour of Constantinople the following year and capture the city.

Limone ✉ 25010

★★★★**Le Palme**, ✆ 0365 954 681, 🖷 0365 954 120 (*moderate*) is housed in a pretty Venetian villa, preserving much of its original charm alongside modern amenities. Named after its two ancient palm trees, it has a fine terrace, tennis courts and a good fish restaurant. *Open April–Oct*. Above the centre ★★★**La Limonaia**, Via Sopino Alto 3, ✆ 0365 954 221, 🖷 0365 954 227 (*moderate*) enjoys a superb position, and has both an adult and a children's pool and playground. *Open Mar–Oct*. Agreeable and small, ★★★**Sogno del Benaco**, ✆ 0365 954 026, 🖷 0365 954 357 (*moderate*) has fairly standard rooms. Above the lake in an olive grove, ★**Mercedes**, Via Nanzello 12, ✆ 0365 954 073 (*cheap*) has a pool and lovely views. *Open April–Nov*.

Riva del Garda ✉ 38066

When German intellectuals from Nietzsche to Günter Grass have needed a little rest and relaxation in Italy they have for many decades flocked to Riva del Garda to check in at ★★★★**Hotel du Lac et du Parc**, Viale Rovereto 44, ✆ 0464 551 500, 🖷 0464 555 200 (*very expensive*), modernized, spacious, airy and tranquil, and set in a large lakeside garden; facilities include indoor and outdoor pools, a beach, sailing school, gym, sauna and tennis courts. *Open April–Oct*.

At the turn-of-the-century ★★★★**Grand Hotel Riva**, Piazza Garibaldi 10, ✆ 0464 521 800, 🖷 0464 552 293 (*expensive*), majestically positioned on the main square, 87 modern rooms look out over the lake; the rooftop restaurant combines fine food with incomparable views. It also has a private beach. *Open Mar–Oct*.

Right on the port in Riva's main square, ★★★★**Sole**, Piazza III Novembre, ✆ 0464 552 686, 🖷 0464 552 811 (*expensive*) has plenty of atmosphere and a beautiful terrace; most rooms have private baths and look out over the lake, though they vary widely in size and quality. Beside the harbour, ★★★**Centrale**, Piazza III Novembre 27, ✆ 0464 552 344, 🖷 0464 552 138 (*moderate*) has fully equipped, spacious rooms and bathrooms; almost as good and slightly cheaper, ★★★**Portici**, Piazza III Novembre 19, ✆ 0464 555 400, 🖷 0464 555 453 (*moderate*) has been competely refurbished and has modern rooms, all with bathrooms. *Open April–Oct*.

Built in 1400, ★**Restel de Fer**, Via Restel de Fer 10, ✆ 0464 553 481, 🖷 0464 552 798 (*low moderate*) has only five rooms and a good restaurant, with summer dining in the cloister. If you seek peace and quiet, a garden and pool in a panoramic spot, the family-run ★**Villa Moretti** 3km up in Varone, ✆ 0464 521 127, 🖷 0464 521 751(*cheap*) fits the bill. A good economy choice, ★**Villa Minerva**, Viale Roma 40, ✆ 0464 553 031 (*cheap*) is very pleasant and very popular. Riva's hostel, **Ostello Benacus**, Piazza Cavour 9, ✆ 0464 554 911, 🖷 0464 556 554, has beds for L19,000 per night. *Open Mar–Oct*.

Arco ✉ 38062

The modern ★★★★**Palace Hotel Città**, Viale Roma 10, ✆ 0464 531 100, 📠 0464 516 208 (*expensive in season*) has a balcony for every comfortable room, a pool, gym and slimming programme, and an optional vegetarian menu in the restaurant.

The best place to eat is the **Belvedere**, Via Serafini 2, ✆ 0464 516 144 (*cheap*), serving home-grown vegetables, local salami, fresh pasta and roast meats. *Closed Wed.* ★★★**Al Sole**, Via Sant'Anna 35, ✆ 0464 516 676, 📠 0464 518 585 (*moderate*) is a popular place to stay, and its restaurant also features local produce—try gnocchi with local prunes. *Closed Mon.*

Torbole ✉ 38069

Beautifully located on a spit of land with water on either side, the modern ★★★★**Lido Blu**, Via Foci del Sarca 1, ✆ 0464 505 180, 📠 0464 505 931 (*expensive*) is an excellent hotel for families, with a private beach, a gym, covered pool, windsurfing school and more.

You can dine well and romantically in a 19th-century Austrian fort in nearby Coe, at **Da Sergio**, ✆ 0464 505 301 (*expensive*), with a menu based on fish, accompanied by a fine wine list. *Closed Wed except in summer.*

Entertainment and Nightlife

Riva enjoys a hectic nightlife in season, much of it geared towards the hordes of Brits and Germans that invade the town. Many can be found in the **Lord Nelson Pub**, Viale Dante 91, ✆ 0464 55412, with its fairly authentic pub interior that becomes a disco in summer. For a more sedate evening's entertainment there are a couple of pleasant piano bars: **Bellavista**, Via Lungolago Verona, with a fairly calm atmosphere, except on Sunday evenings when karaoke takes over, and **Cantina Marchetti**, Piazza Marchetti, which stays open till 4am. The main place in town to get on down is **Tiffany** (*open all year 8pm–3am daily*), in a lovely position in the gardens leading down to the lake. There's usually live music on Fridays.

The East Shore: Malcésine to Bardolino

Garda's east shore belongs to the province of Verona. The silvery groves that grace the hills gave it its name, the Riviera degli Olivi, but its most outstanding feature is Monte Baldo, a massive ridge of limestone stretching 35km between Lake Garda and the Adige valley, cresting at 6989ft. Baldo is anything but bald: known as 'the botanical garden of Italy', it supports an astonishing variety of flora from Mediterranean palms to Arctic tundra; some 20 different flowers first discovered on Monte Baldo bear its name. The southern third of the Riviera degli Olivi is more grapey than olivey, the land of Bardolino.

Getting Around

APT buses run up the east coast from Verona and Peschiera as far as Riva, ✆ 045 800 4129. The car ferry crosses year-round from Torri del Benaco to Maderno.

Malcésine

South of Torbole, the forbidding cliffs of Monte di Nago hang perilously over the lake (but nevertheless attract scores of Lycra-bright human flies) before Malcésine, the loveliest town on the east shore. The Veronese lords always took care to protect this coast and in the 13th century, over the old Lombard castle, they built their magnificent **Rocca Scaligero** (*open April–Oct daily 9.30–8; winter Sat, Sun and hols only; adm*) rising up on a sheer rock over the water; inside are natural history exhibits, prehistoric rock etchings and a room dedicated to Goethe, who was accused of spying while sketching the castle. As well as the Scaliger castle, note the 16th-century **Palazzo dei Capitani del Lago** in the centre of Malcésine's medieval web of streets.

Every half-hour a pair of cableways run vertiginously up **Monte Baldo** (*L18,000 return; ✆ 045 740 0206 for information*); the views are ravishing, and the ski slopes at top are very popular with the Veronese. Malcésine also has pretty walks through the olives, and the shore has lovely places to swim and sunbathe, especially around the cove called the Val di Sogno. To the south, the hamlet of **Cassone** straddles the Aril, said to be the shortest river in the world—although the Fiumelatte on Lake Como begs to differ.

Torri del Benaco and Garda

Further south, past a steep, sparsely populated stretch of shore, there are two pretty towns, one on either side of Punta di San Vigilio, that played minor roles in the 10th century. The first, laid-back **Torri del Benaco**, owes its name to a rugged old tower in the centre which served as the headquarters of Berengario, the first king of Italy, in his 905 campaign against the Magyars. Later, it was defended by another **Scaliger castle** (1383), now a museum (*open April, May and Oct 9.30–12.30 and 2.30–6; June–Sept 9.30–1 and 4.30–7.30; adm*) with displays on olive oil, citrus, fishing, and rock engravings found in the area from *c.* 2000 BC, similar to those in the Valle

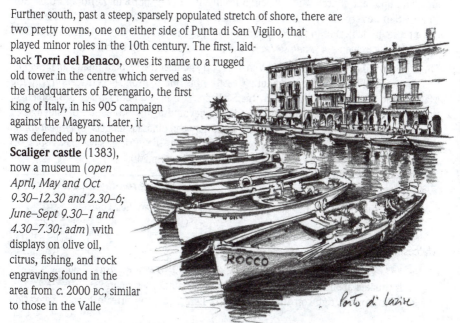

Porto di Lazise

Camonica. The church of **Santa Trinità** has good 14th-century Giottoesque frescoes. One of the many lovely walks in the region is up to the old village of **Albisano**, with beautiful views, then on to Crer and Brancolino, where the largest of Torri's prehistoric etchings can be seen, especially near Crer's church. The first recorded pleasure tourist in Torri was the great Medicean poet Poliziano in the 15th century; more recent fans have included André Gide and Stephen Spender.

Laurence Olivier, for his part, preferred enchanting **Punta di San Vigilio** with its Sirens' rocks, occupied by the beautiful **Villa Guarienti** by the great Venetian Renaissance architect Sammicheli, the old church of San Vigilio, and a 16th-century tavern, now an inn (*see* below). On the other side of a green soufflé of a headland, the Rocca del Garda, lies **Garda** itself, a fine old town with Renaissance palazzi and villas. It gave the lake its modern name, from the Lombard *Warthe*, 'the watch'. After Charlemagne defeated the Lombards, Garda became a county, and in its long-gone castle

the wicked Count Berenguer secretly held Queen Adelaide of Italy prisoner in 960, after he murdered her husband Lotario and she refused to marry his son. After a year she was discovered by a monk, who spent another year plotting her escape. She then received the protection of Otto I of Germany, who defeated Berenguer, married the widowed queen, and became Holy Roman Emperor.

Bardolino

To the south, Bardolino is synonymous with its lively red wine with a bitter cherry fragrance that goes so well with fishy *antipasti*; you can learn all you want to know about it at the Cantine Zeni's **Museo del Vino**, Via Costabella 9 (*open Mar–Oct daily 9–1 and 2–6*) or by following the wine route through the soft rolling hills, dotted with 19th-century villas. There are two important churches in Bardolino itself: the 8th-century **San Zeno** and the 12th-century **San Severo**, with frescoes and a landmark campanile. **Cisano**, south of Bardolino, has a museum dedicated to the Riviera degli Olivi's other cash crop, the **Museo dell'Olio d'Oliva**, Via Peschiera 54 (*open 9–12.30 and 3–7, closed Sun and Wed pm*).

The next town, **Lazise**, was the main Venetian port and near the harbour retains an ensemble of Venetian buildings, as well as another castle, this one built in the 9th century by the Magyars and taken over and rebuilt by the Scaligers. Just inland from Lazise, at Bussolengo, the **Parco Natura Viva** is a private foundation devoted to the protection of endangered species, and is divided into a zoo, with a tropical aviary and dinosaur models (*open year round 9–6*) and a drive-through safari park with animals from the African savannah (*open 15 Mar–Oct daily from 9.30*). Near here too is Gardaland— *see* p.240.

Where to Stay and Eating Out

Note that hotels on the east shore tend to be cheaper than their competitors across the lake.

Malcésine ✉ 37018

★★★★**Val di Sogno**, ✆ 045 740 0108, 📠 045 740 1694 (*expensive*) is situated about 3 minutes out of town in a beautiful setting in its own grounds right on the lake shore. There is a pool, private beach, a lakeside restaurant, and modern rooms with balconies. South of the centre, ****Park Hotel Querceto** at Campiano, ✆ 045 740 0344, 🖷 045 740 0848 (*expensive*) is a romantic place to stay, with lovely views, a pool, garden, and one of the best restaurants in the area, where the cuisine is light and tasty and adapted to the season. *Closed Nov–Mar*.

The inviting ***Vega**, Viale Roma, ✆ 045 657 0355, 🖷 045 740 1604 (*moderate*) offers big, modern rooms, all with satellite TV, minibar, safe and air-conditioning, and a private beach. ***Sailing Centre**, north of the centre at Molini Campagnola 3, ✆ 045 740 0055, 🖷 045 740 0392 (*expensive–moderate*) has a beach, sailing and windsurf schools, sauna, pool, satellite TV and more. *Open end Mar–end Oct*.

The beautifully positioned ***Malcésine**, Piazza Pallone, ✆ 045 740 0173, 🖷 045 657 0073 (*moderate, with some rooms at cheap rates*) has a garden with swimming terrace, pleasant rooms, and an excellent value if average restaurant. Right in the centre, you can sleep where Goethe snoozed in 1786 at the simple **San Marco**, Via Capitanato, ✆ 045 740 0115 (*cheap*); all rooms have a bath.

*Miralago**, Viale Roma, ✆ 045 740 0111 (*cheap*) is good budget option with lake view. By the Porto Vecchio, the **Trattoria da Pace** is a popular place with outdoor tables for seafood by the lake; around L40,000.

Torri del Benaco ✉ 37010

The comfortable **Gardesana**, Piazza Calderini 20, ✆ 045 722 5411, 🖷 045 722 5771 (*moderate*) is right on the harbour with splendid views of lake and castle. All rooms have baths, and breakfast and meals are served on the harbour patio when the weather is good. Near the lake, the plain and simple ***Al Caval**, Via Gardesana 186, ✆ 045 722 5666, 🖷 045 629 6570 (*moderate*) has a park and windsurf rentals, and the best restaurant in town (*moderate*), where the usual lake fish get special treatment in terrines and pasta dishes. *Closed Jan–Mar*.

Garda ✉ 37016

****Locanda San Vigilio**, the little inn hidden out by Sammichele's villa on Punta San Vigilio, ✆ 045 725 6688, 🖷 045 725 6551 (*very expensive*) has seven romantic rooms, a beach and delicious food. *Open mid-Mar–mid Oct*. A lakeside villa, ****Du Parc**, Via Marconi 3, ✆ 045 725 5343, 🖷 045 725 5642 (*expensive*) has recently been entirely refurbished and upgraded. *Open July–Aug*. The large, modern and quite luxurious ****Eurotel**, ✆ 045 6270 3333, 🖷 045 725 6640 (*moderate*) has a fine garden and pool. *Open Easter–Oct*.

An exceptionally well-priced hotel, ***Flora**, Via Giorgione 22 and 27, ✆/🖷 045 725 5348 (*moderate*) is situated slightly above the town in its own grounds, and is slick and modern with pine fittings, spacious rooms, all with balcony, and fantastic amenities—tennis, mini-golf and *two* pools. *Open Easter–Oct*. Next door to the Flora,

***Continental**, Via Giorgione 14, ✆ 045 725 5100, 🖷 045 725 6288 (*moderate*) is also in its own grounds and well-priced, but not quite as modern or comfortable— and with only one swimming pool. *Open Easter–Oct*. *Vittoria**, Lungolago Regina Adelaide, ✆ 045 725 5065, 🖷 045 627 0752 (*cheap*) is the best cheap hotel in

Garda, at the end of the lakefront walk. The rooms are big, and service is very friendly. *Open Easter–Oct.*

On the landward side of Garda, **Stafolet**, Via Poiano 12, ✆ 045 725 5427 (*moderate*) is worth asking directions to, for its wild duck and plump, spinach-filled *strangolopreti* ('priest stranglers'). Less distinguished, but good and cheap, **Al Pontesel**, Via Monte Baldo 71, ✆ 045 725 5419, features stout local cooking.

Bardolino ✉ 37011

You can dine well at **Aurora**, Via San Severo 18, ✆ 045 721 0038 (*moderate*) near the landmark church of San Zeno. Specialities include the produce of the lake, especially trout prepared in a variety of styles. *Closed Mon.*

Atrium: entrance court of a Roman house or early church.

Badia: *abbazia*, an abbey or abbey church.

Baldacchino: baldachin, a columned stone canopy above the altar of a church.

Basilica: a rectangular building, usually divided into three aisles by rows of columns. In Rome this was the common form for law courts and other public buildings, and Roman Christians adapted it for their early churches.

Calvary chapels: a series of outdoor chapels, usually on a hillside, that commemorate the stages of the Passion of Christ.

Campanile: a bell-tower.

Campanilismo: local patriotism; the Italians' own word for their historic tendency to be more faithful to their home towns than to the abstract idea of 'Italy'.

Camposanto: a cemetery.

Cardo: transverse street of a Roman *castrum*-shaped city.

Carroccio: a wagon carrying the banners of a medieval city and an altar; it served as the rallying point in battles.

Cartoon: the preliminary sketch for a fresco or tapestry.

Caryatid: supporting pillar or column carved into a standing female form; male versions are called *telamones*.

Castrum: a Roman military camp, always neatly rectangular, with straight streets and gates at the cardinal points. Later the Romans founded or refounded cities in this form, hundreds of which survive today (Pavia, Como, Brescia are clear examples).

Cavea: the semicircle of seats in a classical theatre.

Cenacolo: fresco of the Last Supper, often on the wall of a monastery refectory.

Ciborium: a tabernacle; the word is often used for large freestanding tabernacles, or in the sense of a *baldacchino* (q.v.).

Comune: commune, or commonwealth, referring to the governments of the free cities of the Middle Ages. Today it denotes any local government, from the Comune di Roma down to the smallest village.

Condottiere: the leader of a band of mercenaries in late medieval and Renaissance times.

Confraternity: a religious lay brotherhood, often serving as a neighbourhood mutual-aid and burial society, or following some specific charitable work (Michelangelo, for example, belonged to one that cared for condemned prisoners in Rome).

Cupola: a dome.

Architectural, Artistic & Historical Terms

Decumanus: street of a Roman *castrum*-shaped city parallel to the longer axis, the central, main avenue called the Decumanus Major.

Duomo: cathedral.

Forum: the central square of a Roman town, with its most important temples and public buildings. The word means 'outside', as the original Roman Forum was outside the first city walls.

Fresco: wall painting, the most important Italian medium of art since Etruscan times. It isn't an easy method; first the artist draws the *sinopia* (q.v.) on the wall. This is covered with plaster, but only a little at a time, as the paint must be on the plaster before it dries. Leonardo da Vinci's endless attempts to find clever short-cuts ensured that little of his work would survive.

Ghibellines: one of the two great medieval parties, the supporters of the Holy Roman Emperors.

Gonfalon: the banner of a medieval free city; the *gonfaloniere*, or flag bearer, was often the most important public official.

Guelphs: (see *Ghibellines*). One of the two great political factions of medieval Italy; supporters of the Pope.

Intarsia: work in inlaid wood or marble.

Narthex: the enclosed porch of a church.

Palazzo: not just a palace, but any large, important building (though the word comes from the imperial *palatium* on Rome's Palatine Hill).

Pantocrator: Christ 'ruler of all', a common subject for apse paintings and mosaics in areas influenced by Byzantine art.

Pietra Dura: rich inlay work using semi-precious stones, perfected in post-Renaissance Florence.

Pieve: a parish church, especially in the north.

Predella: smaller paintings on panels below the main subject of a painted altarpiece.

Presepio: a Christmas crib.

Putti: flocks of plaster cherubs with rosy cheeks and bums that infested much of Italy in the baroque era.

Quadriga: chariot pulled by four horses.

Quattrocento: the 1400s—the Italian way of referring to centuries (*duecento, trecento, quattrocento, cinquecento*, etc.).

Sinopia: the layout of a fresco (q.v.), etched by the artist on the wall before the plaster is applied. Often these are works of art in their own right.

Stigmata: a miraculous simulation of the bleeding wounds of Christ, appearing in holy men like St Francis in the 12th century, and Padre Pio of Puglia in our own time.

Telamon: see *Caryatid*.

Thermae: Roman baths.

Tondo: round relief, painting or terracotta.

Transenna: marble screen separating the altar area from the rest of an early Christian church.

Travertine: hard, light-coloured stone, sometimes flecked or pitted with black, sometimes perfect. The most widely used material in ancient and modern Rome.

Triptych: a painting, especially an altarpiece, in three sections.

Trompe l'œil: art that uses perspective effects to deceive the eye—for example, to create the illusion of depth on a flat surface, or to make columns and arches painted on a wall seem real.

Tympanum: the semicircular space, often bearing a painting or relief, located above the portal of a church.

The fathers of modern Italian were Dante, Manzoni and television. Each had a part in creating a national language from an infinity of regional and local dialects; the Florentine Dante, the first to write in the vernacular, did much to put the Tuscan dialect in the foreground of Italian literature. Manzoni's revolutionary novel, *I Promessi Sposi*, heightened national consciousness by using an everyday language all could understand in the 19th century. Television in the last few decades is performing an even more spectacular linguistic unification; although the majority of Italians still speak a dialect at home, school and work, their TV idols insist on proper Italian.

Perhaps because they are so busy learning their own beautiful but grammatically complex language, Italians are not especially apt at learning others. English lessons, however, have been the rage for years, and at most hotels and restaurants there will be someone who speaks some English. In small towns and out-of-the-way places, finding an Anglophone may prove more difficult. The words and phrases below should help you out in most situations, but the ideal way to come to Italy is with some Italian under your belt; your visit will be richer, and you're much more likely to make some Italian friends.

Italian words are pronounced phonetically. Every vowel and consonant is sounded. Consonants are the same as in English, except the 'c' which, when followed by an 'e' or 'i', is pronounced like the English 'ch' (*cinque* thus becomes cheenquay). Italian 'g' is also soft before 'i' or 'e' as in *gira*, or jee-ra. 'H' is never sounded; 'z' is pronounced like 'ts'. The consonants 'sc' before the vowels 'i' or 'e' becomes like the English 'sh' as in 'sci', pronounced shee; 'ch' is pronouced like a 'k' as in Chianti, kee-an-tee; 'gn' as 'ny' in English (*bagno*, pronounced ban-yo); while 'gli' is pronounced like the middle of the word million (Castiglione, pronounced Ca-stee-lyon-ay).

Vowel pronunciation is: 'a' as in English father; 'e' when unstressed is pronounced like 'a' in fate as in *mele*, when stressed can be the same or like the 'e' in pet (*bello*); 'i' is like the 'i' in machine; 'o', like 'e', has two sounds, 'o' as in hope when unstressed (*tacchino*), and usually 'o' as in rock when stressed (*morte*); 'u' is pronounced like the 'u' in June.

Language

The accent usually (but not always!) falls on the penultimate syllable. Also note that in the big northern cities, the informal way of addressing someone as you, *tu*, is widely used; the more formal *lei* or *voi* is commonly used in provincial districts.

Useful Words and Phrases

yes/no/maybe	*si/no/forse*	Good night	*Buona notte*
I don't know	*Non lo so*	Goodbye	*Arrivederla* (formal), *arrivederci, ciao* (informal)
I don't understand (Italian)	*Non capisco (italiano)*		
Does someone here speak English?	*C'è qualcuno qui che parla inglese?*	What?/Who?/Where?	*Che?/Chi?/Dove?*
		When?/Why?	*Quando?/Perché?*
Speak slowly	*Parla lentamente*	How?	*Come?*
Could you assist me?	*Potrebbe aiutarmi?*	How much?	*Quanto?*
Help!	*Aiuto!*	I am lost	*Mi sono smarrito*
Please	*Per favore*	I am hungry	*Ho fame*
Thank you (very much)	*(Molte) grazie*	I am thirsty	*Ho sete*
You're welcome	*Prego*	I am sleepy	*Ho sonno*
What do you call this in Italian?	*Come si chiama questo in italiano?*	I am sorry	*Mi dispiace*
		I am tired	*Sono stanco*
It doesn't matter	*Non importa*	I am ill	*Mi sento male*
All right	*Va bene*	Leave me alone	*Lasciami in pace*
Excuse me	*Mi scusi*	good	*buono/bravo*
Be careful!	*Attenzione!*	bad	*male/cattivo*
Nothing	*Niente*	It's all the same	*Fa lo stesso*
It is urgent!	*È urgente!*	fast	*rapido*
How are you?	*Come sta?*	slow	*lento*
Well, and you?	*Bene, e lei?*	big	*grande*
What is your name?	*Come si chiama?*	small	*piccolo*
Hello	*Salve* or *ciao* (both informal)	hot	*caldo*
		cold	*freddo*
Good morning	*Buongiorno* (formal hello)	up	*su*
		down	*giù*
Good afternoon, evening	*Buonasera* (also formal hello)	here	*qui*
		there	*lì*

Shopping, Service, Sightseeing

I would like...	*Vorrei...*	money	*soldi*
Where is/are...	*Dov'è/Dove sono...*	newspaper (foreign)	*giornale (straniero)*
How much is it?	*Quanto viene questo?*	pharmacy	*farmacia*
open	*aperto*	police station	*commissariato*
closed	*chiuso*	policeman	*poliziotto*
cheap/expensive	*a buon prezzo/caro*	post office	*ufficio postale*
bank	*banca*	sea	*mare*
beach	*spiaggia*	shop	*negozio*
bed	*letto*	room	*camera*
church	*chiesa*	tobacco shop	*tabaccaio*
entrance	*entrata*	WC	*toilette/bagno*
exit	*uscita*	men	*Signori/Uomini*
hospital	*ospedale*	women	*Signore/Donne*

Time

What time is it?	*Che ore sono?*	today	*oggi*
month	*mese*	yesterday	*ieri*
week	*settimana*	tomorrow	*domani*
day	*giorno*	soon	*fra poco*
morning	*mattina*	later	*dopo/più tardi*
afternoon	*pomeriggio*	It is too early	*È troppo presto*
evening	*sera*	It is too late	*È troppo tardi*

Days

Monday	*lunedì*	Friday	*venerdì*
Tuesday	*martedì*	Saturday	*sabato*
Wednesday	*mercoledì*	Sunday	*domenica*
Thursday	*giovedì*		

Numbers

one	*uno/una*	twenty	*venti*
two	*due*	twenty-one	*ventuno*
three	*tre*	twenty-two	*ventidue*
four	*quattro*	thirty	*trenta*
five	*cinque*	thirty-one	*trentuno*
six	*sei*	forty	*quaranta*
seven	*sette*	fifty	*cinquanta*
eight	*otto*	sixty	*sessanta*
nine	*nove*	seventy	*settanta*
ten	*dieci*	eighty	*ottanta*
eleven	*undici*	ninety	*novanta*
twelve	*dodici*	hundred	*cento*
thirteen	*tredici*	one hundred & one	*centouno*
fourteen	*quattordici*	two hundred	*duecento*
fifteen	*quindici*	one thousand	*mille*
sixteen	*sedici*	two thousand	*duemila*
seventeen	*diciassette*	million	*milione*
eighteen	*diciotto*	a thousand million	*miliardo*
nineteen	*diciannove*		

Transport

airport	*aeroporto*	port station	*stazione marittima*
automobile	*macchina*	railway station	*stazione ferroviaria*
bus/coach	*autobus/pullman*	seat (reserved)	*posto (prenotato)*
bus stop	*fermata*	ship	*nave*
customs	*dogana*	taxi	*tassì*
platform	*binario*	ticket	*biglietto*
port	*porto*	train	*treno*

Travel Directions

I want to go to...	*Desidero andare a...*	Have a good trip	*Buon viaggio!*
How can I get to...?	*Come posso andare a...?*	near	*vicino*
		far	*lontano*
Do you stop at...?	*Ferma a...?*	left	*sinistra*
Where is...?	*Dov'è...?*	right	*destra*
How far is it to...?	*Quanto siamo lontani da...?*	straight ahead	*sempre diritto*
		forward	*avanti*
When does the ... leave?	*A che ora parte ... ?*	backwards	*indietro*
What is the name of this station?	*Come si chiama questa stazione?*	north	*nord*
When does the next ... leave?	*Quando parte il prossimo...?*	south	*sud*
		east	*est/oriente*
From where does it leave?	*Da dove parte?*	west	*ovest/occidente*
		round the corner	*dietro l'angolo*
How long does the trip take...?	*Quanto tempo dura il viaggio?*	crossroads	*bivio*
		street/road	*strada*
How much is the fare?	*Quant'è il biglietto?*	square	*piazza*

Driving

bicycle	*bicicletta*	motorbike/scooter	*motocicletta/Vespa*
breakdown	*guasto* or *panne*	narrow	*stretto*
bridge	*ponte*	no parking	*sosta vietata*
car hire	*noleggio macchina*	parking	*parcheggio*
danger	*pericolo*	petrol/diesel	*benzina/gasolio*
driver	*guidatore*	slow down	*rallentare*speed
driving licence	*patente di guida*	*velocità*	
garage	*garage*	This doesn't work	*Questo non funziona*
map/town plan	*carta/pianta*	toll	*pedaggio*
mechanic	*meccanico*	Where is the road to...?	*Dov'è la strada per...?*

Italian Menu Vocabulary

Antipasti

These before-meal treats can include almost anything; among the most common are:

antipasto misto	mixed antipasto
bruschetta	garlic toast (sometimes with tomatoes)
carciofi (sott'olio)	artichokes (in oil)
crostini	liver pâté on toast
frutti di mare	seafood
funghi (trifolati)	mushrooms (with anchovies, garlic, and lemon)
gamberi ai fagioli	prawns (shrimps) with white beans
mozzarella (in carrozza)	cow or buffalo cheese (fried with bread in batter)
olive	olives
prosciutto (con melone)	raw ham (with melon)
salami	cured pork
salsicce	sausages

Minestre (Soups) and Pasta

These dishes are the principal typical first courses (*primi*) served throughout Italy.

agnolotti	ravioli with meat
cacciucco	spiced fish soup
cannelloni	meat and cheese rolled in pasta tubes
cappelletti	small ravioli, often in broth
crespelle	crêpes
fettuccine	long strips of pasta
frittata	omelette
gnocchi	potato dumplings
lasagne	sheets of pasta baked with meat and cheese sauce
minestra di verdura	thick vegetable soup
minestrone	soup with meat, vegetables, and pasta
orecchiette	ear-shaped pasta, often served with turnip greens
panzerotti	ravioli filled with mozzarella, anchovies, and egg
pappardelle alla lepre	pasta with hare sauce
pasta e fagioli	soup with beans, bacon, and tomatoes
pastina in brodo	tiny pasta in broth
penne all'arrabbiata	quill-shaped pasta with tomatoes and hot peppers
polenta	cake or pudding of corn semolina
risotto (alla milanese)	Italian rice (with stock, saffron and wine)
spaghetti all'amatriciana	with spicy sauce of salt pork, tomatoes, onions, and chilli
spaghetti alla bolognese	with ground meat, ham, mushrooms,etc
spaghetti alla carbonara	with bacon, eggs, and black pepper
spaghetti al pomodoro	with tomato sauce
spaghetti al sugo/ragù	with meat sauce
spaghetti alle vongole	with clam sauce
stracciatella	broth with eggs and cheese
sagliatelle	flat egg noodles
tortellini al pomodoro/panna/in brodo	pasta caps filled with meat and cheese, with tomato sauce/with cream/in broth
vermicelli	very thin spaghetti

Carne (Meat)

abbacchio	milk-fed lamb
agnello	lamb
anatra	duck
animelle	sweetbreads
arista	pork loin
arrosto misto	mixed roast meats
bistecca alla fiorentina	Florentine beef steak
bocconcini	veal mixed with ham and cheese and fried
bollito misto	stew of boiled meats
braciola	chop
brasato di manzo	braised beef with vegetables
bresaola	dried raw meat similar to ham
capretto	kid
capriolo	roebuck
carne di castrato/suino	mutton/pork

carpaccio	thin slices of raw beef served with a piquant sauce
cassoeula	winter stew with pork and cabbage
cervello (al burro nero)	brains (in black butter sauce)
cervo	venison
cinghiale	boar
coniglio	rabbit
cotoletta (alla milanese/alla bolognese)	veal cutlet (fried in breadcrumbs/with ham and cheese)
fagiano	pheasant
faraona (alla creta)	guinea fowl (in earthenware pot)
fegato alla veneziana	liver (usually of veal) with filling
lepre (in salmi)	hare (marinated in wine)
lombo di maiale	pork loin
lumache	snails
maiale (al latte)	pork (cooked in milk)
manzo	beef
ossobuco	braised veal knuckle with herbs
pancetta	rolled pork
pernice	partridge
petto di pollo	boned chicken breast
(alla fiorentina/bolognese/	(fried in butter/with ham and cheese/
sorpresa)	stuffed and deep fried)
piccione	pigeon
pizzaiola	beef steak with tomato and oregano sauce
pollo	chicken
(alla cacciatora/alla diavola/	(with tomatoes and mushrooms cooked in wine/grilled/
alla Marengo)	fried with tomatoes, garlic and wine)
polpette	meatballs
quaglie	quails
rane	frogs
rognoni	kidneys
saltimbocca	veal scallop with prosciutto and sage, cooked in wine and butter
scaloppine	thin slices of veal sautéed in butter
spezzatino	pieces of beef or veal, usually stewed
spiedino	meat on a skewer or stick
stufato	beef braised in white wine with vegetables
tacchino	turkey
trippa	tripe
uccelletti	small birds on a skewer
vitello	veal

Pesce (Fish)

acciughe or alici	anchovies
anguilla	eel
aragosta	lobster
aringa	herring
baccalà	dried salt cod
bonito	small tuna
branzino	sea bass
calamari	squid

cappe sante	scallops
cefalo	grey mullet
coda di rospo	angler fish
cozze	mussels
datteri di mare	razor (or date) mussels
dentice	dentex (perch-like fish)
dorato	gilt head
fritto misto	mixed fried delicacies, usually fish
gamberetto	shrimp
gamberi (di fiume)	prawns (crayfish)
granchio	crab
insalata di mare	seafood salad
lampreda	lamprey
merluzzo	cod
nasello	hake
orata	bream
ostriche	oysters
pescespada	swordfish
polipi/ polpi	octopus
pesce azzurro	various types of small fish
pesce di San Pietro	John Dory
rombo	turbot
sarde	sardines
seppie	cuttlefish
sgombro	mackerel
sogliola	sole
squadro	monkfish
tonno	tuna
triglia	red mullet (rouget)
trota	trout
trota salmonata	salmon trout
vongole	small clams
zuppa di pesce	mixed fish in sauce or stew

Contorni (Side Dishes, Vegetables)

asparagi (alla fiorentina)	asparagus (with fried eggs)
broccoli (calabrese, romana)	broccoli (green, spiral)
carciofi (alla giudia)	artichokes (deep fried)
cardi	cardoons, thistles
carote	carrots
cavolfiore	cauliflower
cavolo	cabbage
ceci	chickpeas
cetriolo	cucumber
cipolla	onion
fagioli	white beans
fagiolini	French (green) beans
fave	broad beans
finocchio	fennel
funghi (porcini)	mushrooms (boletus)

insalata (mista, verde)	salad (mixed, green)
lattuga	lettuce
lenticchie	lentils
melanzane (al forno)	aubergine/eggplant (filled and baked)
patate (fritte)	potatoes (fried)
peperoni	sweet peppers
peperonata	stewed peppers, onions, etc., similar to ratatouille
piselli (al prosciutto)	peas (with ham)
pomodoro (i)	tomato(es)
porri	leeks
radicchio	red chicory
radice	radish
rapa	turnip
sedano	celery
spinaci	spinach
verdure	greens
zucca	pumpkin
zucchini	courgettes

Formaggio (Cheese)

bel paese	a soft white cow's cheese
cacio/caciocavallo	pale yellow, often sharp cheese
fontina	rich cow's milk cheese
groviera	mild cheese (gruyère)
gorgonzola	soft blue cheese
parmigiano	Parmesan cheese
pecorino	sharp sheep's cheese
provolone	sharp, tangy cheese; *dolce* is less strong
stracchino	soft white cheese

Frutta (Fruit, Nuts)

albicocche	apricots
ananas	pineapple
arance	oranges
banane	bananas
cachi	persimmon
ciliege	cherries
cocomero	watermelon
composta di frutta	stewed fruit
datteri	dates
fichi	figs
fragole (con panna)	strawberries (with cream)
frutta di stagione	fruit in season
lamponi	raspberries
macedonia di frutta	fruit salad
mandarino	tangerine
mandorle	almonds
melagrana	pomegranate
mele	apples

melone	melon
mirtilli	bilberries
more	blackberries
nespola	medlar fruit
nocciole	hazelnuts
noci	walnuts
pera	pear
pesca	peach
pesca noce	nectarine
pinoli	pine nuts
pompelmo	grapefruit
prugna/susina	prune/plum
uva	grapes

Dolci (Desserts)

amaretti	macaroons
cannoli	crisp pastry tubes filled with ricotta, cream, chocolate or fruit
coppa gelato	assorted ice cream
crema caramella	caramel-topped custard
crostata	fruit flan
gelato (produzione propria)	ice-cream (homemade)
granita	flavoured ice, usually lemon or coffee
Monte Bianco	chestnut pudding with whipped cream
panettone	sponge cake with candied fruit and raisins
panforte	dense cake of chocolate, almonds, and preserved fruit
Saint-Honoré	meringue cake
semifreddo	refrigerated cake
sorbetto	sorbet/sherbet
spumone	a soft ice cream
tiramisù	sponge fingers, mascarpone, coffee and chocolate
torrone	nougat
torta	cake, tart
torta millefoglie	layered pastry with custard cream
zabaglione	whipped eggs, sugar and Marsala wine, served hot
zuppa inglese	trifle

Bevande (Beverages)

acqua minerale con/senza gas	mineral water with/without fizz
aranciata	orange soda
birra (alla spina)	beer (draught)
caffè (freddo)	coffee (iced)
cioccolata (con panna)	chocolate (with cream)
gassosa	lemon-flavoured soda
latte	milk
limonata	lemon soda
succo di frutta	fruit juice
tè	tea
vino (rosso, bianco, rosato)	wine (red, white, rosé)

Cooking Terms, Miscellaneous

aceto (balsamico)	vinegar (balsamic)
affumicato	smoked
aglio	garlic
alla brace	on embers
bicchiere	glass
burro	butter
cacciagione	game
conto	bill
costoletta/cotoletta	chop
coltello	knife
cucchiaio	spoon
filetto	fillet
forchetta	fork
forno	oven
fritto	fried
ghiaccio	ice
griglia	grill
in bianco	without tomato
limone	lemon
magro	lean meat/or pasta without meat
marmellata	jam
menta	mint
miele	honey
mostarda	candied mustard sauce, eaten with boiled meats
olio	oil
pane (tostato)	bread (toasted)
panini	sandwiches
panna	cream
pepe	pepper
peperoncini	hot chilli peppers
piatto	plate
prezzemolo	parsley
ripieno	stuffed
rosmarino	rosemary
sale	salt
salmi	wine marinade
salsa	sauce
salvia	sage
senape	mustard
sartufi	truffles
tazza	cup
tavola	table
tovagliolo	napkin
tramezzini	finger sandwiches
umido	cooked in sauce
uovo	egg
zucchero	sugar

80,000 BC	Give or take a couple of 10,000 years: Palaeolithic settlements along the Riviera
8000 BC	First rock incisions in the Val Camonica
236–22 BC	Romans conquer Po Valley from Gauls
222 BC	Celtic Mediolanum (Milan) comes under Roman rule; Roman colony of Ticinum (Pavia) founded
219 BC	Hannibal and his elephants cross the Alps
70 BC	Virgil born at Mantua
87 BC	Catullus born at Sirmione
23–79	Pliny the Elder, of Como
62–120	Pliny the Younger, of Como
284–305	Diocletian divides Roman Empire in two; Milan becomes most important city in West, pop. 100,000
313	Edict of Milan: Constantine makes Christianity religion of the empire
374–97	St Ambrose, bishop of Milan
387	St Ambrose converts and baptises St Augustine in Milan
539	Goths slaughter most of male Milanese
567	Lombards overrun most of Italy, and make Pavia their capital
590s	Pope Gregory the Great converts Queen Theodolinda and the Lombards to orthodox Christianity
c. 730	Desiderius, King of the Lombards, born near Brescia
778	Charlemagne defeats Desiderius, repudiates wife, Desiderius' daughter; crowned King of Italy at Pavia
888	Berengar crowned King of Italy at Pavia
1109–55	Arnold of Brescia, monk and preacher against worldly Church, only to be hanged by Pope
1127	Como destroyed by Milanese, rebuilt by Barbarossa
1154	Milan sacked by Barbarossa
1155	Barbarossa crowned king of Italy at Pavia
1156	Barbarossa does it again
1158	Milan obliterates rival Lodi; Lodi rebuilt by Barbarossa
1176	Lombard League defeats Barbarossa at Legnano
1183	Treaty of Constance recognizes independence of Lombard cities
1252	Inquisitor St Peter Martyr axed in the head by Lake Como
1277	The Visconti overthrow the Torriani to become *signori* of Milan
1334	Azzone Visconti captures Cremona
1335	Como becomes fief of Milan
1348–9	The Black Death wipes out a third of the Italians
1386	Gian Galeazzo Visconti begins Milan cathedral
1396	Gian Galeazzo Visconti founds the Certosa of Pavia
1402	Gian Galeazzo Visconti, conqueror of northern Italy, plans to capture Florence but dies of plague
1421–35	Genoa under Filippo Maria Visconti; the Genoese fleet crushes Aragon
1428–1797	Bergamo and Brescia ruled by Venice
1441	Bianca Visconti weds Francesco Sforza, with Cremona as her dowry
1447–50	Ambrosian republic—Milan's attempt at democracy
1450	Francesco Sforza made Duke of Milan
1494	Wars of Italy begin with French invasion of Charles VIII
1495	Battle of Fornovo; Leonardo begins *Last Supper*
1500	Duke of Milan, Lodovico il Moro, captured by French at Novara
1509	Defeat of Venice at Agnadello by Louis XII of France, Pope Julius II, Emperor Maximilian and the League of Cambrai; Venice loses new acquisition of Cremona, but soon regains Brescia and Bergamo and other *terra firma* real estate
1525	Battle of Pavia; Spaniards capture French King Francis I
1527–93	Giuseppe Arcimboldo, first surrealist, of Milan
1533	Federico Gonzaga of Mantua picks up Monferrato by marriage
1538–84	St Charles Borromeo, Archbishop of Milan

Chronology

| 1559 | Château-Cambrésis Treaty confirms Spanish control of Italy and returns Turin to the House of Savoy |
| 1567–1643 | Claudio Monteverdi, opera composer, of Cremona |

1573–1610	Michelangelo da Caravaggio
1596–1684	Nicolò Amati, violin maker, of Cremona
1620	Spanish governor of Milan orders 'Day of Holy Butchery' in the Valtellina; Catholics massacre Protestants, initiating 20 years of war
1630	Plague in Milan (described by Manzoni in *I Promessi Sposi*)
1644–1737	Stradivarius, violin-maker, of Cremona
1665	Carlo Emanuele II and Louis XIV persecute Waldensians in Piedmont; Cromwell and Milton protest
1683–1745	Giuseppe Guarneri, violin-maker, of Cremona
1700–13	War of the Spanish Succession
1713	Austrians pick up Milan
1745	Alessandro Volta, the physicist, born in Como
1778	La Scala inaugurated
1785	Alessandro Manzoni, author of *I Promessi Sposi*, born in Lecco
1790	Wordsworth lives by Lake Como
1796	Napoleon first enters Italy, defeats Austrians at Lodi, makes Milan capital of his Cisalpine Republic
1798–1848	Gaetano Donizetti, of Bergamo
1800	Napoleon defeats the Austrians at Marengo
1805	Napoleon crowns himself with Iron Crown of Italy in Milan Cathedral
1813	Rossini composes *Tancredi* on shores of Lake Como
1814	Overthrow of French rule
1816–17	Queen Caroline of England at Lake Como
1831	Mazzini founds *Giovane Italia*; Bellini composes *Norma* on the shores of Lake Como
1848	Revolutions across Italy; Austrians defeat Piedmont at war
1849	Restoration of autocratic rule
1852	Cavour becomes Prime Minister of Piedmont
1853	Verdi composes *La Traviata* in a villa on Lake Como
1854	Piedmont enters Crimean War
1859–60	Piedmont, with the help of Napoleon III, annexes Lombardy at battle of Solferino; in return gives France Nice and Savoy; while Garibaldi's 'Thousand' conquer Sicily and Naples
1860–65	Turin is capital of Italy; in 1865 moved to Florence
1870	Italian troops enter Rome; unification completed and Rome becomes capital
1871	Mont Cenis (Frejus) railway tunnel, first great transalpine tunnel, opened between France and Italy
1879	Queen Victoria takes a holiday by Lake Maggiore
1881	Angelo Roncalli (Pope John XXIII) born at Sotto il Monte, near Bergamo
1900	King Umberto I assassinated by anarchist
1901	Verdi dies in his hotel room in Milan
1902–7	Period of industrial strikes
1905	Simplon Tunnel, the longest rail tunnel in the world, completed
1910	Peruvian Georges Chavez makes the first flight over the Alps, killed in a crash near Domodossola
1915	Italy enters First World War
1925	Mussolini makes Italy a fascist dictatorship
1925–7	D.H. Lawrence at Lake Como
1938	Gabriele D'Annunzio dies at Il Vittoriale, by Lake Garda
1940	Italy enters Second World War
1943	Mussolini deposed; rescued by Germans to found puppet government of Salò; Milan burns for days in air raids
1944	Vittorio Emanuele III abdicates
1945	National referendum makes Italy a republic; King Umberto II exiled in Switzerland; new Italian constitution grants the Valle d'Aosta regional and cultural autonomy
1956	Italy becomes a charter member in the Common Market
1965	Completion of Mont Blanc motorway tunnel
1980	Completion of Mont Cenis (Frejus) motorway tunnel
1983	Major landslides wreak havoc in the Valtellina
1988	More landslides and floods in the Valtellina
1990	Emergence of Umberto Bossi's Lombard League
1994	Election of Silvio Berlusconi, Milanese media magnate, as Prime Minister at the head of Forza Italia

Note: Page numbers in *italics* indicate maps. **Bold** references indicate main references and chapter headings.

Index

Also Available from Cadogan Guides...

Country Guides

Antarctica
Belize
Central Asia
China: The Silk Routes
Egypt
France: Southwest France;
    Dordogne, Lot & Bordeaux
France: Southwest France;
    Gascony & the Pyrenees
France: Brittany
France: The South of France
France: The Loire
Germany: Bavaria
India
India: South India
India: Goa
Ireland
Ireland: Southwest Ireland
Ireland: Northern Ireland
Italy
Italy: The Bay of Naples and Southern Italy
Italy: Lombardy, Milan and the Italian Lakes
Italy: Venetia and the Dolomites
Italy: Tuscany and Umbria
Japan
Morocco
Portugal
Portugal: The Algarve
Scotland
Scotland's Highlands and Islands
South Africa, Swaziland and Lesotho
Spain
Spain: Southern Spain
Spain: Northern Spain
Syria & Lebanon
Tunisia
Turkey
Western Turkey
Yucatán and Southern Mexico
Zimbabwe, Botswana and Namibia

City Guides

Amsterdam
Brussels, Bruges, Ghent & Antwerp
Florence, Siena, Pisa & Lucca
Italy: Three Cities—Rome, Florence & Venice
London
Manhattan
Moscow & St Petersburg
Paris
Prague
Rome
Venice

Island Guides

Caribbean and Bahamas
NE Caribbean; The Leeward Is.
SE Caribbean; The Windward Is.
Jamaica & the Caymans

Greek Islands
Crete
Mykonos, Santorini & the Cyclades
Rhodes & the Dodecanese
Corfu & the Ionian Islands

Madeira & Porto Santo
Malta
Sicily

Plus...

Southern Africa on the Wild Side
Bugs, Bites & Bowels
Travel by Cargo Ship
London Markets

Available from good bookshops or via, in the UK, **Grantham Book Services**, Isaac Newton Way, Alma Park Industrial Estate, Grantham NG31 9SD, ℗ (01476) 541 080, ℗ 541 061; and in North America from **The Globe Pequot Press**, 6, Business Park Road, Old Saybrook, Connecticut 06475-0833, ℗ (800) 243 0495, ℗ 820 2329.